Tisha is a true love story you will never forget, a thrilling adventure full of all the struggles and joys of a young, attractive woman in the Alaskan wilderness, battling for the half-breed man she loved and the two half-Indian children who had become her own.

TISHA

"The memoir reads like an old-fashioned novel, a heartwarming love story with the added interest of frontier hardships and vividly portrayed characters."

—*Publishers Weekly*

TISHA

The Story of a Young Teacher
in the Alaska Wilderness

as told to
Robert Specht

CARLE PLACE HIGH SCHOOL LIBRARY
CARLE PLACE, NY 11514

BANTAM BOOKS
TORONTO • NEW YORK • LONDON • SYDNEY • AUCKLAND

*This low-priced Bantam Book
has been completely reset in a type face
designed for easy reading, and was printed
from new plates. It contains the complete
text of the original hard-cover edition.*
NOT ONE WORD HAS BEEN OMITTED.

RL 6, IL age 13 and up

TISHA: THE STORY OF A YOUNG TEACHER
IN THE ALASKA WILDERNESS
A Bantam Book

PRINTING HISTORY
*St. Martin's edition published May 1976
2nd printing . . . May 1976
Book-of-the-Month Club edition published June 1976
A selection of the Christian Herald Book Club in June 1976
A selection of Reader's Digest Condensed Book Club, June 1977
Bantam edition / March 1977
12 printings through July 1985*

*All rights reserved.
Copyright © 1976 by Robert Specht.
This book may not be reproduced in whole or in part, by
mimeograph or any other means, without permission.
For information address: Bantam Books, Inc.*

ISBN 0-553-24771-9 √

Published simultaneously in the United States and Canada

*Bantam Books are published by Bantam Books, Inc. Its trade-
mark, consisting of the words "Bantam Books" and the por-
trayal of a rooster, is Registered in U.S. Patent and Trademark
Office and in other countries. Marca Registrada. Bantam
Books, Inc., 666 Fifth Avenue, New York, New York 10103.*

PRINTED IN THE UNITED STATES OF AMERICA

H   21 20 19 18 17 16 15 14 13 12

For
Judith, Raphael, and Allegra

DISCARDED

CARLE PLACE HIGH SCHOOL LIBRARY
CARLE PLACE, NY 11514

author's note
and acknowledgments

Throughout this work I've tried to keep as close to actual occurrences and facts as I could, adding to them or altering them only when I deemed it dramatically necessary.

Many Alaskans, particularly those who live in the Forty Mile country, will note that I've taken some license with geography. For instance, the Indian village in these pages is described as being located on the Forty Mile River. The actual Indian village from which Chuck and Ethel came was, and still is, located on the Yukon. Today there is a modern, well-equipped school there. In 1927, however, it was pretty much as I described it.

There are many who helped in the creation of this book, both in Alaska and in the Lower 48:

To Charles Bloch go my deepest thanks both professionally and personally. More than an advisor and supporter, he has been a friend and a guide. Without him this book would not have been completed.

To Linda Price, my editor at Bantam Books, I owe a special debt of appreciation. Her patience and judgment were indispensable.

Nor could I fail to mention Julie Garriott of St. Martin's Press for her incisive criticism and enthusiastic support. She is a gifted editor.

Among others who helped in different and important ways are: Grace Bechtold, Orrin Borsten, Leonard Brean, Jackie Carr, Everett Chambers, Van Dempsey, Julia Fenderson, John and Dora Funk, "Dean" Galloway, Jack Guss, Borgil Hansen, Lynne Specht Klein, Martin Lowenheim, Charles Mayse, Sanford and Patricia Mock, Isabelle Purdy, Michael and Georgina Ritchie, Marjori Rogers, Zelma Rose, Walter Schmidt, Dee Sclar, Beulah Thornburg, Norman and Erna Toback, Vernon and Beth Weaver, Marguerite Wilson, Jack Young.

I am grateful to them all.

—R.S.

I've lived in the Forty Mile country of Alaska for a long time, but even now, every so often when I'm out rock-hunting or looking for fossils, I get lost. Sometimes I'll have to wander around for a while before I get my bearings. That's what happened to me when I first started to think about telling this story. I wasn't sure which direction to take, until I finally realized that the only way to tell it was the way I might have told it when I first came to Alaska.

That was back in 1927, when I was a prim and proper young lady of nineteen. From the time I'd been a girl I'd been thrilled with the idea of living on a frontier, so when I was offered the job of teaching school in a gold-mining settlement called Chicken I accepted right away.

The first time I heard the name Chicken I laughed. I didn't believe there could really be such a place. Sure enough, though, when I looked at a map of Alaska there it was (and still is), right up near the Yukon Territory.

Green as goose grass and full of lofty ideals, off I went, thinking of myself as a lamp unto the wilderness. The last thing I expected was that the residents of Chicken weren't going to think of me in that way at all. Far from it: before my first year of teaching was over half the population wanted to blue-ticket me out of the place.

All that was forty-eight years ago, yet I can still remember how excited I was on the day I set off for Chicken by pack train. For me it was the final leg of a long journey, and the pack train left from a village called Eagle . . .

September 4, 1927

I

Even though it was barely eight o'clock and the sun had just come up, practically the whole town of Eagle had turned out to see the pack train off. Counting the Indians, who'd come down from their fish camp for the dance the previous night, there must have been close to a hundred people gathered around—miners in hip-length boots, old sourdoughs in battered Stetsons, even women and children. In a few minutes I'd be leaving, going off into the wilderness, and I was kind of excited. I was scared too, and I must have showed it, because Mrs. Rooney asked me if I was feeling well.

"Yes, ma'am," I said. "I feel just fine."

"You look a little pale. You're not afraid of the trip, I hope."

"No. I guess I just didn't expect there'd be all these people," I said.

Mrs. Rooney dismissed them with a wave of her hand. "One thing you'll learn is that it doesn't take much to collect a crowd in Alaska. As for the trip, you don't have a thing to worry about. It's only ninety miles and you'll be perfectly safe. Mr. Strong will take good care of you."

But it really wasn't the crowd that was bothering me. Hardly anybody was paying any attention to me.

To the people here this was just a little event, nothing like the riverboat coming in, which was really exciting to them. And I wasn't afraid of the trip, either. It was the horse I'd be riding for the next four days that was scaring me. I'd have felt silly admitting it, but he was making me so nervous I could hardly concentrate on what Mrs. Rooney was saying. It wasn't as if I'd never been on a horse before. Eight years ago, when I was living with my grandmother on her farm, I used to ride around on old Tom bareback. I was only eleven then, and Tom was a pretty big horse, but he always moved so slow and he was so gentle that you could almost curl up on his broad back and go to sleep and you wouldn't fall off. This one was mean.

He was called Blossom, but where he got that name I would never know. Maybe he looked like a blossom when he was a colt, but it was the last thing he looked like now. He was so huge that even if I stood on my toes I wouldn't have been able to see over the saddle, and he was scarred and wild-looking. From the minute Mr. Strong handed his reins over to me I'd been afraid of him. And Blossom knew it. He started rolling his eyes at me right away and tried to nip me a couple of times. After he caught the sleeve of my jacket once I made sure to hold the reins close to the bit and keep him at arm's length. But every time I thought he'd settled down, he'd jerk his head up and nearly pull my arm out of its socket.

From the corner of my eye I could see Mr. Strong moving toward me down the line of horses and mules that were tethered together.

I wished I wasn't the only passenger. In another minute I'd have to mount up, and as scared of Blossom as I was, I was sure I'd make a spectacle of myself. We weren't getting along too well just standing side by side, so I couldn't foresee our relations improving when I was up on top of him.

The other animals in the train were loaded down with just about everything in creation: washboards, sacks of dried beans, bolts of canvas, even windowpanes. One mule started bucking, trying to shake off his burden of shovels and stovepipes and whatnot. The load shifted and it looked as if it was going off until somebody grabbed it at the last minute. The rest of the animals stood patiently while Mr. Strong adjusted a rope here and there or tightened a cinch.

". . . And if you have any problems at all," Mrs. Rooney was saying, "write to me and I'll be glad to give you any advice I can." She fingered the cameo brooch on the front of her dress. "And remember what I said—spare the rod and spoil the child. Show those kids right off that you're the teacher and you won't have a bit of trouble."

"I will."

"If you have to smack a couple of them do it."

Somebody went over to Mr. Strong's stable and started to close the doors. I caught a glimpse of the big sled that was in there. It was the size of a hay wagon, and I wondered how many horses it took to pull it. In a couple of months from now, after the first heavy snowfall, Mr. Strong would be bringing my trunk out on it.

The doors slammed shut and the odor of hay and manure drifted over. And then Mr. Strong was beside us, clearing his throat. Even though it was sunny and comfortable, he was wearing a mackinaw. It was open, and I could see the top button of his long underwear under his flannel shirt.

He was a tall, stoop-shouldered man, and he had such a courtly way about him that if he wore a beard he'd have made me think of Don Quixote. When I'd first met him yesterday his manners had seemed so out of place in this rough country that I thought he was joking and almost laughed. I was glad I didn't, though, because he acted that way with almost everyone. I'd been waiting over two days for his pack train to come in, but when I'd asked him if he could take me to Chicken all he'd said was, "Yes, madam, I can."

"Will you be going soon?" I'd asked him.

"Yes, madam. My pack train leaves for Chicken on the fourth, the fourteenth and the twenty-fourth of each month. I shall, therefore, be leaving tomorrow. Eight a.m. sharp."

"I'd like to go," I'd told him.

3

"The rent for your horse will be ten dollars per day. That will include your meals along the way and your lodgings. The journey will take four days. I hope that will be satisfactory."

I'd told him it would be fine and that was that.

"If you are ready, madam," he said to me now, "I shall assist you to mount."

Mrs. Rooney smiled up at him. "You will take good care of her, won't you, Mr. Strong?"

"I shall do my best." Compared to him, President Coolidge was a nonstop talker.

Mrs. Rooney looked at him coquettishly and brushed at the front of her dress. It had a lot of shiny spots where her corset poked against it. She'd been a widow for ten years, she'd told me, and I had a feeling she would have liked to marry him, but he wasn't interested.

He took the reins from me and dropped them over Blossom's head, then he bent forward with his hands locked together. I grabbed the saddle horn and he boosted me up. Once I was in the saddle the ground looked pretty far down. Blossom started to dance around and a few people laughed. I thought they were laughing at the trouble I was having trying to get him to stand still, but as soon as he settled down I saw they were laughing at my legs. The saddle was so big and wide that they stuck out like wings.

"Better do somethin' about them pins a hers, Walter," somebody called out, "or she'll be knockin' down every tree in the Forty Mile."

Mr. Strong shortened the stirrups until I could get my feet into them, but I was still spread out pretty wide. Some good-natured suggestions were offered by people close by, such as tying rocks to my feet, but Mr. Strong didn't see anything funny about them.

"When we stop over at my camp in Liberty tonight," he said to me, "I will have a smaller saddle for you." He looked at my clothes skeptically. "Are you sure, madam, you will not reconsider my offer of the coat?" A little earlier, when he saw how I was dressed, he had offered to lend me a coat, saying that the weather was

4

very changeable. But I'd told him I didn't think I'd need it.

"I'm really very comfortable," I said now. "I mean it's such a lovely day."

If I was back in the States I'd have felt ridiculous, but here in Alaska nobody cared how you dressed. I was wearing the jacket of my pink Easter suit, a pair of boy's corduroy knickers I'd bought for the ride, cotton stockings and some old sport brogues. I knew that the flowered hat I'd bought in Portland the past summer would end up crushed if it was put on the pack animals with my other things, so I wore that too. My ensemble was completed by a nickel-plated revolver that a fellow had given me at the dance last night.

Mr. Strong was still skeptical. "Should you change your mind, let me know."

"Now, Walter," an old-timer called out, "why you want to go and hide all that nice young beauty under that old army coat?"

Mr. Strong started for the front of the pack train and I looked around, able to see the whole crowd for the first time. A few old men were sitting on the rail of the schoolhouse porch, giving encouragement to a couple of little boys on a small dogsled. The sled was outfitted with some old baby-carriage wheels and the boys were trying to teach the malamute puppy that was pulling how to gee and haw.

Aside from Mr. Strong's stable and the stables of a couple of other freighters, the schoolhouse was the only other building here at the edge of town. Mrs. Rooney had showed me the inside of it and I was looking forward to teaching in it when I took over from her next year. Made of squared-off logs, it was good and sturdy. I only hoped the schoolhouse I was heading for now would be as nice.

Farther up the line of pack animals a few men were rechecking some of the loads, making sure that whatever they were sending out to mining partners or friends wouldn't fall off. But most people were just gathered around talking.

The Indians stood apart from the whites, and I wondered where they'd spent the night. There were about twenty-five of them, mostly men. Compared to the whites, who were laughing and joking about how much they'd drunk and danced, the Indian men were quiet, just watching what was going on or making an occasional comment to each other. They looked so serious, all of them, that if I hadn't seen them having such a good time last night, I'd have thought they were angry or resentful. That was what I'd thought about them when I'd first seen them standing around in White Horse and Dawson. But now I knew better. They'd laughed more and danced better than almost all the whites in Eagle. And probably had more fun too. They were just different from the whites. When they didn't have anything to say they didn't say anything.

I felt kind of sorry for the Indian women, especially the girls. Most of them had changed to moccasins, but a few still had on high heels and bright shawls. In the crisp morning air they looked out of place, their silk stockings full of runs and their makeup all smeared. For all the attention the white men paid them now they might just as well have not existed. It hadn't been that way at the dance. The white men had been pretty free with them then—a little too free. The Indian women hadn't minded it, or the Indian men either, but the white women hadn't liked it at all. Only one or two of the white women had even danced with the Indian men. The rest looked down their nose at them or, like Mrs. Rooney, disliked them outright. "Dark faces all packed full of bones," she complained to me, "you never know what they're thinking." She hated the Indian women, saying that the way they carried on with white men it was no wonder the women like herself who were matrimonially inclined couldn't find a husband.

"How's the weather up there, Teacher?"

"Cabaret" Jackson's hatchet face grinned up at me, his Adam's apple looking as though it was going to pop through his skin. One of his eyes was closed and there was some dried blood in his nostrils, but he'd cleaned himself up pretty well and he didn't look too bad.

I wished I could give him a clever answer, but I

6

never could think of the right thing when it came right down to it. "The same weather you have down there," I told him.

"Hate to see you leavin' here," he said. "Don't suppose you'd change your mind about what I asked you last night?"

"Thanks, Cab, but I don't think so."

He was the one who'd given me the revolver, telling me that I shouldn't be going into the wilds without a little protection. Last night, before he got too drunk and had a fight, he'd proposed to me, promising he'd give me everything under the sun. He'd been a real gentleman, but as soon as he got drunk he turned mean. In the fight he'd had, he'd beaten the other man bloody and got so wild he tried to bite the man's ear off. The whole thing had made me sick to my stomach. He probably wasn't a bad fellow at heart, but he wasn't the type I'd want to keep company with.

"Well," he said, "I'll be mushin' out there to Chicken some time after the freeze-up, and I'll just try you again when I do." He grinned. "Take care, Teacher."

"Teacher?" A girl with kinky hair and close-set eyes had come up near me along with her husband. I couldn't remember her name, but there was something so nice about her, a kind of a sweet smile she had, that I'd liked her right away. She was going to have a baby and she was a little embarrassed about her big stomach, so she kept kind of stooping over all the time. "Teacher, do me a favor, will you?"

"Sure." I liked that—the way everybody called me Teacher.

"My ma runs the roadhouse out to Chicken—Maggie Carew. Tell her I'm comin' along real good an' that I'm expectin' middle of December."

"And tell her it'll be a boy," her husband said. He was about as young as she was, a big stringbean. Last night he'd had to practically drag her out on the floor to fox-trot with him, but she'd been so embarrassed by her stomach she didn't even finish.

"You tell her it's gonna be a girl. I know it. My name's Jeannette," she said to me. "Jeannette Terwilliger. And this here's Elmer."

7

"Maggie Carew," I said. "Middle of December. I'll tell her."

At the front of the line Mr. Strong had mounted up. Holding a coiled bullwhip, he wheeled his horse and slapped a few of the animals on the rump. To the accompaniment of whoops and hollers from the crowd, the pack train slowly moved out.

"Don't you fall in love with any a them gum-boot miners out there, Teacher," I heard Cab yell to me, "they'd marry ya just for a grubstake."

"Make sure you come on back after break-up," someone else called, "and don't ride ol' Blossom too hard."

There was no chance of that, for after all his fussing and dancing around, Blossom wasn't moving. I kept trying to kick him in the ribs, but my feet were out too far, and he hardly felt it. So all I could do was jiggle the reins and tell him to giddap.

Then someone behind me whacked Blossom across the rump and I grabbed for the saddle horn as he plunged forward. Cries of encouragement went up from the crowd and I held onto Blossom for dear life as he caught up with the pack train and kept going. I felt my hat slowly lifting from my head, and then it was gone. But I didn't care. All I wanted to do was stay on. By the time we passed Mr. Strong I was sliding off and I braced myself for a fall. And then miraculously Blossom slowed down and stopped just short of a corridor of birches that led into the forest.

Shaking, I watched Mr. Strong ride back and pick up my flowered hat. I knew I was as white as flour when he rode up and presented it to me, and I was ready to burst into tears. But he was a gentleman, not even giving the slightest sign that he noticed it. "Madam," he said graciously, "since you're not familiar with the trail, I think it better if you allow me to lead."

As he went past I looked back at Eagle. There were a few people waving good-bye, including Mrs. Rooney, and I felt sad. For the past two weeks I'd done more traveling and met more friendly people than ever before in my life. Up to now the longest trip I'd ever made had been from Colorado, where I was born, to Oregon, where I'd been teaching. But in the past couple of weeks I'd traveled to Seattle, taken a boat up the Inside Passage to Juneau, then come North through places I'd only read of but never thought I'd see—Skagway, the Chilkoot Pass, White Horse, Dawson, the Yukon Territory, and finally here.

Along the way I had so much attention paid to me by men that sometimes I didn't think I was me. Even though I'd heard that there weren't too many women in the North, I hadn't expected to be treated like a raving beauty wherever I went. But I was. In White Horse and Dawson, when I checked into a hotel overnight, the clerk told me there'd be a dance given in my honor. And during the week that I'd spent on the riverboat, sailing north down the Yukon, I'd been invited to sit at the captain's table every night. A couple of times, in my cabin, I'd look at myself in the mirror thinking that maybe I'd changed in some way, that maybe I was really much prettier than I'd always thought I was. But after a good examination I knew I was just the same plain Anne Hobbs—same gray eyes, not a bad nose, good white teeth. One of the front ones was a little crooked, so about the best I could say was that if I didn't open my mouth and if my hair were still long I might have a faint resemblance to Mary Pickford. But even here in Eagle, where the riverboat had left me off, there'd been a dance given for me.

The last of the pack animals passed me and I took one more look at the town. People were moving off now, and beyond them the log cabins and white frame houses looked snug and comfortable. It was a beautiful place and I was sorry to leave. I couldn't see the wharf from here, but I could see the green waters of the Yukon River snaking for miles in each direction.

Blossom started to move, following the pack animals along a rutted wagon road that disappeared into the corridor of birches. The birches were beautiful, flaming with the colors of autumn, and they grew so thick on each side that I couldn't see the mountains beyond them. Wanting to ride alongside Mr. Strong, I gave Blossom a little kick, but he didn't pay any attention. I tried giving him a few more, then I gave up.

9

It was easy going for the first couple of miles, the wagon road gently curving through the forest, the only sounds the clatter of the pack animals' cowbells and the clop of their hooves. After a while my backside began to ache a little and I felt some stiffness in my shoulders, but I didn't mind. Blossom wasn't giving me any trouble and it was warm enough so I could open my jacket. It was hard for me to believe this was Alaska. Even though it was only the beginning of September, somehow I'd expected to find snow on the ground and cold weather. So far, except for a few nippy days and some nights when it came near to freezing, it hadn't been much colder than it would be back in Forest Grove, Oregon.

The wagon road ended suddenly and turned into a trail that was barely wide enough for one horse to pass through at a time. Trees and buckbrush pressed in on each side. Branches and bushes tore at my jacket and pulled the threads out. Now I realized why Mr. Strong had offered me the coat. If I could have I'd have ridden forward and asked him for it before my jacket was ruined, but even if I could get Blossom to move faster, the trail was too narrow for me to pass the animals ahead. Most of the time I couldn't see more than half a dozen of them because the trail twisted and turned so sharply. Twice when I caught sight of Mr. Strong through the trees I yelled to him, but the growth was so thick and the cowbells made so much noise that he couldn't hear me. Once I thought he saw me and I waved to him frantically, but he just gave me a pleasant wave back and went on.

The farther we went the more uneven the trail became and I kept slipping and sliding all over the saddle. The muscles in my legs were aching from trying to hold on. After a while I tried to stop Blossom so that I could get off, but no matter how hard I pulled on the reins he kept going. When I kept it up, he turned and tried to bite my foot.

An hour later when we were climbing up the side of a steep hill, I knew I wouldn't be able to hold on much longer. We'd been climbing for about fifteen minutes, and I was hoping that when we reached the top I might be able to jump off. But as soon as we did the land dipped suddenly and Blossom started down a canyon side that was so steep I was afraid I was going to go tumbling over his head.

By the time we were halfway down my hands were hurting so badly I could barely hold onto the saddle horn. My jacket was just about ruined and all I wanted to do was whimper. Then things became worse. Without warning the sun disappeared and everything was gray and chill. A few minutes later big feathery snowflakes were drifting down and it was like being in the middle of winter. When I finally reached the bottom of the canyon, my teeth were chattering. My hands were so numb I couldn't move my fingers.

The pack train had stopped and so did Blossom. Mr. Strong came riding back, the olive-drab coat over his arm. He shook his head when he saw how I looked, but he didn't say anything. If he'd asked me how I was I would have started crying. Leaning over, he helped me on with the coat. "I believe you'll be more comfortable now," he said. "There are mittens in the pockets."

"Could we stop here for a while?"

"I'm afraid not, madam, I have U.S. mail to deliver and we have twenty-five miles to cover before nightfall. I must stay on schedule. We'll have a rest stop at Gravel Gulch."

"How far is that?"

"Seven or eight miles."

I knew I wasn't going to make it without a rest and maybe he suspected it, because whenever he could he rode back to see how I was. Snow kept drifting down, melting as fast as it hit the ground. Finally it stopped. Once when he rode back he complimented me on how much better I was sitting. "You're not sliding all over the place now."

"Thanks," I told him, "but it's not me. The snow melted on the saddle and my pants are stuck."

He smiled for the first time since I met him. "Are you hurting badly?"

"Kind of."

I wasn't a crybaby, but for the third time in as many hours I was ready to burst into tears.

He thought for a moment, then he said, "We'll stop at the next creek for about twenty minutes and you can stretch your legs."

The twenty minutes went like twenty seconds. Then I was back in the saddle again. I tried as hard as I could not to cause Mr. Strong any bother or hold up the pack train, but I just didn't have the strength in my legs to keep holding on without a rest once in a while. Besides that, the saddle was rubbing me raw in a couple of places. We finally figured out the best thing to do. Every time we came to the top of a hill or canyon Mr. Strong took Blossom's reins and led him while I walked or slid down by myself. It worked out fine because I could make it down five times faster than the pack animals. By the time I got to the bottom my shoes were full of dirt and stones and I had to spend some time getting stickers and foxtails out of my stockings, but it gave me a rest.

When we'd started out from Eagle I'd been looking forward to what I'd see along the way, but long before we reached Gravel Gulch I was aching so badly that I didn't care about anything except getting there. I had leaves and all kinds of twigs down my back and I'd been slapped by branches and brush so many times my face was raw. On top of that I was getting so hungry my head was aching. So when Gravel Gulch came into view I hardly minded when Blossom speeded up, even though it hurt.

It was only a few cabins nestled in a gulch, the slopes around them thick with willow and tamarack, but it looked beautiful. Before we came to them we crossed a few acres of ugly ground that was dotted with excavated mounds of yellow-looking dirt. They were tailing piles, I found out later, the gravel that was left over after gold had been taken from the ground. But then I didn't care what they were, all I wanted to do was get off Blossom before I fainted or died.

Four men and a woman were waiting for us. The sod roof of the cabin they were standing in front of must have been over a foot thick. There were still some vegetables left in the garden that had been growing on it, and I thought to myself that my Grandmother Hobbs would sure like to have seen a garden growing up in the air like that.

The men were glad to see us, but they seemed a little shy when they saw me and went right to the pack animals instead of saying hello. The woman wasn't shy at all. Her name was Mrs. Ross. Short and fat, with jolly red cheeks, she was stuffed into a lumberjack shirt and a pair of Levis rolled up at the bottoms. She came right up to me, took in my flowered hat and the apparition underneath it and said, "Good Lord, what'na hell happened to you?"

She wasn't expecting an answer and I didn't give her any. "One of you galoots get this poor thing down from there," she said. A man came over to me and lifted me out of the saddle as if I was a toy. When he set me down my knees gave way, and the next thing I knew the woman was practically carrying me into the cabin.

She sat me down beside a cookstove that had all kinds of things warming on it, took off my coat and jacket and told me not to move. I didn't have to be told. If she'd have wanted to kill me I wouldn't have raised a finger to stop her. She was swabbing my arms and hands with a washcloth when somebody started to come in. Whoever it was shut the door right away when she told him and everybody else to stay out until I came back to life.

I told her my name while I dried myself off with a towel she gave me, and she asked me where I was headed.

"Chicken," I said. "I'm the new teacher."

"Chicken! Honey, from the looks of you, you ain't even gonna make it to Liberty."

She was so hearty and outgoing that she made me feel better right away. If she'd been wearing a shirtwaist and long skirt she'd have reminded me of Miss Ivy, a teacher who'd taken me in when I was still in high school.

She didn't let the men in until she was sure I wasn't

13

going to faint or cry, then she served up a delicious lunch of hot bear soup, hot sourdough bread and moose pot roast.

The men at the table didn't have too much to say, talking a little with Mr. Strong about their "clean-up" —the gold they'd taken from the ground—and speculating about the kind of winter they thought they were in for. I could tell they'd have liked to talk to me, but they were being polite and letting me eat. I was starved and ate so much finally that I could hardly move when I was done.

Mrs. Ross shooed them outside as soon as they finished so that I could lie down for a while. A half hour later when it was time for me to get up, I was glad the men weren't around. The insides of my thighs were so chafed I waddled around like a duck for a few minutes.

Before I got on Blossom again Mrs. Ross gave me an old stained pillow to put under me. It made it a little harder for me to balance myself, but it helped.

Once we were out of Gravel Gulch the going was easier. The country smoothed out into a series of gently sweeping hills, and I wished I weren't so saddle sore, so that I could really appreciate it. Sometimes, when we'd be riding across the crest of a hill I could see for hundreds of miles in every direction and I'd feel expectant and afraid at the same time. It was all so big that it made me feel as if something exciting was going to happen, yet so quiet and lonely I felt lost in it. But as big as it was, when we'd stop to water the horses at a creek and have a drink ourselves, there'd always be an old tin cup sitting between some rocks or hanging from a nail driven into a tree.

Darkness came slowly after a long twilight, but once the sun was down it became cold fast. It was past eight o'clock when we reached Liberty, and I was so bone-weary I hardly paid any attention to what was going on. Even if I had there would have been nothing to see but an old sagging cabin and a smelly stable nearby.

All I wanted to do was get into a bed and never wake up, so when Mr. Strong told me that after the horses were unloaded and stabled we'd have something to eat, I asked him just to show me where I was going to sleep. An old man who tended the stable for him hobbled ahead of me to a one-room cabin that smelled stale with sweat. He took three bedrolls down from a shelf and laid them out, then put some horse blankets on them. Before he left he told me that I'd be most comfortable nearest the stove. There was a kerosene lamp hanging over a homemade table, and some water warming on the small stove, but I didn't even bother to turn the lamp down or think about washing or brushing my teeth. I just lay down on the bedroll, pulled a couple of blankets over me and tried to sleep.

From the start I kept drifting in and out, too exhausted to wake up and too sore to fall into a deep sleep. I felt the floorboards move under me when Mr. Strong and the old man came in and lay down, and during the night I heard one of them snoring.

I kept dreaming that I was still on Blossom and that he was walking all the way back to Eagle with me. No matter what I did I couldn't stop him. When we arrived I felt terrible. I'd been riding for two days and I was back where I started.

II

It was dark and cold the next morning when Mr. Strong shook me. "There's hot water on the stove, madam," he said. "You will have twenty minutes to wash up and prepare yourself. Then we shall have breakfast and be on our way."

Ordinarily I loved getting up early and starting a new day, but after he went out I had to force myself to move. It took me five minutes before I could even stand. I had charley horses in both my legs and I didn't know which part of me hurt most. On top of the

15

potbellied stove there was a kettle of water. I limped with it over to a wooden counter, poured some hot water into a basin, then got some cold water from a big barrel. The water didn't look that clean so I decided I'd skip brushing my teeth.

It was just starting to get light when we finished breakfast and were ready to go. But this time when Mr. Strong cupped his hands to boost me into the saddle I was too stiff to raise my foot. He and the old man had to get together and lift me.

Our next stopover for the night, Mr. Strong told me, would be Steel Creek, twenty-four miles away. "We'll stop at Dome Creek for lunch," he added.

"Everybody here in Alaska seems to live either on a creek or a river," I said.

He didn't think too much of my observation. "It's natural enough, madam. If they didn't they wouldn't have any water."

I was tempted to say they could always dig a well, but I didn't.

He'd found a smaller saddle for me as he'd promised, and it helped a lot at first by not rubbing me where I was raw, but after a while it started new raw places.

I'd thought Blossom had been mean the day before, but today he was even worse. Now that I had a smaller saddle I thought I'd be able to make him mind me. Instead he showed me right from the start who was boss. He'd stop whenever he felt like cropping some late grass or a few leaves that were still green, then to make up for lost time he'd jog along till he caught up with the pack train, punishing every bone in my body. I told Mr. Strong about it and he gave me a small box of chocolate creams. "Feed one to him every so often. It will keep him in a good mood."

They kept him in a mood, but it wasn't good. He was as smart as he was mean. After I gave him the first chocolate he kept turning his head every few minutes for another, whinnying and making terrible throaty sounds until I gave in. Twenty minutes later I gave him the last chocolate, showed him the empty box and tossed it away so he knew there was no more. After that he was worse than ever. I couldn't do anything to make him obey, until finally I just stopped caring. I rode hunched over, only seeing the creeks we crossed as Blossom splashed through them, and once I watched his legs turn blue as we sloshed through a patch of late blueberries. Sometimes I fell as much as a quarter of a mile behind the pack train.

It was about an hour after we left Gravel Gulch that I looked up to see the pack train halted and Mr. Strong waiting for me. Up ahead was what looked like a field of cotton. A light wind rippled its surface, and it was so beautiful that it made me forget how bad I was feeling.

"What's that?" I asked Mr. Strong.

"Tundra."

"I mean the white stuff." I didn't think it could be cotton, but it was.

" 'Alaska cotton,' " Mr. Strong said. "From this point on, madam, you'll have to look where you're going. We're going to cross all that."

"I don't mind at all," I said.

He stared at me owlishly. "Have you ever crossed a niggerhead flat?"

"No . . ."

He wheeled his horse and the pack train started forward. I soon found out what he meant. At first I enjoyed myself. We rode through acres and acres of silvery bolls, their long silky fibers waving like pompoms atop a slender stem. Then we hit swamp. Out of it grew big hummocks of matted grass that looked like giant mops. They grew so thick that I thought of getting off Blossom and walking on them. Like the other animals, he wasn't having easy going. The mud sucked at his hoofs, and he kept slipping all over the place and stumbling over submerged roots. We slowed way down and soon fell behind the rest of the pack train.

I was so busy holding on that I didn't see the herd of caribou until we were almost on top of them. I heard them first, making peculiar coughing sounds. Then, as though they'd come out of nowhere, there they were a few hundred yards ahead on solid ground. They were grazing, eating some kind of white moss, a forest of antlers over their heads and a shawl of white around

17

their shoulders. The closest of them lifted their heads, big eyes staring curiously. Then they went back to grazing as if they hadn't seen a thing.

What happened next went so fast that it was over before I knew it. We were about forty feet away from a caribou mother and a calf that were separated from the rest of the herd. All I saw at first was something moving fast—a humpbacked shape that was charging down on the calf in one moment and in the next was launching itself through the air.

It was a huge grizzly, and it landed on top of the calf with a terrible bone-crushing sound. The calf tried to get out from under but it didn't have a chance. I watched, horrified as the grizzly, snarling and raging, held the struggling calf down with one paw. Then, like a wrestler, it wrenched the calf's neck back, snapping it.

Blossom reared and I went tumbling into the mud, praying he wouldn't fall on me. Scrambling and stumbling, he managed to stay on his feet, then ran off. The whole herd started to move at the same time, antlers clacking, all of them pushing and shoving at each other in a panic to get away. A few stumbled and fell, but were back on their feet in a moment. Then the whole herd was bounding off.

Only the mother stayed, watching as the grizzly tore a great chunk of flesh from the twitching body. I started to back off, but I must have moved too fast. The grizzly dropped what he was eating and snarled at me, flashing bloody fangs.

I was too scared to move until I was sure he was more interested in his meal than in me. Then I started to black off slowly, the mud sucking at my shoes. Finally I turned and stumbled away.

After I felt I'd gone a safe distance, I turned around. My heart almost stopped as I stared into a pair of eyes.

The caribou mother had followed me. Only ten feet away, she looked enormous now that I was on foot. She let out a mournful wail that scared me even more and I screamed at her hysterically. "Go away! You hear me? Go away!" I started to cry.

At that she wheeled and loped off. I saw why a few

18

seconds later: Mr. Strong was riding toward me, leading Blossom. Covered with mud from head to toe, aching all over, I couldn't stop crying. There was even mud up my sleeves. Mr. Strong got down from his horse and came over to me and I threw my arms around him. He stood straight as a statue, giving me a soft pat on the shoulder once or twice. "Now, madam," he said after a couple of minutes, "you mustn't take on so. Whatever happened you seem to have weathered it."

Finally I was able to blubber out the whole story.

"It is something you must get used to in this country," he said. "We will find some dry ground and after you change clothes you will feel better. Can you ride now?"

"I guess so."

"Madam, where is your hat?"

"Back there somewhere. I don't care about it anymore."

He rode back a ways before he found it. When he returned with it and I saw the shape it was in I told him to throw it away. He said he'd prefer not to.

"It is very becoming on you. Perhaps we can wash the mud off at the next creek."

The revolver lay heavy against my thigh. I hadn't even thought to use it, I realized. I mentioned it to Mr. Strong.

"It was fortunate you didn't. That grizzly would have torn you to pieces."

As soon as we reached some dry ground he unpacked the horse that had my things on it, then turned around so I could change. Luckily, I'd bought an extra pair of knickers back in Eagle, but having to put on a pair of practically new pumps, I wished now that I'd bought some boots. Mr. Strong had advised me to, but I wanted to save the money.

"After this," he said before we mounted up again, "I want you to keep up with the pack train."

"I'd like to, but I just can't get Blossom to mind me."

That made him mad. Without saying a word he walked over to a tree and broke a branch from it. He

19

swished it around a couple of times, then grabbed Blossom's rein. First he jerked Blossom's head from side to side, punishing his mouth with the bit, then pushed him backwards until he almost fell. Blossom was scared and so was I. He tried to rear, but Mr. Strong held onto the rein. Then he lashed out at Blossom's neck with the switch while he held the rein tight. Blossom snorted and whinnied in panic, but Mr. Strong wouldn't stop. Dirt and stones were flying all over the place. How he held onto that big animal I didn't know, but he must have hit Blossom on the neck and face about twenty times. When he was done Blossom was quivering so badly I felt sorry for him. Mr. Strong's hat had fallen off. I gave it to him when he handed me the switch. He was sweating, and with his hat off, the top of his head bald, he didn't look so forbidding.

"If he gives you any trouble after this, whack him on the neck. He'll mind."

I didn't have to. All I had to do from then on was tap him and he did what he was supposed to do.

After that Mr. Strong became more friendly. Up to then I didn't think he liked me, but after a while he even asked me where I'd come from and how I happened to come to Alaska.

I told him about how I'd been teaching in Forest Grove Elementary in Oregon when the territorial commissioner of education visited there last year. "He gave a lecture in the auditorium about teaching here, and he made it sound so exciting and adventurous that I made out an application. And here I am."

"Where were you brought up?"

"In Colorado. My father was in the mining business," I said. Somehow it sounded better than saying he'd just been a coal miner.

"You seem a little young to be out on your own."

"I'm almost twenty," I said.

"You don't look it."

I knew he was going to say that. Just before I'd left Forest Grove I'd gone into a barbershop and had my hair bobbed. I'd figured that since I was going to be teaching somewhere in the wilds, it would be easier to take care of if it was short. Up to then people always

20

took me for being older than I was, but from then on they kept telling me I looked like a kid.

"I meant no offense by that, madam," he said. "I was twelve when I left home myself and the experience hasn't hurt me yet."

"I was an old woman compared to you. I was sixteen when I left Colorado and started teaching in Forest Grove."

As we rode he told me a little about himself, of an unhappy childhood in North Carolina, then running away to go to California. He was in his late twenties when he came to Alaska to look for gold, and he'd been in the Forty Mile country for twenty-one years now. He was on the town council and was a member of the school board in Eagle.

The two of us having left home early gave us something in common. He didn't stop calling me madam, but I could tell he felt kind of fatherly towards me. All the rest of that day, seeing how badly off I was, he helped me down and let me walk a little even when we weren't going down a steep hill. It meant that the whole pack train had to slow up and I really appreciated it.

It was getting towards dark and I was thinking that we were never going to reach Steel Creek, when we came to the foot of the steepest trail we'd come across so far. The brush around it was so thick and high that it formed a tunnel. Even without packs it would have been a tough trail for the animals to climb. Now since it was the end of the day and they were tired, they balked at it and I didn't blame them.

They weren't the best animals to begin with—I'd seen finer horses pulling vegetable wagons—and they were overloaded. Besides that, most of the loads weren't packed on them right and half of them had sores full of pus and blood where the loads were rubbing against them. One of the mules whose back was the worst of all kept trying to knock his pack off against every tree he passed. I mentioned it to Mr. Strong, but he said they'd be all right.

Now he kept smacking the lead animals on the rump with his coiled whip and yelling at them, but it didn't do

21

any good. They were played out. I'd thought he was mad when he'd whipped Blossom earlier in the morning, but this time he went into a rage.

Dismounting, he searched around in the brush until he came up with a length of dead limb as thick as a two-by-four. Then helling and damning to beat the band, he clubbed the first few animals all over their bodies. I thought he'd gone crazy and was going to kill them, but they moved. One after the other they disappeared up into the tunnel of brush, dirt and rocks coming down behind them. When Mr. Strong reached me, he threw the limb aside and took Blossom's reins.

Leading Blossom to his own horse, he mounted up. "This will be a tough climb, madam. You're going to have to hold on."

Before I could say anything, he'd spurred his horse forward, jerking Blossom's reins, and the next thing I knew I was charging up through the tunnel after him. It was so steep I couldn't see how we were going to make it to the top. I could barely see ahead with all the dust that had been raised, and a couple of times I was almost blinded by branches. It was a full five minutes before we broke out of it. When we did the horses and mules were dripping sweat onto the ground and breathing so hard they sounded like bellows. My backside was raw and I was all for just dropping off Blossom and giving up then and there, but when I asked Mr. Strong if I could get off, he shook his head, too winded to talk. It took him a minute before he could say, "Walk your horse over there." He pointed to a spot about a hundred yards away and I nudged Blossom over to it.

I didn't know what to expect, but what I saw made me forget every ache and pain I had. The sun was below the distant mountains, and the land in between was covered with a strange veil of gray. Pine and spruce loomed up from the slopes below me, and beyond there was so much land, all of it bursting with spruce and tamarack, that I felt like a speck of dust that could be swept away in a second. Winding through it for as far as I could see were the waters of the Forty Mile River. And directly below, on the other side of the river, looking almost unreal, were twenty acres of tilled farm

22

land. A big red barn was set to one side of them, and near that was a log building with bright patches of flowers all around it. Another half acre, directly behind the building, was lined with the orderly green rows of a vegetable garden.

"Steel Creek," Mr. Strong said, riding up beside me. "That's the creek, branching into the river down there. And that's the Prentiss roadhouse."

There was no problem getting the pack animals down to the river. Once they saw what was below they came to life, knowing that feed and a warm stall were waiting. They were so anxious that Mr. Strong had to keep holding the lead horse back, afraid that once the animals started to move fast there'd be no stopping them. If one of them was to fall he was liable to drag all the rest down. I knew how they felt. I couldn't wait to get there myself. Mr. Strong had told me I'd be able to take a hot bath when we reached Steel Creek.

As we kept going down and drawing near the river, I wondered how we were going to cross. The river wasn't high, but it was flowing pretty fast. When we reached the bank I was glad to see a thick cable stretched across the water. It was anchored to the cliff face on this side and to a big iron tripod on the other. There was a raft pulled up on the opposite shore that had a line attached to the cable.

No sooner did we arrive at the river than about a half a dozen people appeared on the other bank. Except for a girl in bib overalls, they were all men. One of them hallooed and yelled a question, but what with the rushing water and the animals milling around, I couldn't hear. Mr. Strong understood. He shook his head violently from side to side and waved a hand to make sure they understood he was saying no.

Almost as soon as we were at the bank, Blossom began to give me trouble for the first time all day. He kept heading for the water, and each time I turned him away from it he'd try again. He'd been so good that I'd dropped the switch a long way back. Now I wished I had it.

Mr. Strong dismounted, and I thought he was going to grab Blossom and help me down. Instead, he started untethering the pack animals. As each one was untied it splashed into the waist-deep water. After the third one went in Blossom was so mad at my holding him back that he started trying to bite my foot again, his teeth clicking evilly.

"Mr. Strong, can you help me? I can't hold Blossom!"

"Give him his head, madam. He knows what to do."

"You mean let him go in the river?"

"That is correct."

"Can't we use that raft?"

"We don't need it. Rest assured, madam, it's not necessary. I've been doing this for years."

You may have, I thought, but I haven't, and I wished I had the courage to tell him that. The lead animals had reached the middle. Almost up to their haunches, they had to fight to keep their feet in the powerful current. I couldn't swim, but even if I could cross the Channel like the champion Gertrude Ederle I still wouldn't be too anxious to do it with Blossom. But I took a deep breath, eased my hold on the reins and let Blossom go. Hungry and bad-tempered, he plunged right in.

To my surprise, it was easy. Once I stopped caring about getting splashed, I began to enjoy it. I'd seen cowboys cross rivers in picture shows and they'd done it in deeper water than this. I was feeling so good that I even waved once to everyone on the opposite bank.

Then Blossom slipped.

He went down on his hind legs and I almost slid off. While he was down the water hit us in the side with so much force that we almost went over. Blossom held his feet, but he started losing ground. The current was pushing us into deeper water. As hard as he tried, Blossom couldn't hold out against it. He slipped again, and I felt the shock of cold water up to my waist. I began to panic. With Blossom not able to get any purchase on the slippery bottom, it was only a matter of time before we'd be swept away.

He knew we were in trouble and fought harder than ever to make it to the opposite bank. If I wasn't so busy just holding on, I'd have had the sense to point

24

him downriver and ease him over to the bank gradually, but I was too scared to think. Suddenly he stumbled. His forelegs went down and I was pitched forward at the same time that his head snapped back and it cracked against my forehead. Dazed, I hardly knew what was happening after that. All I knew was that I couldn't faint and I had to hold on.

I grabbed a handful of mane and had a quick flash of the people on the opposite bank whirling away from us. Then they were gone. A big blood-red blotch kept coming between me and everything else. I heard Blossom blowing and snorting, and once I felt the two of us being pulled down, only to be pushed right back up again.

I couldn't tell how long it was before I realized that Blossom had calmed down. The red blotch in front of my eyes had disappeared and left me with a headache, but somehow I was still in the saddle. Blossom was swimming. Moving along smoothly, he was heading for the bank. I felt him touch bottom, and a few seconds later he heaved himself up out of the water. Once we were on dry land he shook himself so hard that even if I'd wanted to I couldn't have stayed on him. I slid to the ground and landed hard.

It took me a minute before I started telling myself that I'd better get up. I was shivering with cold, but didn't have the strength to move.

I'd finally managed to sit up when I heard someone coming. It was a girl. Breathing hard from running, she leaned down, one of her braids dangling in front of me.

"You all right, ma'am?"

I managed a nod.

"Can you walk if I help you?"

She got me to my feet and we were making our way along the bank when Mr. Strong came riding up. He wanted to put me up on his horse, but I wouldn't let him. I didn't want to look at another horse right then. Between the two of them they brought me to the Prentiss roadhouse.

Inside, a stocky woman with gray hair and a bossy manner took me in charge right away. Holding me away from her so she wouldn't get wet, she told the girl to unfold the canvas tub, and then ushered me into a room. There she told me to take off my wet clothes, and dry myself off. She came back with an old flannel bathrobe a few minutes later, steered me into a bathing room and eased me into a portable tub that was full of steaming water. It burned me where I was raw, but it felt wonderful everyplace else. She was furious at Mr. Strong. "That old tight-fisted sonofabitch," she said, when I leaned back against the wooden frame of the tub, "—it was his fault you went in. If he'd of let us send the raft over it wouldn't of happened. But he wanted to save the money."

The girl came in then carrying a big copper kettle. "This is my daughter Nancy," the woman said. "I'm Mrs. Prentiss. This isn't the first time this kind of thing's happened." She turned to her daughter, "You remember when he lost those two mules loaded down with parcel post?"

"Yes'm." The girl let the hot water into the tub slowly.

"You stay here with her. I got supper to make and I don't want her falling asleep in there. Be a hell of a thing if she ended up drowning in *here* after all that."

She left. Nancy finished pouring the water and sat down in a homemade chair. I slid further down along the smooth rubber lining and let my head rest against the frame. I'd rather have been left alone, but Mrs. Prentiss wasn't the kind of person you argued with. Nancy was uncomfortable. Her green eyes kept looking everyplace but at me.

"Thanks for helping me," I said.

She made a little motion with her head to say it was nothing, then looked down at her fingers. She had on an old middy blouse under her overalls and her fingernails were bitten down to the quick. She could have been pretty if she didn't keep her mouth pursed so tight.

"We didn't think you were gonna make it."

"Neither did I."

"Everybody figured Chicken was gonna have to do without a teacher for another year."

When she saw me smile she grinned, trying to hide

the cavities in her front teeth. I told her she didn't have to stay. "I won't fall asleep."

"You sure?"

"Positive. It feels too good."

I stayed in the tub for another hour, until Mrs. Prentiss came for me and brought me back into the room. She'd already laid out bandages on the top tier of a bunk bed and made me lie down on my stomach on the bottom tier. Then, even though I told her I could do it myself, she insisted on bandaging all the places where I was raw. "I've raised eight kids," she said. "You don't have anything they don't. In some places they got more, so settle down. You got two more days before you reach Chicken. You won't make it with a raw behind."

She was none too gentle, but she was thorough. After she finished, she handed me a suit of boy's Stanfield underwear. "It's scratchy," she said, "but it's warm."

She ordered me to stay awake until she brought me some dinner. I found out later that the meat was bear cub, but it tasted like pork and it was delicious. No sooner had I finished it than I fell asleep.

Breakfast the next morning was solemn. The big main room of the roadhouse was cheerful and clean, the board floors almost bleached white. There were flower boxes on the window-sill. The whole place was so spick-and-span it made me uncomfortable, but not half as uncomfortable as the Prentisses did. All ten of them, including Nancy, sat at the long table sullenly, as though someone had cheated them and they were angry about it. I wished Mr. Strong was here, but he'd eaten already and was out getting the animals loaded up. After Mrs. Prentiss introduced everyone in the family to me they didn't say a word. She seemed to dominate them like a circus lion tamer with a cage full of cats. After a couple of minutes of silence, she looked at them with cold green eyes. "Ever see a finer lookin' bunch?" she said contemptuously. "Talk your ear off, don't they? My nine mules—happy as sunshine, the whole lot of 'em."

"How long you been teaching?" she asked me a minute later.

27

"Two years."

"You must have started when you were in diapers."

"I'm older than I look," I said.

"What do you think of somebody who's had plenty of schooling and still can't read?"

"I don't know," I said. "There could be a lot of reasons."

As soon as Mr. Prentiss finished his breakfast and got up, the rest did also. I thought at first that maybe none of them wanted to be left alone with her. But as soon as they were gone I realized they knew she wanted to talk to me alone.

"I got a favor to ask you," she said. "I want my Nancy to stay with you at Chicken."

I was too surprised to answer.

"I'm willing to pay, mind you," she went on, as if that meant I didn't have any excuse for refusing. "I'm not asking nothing for nothing."

"But Nancy and I don't even know each other, Mrs. Prentiss."

She brushed that aside. "That doesn't matter. You're a teacher. My Nancy can't read too good and I think you could help her."

"But I don't even know if I'll have room for her. I've never been to Chicken."

"There'll be room. And if there isn't she'll sleep on the floor." When I didn't say anything, she found another argument. "Look, Teacher, you're a cheechako. You don't know the first thing about this country. Nancy could be a big help to you."

"Let me think about it," I said, wanting to get away.

Mrs. Prentiss' tone changed. She stopped pushing. "I'll give it to you straight, Teacher. I don't know you, it's true. I don't know anything about you, but I think you'd be good for Nancy. I'm talking to you because she asked me to. I could send her to school in Eagle, but she doesn't like that Mrs. Rooney, says she's more interested in men than in teaching. Besides, the kids there call her bonehead because she can't read."

The door to the kitchen was ajar and I had the feeling Nancy was behind it, listening. I got up. "Let me think about it," I said again.

28

The stable next to the roadhouse was almost as neat as the roadhouse itself, with plenty of fresh hay all around, and a clean stall for a cow. Mr. Strong was almost ready to lead the animals out. When I told him the story, he didn't seem surprised at all. "It's a good idea," he said.

"But we're complete strangers."

"That has nothing to do with it, madam," he said. "If I were you I would take her."

"Why?"

"You're new to this country. You're going to be all alone. Living in the bush isn't easy for anyone, much less for someone like you. Nancy can teach you a great deal."

"Suppose we don't get along?"

"You can always send her home."

I stayed in the stable, trying to decide what to do. I thought about Miss Ivy. If she was in this situation, I knew, she wouldn't have thought twice about taking Nancy. She'd been my teacher in high school, and if it hadn't been for her I'd probably never have become a teacher myself. When my family had broken up and my mother couldn't support me anymore she'd taken me in and treated me as if I were her own daughter. She hadn't made any bones about it either, just took me in and kept me with her until I graduated, as if she wasn't doing anything but what was simply right and proper.

When I thought about it that way it seemed to me that taking Nancy to live with me wasn't a big thing at all—especially since what Mr. Strong had said was true. I *didn't* know anything about living in the wilds. Having someone like Nancy to show me the ropes would make things a lot easier. I could help her and she could help me.

Before the pack train left I told Mrs. Prentiss that it was all right, and she said she'd send Nancy out with Mr. Strong some time in the next few weeks.

I hadn't seen Nancy around at all, but as we were moving out she appeared around the corner of the roadhouse. "Bye, Teacher," she called.

"Bye, see you soon." I smiled.

She didn't smile back.

III

From Steel Creek on the going was easier. Right from the start I felt better. The air was nippy, but I was well bundled up. Besides the suit of long underwear I was wearing, Mrs. Prentiss had given me a pair of bib overalls one of her boys had outgrown, a pair of his boots and a flannel shirt. With Mr. Strong's coat on top of it all, I didn't have to worry about being cold.

My flowered hat was in such bad shape that I gave it to Blossom. With a couple of holes cut in it to let his ears through, it really looked almost rakish on him. I settled for an old wool pom-pom hat that I could pull down over my ears. I was feeling so good I started paying attention to the country.

All during the trip down the Yukon I'd kept wondering what it was that made this country so different from what I'd known so far. I'd thought it was the bigness, but it wasn't only that. It was the rawness. Back in Oregon the trees billowed out fat and heavy even at this time of year. Here they were tattered, leaner and tougher—the tall spruce looking like huge giants ready for a scrap. Everything was that way, like the thick groves of willow that some animal had chewed half up, stripping the bark from them. They just kept on growing anyway, unkillable. Even the clouds overhead seemed to move faster. The air was all charged up, as if something was going to happen.

I'd have thought that with all the noise the cowbells were making, we wouldn't see hide nor hair of any wild animals, but it was just the opposite. The noise made them curious, and every so often I'd look off and see something watching us. Once it was a whole bunch of foxes. They were frisking on a shelf when we came on them, two blues, a couple of blacks and one cross fox. They stopped fooling around and just stared at us as nervy as you please, then went right back to what they were doing.

I'd always thought wolves traveled in packs until I saw one all by himself maybe a hundred yards off the trail. I'd never seen one before, but I knew right away it had to be a wolf. It looked bigger and meaner than I'd imagined, long snout, heavy ruff around the neck and eyes as calculating as the Devil's. He paced us for almost a mile, sometimes showing up ahead of us, and I'd have sworn he was thinking as clearly as I was. "You can bet on that," Mr. Strong said. "He smells the horses—hopes maybe one of them will drop dead."

He gave up hoping finally and disappeared.

We were a few hours out of Steel Creek when a settlement appeared in the distance—a line of about fifteen cabins set back from the banks of the Forty Mile River. A few small boats were pulled up on the bank and there were some food caches standing on poles in back of the cabins.

"An Indian village," Mr. Strong said. "We'll stop there."

I'd seen a couple of Indian villages from the riverboat coming down the Yukon, but never close up. Before that I hadn't even known there'd be Indians in Alaska. I thought there'd be Eskimos. This village looked so picturesque I couldn't wait to get there.

But when we drew near I was shocked. It was a shanty-town, worse than any of the worst sections I'd seen in all the coal towns I'd lived in. There might have been three or four decent-looking places, but the rest were hovels, sway-backed cabins and sagging shacks that were patched with everything the owners could get their hands on—tarpaper, rotting planks, scraps of galvanized iron, even old animal hides. The whole place looked as if all the garbage and slop from Eagle had been dumped here. Rusting tin cans, rags, paper, shreds of hide, bottles and fishbones littered the ground. There was no breeze blowing and the stench that hung over everything was nauseating. I was glad it was chilly. If it had been hot it would have been unbearable.

As we rode in people stared at us from doorways. I'd thought that the Indians I'd seen at Eagle were poor, but these people had nothing. They made me think of pictures I'd seen in a stereoscope once of starving Negro sharecroppers, except that these faces looked Oriental. The clothes were the same, though: worn dresses that hung like sacks on the women, patched and baggy overalls on the men. On one man we passed I recognized the frayed jacket of a riverboat captain.

Mangy dogs, half starved and chained to stakes, snarled and leaped at us as we went by. They were jerked back and landed in their own dung. A few children kept pace with us, giving the horses plenty of room. Barefoot and in rags, noses running, they were having a good time. One little boy, with open running sores all over his head, tripped over one of the dogs and barely avoided being bitten. Another boy had the same kind of sores all over his neck. They were from tuberculosis, I found out later.

We stopped in front of a frame house that had paint peeling all over it. I thought that maybe it was where the chief of the village lived because a lot of the Indians were gathered in front of it. Mr. Strong seemed to know everybody, greeting a few people by their first name.

"Betty, how's little Charles Lindbergh?" he asked a mahogany-colored woman who was holding a tiny baby. The dogs all over the village were making such a racket he almost had to yell.

"He's fine," she yelled back, lifting the baby a little to show him off. "Strong like bear."

"*Skooltrai* here?" Mr. Strong said.

The woman nodded and at almost the same time the door to the house opened. An Indian and a white girl came out, and no two people could have looked more different than they did. Maybe it was because the girl was so beautiful, but I thought the Indian was one of the ugliest men I'd ever seen. He was tall and thin, the skin over his cheekbones drawn so tight that it glistened, and his eyes were small and set wide apart. His shirt was open at the throat and his neck looked as

32

though somebody had once wound barbed wire around it, it was so covered with scars.

They were followed by a little boy. He must have been about eight years old and you could see he was part white. Like the other kids, he was as skinny as a rail.

"Good day, Miss Winters," Mr. Strong called to the girl. Up to then he'd been smiling and friendly with everybody, the way you'd be with children. But he didn't look friendly now. "This young lady is bound for Chicken," he went on, "and she needs a short rest. I would appreciate it if you would accommodate her."

The girl didn't act any friendlier to him than he did to her, but she came right over to me.

"I'll give you a hand," she said, reaching up.

She was really lovely, with bright blue eyes and long black hair tied back with a red bandanna. She was wearing moccasins, but even then she was taller than I was.

"I'm Cathy Winters," she said, after I was able to stand by myself.

"Thanks," I said. "I'm Anne Hobbs."

She indicated the tall Indian beside her. "This is Titus Paul."

I told him I was glad to meet him, but he didn't return the compliment.

She asked the little boy to get her mail, then brought me into the house. Her place was less than half the size I'd thought it was from the outside, one dingy room with a cracked brown linoleum on the floor and a tiny bedroom. She helped me off with my coat and I plopped down on a battered couch.

"I hope I'm not putting you out."

There was a small table in the center of the room with the remains of a meal on it and I smelled the delicious odor of fried fish.

"Not at all. Titus and I just finished eating some grayling he caught this morning. Plenty left over if you're hungry."

"Thanks. This is all I need."

"Want to wash up?"

33

"I sure do."

She set about getting a basin and a washcloth and I just sat back and watched her move around. She had on a dress that was as beautiful as her figure, some kind of homespun embroidered with Indian designs around the hem and the half-length sleeves. It was tied with a leather thong at the waist. She looked so smart and neat that even if I hadn't been so sweated up and grimy I'd have been jealous of her.

The little boy came in then and put her mail on the counter.

"This is Chuck," Cathy said, taking a pitcher and dipping it in a barrel of water. "He'll be keeping you company the rest of the way. Chuck, I'd like you to meet Miss Hobbs."

He was too shy to look at me.

Cathy tipped the pitcher over the hand basin and poured the water in. "Oh come on," she said to him. "Is that the way I taught you to say hello? Go on," Cathy encouraged him. "She won't bite you. She's a teacher just like me."

"Please . . . to . . . meet you," he said gravely.

"I'm pleased to meet you too," I said.

She told him to run along and he went out, grateful to get away.

After I washed up I felt a little better, and over a cup of coffee I found out why her place was so small. She was the schoolteacher here and these were her living quarters. The rest of the house was the schoolroom. I admired her. She didn't have much of a place, but she'd certainly made it comfortable. There were books all over and all kinds of Indian articles on the walls—a quiver full of arrows, bows, a couple of wooden ceremonial masks and dozens of other things. A colored framed print of Jesus that hung on one wall looked out of place.

"Are you here all alone?" I asked her.

"Sure." She must have realized what I was thinking because she said, "I know how you feel. I felt the same way when I first came. But there's nothing to be afraid of here. If you like, I'll show you around. You should walk a little anyway—get the kinks out."

Outside, Mr. Strong had untied a badly sagging load on one of the animals and laid the contents out on the ground. He and the Indians who'd ordered stuff were stooped around it. They had their money ready as he handed them their goods: a frying pan for one, kerosene lantern for another, canned milk, a teapot. The others just looked on.

The onlookers made way for Cathy and me when we came out, and Cathy introduced me to them in their own language. I caught the words *"skooltrai"* and "Chicken" as she explained who I was. Then she reeled off their names to me, almost all of them Biblical: David Solomon, Paul Joe, Ruth James, Isaiah John. The older people nodded pleasantly. The younger ones, especially the girls, were kind of shy. They giggled when they were introduced. The ones with babies carried them on their back in a blanket. The older women, like most of the men, looked listless and tired, half of them with cheeks that had a hectic flush and eyes that glistened. I didn't know until Cathy told me a little later that they were the symptoms of TB. Half the village had it. The sores on some of the children were from glandular TB, Cathy said.

"You got chewing gum?" a squat, flat-featured woman asked me after Cathy introduced her as Mary Magdalene.

"Mary, where are your manners?" Cathy said.

"Hunh," Mary said. "I not need manners. Need chewing gum."

Cathy took me from one end of the village to the other. There wasn't much to see, but the more she showed me of it the worse I felt. I'd always thought of Indians who lived in the wilds as being strong, proud people able to live off the land, but here there were up to seven and eight people huddled in small one-room cabins. Through a couple of open doors I could see that except for some crude bunk beds, a stove and a few chairs and boxes, most of them were bare. The caches that squatted on poles in back of many of them should have been packed with dried meat and fish. Most of them held pitifully little, Cathy told me.

"They won't be empty in the winter, though," Cathy

35

said bitterly. "We'll be using them for the dead, keep them there until we can bury them in the spring." She saw the look on my face. "Sorry," she said. "It doesn't take much to get me started. You've got your own troubles."

I couldn't understand it. "Why do they live this way?"

"It's not an easy question to answer. Anyway it's too long to go into now. The main thing is not to judge what you see here by white standards. Most of these people didn't meet whites until about thirty or forty years ago. Up to then they were living in the Stone Age."

"What kind of Indians are they?" I asked her.

"Athapascans. That's the general designation for all the Indians up here. Then that's broken down into tribes. These people are Kutchins—Takhud Kutchins."

On the way back we passed a huge caldron boiling over an open fire. The odor from whatever was bubbling around in it was awful. An old crone, her spindly legs bowed so badly they looked like they were going to snap, was trying to get something out with a wooden spoon. But she was too short and couldn't reach over without almost falling in. Cathy said something to her in Indian, took the spoon and tin enamel plate from her and scooped out some pieces of salmon. When she handed it back the old woman took it gratefully. She had only a couple of teeth in her mouth and two lines of tobacco juice ran down each side of her chin.

"What's that cooking in there?" I said.

"Fish head, animal guts, rice. It's the dog pot. For them." She waved a hand toward one of the dogs. The old woman sat down on the ground and began eating. "That's Lame Sarah. That little boy who's going along with you—Chuck—he's been living with her. As you can see, he hasn't been eating steak and potatoes. She can barely take care of herself. Thank God he's getting out of here."

When we were ready to leave, the old woman and Chuck were standing by one of the mules, which had an old beat-up saddle on it. She was buttoning up Chuck's mackinaw. When she finished, she hugged him to her, murmuring endearments. He was only half listening, though. His eyes were on the mule and he looked worried. It towered over him the way Blossom did over me, and I knew exactly what was on his mind. The old woman let him go.

"Up we go, Chuck," Cathy said to him. She tried to lift him into the saddle, but he pulled away from her. "No!" he yelled. He was scared and I didn't blame him. A few of the kids were looking on, kind of anxious and envious at the same time. Cathy kneeled down in front of him. "Chuck, if you want to see your mother you're going to have to ride that mule."

Mr. Strong came over and asked what the matter was.

"He's a little afraid to get on," I said.

"Is that right," he said. Without another word he grabbed the back of Chuck's mackinaw, lifted him bodily and plunked him down on the mule's back. "You stay put," he warned him, "savvy?"

Terrorized, Chuck didn't answer, but he looked as though he were about to cry.

"You didn't have to do that," Cathy said. I didn't say anything, but I agreed with her. Mr. Strong acted as if he hadn't heard her.

"We are about ready to go, madam," he said to me. He glanced down at Cathy's feet. "Are you too destitute to buy shoes, Miss Winters?"

Before we left her house she'd slipped on a pair of black rubbers over her moccasins. I noticed that a few of the Indians were wearing the same thing.

"What makes you ask?" Her voice was cold as ice.

"I know the Indians are accustomed to wearing such footgear, but I've never seen respectable white women do so. They prefer shoes. From the rear I might have taken you for a squaw."

"Nobody asked you to look at my rear."

He got red, and I almost blushed myself. I would never have been able to say anything like that to an older person. Not that Cathy was being fresh or disrespectful. She was just giving tit for tat, but if it had been me I would have just shut up.

"Are you ready, madam?" he asked me.

37

After he boosted me up, he went down the line once more for a last check of everything.

"Do me a favor, Anne," Cathy said. She tossed her head in Mr. Strong's direction. "For all he cares, Chuck is just another piece of baggage—maybe less. Look after him, will you? He's hardly ever gone further than a few miles out of this village and he'll be scared to death."

"I'll look after him."

Cathy spoke to him in Indian, pointing to me a couple of times. "Remember," she said, "if you need anything you speak English. If you get scared, or you have to go to the toilet, you tell the teacher here, savvy?"

"*Aha*," he said.

"No more *aha*," Cathy said. "From now on it's yes, understand?"

He nodded.

"I say yiss and I tell Tisha."

She reached a hand up to me. "Good luck."

"Good luck to you, Cathy. I wish we'd had more of a chance to talk."

"Drop me a line when you get to Chicken if you feel like it."

I told her I would.

The pack train moved out then. We followed the curve of the river, and the last I saw of the Indian village before it disappeared behind us was the white wooden cross that stood on top of the church. Then that disappeared over the tops of the trees. I was glad when it was gone. The whole place was awful, and I just couldn't see any reason why they couldn't clean it up. I didn't want to say it to Cathy, but I wouldn't have stayed there for five minutes.

Mr. Strong slowed down and let the pack train move ahead. "I trust you're feeling much better, madam," he said when Chuck and I reached him.

"Much."

"Good. I would like to make up for some of the time we have lost."

"It's all right with me, but I don't know about Chuck."

He was still scared stiff, just barely managing to hang on.

"Don't worry about him," Mr. Strong said. "These Indians can take anything . . . What did you think of that young lady back there?"

"I liked her."

He was still angry, and I thought he was going to say something about her, but he changed the subject. "We will stop for lunch in a couple of hours, then push on until nightfall. We will spend the night at the O'Shaughnessy roadhouse. I trust you will bear up until then."

I would, but I didn't know about Chuck. Indian or whatever, he was only a little boy and he was going to need rest along the way.

He made out all right as long as we stuck to the river bank, but once we veered off and started going through rough country he looked as though he was going to be sick.

"Do you want to stop, Chuck?" I asked him. Pale and sweating, he was too miserable to answer.

A few seconds later the mule jumped over a dead tree and he went tumbling off. He landed on his hands and knees and didn't get up. Instead he started to retch. By the time I was able to get Blossom to stand still long enough to get off, Chuck had thrown up and was crying.

I led him over to the tree, sat down with him and put an arm around him.

Mr. Strong made his way back to us a few minutes later leading both Blossom and the mule.

"He fell off," I said.

Mr. Strong wasn't too happy. "Is he hurt?"

"No, but he's pretty badly upset."

Mr. Strong waited until he was able to stop crying, then he said, "Chuck, I think maybe you go back home, huh? I give you your stuff, you go home."

Chuck looked stricken. "You no want me?"

"You fall off mule. No can ride. We ride far, sleep tonight long distance from here, ride more tomorrow. Too tough for you."

"I ride," Chuck promised. "You take me I no fall down no more."

Mr. Strong raised a finger. "You fall once more you go home, savvy?"

He tried as hard as he could and my heart went out to him for it, but it was a losing battle. He managed to stay on for another mile before he fell off again. It made me wince, but he scrambled right to his feet and ran after the mule, trying to get it to stop. It wouldn't though, and he stood in the trail, tears of anger streaming down his face. "Sumbitch mool!" he called after it. "Dirty black sumbitch white mool!"

I stopped Blossom. In a couple of minutes Mr. Strong would be coming back. "Chuck, do you know your way back to the village from here?"

"Yiss," he said.

"Maybe you can try again when Mr. Strong comes through next time."

He wrung his hands. "Tisha," he said earnestly, "you talk Mista St'ong me? You talk him? Say one more time Mista St'ong he let me come I stay on goddamn mool. I stay on, Tisha, I stay on."

"I'll talk to him, but I don't think he'll listen to me."

He wrung his hands again, glancing up the trail, then dropped his hands in defeat. I felt terrible for him.

There was a big boulder a short distance away. I headed Blossom over to it and stopped him beside it.

"See if you can climb up and get on with me."

He clambered up and somehow we got him on in back of me. Then we rode on, his arms tight around my waist. Up ahead, Mr. Strong came in sight. He looked at me questioningly.

"He asked me if he could ride with me for a while," I said. "I'm getting pretty good now. I don't mind."

Whether he believed me or not, he wheeled his horse without saying anything. Chuck's head leaned against my back.

"Tisha?"

"Yes?"

"You one helluva good white woman," he said, tightening his arms around my waist. It made me feel good when he did it.

Somehow we made it to the next rest stop. How I didn't know, but we did. This time it was a sagging old

40

cabin that had sunk into the ground about a foot. I had to stoop down when I went through the door. Inside it was dark and dingy, half of it floored with planks and the other half dirt. A man and his wife owned it and from the way they acted you'd have thought they'd taken vows of silence. After the man asked Mr. Strong how the trip had been they hardly said anything. The man gave Mr. Strong and me a basin of water to wash with while the woman began ladling out some stew she had on the stove. When Mr. Strong finished washing, the man threw the water outside. He didn't fill the basin for Chuck. I said that Chuck would probably want to wash up too, but he didn't pay any attention to me. Mr. Strong sat down at the table and indicated the other place that had been set. "Sit down, madam."

"Isn't Chuck going to eat?" He'd sat down on the floor beside the stove and was leaning against the wall.

"You hungry, Chuck?" I asked him. He nodded up and down a few times.

Mr. Strong said, "I am not being paid for his transportation, madam. I'm doing it out of charity. Rest assured, he can take care of himself."

"I'll be glad to pay for his meal," I said. "Is that all right?" I asked the woman. She looked at Mr. Strong and he nodded, so she got a bowl for Chuck, cut a slice of bread and handed them to him where he sat. He finished off every bit of it.

We had a half hour before we were to leave and I spent part of it showing Chuck how to ride the mule. "You say whoa when you want him to stop, say giddap and give him a little kick when you want him to go." It took a little while for him to get it, but once he saw he could control the animal, he stopped being afraid. By the time we were ready to go, he was having fun. "Giddap, mool," he said, and we were off.

The longer we rode together, the more I liked him. If he was sore—and he had to be—he didn't complain about it. Instead he'd jump down every so often and lead the mule along. Walking didn't seem to bother him at all. Sometimes, when the horses had tough going, he even drew way ahead of us. When we caught up with him, he'd lead the mule over to a rock or a log and clamber back into the saddle without any help.

"I told you, madam," Mr. Strong said to me the first time he did it. "These Indian kids are hardy."

Our next overnight stop was the O'Shaughnessy roadhouse. It was run by a pleasant Irishman with a thick accent. Since I was a woman he gave up his bedroom, and I shared his bed with his wife, a plump Indian woman who saw to it that Chuck was well fed and bedded down in a warm sleeping bag in our room. I tucked him in and was going out when he called to me. "Tisha . . . You talk me?"

He wanted company. He was scared being in a strange place. I sat down on the sleeping bag. "I bet you'll be glad to see your mother," I said.

"Oh yiss," he said.

"She must be very nice."

"She beyoodeeful, Tisha—like you."

"I'll bet. Is your father in Chicken too?"

"Yiss."

"What kind of a man is he?"

"Big man," he said. "Got plenty guns, lotsa things. Got big glass eyes see far." He curled both his fists in front of his eyes to make binoculars. "I no like him," he added.

"Why not?"

"He no like me and Et'el."

"Is Ethel your sister?"

"Mmm . . . You got nice school?" he asked drowsily.

"I don't know. I haven't seen it yet."

"You let me come?"

"Sure. Do you like school?"

"Like too much," he said enthusiastically. "School plenty warm. Big. Miss Wintuhs make good grub for kids. You make good grub you school?"

"I never have, but I probably could. What do you like to eat?"

He didn't answer. He'd fallen asleep.

IV

We were up at five the next morning and on our way an hour after a hearty breakfast.

Right from the start Chuck was lively as a squirrel, riding that mule as though he'd done it all his life. In fact a couple of times he gave me a turn, slapping the mule to make him jog and pretty near falling off in the process.

He was comfortable around me, but not around Mr. Strong. For the whole trip I never heard him say a word when Mr. Strong was in earshot. Not that he talked much when we were alone either. Aside from the talk we had before he went to sleep the previous night, the only real conversation we had was about George Washington.

"You know Geo'ge Wash'ton?" he asked me.

"I've heard of him," I said.

He started giggling. "He chop down cherry tree."

"What are you laughing at?" I asked him.

"Cherry *tree*. Fun-ne-e-e." He kept giggling.

"Why is it funny?"

"Cherry grow on *tree*. I no believe."

"They do, though."

"You see?"

"Oh, yes."

"See *apple tree*?"

"Loads of 'em."

That really made him laugh. "How apple get on *tree*?"

"They just grow there. Oranges, pears—they all grow on trees."

He shook his head. It was hard for him to accept. "Potato?" he said mischievously.

"No, not potatoes."

"Leddus?"

"No, lettuce grows right out of the ground. You know that."

He laughed so much he had *me* giggling about it. When you saw it from his point of view, big pieces of fruit hanging from a spruce tree, or a birch, it did seem kind of funny.

Around noon, Mr. Strong stopped the pack train as we were making our way through a dense growth of cottonwood. The cowbells that had been clanking all the way down the line were quiet all of a sudden, and all I could hear were the merry waters of the meandering creek we'd been crossing and recrossing for a while.

"There it is, madam," Mr. Strong said. "That is Chicken."

I could barely make it out through the trees—a settlement about a mile away and a little below us. It was too far to really see what it was like.

"If you don't mind, Mr. Strong, I'd like to change my clothes."

"What is the matter with what you have on?"

Miss Ivy had always told me that first impressions were important. "Always look your very best," she said to me once. "No matter where you are you must try to be a lady."

"I'd feel more comfortable if I were more properly dressed."

Mr. Strong dismounted. "Will you want to wash up too?"

"I'd like to."

He was nice about it, unpacked the suitcase I asked for and brought it to the edge of the creek.

"We camp here?" Chuck asked.

"No," I said, "I'm going to change and wash up." I took off the army coat, Chuck watching me, interested. I asked him to turn around before I took off my shirt and knickers. "And don't look until I tell you to."

"Why I do this, Tisha?" he asked with his back to me.

"It's not important," I said. "Just stay that way until I tell you it's all right." It would have been too much

44

trouble to explain. When it came to modesty he didn't have any, urinating and moving his bowels in full view without embarrassment.

After I finished I put the army coat back on and brought my suitcase back. I'd changed into a long black skirt, cotton stockings and white blouse. "You look quite nice, madam," Mr. Strong said gallantly.

He put my suitcase back, then started moving down the line, checking the loads for the final time. "When we break out of these trees," he said, "the animals are going to be in a hurry."

There weren't as many as we'd started out with, about ten left now. The rest had been left along the way.

I looked off at the settlement, my stomach doing flip-flops. This is it, I thought. I'm almost there. I'd come to a far place, just as my Grandmother Hobbs used to tell me I would. When I was a little girl back in Colorado I used to hate the places I lived in: Blazing Rag, Big Four, Laveta, Evansville. Mining towns full of company shacks, they were all ugly. I felt sure I'd be living in them forever, but Granny said no I wouldn't and she'd been right.

"You be a teacher, Annie," she used to tell me, "an' you can go anywhere in the world you want."

When I thought about her now I could see her as clearly as if she were right in front of me. As a little girl I used to wish that when I grew up I could be just like her. She wasn't like anybody else in our whole family. The rest of us were light skinned and had blue eyes—or gray eyes like mine—and we were all very serious most of the time. But not Granny. She was a full-blooded Kentuck Indian and her face had been brown and broad, with wonderful black eyes that usually sparkled and laughed. If it hadn't been for her I couldn't think of what might have happened to me. More than likely I'd be sitting around somewhere feeling sorry for myself—the one thing Granny wouldn't ever let me do.

My father had never cared anything about me, nor my mother either for that matter, but Granny had adored me. Every time my father lost his job or left the house I was sent to live with her, and I couldn't wait to get there. I'd sit on the train coach overnight with my cardboard suitcase on the seat beside me and I could barely sleep for being so happy. She had a little farm in Deepwater, Missouri that had hardly any kind of a house on it at all, just a little ramshackle place in the backlands, but I thought it was wonderful. It made me smile just to think about it now. All the house had was one tiny bedroom that, even though it was three feet above the kitchen, had no stairs to it. Whenever Granny and I went to bed we had to shinny ourselves up. She must have been close to seventy the last time I was there, but she was able to scramble up almost as fast as I.

Living with her had been like living with another little girl who was just older and smarter than I was. There wasn't anything she couldn't do, except maybe handle a plow. At home my father had never let me help him because he said that I couldn't do anything right, but Granny had let me help with everything—milking the cow, tending the chickens, cooking and baking. She even let me help plant the vegetable garden, another thing my father wouldn't let me do. I couldn't keep the rows straight, he used to tell me. But Granny said she didn't give a hoot about straight rows. The potatoes I planted in her garden grew all over, sometimes crossing into the spinach, which curved around behind the tomatoes. It was less of a garden than a living salad, but when it all came out of the ground Granny couldn't get over how smart I was to have performed such a miracle, or so she told me.

I'd lived with her for a whole year that last time, and I'd never forget how terrible I'd felt when my mother finally wrote me to come home because my father was working again. Granny couldn't read, so I'd even thought of not telling her what was in the letter, but I couldn't lie to her. She felt as bad as I did, but there wasn't anything we could do.

That last night we'd spent together we tried to pretend that it was just like any other night. We went to bed right after supper the way we always did and I read to her from the Bible for a while. I knew the Book of Psalms was her favorite, so I was reading from that. Granny had decided she couldn't abide beds after my grandfather died, so we were lying on thick patchwork quilts on the floor. It was warm enough so that we didn't need a blanket, and she was curled up beside me, her knees pulled up and poking at her cotton nightie, her hair done in a long braid down to her waist. Her eyes were closed, and after a while I thought she was asleep, so I put the Bible away.

Before I leaned over to turn down the oil lamp I looked at her face, seeing the deep lines in it. It was so dark and looked so Indian that I could almost imagine her living in a tepee, sewing hides and things like that. She wasn't asleep, though. Her eyes popped open and she smiled at me. She was a tiny little thing, thin in the shoulders and heavy in the waist. Even though I was only eleven I was bigger than she was.

"You fooled me," I said.

It was a game we played sometimes. If she fell asleep while I was reading I could go without washing my hands and face the next morning. But if she caught me I had to wash my neck and my ears.

"No, I jus' dozed off. I really did."

She took my hand and squeezed it. I could feel the calluses on hers. "I'm gonna miss you, Annie."

I'd tried hard not to whine or cry up to then, but I couldn't keep it up. I managed to blurt out, "Granny, I don't want to go home ever again. I just don't want to. Please let me stay." Then I started to bawl so hard I didn't think I'd ever be able to stop. Granny got up and held onto me the whole time. She didn't say a word until she knew I was done.

"Annie . . ."

"Uh-huh."

"You know I don't want you to go home . . ."

"Yes."

"An' you know I never told you a lie."

"I know."

"Then you know if I tell you you're a lucky girl, that's the truth."

"How can I be lucky?"

" 'Cause a lot of people when they unhappy, they

47

can't do nothin' about it. But you can, 'cause you're smart. You got brains. An' when a person's got brains they got a ticket to any place they want to go—a ticket to the whole world."

"What kind of a ticket?"

She tapped her head. "Right up here. Didn't you tell me that if you was to work hard an' really study you could be teachin' school by the time you're sixteen?"

"That's what my teacher said."

"Then that's what you got to think about, about bein' a teacher an' gettin' outta them dirty minin' places."

"I'll never be able to do it, Granny, never." I was ready to start crying all over again, but Granny told me to stop right away. "An' listen to me, 'cause I ain't gonna say this twice."

She told me to sit up. "You're gonna do big things some day, Annie—real big things. But you can't do them big things if you're gonna go round feelin' sorry for yourself." She stopped for a second and she looked a little sad. "Your pa's my son, child. He ain't an easy man, but he ain't a bad man neither. Whatever you think about 'im you just remember he always stood on his own two feet an' he learned you the same. An' he always paid his own way. That's what the Hobbses is like—all of 'em. Maybe him and your ma ain't been too understandin' of you, but they fed you good an' give you a roof. That's more than many's got . . ."

"But they don't really want me, Granny."

"Yes they do. They jus' don't know how to show it. But never mind that. If you got just *one* person in the whole world who loves you an' believes in you, why that's wonderful, don't ya see. An' you got one—me. *I* love you, an' I believe in you. So anytime you get to thinkin' you ain't gonna make it, or that you can't do somethin' for your own self's sake, you do it for my sake. Will you?"

"Yes."

"Promise?"

"I promise."

"That's what I want to hear. You'll see, Annie. Some

day you're gonna go off to a new land just like a pioneer—just like your grampa an' me did. 'Cause you're that kind—a big person. An' that's the kind that goes to a new land."

"But there's no new lands, Granny. They're all gone."

"Shoot, child, there always be new lands."

"Where?"

"California maybe, I don't know. Or Alaska . . . Now there's a new land, Alaska."

I asked her what she knew about it, but she'd begun to get sleepy and so had I. A few minutes later we were asleep.

"Madam?" Mr. Strong had finished checking the animals over and had mounted up again. "I asked you if you are ready."

"Yes," I said, "I am."

As we moved forward I thought of that last morning I'd spent with Granny. When it was close to train time a neighboring woman had ridden into the yard with a buckboard. Granny had gone as far as the main road with us, then we hugged each other good-bye. She'd felt like a strong little bird.

As the buckboard drove off and I turned around to see her waving to me I had to fight to hold in the tears. "Don't worry," the driver said, "you'll be back some day."

I hadn't answered her, not knowing how to explain that I wasn't crying because I was going away, but because my grandmother had looked so small and alone as she stood in the middle of the road gently waving good-bye.

I'd never seen her again after that. She'd died during the first year I'd been teaching. I hadn't found out about it until three weeks after it happened. She had died in her sleep, my mother wrote me, and she had left me a legacy.

She sure had, but it wasn't the legacy my mother had written me about. It was one she'd given me a long time ago when I needed it most. And for that I'd never forget her.

"You'd best keep a tight rein on him, madam," Mr.

Strong was saying. As soon as we'd broken into the open, just as he'd predicted, the pack train speeded up and so did Blossom. I pulled back on the reins.

We'd descended into a small level valley. About a quarter of a mile ahead were maybe twenty-five or thirty buildings strung along the same side of the creek we were on.

"Is that all of it?"

"Just about."

I'd imagined it would be something like Eagle—a town—but from this distance it looked more like the Indian village we'd gone through. It couldn't have been built in a better place, though, set down snug on the valley floor. Low hills ringed the valley, rolling away from it into a blue haze of high mountain peaks. The creek was deep and narrow here, spilling down from the slope behind us. It got wider as it went, and right smack in the middle of the settlement a wooden bridge arched across it.

Blossom was just aching to break into a gallop and I had all I could do to hold him to a walk. It must have rained here recently, because halfway there we started winding around craters filled with muddy water.

"Keep away from those holes, madam," Mr. Strong cautioned me sharply when Blossom came close to one. "Some of them are deep. Fall in and you're liable not to come out."

I told Chuck to be careful too, then I asked Mr. Strong what they were.

"Prospect holes. Some of them go down forty feet. These miners don't bother to fill them up after they've dug them."

The ground was pock-marked with them all the way into the settlement and the ground got muddier as we went.

"Looks like everybody's waiting for us," I said. There was a whole crowd of people, maybe twenty or thirty, gathered in front of a tiny cabin. It wasn't much bigger than a hut, but with the American flag fluttering over it I figured it for the post office.

"They don't have much else to do but wait. It's a

big day for them. The women curl their hair, everyone spruces up. Some of them even take a bath."

Whether he was being sarcastic or not, I started grinning. The sweet fragrance of wood smoke wafted over and I felt proud enough to burst. I'd really done it, I thought, I was really a caution. I'd traveled through the wilderness just the way Granny Hobbs had done. Now here I was riding toward a frontier settlement as though it was the most natural thing in the world. Mr. Strong saw the look on my face and he smiled.

"What do you think of it?"

"It looks wonderful," I said.

It wasn't anything like the Indian village at all. The street between the creek and settlement was wide, with patches of late grass here and there, no tin cans, no trash. Even from here I could see vegetable gardens in a few backyards, along with dog kennels and stacks of corded wood. As soon as we neared the edge of the place the crowd started calling and waving. Between their hollering and sled dogs doing the same thing in their own way you'd have thought it was the Fourth of July.

The whole place was about three city blocks long, the post office right in the middle, opposite the wooden bridge. The first couple of cabins were a letdown. They were in bad shape, one just a rotted skeleton, roof gone and weeds spilling out the door, the other all boarded up. As far as I could make out, a few others down the line weren't lived in either. The ones that were lived in, though, were solid and sturdy, with traps, harness, washtubs and all kinds of stuff hanging from posts and railings. One of them even had a dogsled leaning against the side of it.

No sooner did we pass the first few cabins than Blossom broke into a jog and I couldn't hold him back. We jittered past a cabin that had a young birch tree growing from the sod roof, then almost ran into half a caribou carcass that was hanging from a tripod. Blossom was heading right for the stable, which was on the creek side of the road a little beyond the crowd. Somebody was way ahead of him, though. A man in knee-length boots ran out to cut him off, yelling and waving a beat-up fedora. Blossom gave up. It was too muddy for him to risk trying to dodge, so he just slowed down and ambled up to the crowd as though that's where he was headed all along.

A little old man appeared under him and grabbed his rein. "Steady as she goes." He smiled up at me from under the brim of a yachtsman's cap, a shrunken pug-nose face and teeth stained from chewing tobacco. "There y'are," he said, "safe in port. Hop right on down, little lady."

"Goddamn fool," another old man said to him. "Can't ya see she can't make it by herself? Wait'll I get a box."

Everybody who hadn't moved out to stop the pack animals and help Mr. Strong unload them stood around and stared up at me. If I hadn't been in Alaska for a couple of weeks I wouldn't have realized that most people were wearing their dress-up clothes. But now I was used to how drab everybody looked and how old-fashioned their clothes were, so I knew that even though the men's shirts were wrinkled and you could hardly tell what the original color was, the fact that they had a tie on meant they were dressed up.

Chuck had found his mother, I saw—a slight dark Indian woman who had a little girl by the hand. From the quick glimpse I caught of her as she kneeled down to hug him she looked like a beauty.

I kept smiling and getting smiles in return. A heavy-set Indian woman wearing a shawl gave me a big grin and waved. She had a little girl with her—half-white, I could see. I waved back to her. There were a few other children around, and one little boy in a gray cap and knickers looked away when I smiled at him.

I tried to figure out which building was the school-house, finally realizing that it had to be a big frame house with a homemade flagpole in front of it. It was opposite the stable a little further up. Mr. Strong had described it to me and I knew that my living quarters were in it too, so I was glad to see that it was larger than Cathy's place.

The second old man came back with a box and set it down. "Here you be, missis." He was almost hunch-backed, he was so stooped over, with a beard that hung from him like weeping willow.

What with everything else that had gone wrong on this famous trip, I should have known I wasn't going to make a dignified entrance. I let one foot down while the bearded man tried to steady me. As soon as I put my weight on the box it collapsed right under me and the next thing I knew I was sitting in the mud and everybody was staring down at me. I could hear a cou-ple of the kids laughing and I was so embarrassed I wanted to disappear right then and there.

The old men helped me up and fussed around trying to get some of the mud off me until they were pushed aside by a big burly woman.

"Awright, awright, for Chrissake. Leave 'er alone be-fore you wind up killin' 'er. I'm Angela Barrett," she announced. "You're the new schoolmom, I take it. What's yer moniker?"

I told her, and she led me over to another woman who was wearing a long navy blue coat buttoned up to the neck. She had a broken nose. "She's the new schoolmom, awright," Angela said to the woman.

"I'm Maggie Carew," the woman said. "What's your name, honey?"

"Anne Hobbs." My skirt was clinging in back of me and I could feel water trickling down my legs. I just hoped it didn't make me look ridiculous.

"Let's get you over to the schoolhouse."

I'd been right about which building it was. When we stepped up onto the porch, Angela Barrett moved to the closer of two doors. It was studded with mean-looking nails that stuck out about three inches. "This here's the schoolroom," she said, opening it. "The oth-er door there's to your quarters. Watch out for them nails."

As I followed her in my heart sank. The room was big, but it wasn't like any schoolroom I ever saw, and it was in a shambles. A few assorted tables and chairs were piled in one corner, and some boxes in yet another corner held old books and papers. Piles of dust and dirt were everywhere, and a few yellowed papers littered the floor, mice droppings all over them. The plank flooring was buckled and warped, higher in the center than it was at the walls. The tables and chairs all sat at an angle and I felt seasick just looking at them. Light came in through windows fogged with smoke and grime.

"Needs a little cleaning up," Maggie admitted, "but I'll give you a hand with it." Her broken nose made her look tough, but I had a feeling she was pretty decent. I guessed she was about forty.

The other room was neater, the same size as the schoolroom, but except for a brass bed that had no mattress, two chairs, and a big potbellied stove, it was empty.

"How do you like 'er?" Angela Barrett asked. She must have weighed two hundred pounds and she towered over me. Her voice was rasping, and there was a red rash on her nose and all around it. I tried to think of something nice to say.

"It's a good big room."

"Glad you feel that way," Angela said. "You're the one's gonna be livin' in it."

"Do you think it will take much time to get it ready?"

"What do you mean ready?" Angela asked. "It's ready now."

Both women were staring at me as if there was something wrong with me. I was almost afraid to ask the next question. "Don't I have to have a mattress?" I said. "Or blankets, or a table?"

It took a moment before they seemed to realize that I had a point.

"Where'na hell'd it all go?" Angela said, as if she'd turned her back for a minute and somebody had snatched everything away. "It's your fault, Maggie, you're the school janitor. It's your responsibility."

"When there's no school there's no janitor," Maggie said tartly, "and there ain't been a school here in well over a year."

"What are we gonna do?" Angela said.

Maggie thought for a minute. "Come on," she said finally.

Angela and I followed her outside. At the post office, almost all the pack animals had been unloaded. The stuff everyone had ordered was lying on the ground: boxes of candles and flashlight batteries, sacks of flour, crated gasoline cans and cans of kerosene, tied-up bundles of dried fish and a whole bunch of packages of parcel post.

"How about my cornflakes?" the bearded old man who'd tried to help me was saying to Mr. Strong. He could just straighten up enough to look Mr. Strong in the eye. "I had a dozen boxes of cornflakes on order an' you didn't bring 'em."

"They'll arrive in due time, Mr. Spratt."

"That's what you told me the last three times. I ordered them cornflakes by parcel post four months ago an' they should be here. You got 'em stuck there in the warehouse at Eagle, now don't ya?"

A lot of people were beginning to mutter that the old man was right, and Mr. Strong was getting mad. "You heard what I said, Mr. Spratt."

"I heard you. An' I know you ain't brought'm 'cause it don't pay you to bring'm out with the rest of the parcel post right now—take up too much space on them precious horses a yours. Well you damn well better bring'm out next time, or I'm writing to Washington D.C. You got a mail contract says you bring out *all* the mail—not what personally suits ya."

"Uncle Arthur, hold on a minute if you can," Maggie broke in. "We got a problem that needs everybody's attention . . . This is Anne Hobbs, our new teacher," she said to the crowd.

"I don't doubt she's a teacher," a quiet voice said from somewhere, "but she sure don't look new."

There was some laughing, but Maggie cut it short.

"Miss Hobbs here needs some help," she went on. "Some of you mutts have borrowed everything there is in the teacher's quarters. There's nothin' left in there and I mean nothin'. I ain't sayin' who took what, but it's got to be packed back here pronto. The poor girl's got an empty cabin."

55

"What do you need, Miss?" a tall good-looking man asked. He was trying on a heavy fleece-lined jacket he must have ordered.

"Just about everything."

"I've got a couple of good Hudson Bay blankets I can spare."

Angela Barrett snorted. "Leave it to Joe. Gives you a couple of blankets one day, tryin' to climb under 'em the next."

"How about the rest of you?" Maggie said.

"We got a good set of tin dishes she can borrow," a girl of about ten said. She was with two older girls who looked like twins, both of them rawboned and husky. "Can she, Pa?" she asked. A red-haired man beside her nodded.

After that the offers came thick and fast—a broom and pan, a rocking chair, a wash boiler and a dozen other items. One man said he'd taken the chifforobe and would return it. Everybody got into the spirit of the thing, telling me not to worry, they'd take care of me. It made me feel so good that when Maggie Carew asked me if I wanted to say a few words, I was just about able to say thanks and that I was glad to be here.

The men were as good as their word. While I kept busy cleaning and scrubbing up the place the rest of the day, everybody kept trooping in carrying things. Within a few hours I not only had a firm straw mattress for the bed, but also a blanket, a pillow, a table and some chairs. Someone even thought to bring a water barrel. My prize possession was a wood-burning cookstove. It took four men to carry it in, and it was a beauty. Black wrought iron with shining nickel-plated fittings, it had hardly been used. All I needed was a stovepipe and I could start cooking.

The two old men who'd helped me down from Blossom brought me presents. "Uncle Arthur" Spratt, the little bent-over man who'd been angry about his corn flakes, came by with a few jars of wild cranberry jam he'd preserved himself. The man in the yachtsman's cap gave me a can of bear lard. "It's kinda sweeter'n the lard you're used to," he said, "but you just add a little salt to it and it's just as good."

56

Granny sure knew what she was talking about, I thought. People who go to a new land *are* big people, kind and generous.

I didn't even have to clean the place alone. Five of my pupils showed up to help. The three Vaughn girls were first—Elvira, the girl who'd asked her father for the tin dishes, and her older twin sisters, Evelyn and Eleanor. Then Maggie Carew's two children came over. They all went to work with a will, so that by late afternoon the windows were sparkling and the whole place looked and smelled clean. While we were working the man who'd promised me the blankets rode up. "I'm Joe Temple," he said when he came in. The two blankets he'd brought were almost new. I offered to pay him for them, but he said forget it. "Use them for as long as you like."

He was good-looking and he knew it. He was too old for me—I figured he was about thirty-two or thirty-three—but I could have thought of half a dozen teachers in Forest Grove that would have taken to him right away. "You've got your work cut out for you," he said, looking around the room. He was still holding onto his riding crop and he slapped it against his boot a couple of times. I'd unpacked all my dresses and hung them wherever I could find a nail. "I haven't been Outside in a couple of years," he said, looking at them, "but I thought they were wearing dresses shorter than that."

"They are. I guess I'm pretty conservative."

"Not all the time, I hope." I didn't know how to take that so I didn't say anything. "You'll have to let me take you out to dinner," he said.

"I didn't see any restaurant signs coming in."

"Right down the street—Maggie's roadhouse. She's the best cook in town."

"Maybe after I get settled."

"Settled or not you're going to have to eat dinner. How about tomorrow night? I won't bite you."

"All right, you're on."

He whacked his crop against his boot again. "See you around six," he said, going out. "I'll go over and tell Maggie now."

Wow, I thought, things really happen fast around here. I haven't been in Chicken more than a few hours and already I have a date.

Maggie Carew came by a little before dark and sent the children home. "Place looks a lot better," she said.

"Thanks to you. I appreciate your helping me."

"Don't mention it. Joe Temple tells me you're comin' over the roadhouse with him tomorrow night. Fast worker, that one," she said admiringly.

"What does he do?"

"Mines, like everyone else. Damn good miner too. Got a college education to boot. Do 'im good to go out with a white woman for a change. You hungry?"

"Starved."

"Come on over the roadhouse when you're ready and I'll fix you some supper. On the house."

"Thanks, but Mr. Strong said he'll be coming back with some food and I was to wait for him."

She went to the back of the room and opened the door that led into a small storage room—the cache. Her high-buttoned shoes made a lot of noise on the plank floors. "You'll have plenty of room for your outfit," she said.

"Outfit?"

"Your grub for the winter, flour, sugar, all a that."

"I don't have any."

"Didn't they tell you to have an outfit shipped in when you were hired?"

"No."

Now that she'd mentioned it, I realized I didn't have even a bit of food.

"That makes sense. Well, don't worry, you won't starve. When the freeze-up comes Walter Strong'll bring one in for you. It'll cost you a little more, but not that much. We'll help you out in the meantime. Well, I got supper to make. Drop by the roadhouse later if you like."

Just then I remembered her daughter. Her face lit up when I told her what Jeannette had said. "Thinks she's gonna have a girl, eh? Well, I hope so. If she's anything like Jennie that'll be two good things I got outta this life."

As she went out I asked her what all the nails in the doors were for.

"Bear," she answered. "Last teacher here threw a fit when one came sniffin' at the door one day. I'd have'm hammered down if I was you. Kids might hurt themselves."

Alone, I sat down on the bed and looked the room over. It needed a lot of work. The floor was as bad in here as it was in the schoolroom. In some places it had dropped below the walls and I could see the ground outside. The walls were in bad shape, too. They were just rough planks with canvas stretched over them like wallpaper, and the canvas was peeling in places. But I didn't care. This was the first place I'd ever had to myself. Right now, with everything piled all over, it looked like a secondhand store, but when I fixed it up it would look nice, nicer even than Cathy Winters' place.

It was getting chilly, drafts coming in from the spaces around the molding. I went over to check the potbellied stove. Maggie Carew's son Jimmy had built a fire in it to get the dampness out, but I'd forgotten to keep it up. Opening the door, I saw that the wood he'd put in was just embers now. I tried to start it up again, but I didn't have any kindling. There was no water left either, so I took a pail and went outside.

In the Vaughn cabin, next door, pots and dishes were rattling as the girls prepared supper. A couple of them were talking, but I couldn't make out what they were saying. Standing there outside, the darkness falling fast, I felt lonely all of a sudden. Except for the sounds from a few cabins, everything was quiet. There weren't as many people here as I thought there'd be. Out of all the buildings on each side of me there were maybe only six that had people living in them—the Vaughns' next door, the Carews' roadhouse, Angela Barrett's cabin and a couple of cabins way down at the far end.

The only other cabin that was occupied was on the other side of the creek. The unoccupied ones were shells, most of them—the windows taken out, the doors gone. The rest were outbuildings, privies, stables, tool sheds and the like. Most of the people who'd been waiting at the post office lived on the outlying creeks.

It was a little like being in a ghost town. Twenty and thirty years ago this had been a thriving settlement, men had streamed in here looking for gold, built these cabins and dreamed about making a big strike. Most of them were gone now. Almost everyone here now had come after the rush was over, like me.

The sun was gone, a faint orange glow in the purple sky.

I filled the pail with water and started lugging it back, stopped halfway to rest. I could even see inside my quarters it was so dark. I felt a little scared. Maybe it was because everything looked so rough and bare, I didn't know. Suddenly it didn't seem so friendly. Back in Oregon, where I'd taught up until last June, the nights were made for a nice walk or a soda at the drugstore. Here it was all wilderness. At night everything went into hiding. I picked up the pail and hurried back into my quarters.

Inside, it was almost too dark to see. I thought about going next door to the Vaughns and asking if I could wait there for Mr. Strong, but I didn't want to bother them. Besides, if I was going to get used to being on my own I might as well start now.

I thought I remembered seeing a couple of stubs of candles somewhere. I was lucky. I found them right away, along with a box of matches, in one of the fruit boxes nailed above the counter. Lighting the candles, I put one on the counter and the other on my table. Then I sat down to wait.

The candles didn't give too much light and they made shadows go jumping all over.

After a while I began to get cold, so I got up and walked around, stopping to listen for the sound of Mr. Strong returning. But it stayed quiet outside. Too quiet, I thought. I couldn't hear a sound.

A slight wind shook the door and for some reason I thought right away of the grizzly that had pounced on the caribou calf. I caught myself listening for the soft pad of an animal outside.

The door to the schoolroom was open and it looked

like a big dark hole, so I closed it. My footsteps sounded hollow on the plank floors and I realized suddenly that I had no protection here at all. All I had between me and the wilderness outside was a few walls. I didn't even have locks on the doors. Anyone who wanted to could walk right in through the schoolroom or my front door. They could even come in through the cache, since it had a door that led outside. I tried lodging a chair in front of the doors, but the knobs were too high.

My nickel-plated revolver, still holstered, lay in a box beside the bed. Tying it around my waist, I felt a little better.

A half hour later Mr. Strong still hadn't come back. One of the candle stubs was flickering out and the other had only two inches to go. Once it was gone I'd be left in complete darkness. There was a gas lantern hanging from the ceiling, but there was no gasoline for it. Even if there had been, I wouldn't have known how to work it.

Then I heard footsteps outside.

I knew they didn't belong to Mr. Strong. He'd gone to make some deliveries on some outlying creeks and I'd have heard his horses. The footsteps couldn't belong to a neighbor either, because they were coming from the brush back near the outhouse. They padded closer, moving around the side of the house. I waited, hoping they'd pass by, and yet something told me that whoever they belonged to was coming after me.

I was right. They stopped in front of the porch. I got to my feet, wondering if maybe I ought to slip out through the cache and run next door. Before I could make up my mind the footsteps came up on the porch and I was too scared to move. A second later I almost jumped as the ghostly outline of a face appeared at the window, then ducked away. Then there was a soft knock at the door.

Taking the revolver out, I stayed still as a rabbit, hoping whoever it was would go away. When the knock came a second time, I decided that whoever was out there could get in just by turning the doorknob anyway. He'd be less antagonized if I invited him in than if I didn't. The revolver was too heavy for me to hold in one hand, so using both I pointed it at the door. "Come in," I said, "but be careful."

The chair I'd left in front of the door slid forward and I could just make out a dark man with thick black hair staring at me from the porch. As soon as he saw the gun he raised his hands. He was nervous, but he smiled. He was darker than a Spaniard, and his teeth looked deadly white.

"You better be careful," I said. "I shot a bear with this once." I was so scared I didn't know what I was saying.

He stopped smiling. "I can believe that," he answered.

"Did you come to see me?" I asked him.

I was hoping he'd say he got the wrong cabin by mistake, but he didn't. He said, "Yes."

"Well, you can come in if you want, but I'd much rather you didn't." That sounded silly, I realized.

He stayed at the threshold and kept his hands up. "I just came to talk to you," he said.

"What about?"

"My mother sent me over to see if you'd like to have supper with us."

As soon as he said that I realized how silly I was being. He wasn't even much older than I was, I could see now, and he was embarrassed. So was I. "Oh."

"Can I put my hands down?"

I nodded yes.

"I won't come in," he said, "so could you point that gun away?"

"Sure," I said. "I'm sorry. You can come in if you want." I meant it this time.

"That's all right. I'm sorry I scared you. My father said you came in with the pack train today, and my mother thought this being your first night, you wouldn't be set up to cook. She thought maybe you'd like to eat with us."

"Oh," I said again. "That's awfully nice of her, but I better not. Mr. Strong is coming back soon and he'll be bringing dinner with him."

He looked uncomfortable. "Well, my mother said to

tell you that if you need any help at all you just let us know."

He looked the room over, not able to think of anything else to say.

"Do you live here in the settlement?" I asked him finally.

"No, a little further up Chicken Creek," he said.

I tried to think of something else to say, but for the life of me I couldn't.

"I guess I better be going," he said.

I was disappointed. Now that I wasn't afraid of him I wished he could keep me company until Mr. Strong came back. But he said good-bye and closed the door before I could even think to ask him his name.

"That was young Fred Purdy," Mr. Strong said when he finally came back. He seemed pleased that I hadn't accepted the invitation. Later, as we were finishing the cold chicken he had brought, he smiled when I mentioned how I'd held the gun on Fred.

"You'd have been more than safe with him. Fred undoubtedly will never amount to anything, but he is a fine young fellow . . ."

"Why won't he ever amount to anything?"

Mr. Strong nibbled the last piece of meat from the chicken bone he was chewing and laid it on the plate, satisfied.

"Couldn't you see? He's a half-breed," he said, wiping his hands. "Mother's Eskimo, father's white."

"He seemed very nice."

"He is. Smart too. Smarter than most breeds. The whole family is as good as they come."

"Then why won't he ever amount to anything?"

He got up and began to collect the plates. "I told you," he said patiently, "he's a breed—a product of race mixture. That's what happens when you mix the races. I've seen it all my life—seen it in the South, see it here. It's always the same—the offspring have to suffer."

He made it sound as if anybody who wasn't all white had some kind of a disease. It kind of disappointed me in him a little. I wondered what he'd think of me if he knew my grandmother had been Indian.

"What is Chuck's father like?" I asked him, changing the subject.

"Joe? Good miner, good trapper. You can bet your bottom dollar he regrets ever having involved himself with a native woman."

"Joe Temple is Chuck's father?"

"Why do you look surprised?"

"He's supposed to take me to dinner tomorrow night."

"Well, it's nothing for you to be concerned about. Mr. Temple is a gentleman and he will treat you like a lady."

"But he's married."

"No, he is not and I'm sure he thanks God for it."

Married or not, I still felt funny about going out with him.

Before Mr. Strong left I knew just about everything there was to know about everyone here. As far as the Purdys were concerned, he respected Mr. Purdy even though he felt he'd lowered himself by marrying an Eskimo woman. He advised me to act towards them the way he did himself—"the way you'd act towards anybody who abides by the law no matter what their color is . . . You know what I mean, just about the same way you'd act towards niggers."

V

After Mr. Strong left I was so tired I could hardly keep my eyes open. Leaving the gas lantern on, I lay down on the bare mattress with my clothes on, and pulled a couple of blankets over me. But I couldn't sleep. It was so quiet outside that the creek sounded as though it was right in the room. The slightest draft made the doors rattle. It was cold out too. I could feel it slipping in through the cracks in the floor and walls. Then a small animal began moving around the side of the house, and every time I closed my eyes I imagined that something was going to charge into the room and pounce on me.

Finally I got up, pumped up the light in the lantern and got my Bible. But I couldn't concentrate on it. My ears perked up every time one of the horses snuffled in the stable across the way or kicked the side of the stall. I wished I was in Blossom's place. At least he had a bar across his door and plenty of company.

I started to think about the next few days. Besides having to get these quarters into shape, I had a lot of work to do in the schoolroom before school started. There were hardly any supplies, no blackboard, no paper that I could find, and not many books. When I had mentioned the shortages to Maggie Carew, she didn't seem to think anything of it. "You'll make out," she said.

It was almost the same thing Lester Henderson had told me when he interviewed me in Juneau. He was the commissioner of education for the whole Territory and when I told him I was worried because I'd never taught in a one-room schoolhouse, he'd told me not to be.

"Forget it," he'd said. "You're going to do fine." He was a big, broad-shouldered man, as easygoing as a Saint Bernard.

I could remember looking out the window of his office and seeing all the ships moored in Gastineau Channel far below. The *Dorothy Alexander* had been among them, the boat that would take me to Skagway.

"It'll be much easier than you think," he'd gone on. "I doubt that you'll have many more than ten pupils, and I know you'll be able to handle them. What does concern me a little is your age. May I be frank with you?"

"Of course."

"You're just about one of the youngest teachers I've ever sent into the bush. Ordinarily I'd place you here in Juneau first, or some other more well-populated place. The only reason I haven't is that it's not easy to find qualified people who will go into the bush. Does that surprise you?"

"Yes." I really was surprised. "When you lectured at my school I figured you'd be swamped with applications."

"Well I'm not. I hope that doesn't make you less enthusiastic."

"Not at all."

"Good. You see, I fought hard to get these Territorial schools established. It wasn't easy, but I did it because I believed that where there is even one child who needs schooling—not ten as the law says there must be—there should be a school for him. What I'm trying to say, Miss Hobbs, is that education is so important to me that despite my misgivings about sending a nineteen-year-old cheechako into the bush country, I'm going to send you anyway."

"A cheechako is a greenhorn, isn't it?"

"The greenest. You've done some reading about Alaska, I see . . ." He paused, then went on. "Before you leave this office I'd like to give you a bit of advice. I have the feeling that you are a pretty tolerant young lady—young enough to be open to new ideas. Where you're going you'll find that most people are not. They have their own code and they don't take to anybody who tries to go against that code or change it. In short, I hope you're not going into this job with, well . . . shall I say missionary zeal?"

"I don't think so," I said, but I'd gotten all red. More than once I'd thought of myself as being like a young Florence Nightingale. I had even imagined the smiles on the faces of hardy backwoods parents as their children came home from my log-cabin school brimming over with the learning I'd given them. "I've tried to keep my mind open," I added maturely.

We talked a while longer and he shook my hand warmly before I left. "I want to hear from you," he said, "and I don't mean that I want to hear from you only in your regular monthly report. Write to me anytime you need help or advice. Alaska's a big place, but it's just like the small town you've been teaching in.

We all know each other, and we're concerned about each other. If there's anything I can do for you, let me know immediately."

He'd meant it, I knew, and it made me feel good even now. I'd write to him tomorrow about the books and supplies before Mr. Strong left. But now that I was here I was more worried than ever about being able to handle the job. Teaching in Forest Grove, I'd had everything mapped out for me. There was a system, a time for study, for recess, for lunch, for auditorium, for everything. There was order and routine. Here I didn't even have a register, I realized, or report cards. I wondered what I would do if I couldn't control the class. What if they didn't like me or didn't want to listen to me?

The more I thought about it the worse I felt. All I had was a high-school education. I knew my subject matter pretty well, but suppose a couple of the children were smarter in some subjects than I was? I didn't even have a library I could go to for more advanced materials. Suddenly the whole idea of coming here seemed like a big mistake. I was going to fall on my face, I was sure of it ...

The sun was streaming through the window when I woke up, but the room was so chilly and damp that my breath steamed. There was still some water left, and Mr. Strong had brought coffee, so I set about making a fire. Five minutes later the room was so full of smoke I had to go out on the porch.

Outside, the sun shone down on hills covered with frost. As though there had been a shower of diamonds the night before, the whole valley sparkled and glittered with the reflected colors of autumn.

Across the road Mr. Strong's stable was open and I heard him murmuring to the horses and moving around. A few moments later he came out leading four of them, but stopped when he saw the smoke billowing out of my doorway.

"It's only the stove," I told him. He nodded and continued to lead his horses to one of the big prospect holes filled with rainwater. Breaking the light crust of ice in a few places, he left them to drink, then made his way past me. In a few moments he had cleared the smoke from the house.

After he started a fire in the stove, he took me over to his store, a small log building about five cabins away.

The inside of the store was so crowded with things that except for a narrow path to the counter and some sitting space around an oil-drum heater there was hardly room to walk. Canvas parkas, snow shoes, animal traps and just about everything else hung from the ceiling. Odors were all over the place—of wool and cotton from a counter loaded with pants, overalls and long underwear, of furs and hanging slabs of bacon. In front of the heater a deep pan of yellow water gave off the rank smell of cigarette butts and tobacco juice.

Looking the shelves over, I felt a lot better. There was everything here, even tins of butter. Inside of a few minutes, Mr. Strong and I had loaded up two sacks with canned goods, cereal, flour, sugar and other staples. A little while later, after I'd rustled up some bacon, eggs and hot coffee for us on top of the potbellied stove, he paid me my first compliment. "It is heartening to know, madam, that there are still girls around who can make a proper breakfast." He gave me the key to the store, something he said he'd never done with anyone else. I was to take what I wanted as I needed it, and we'd settle up once a month. In return I agreed that if anyone wanted anything while he was away I would give it out and keep a record of what was bought.

By mid-morning I had the furniture in my quarters arranged fairly nice. I was working in the schoolroom when I heard footsteps on the porch. It was Fred Purdy and what I thought at first were two younger sisters with him. Only one of them was his sister, though. The other was his mother. I doubted she weighed more than ninety pounds. She was even smaller than Granny Hobbs, and cute. She was Eskimo for sure—round dark face, wide mouth and strong uneven teeth. She just seemed to light up when she saw me and I liked her right off.

"Ah, the teasher," she said. "I am so happy to meet

you. I am Mrs. Purdy, and this is my daughter, Isabelle."

She put a hand out and it felt small and capable. "My son Frayd have tell me how pretty you are," she said after I introduced myself. "Before he say only lynx is pretty. Now I see for myself. Indeed, you are very lovely."

She was like a little queen, and she wasn't putting it on. She was dressed beautifully too—in a cloth parka that looked like a Fifth Avenue design, and a soft fur hat.

When I invited them in she complimented me on how much I'd done with the cabin. We all sat down and had a cup of tea and talked for a while. Before I knew it I was telling them about the trip out on Blossom, but instead of it coming out the way it really was, it sounded funny, especially the part about my landing on my behind in the mud outside the post office. I never heard anybody laugh the way Fred did when I told the story—with so much fun and enjoyment that it made me laugh myself. By the time I told how I'd walked in here to find hardly a stick of furniture we were all doubled over.

"Indeed, Ahnne," Mrs. Purdy said, wiping away tears, "there is mush work to do in this place." She grew serious. "You cannot live here in sush . . . sush . . ."

Fred supplied the word. "Conditions."

"Conditions, yes. Thank you, Frayd."

"Do you really think it's so bad?"

"It is not terreebul, yet it is not good. There are many things to do here." She sent Isabelle out to play, then went around the room, shaking her head. "If you are to live here, you must have home that is comfortable, warm." She pointed to the baseboard where light was coming in. "This must be fixed or in winter you will freeze to the death. No, this will not do." She reeled off all the other things that had to be fixed—sagging shelves, loose floorboards, crippled tables in the schoolroom.

"You will work here," she said to Fred, "and Father will do your chores at home."

Fred grinned. "Yes, boss."

"How mush work, you think?"

"Oh . . . Couple months maybe."

She smiled. "You wish to open school when, Ahnne?"

"In a few days if I can."

"You will do it in a few days, Frayd, no?"

"I will do it, boss, yes."

Before they left Mrs. Purdy asked me if I'd like to come to supper that night. I couldn't because Joe Temple was taking me over to the roadhouse, so we made it for the next night.

A couple of hours later Fred came back driving a wagon that looked like a long thin buckboard. It had a load of rough boards on it and a big tool box.

We were a little shy with each other at first, but after we worked together for a while we were gabbing about everything under the sun, from the Marines in Nicaragua to Lindbergh's trip across the Atlantic. I told him I was surprised he knew as much about what was going on in the world as I did.

"One thing everybody does plenty of around here is read," he said. "There's not much else to do at night."

By noontime he'd connected a stovepipe to the cookstove and run it up through the roof. After we had a fire going in it I made lunch for the two of us—canned ham and sweet potatoes. "There has to be something else people do here at night besides read," I said while we were eating.

"Every other Friday night there's a dance. We've been having them at the roadhouse, but as soon as the schoolroom's in shape we'll have them there."

"When will the first one be?"

"You call it. You're the teacher."

We decided on a week from the following Friday.

While we worked people kept dropping by to lend me more things they thought I might need, a kettle, some spoons and knives, even an old encyclopedia. I told Fred that I knew people in Alaska were hospitable, but I hadn't expected it to be like this.

"Everybody wants to do what they can to make you stay," he said.

"Why should they think I won't?"

"For the same reason the teacher who was here last didn't. This is tough country, especially for a cheechako."

"When do I stop being a cheechako and become an Alaskan?"

"Maybe by the time the river goes out in the spring."

"What do you mean—maybe?"

He looked at me almost the way Mr. Strong did that day when he'd ridden back to give me his army coat —as if I was a foreigner. Only Fred's look was a little different. The only thing I could liken it to was the way one forest animal might look at another to see if it was its own kind. If it wasn't there was no offense taken. The animal just loped off. It gave me a funny feeling.

"Well," he said, "some people never really become Alaskans. They never get to like it the way it is. They just tolerate it."

"I don't know what you mean."

"It's hard to explain, maybe because it's something you have to feel inside. All these old sourdoughs around here—they're real Alaskans. They came here way back before I was born, when there was nothing out here but raw land. They fought the cold and the rivers, built cabins and barely stayed alive. They were lonely and went hungry, froze their feet and their hands and hardly ever took enough gold out of the ground to keep themselves in grub, but they made it."

"You think I'll make it?"

"No reason why you shouldn't. Just make sure you've got good footgear and plenty of warm clothes —and take people's advice."

"When they give it to you, you mean. Up to now I keep finding things out hit and miss." I told him about Mr. Strong offering me his old army coat back in Eagle. "When I turned it down he didn't try to convince me I was wrong."

"That's the way it is. If somebody tells you something you have to listen the first time. They won't tell you twice. They'll let you find out for yourself."

"What do you think of Mr. Strong? You think he's an Alaskan?"

71

"He sure is. He cuts it a little thin sometimes and he's tough on horses, but he's skookum—he's got guts. The people around here don't appreciate him much because once in a while he'll lose some mail or other stuff in the river."

"Stuff like me you mean."

That made him laugh. "I heard about that," he said. Then he went on as though it wasn't anything out of the ordinary. "What most people don't realize is that he's been mushing that trail for over twenty years and no matter what it's like—blown in, flooded or frozen—he shows up here on time if he possibly can. Twenty-four days out of every month he's on trail all alone and he's usually here like clockwork on the eighth, the eighteenth and the twenty-eighth. But if he shows up a day late once in a while, or he won't pack parcel post out here in summer, people get all riled up at him and start sending letters to Washington D.C. saying the mail contract ought to be taken away from him. Well, he's still got it—because there's nobody else can do the job better. You'll see what I mean after the freeze-up."

I wondered if he knew what Mr. Strong thought of him and his family, and I had a feeling he did.

We kept working all day and he didn't go home until a little before Joe showed up.

Joe came in wearing the fleece-lined jacket I'd seen him trying on when I arrived, and he had a tie on. He was surprised I was ready. "I was ready an hour ago," I said.

"You're still operating on Lower 48 time," he said, helping me on with my coat. "You're going to have to get used to Alaska time."

"What's Alaska time?"

"An hour or two early or an hour or two late. Maybe more depending on the weather. If somebody doesn't come at all you know something held them up and they'll be along the next day, or the next."

"I hope the school won't work that way."

The roadhouse was about five cabins down from me. Inside it reminded me of a frontier stagecoach stop I'd seen once—rough plank floors, ceiling black with wood-smoke, a couple of long tables covered with oilcloth and a bunk room and stable in the rear. I wished I had the old upright piano in the corner, though. I could have used it in the schoolhouse for music appreciation and singing. I made a mental note to ask Maggie if she'd let me bring the class in occasionally.

There wasn't anybody else in the place, so except for Maggie and her family, Joe and I had the place to ourselves. Maggie gave us a small table against the rear wall. The stable was on the other side of it and it took me a little while to get used to the horses that kept snuffling and sniffing the whole time we ate.

The boiled moose tongue she made was delicious, and while we ate I found out that Joe had gone to Washington State University. He'd come to Alaska in 1920, right after he got out of the Army. After we finished eating, Maggie and her husband sat down with us while her two little boys sat at one of the big tables listening.

"Heard you dropped in for a visit with Cathy Winters," Maggie said. "Did you see that Indian buck she's living with?"

"I was in her place. It didn't look to me as if anybody was living there but her."

"I don't mean *living* with," Maggie said impatiently. "I mean doing things she shouldn't with." Her two little boys, Jimmy and Willard, were all ears. "He's a tall lean thing, ugly as sin and scars all over his neck. What's his name?" she asked her husband, raising her voice a little because he was hard of hearing.

"Titus Paul." He was a small intense man. His false teeth were uncomfortable and he kept clicking and grinding them.

"I just saw him for a second," I said. "I wasn't there for very long."

"Well I'll bet a Stetson to an old spud she's living with 'im," Mr. Carew said. "She don't act like any white girl *I* ever saw. Spoils them Indians rotten."

"She's one a them communists," Maggie said, "—believes in free love an' all that. She won't be around much longer. Comes spring they'll send her Outside on the first water—kick 'er right up the Yukon. How's the Purdy kid comin' along fixin' your place up?"

73

"Fine. It won't look like the same place when he's done."

"He's a good kid for a half-breed," she said.

"Mr. Strong didn't seem to think too much of him, or his family for that matter."

"Mr. Strong's a little old-fashioned," Joe said to me. "You know, white man's burden and that sort of nonsense. The last I heard he was trying to get the town council in Eagle to pass a law saying the Indians had to be out of there by sundown."

"Who says that's a bad idea?" Mr. Carew asked. "I'm no crazier about siwashes than he is. Half-breeds either for that matter."

While we were talking Mr. Vaughn came in. Living right next door to me, he'd dropped in a couple of times while Fred and I had been working. He'd stayed about an hour each time, offering advice and telling Fred how things should be done, but he hadn't lifted a finger to help out. A widower, he told me he'd raised his three girls practically by himself. I'd heard him yelling at them once or twice, and just before Joe had come over earlier I'd heard him slap one of the twins when she dropped something and it broke.

After Mrs. Carew poured him a cup of coffee he just sat and listened for a while. Finally he asked me what kind of teaching I was going to do. "Are you going to get fancy and teach a lot of tripe, or are you going to teach the three R's?" Somehow, the way he said it put me on the defensive.

"I'll teach the best way I know how, I guess. Arithmetic and reading are important, but there are other things too."

"Such as?" Mr. Vaughn asked. He had a goiter as big as an orange on one side of his neck and I kept trying not to stare at it.

"Literature and poetry. Civics, music."

"Sounds pretty fancy, all right," Mr. Carew put in.

"Sounds that way to me too," Mr. Vaughn said.

"Hey, give her a chance, will you?" Joe said. "She hasn't even started yet."

"What's wrong with us being interested?" Mr. Vaughn said. "That's why we have a school board."

74

"I'm glad you are," I said. "Does the school board meet very often?"

"When we think it's necessary," Mr. Vaughn answered. "We'll let you know when we think we should have a meeting."

A little while later Joe walked me back to my place. It was clear out when we'd gone into the roadhouse. Now it was so misty you could hardly see three cabins ahead.

"What's a sy-wash?" I asked him.

"Siwash? An Indian."

"That's what I thought. Is it an Indian word?"

"French. *Sauvage*. Savage. The old-timers weren't too finicky about their accent."

He came in with me and built up the fire in the stove. I thanked him for the supper.

"My pleasure," he said. "We'll have to get together again soon."

"Maybe after I get settled."

"I have plenty of time till trapping starts. You name it."

"I'll tell you the truth, Joe. I feel a little funny about going out with you."

"Why?" He saw I was embarrassed. "I see . . . Mary Angus?"

"I guess so."

"Don't let that worry you. We split the blanket a while back."

We dropped the subject and after a couple of minutes he left.

The next day while Fred and I were working I asked him about Joe and Mary.

"It's pretty much of an old story," he said. "Mary lived in the Indian village and Joe was doing some mining near by. They fell in love and took up housekeeping. They were like man and wife for a long time until they finally broke up about a year ago. Then a few months ago Mary came out to be with him. I don't think he really wanted her to, but she's still in love with him, so she did."

"Where does she live?"

"About a half-mile from here, on the way to my house."

Later on we stopped off at her cabin when Fred took me over to his house. It was a lovely walk, the sun settling down behind the mountains in a sea of liquid gold. The woods were silent except for here and there a few camp robbers hopping around in the trees, having some last minute arguments. We followed a wide trail alongside Chicken Creek, then turned north after a quarter of a mile.

Mary Angus' place was stuck back off the trail. There was so much buckbrush and willow growing up around the back of it that I didn't see it until Fred pointed it out. He'd said it was just an old line shack, a place put up by a trapper to stay in overnight as he moved along his trapline, so I hadn't expected it to be much. But it was awful—an old weathered shack that looked as if one good wind would blow it right over. A stovepipe leaned out of the roof and a couple of broken window panes had rags stuffed in them. It made me think of the greasy little shed the Rag Man used to live in when I was a little girl back in Evansville. None of us kids even knew the Rag Man's name, but every so often we'd go over to the junkyard where his shed was and throw stones at it until he came hobbling out on a heavy old cane. Then we'd run away screaming. We were so afraid of him that whenever I did something bad my father used to threaten to give me to him.

Mary Angus was out in front sawing some wood, and when she turned around it was hard for me to believe she was the same woman I'd glimpsed a few days ago. I'd had the impression then that she was beautiful. And at one time she must have been, with a lovely long face and dark eyes that were slanted a little. Now, although she was probably in her mid-twenties, she was old and tired. Her face was pock-marked and there were dark circles under her eyes. She was flushed and perspiring from the work she'd been doing. When Fred introduced us she smiled and I felt worse than ever. Most of her back teeth were gone. "I . . . am . . . happy . . . to . . . see . . . you," she said in this tiny little voice. It was like a little girl reciting. Fred had told me she didn't speak English too well, so I spoke slowly.

"I'm glad to meet you too," I said. "Is Chuck around?"

"In cabin. He sick."

"Can I say hello to him?"

She gave Fred a quick questioning look and he nodded slightly. When I asked Fred about it later he told me that white people didn't usually go into Indians' cabins, at least not white women.

Inside, the odor was so bad I almost gagged. It was like being in a tiny foul hell. The floor was dirt, and Chuck was lying on some kind of fur robe, a couple of dirty blankets pulled over him. The small Yukon stove was going full blast and there was some gray stew bubbling in a coffee can on top of it. An oil lamp on a shelf gave off a faint yellow light. It was a nightmare, the smell from a slop jar so foul I had to breathe through my mouth. Chuck had a cold. I stooped down alongside him.

"How are you feeling?" I asked him.

"Bad sick," he murmured.

He looked it too. If I could have I'd have taken him home with me right then and there. He needed a clean bed, some good nourishing food and a place where he could breathe.

I heard a little sigh. It was from his sister. She was lying fully clothed on some kind of small wooden frame lashed together with leather strips. She was asleep.

"You take care of yourself," I said. "I'll see you in school when you're better."

He didn't answer. He wasn't in any shape to be interested in me, school, or anything else. I went outside so furious at Joe Temple I wanted to scream.

"How can he let them live like that?" I asked Fred when we went on. "Can't he help them out at all?"

"He probably would if Mary would go back to the Indian village," Fred said.

"Couldn't he at least move her into one of those empty cabins in the settlement? A couple of them are ten times better than that shack."

"The people there don't want her."

"Fred, that's inhuman. Joe lived with that woman. Those are his children. It's all wrong."

77

"There's nothing anybody can do about it."

"There has to be."

"What Joe does is his business—his and Mary's. That's the way it is."

He didn't seem to want to talk about it, so I didn't say anything more, but I was a little disappointed in him for saying something like that.

His own house was beautiful, a big log cabin that was built on a knoll. A few outbuildings were around it, and telescoping out from the rear of it were a couple of smaller cabins. I'd seen other cabins built the same way, added on to like that. I asked him why people did it.

"The only time you can build is during the season— that's about four months. So you build your main cabin, then keep adding on every year."

As soon as I walked in I realized why his mother had thought my place looked so terrible. She had a lovely home. The whole place sparkled with friendliness and good cheer. Potted plants and growing herbs lined the windowsills and three braided rugs lay on the highly polished floor. I couldn't get over it, especially since the Purdys had made just about everything that was in it themselves, from the glass-fronted cupboards in the kitchen area to the bright curtains on the window sewn from flour sacks.

It was a nice evening, with everybody talkative and good-humored—and a delicious dinner to boot. The only one who didn't have much to say was Fred's father. After I was introduced to him, he disappeared into one of the back rooms, and during supper I almost had the feeling that if he could have he'd have eaten by himself. The only time he really said anything was when I asked him where he was from. "New England," he said. Then, as if he didn't want me to ask any more questions, he asked me where I was from. I told him, and that ended the conversation between us. Right after dinner he excused himself and went into the next room. For the rest of the evening I could see him through the curtained doorway, working on a crystal radio he was making.

Before I left Fred asked me if I'd ever seen gold in

the raw. I told him no, so he took a preserve jar down from a shelf. He handed it to me and everybody laughed when I nearly dropped it. It was about ten times heavier than I'd thought and it was filled with dull yellow flecks mixed with black powder. "That's flour gold," Fred said. He brought over another jar that was filled with nuggets ranging in size from pinheads to little pebbles. The two jars had their whole season's cleanup in them—maybe two thousand dollars worth of gold. It wasn't very much for a family to live on, but Fred said they expected to do better next year. They were going to prospect some ground during the winter that they thought would have some real good pay in it.

The next afternoon I got to see some gold mining done. Fred took me over to Lost Chicken Hill, where Uncle Arthur and Mert Atwood were going to be sluicing for the last time. "They don't have much of a set-up," he told me on the way, "but you'll be able to see what it's all about."

"How come they're the only ones still mining?"

"They have a little water left. Nobody else has. No water, no mining."

"What do you mean 'no water no mining'?"

"Well," he said, "you've got to wash tons of dirt to get a few ounces of gold. You can have the richest ground in the world, but if you can't pipe water to it it's not worth a cent. The run-off's all gone now. The rivers, the creeks—they're all low. There won't be enough water for mining again until after the winter's over and the snow starts to melt."

"How about for bathing? I notice the creek in front of the schoolhouse is low too. Suppose it dries up?"

"It'll freeze before that happens."

"Then what do we do?"

"Chop ice or go bathless."

"I'll let you know what I decide."

"Oh I'll know, don't you worry." He laughed. "Everybody'll know."

It took us a half hour to get there, through a couple of canyons and over a stretch of tundra, then across a hillside that blossomed red with waist-high fireweed.

The two men were waiting for us, their sluice box set up on a slope. About ten feet long and open at both ends, it looked like a small gangway. Alongside of it was a big heap of pay dirt they'd excavated with pick and shovel. There must have been a couple of tons of it.

I was afraid I'd be in the way, but they went out of their way to make me feel welcome. I liked Mert the best. He was the one who'd brought me the bear lard. A barrel-chested little man, he was so shy that the first few times I asked him something he took off his yachtsman's cap each time he answered. They'd dammed up a stream farther on up the slope, he explained to me, then they'd dug a trench from it all the way down to one end of the box. As soon as I was ready, he said, he'd go up and let the water go.

"You worm-eaten dub," Uncle Arthur bawled, "why you think she came over—ta spend the day with ya?"

Mert started up the slope apologetically. "Somethin' wrong with his cerebral machinery," Uncle Arthur complained. "Been goin' around with 'is hat off too long. Froze 'is brain box." He rested a hand on the sluice box. It was like a claw. The two last fingers were gone and the rest looked as though they'd been badly burned. Fred told me later that they'd been frozen.

Mert didn't come back for ten minutes. A few minutes after he did the water began to seep down the trench. Before long it was gushing down and running through the box pretty fast, gradually building up force. As soon as it had a "good head," as Uncle Arthur called it, the two men started shoveling in the paydirt. The water swept it right through the box. Even rocks as big as a fist clattered along easily. And that was all there was to it, Fred said, whatever gold was mixed in the dirt would drop to the bottom of the box where it was caught in the "riffles," wood slats. The dirt and rocks were washed through, running down to the bottom of the slope, where they added to the other tailing piles already built up by earlier sluicings during the season. Now I understood what Fred had meant. Pay dirt without water was just ordinary dirt.

It was over in about twenty minutes, when the water ran out, and Uncle Arthur and Mert leaned against the box, sweat staining the back of their shirts. They were both staring down at the muck in the bottom of it. Their final cleanup was down there. Four months' work with pick and shovel was ended.

I thanked them for letting me come over, then we left. On the way back I asked Fred if he knew how they'd done.

"Not too good," he said. "They never do."

"Never?"

He shook his head.

"Then why do they do it?"

"It's better than working for wages."

When you looked at it that way, maybe he was right. My father had worked down in the mines all his life, six days a week, and he had nothing to show for it. However little Uncle Arthur and Mert had, at least they were their own men.

"Now that everybody's done mining, what do they do?"

"Get ready for winter. Trapping'll start around the beginning of November."

"Why wait so long?"

That made him laugh.

"What are you laughing for? Is that a dumb question?"

He said, "No," but he was as amused as Chuck had been at the idea of fruit growing on trees. "You see, when you go out trapping," he explained, "you've got traps to tote, food and supplies, and sometimes you go pretty far. Then you've got to tote the furs back. You need a sled for all that."

"And for a sled you need snow."

It was a dumb question, all right. We both tried to keep a straight face, but it was no use. One look at each other and we were laughing.

Later on I asked him why the place was called Lost Chicken.

"Somebody found it once, then lost it. By the time they found it again they'd named Chicken Chicken."

"They must have lost a lot of places, those old prospectors." Besides Lost Chicken I'd heard of Lost Delta and Lost Fork.

We worked for another two days before my quarters and the schoolroom were finally finished. When they were done you could see the difference right away. Fred had glued the canvas back on the walls where it had been peeling and patched the bad spots, the tables and chairs in the schoolroom were sturdy, and I even had a "blackboard"—a couple of dark green window shades tacked to beaver board. He'd also made me a couch for my quarters by nailing three boxes together. Maggie Carew gave me a mattress for padding, and covered with a blanket and pillows it looked fine. He stayed for supper, and before he left we had a cup of cocoa and some cookies to celebrate.

"I'm really grateful to you," I told him. "I don't know what I'd have done if you hadn't helped me so much." I meant it too. A lot of people had loaned me things and even lent a hand once in a while, but he'd done just about all the work.

"Forget it," he said. "I was glad to help out. Maybe I'll drop by after school tomorrow and you can tell me how you did."

"Will you?" I'd told him how scared I was.

"Sure."

We sat talking for a while longer. He didn't want to go and I didn't want him to either, which really surprised me. Usually I never knew what to say to boys when I was alone with them. But with him it was just the opposite. Here we'd been together for practically three whole days and I felt I could have gone on talking to him the whole night. I'd never met any boy like him. He said he'd only gone as far as the sixth grade in school, but he read everything he could get his hands on and he was interested in everything—history, current events, motors, even metallurgy. He'd taken me for a walk to show me around and pointed out all kinds of rocks and minerals, white quartz with glints of pyrite in it, lodestone, feldspar. I'd never heard of most of them. He said he had a book about them and when I asked him if he'd lend it to me so the class could start a rock collection he said he'd be glad to.

He was just getting ready to leave when there was a knock at the door. It was Mr. Vaughn. "I brought you over the flag," he said.

It was for the pole outside. He'd had one of his daughters wash it for me.

"Thanks," I told him. "You didn't have to bring it over special, though. The girls could have brought it with them in the morning."

"No trouble," he said.

He kept standing in the doorway. "Schoolroom all done?"

"Ready and waiting. Did you want to see it?" I asked him.

"Wouldn't mind at all."

He came in and nodded to Fred. Fred said hello, then he said he'd better be going.

"Not before we show off your handiwork," I said.

I brought the oil lamp and the three of us went inside. I showed him the blackboard Fred had made, the shelves. He'd even made a couple of shelves low down for the two little kids I'd have. Mr. Vaughn just glanced around. He didn't seem too interested. "It'll do," he said.

I was a little disappointed. The least he could have done was tell Fred he'd done a good job, but all he said to him was, "Well, you'll be able to get back to your own work now."

Then I realized he'd come over just to see what we were doing. It embarrassed me and it made Fred feel uncomfortable too. He walked out right after Mr. Vaughn did. "I'll see you tomorrow," I called after him.

Before I went to sleep I went into the schoolroom again. I stood behind my table and imagined the kids sitting in front of me. It felt exciting. The room looked wonderful. I'd scrubbed the Yukon stove so it looked almost new and it was all ready with kindling and logs. On one of the shelves there was a whole row of books —a few readers, a dictionary I'd brought with me, and the old encyclopedia someone had contributed. I'd kept a few of the rocks Fred had pointed out to me when we took a walk, and they were sitting on another shelf. It was just a big bare room now, I thought, but in a few weeks, after the children began to draw and make things, it would look more like a schoolroom. Looking at the empty tables and chairs, I thought of so many things I wanted to say to the class that I went back inside my quarters and started jotting them down. They were things like our being as much a part of America up here as the people in any of the forty-eight states, and how important it was for all of us to be fine, well-educated citizens. When I went to bed I was so keyed up it was hard to fall asleep.

VI

School was supposed to start at nine, but by a quarter to they were all outside, so I went out and brought the folded flag with me.

With the oldest boy helping me, I ran it up to the top of the pole and then we all said the Pledge of Allegiance. Right then and there I knew I couldn't say one of the things I'd planned on. They all sounded too high-falutin' and phony. In fact, once we were in the schoolroom I couldn't say anything at all. I had stage fright. For a full minute the whole class stared at me silently and, completely tongue-tied, I stared back at them. The only sound was everybody's breathing and the squeak of the floorboards.

"How do you like the schoolroom?" I finally managed to croak.

"Real spiffy," Jimmy Carew said. He and his little brother and the Vaughn girls had seen it already, and so had Isabelle. Robert Merriweather and Joan Simpson hadn't. They all looked around, murmuring their approval. I was proud of it. Fred had done a wonderful job. All the tables were covered with oilcloth and he'd painted the place with some pale green paint we'd found in Mr. Strong's store. The color was a little on the bilious side, but it brightened the room up and made it look larger.

"It smells good," Joan Simpson said. She was six years old, blue eyes, blond hair. I'd have to teach both her and Willard Carew to read.

After we found seats for everyone I wrote my name across one of the shades and said I was glad to be here. Then I shivered. "Before we go on," I said, "does anybody know how to build a fire in that stove?"

The schoolroom was so chilly that everybody sat with coats and parkas on. I'd tried to work the Yukon stove, a squat black metal affair a little bigger than an orange crate, but couldn't get a fire going in it. Out of the many hands that volunteered I picked Robert Merriweather. Twelve, he was the oldest of my three boys and big for his age.

He showed me right away what was wrong. I hadn't used enough kindling. "Also," he said, "you didn't open the damper enough. You need a good draft when the fire first starts." After he filled the stove with more kindling, he placed a couple of slender logs inside, then a couple of hefty three-foot logs on top of them. "You see," he said, "this kind of stove is made for long logs, so you don't have to keep feeding it so much."

"What do you know about that?" I said. "I thought all stoves were alike."

"Oh, no," a few children protested.

"Some you have to put small pieces in, like a cookstove, some large like this one," Elvira Vaughn said.

"That one's real ornery," Jimmy Carew said.

They loved the idea that here I was a teacher and I didn't know something. I'd intended to spend the morning getting acquainted and had rehearsed how I was going to start off asking them about themselves, but I didn't have to. Since they'd already taught *me* something, they didn't think twice about asking me questions.

"How come you don't know anything about stoves?" six-year-old Willard Carew asked. *"Every*body knows about *stoves."*

"Well, they don't use wood stoves very much where I come from."

"Then how do they cook?"

"Can anybody tell Willard?"

Robert Merriweather raised his hand. "I can. They use gas stoves. We had one before we came here to Alaska."

"What's a gas stove?" Willard asked.

Robert looked at me to see if I'd let him go ahead. He seemed to be the kind of a boy who'd always been kept in check, and he was self-conscious. I nodded to him.

"You turn on a switch and put a match to the burner and it lights right up. It's a million times better'n a wood stove."

From there we went on to talk about furnaces and steam heat and fireplaces.

"My father says a fireplace is the biggest waste of wood there is," Eleanor Vaughn said. She turned to her twin sister Evelyn, who was as husky as she was. "Isn't that right?"

"That's right."

"Ah, your father knows everything," Jimmy Carew said sarcastically.

After we decided which chairs and tables would be most comfortable for everybody and who would sit with whom, I asked them what they thought they were coming to school for.

" 'Cause we have to," Jimmy answered. That brought a laugh.

"All right, that's one reason. How many want to?"

Everyone's hand went up.

"Wonderful. Why?"

The hands went up again. I called on Jimmy's brother Willard. "There's nothin' else to do," he said with typical six-year-old honesty.

"Another reason. Next."

"To learn readin', writin' and 'rithmetic," Eleanor

Vaughn said. She and her twin looked exactly like their father, the same big teeth and stern frown.

"Fine," I said. "What else?"

Silence.

"Nothing else? Anybody here know how to play the harmonica?"

"I do," Robert answered.

"Anybody want to learn?"

"Me," Jimmy said.

"All right, you'll learn."

"Here in school?"

"Certainly. That's what school's for—to learn what you want to learn."

"I'd like to learn sewing," Elvira Vaughn said.

"Me too," I said. "I'm terrible. Any good sewers here?"

Isabelle Purdy raised her hand.

"Think you can show Elvira how?"

"Sure," she said.

"That takes care of sewing. Anything else anybody wants to learn, they can learn it—as long as they keep up with their work. Maybe we can even learn a little bit about each other, like where we're all from."

The Purdys had come from Canada, we found out, the Carews from Pennsylvania. It gave me a chance to use one of the few teaching aids I had—a big map of the U.S. and Canada. It was my pride and joy and I wasn't about to pass the chance up.

"Where are you from, Teacher?" Elvira Vaughn asked me. Like her two sisters, her first name began with an E, but there the resemblance ended. She was slender and demure, not as sure about everything as they were, and more curious.

"I was brought up in Colorado."

"Where's that?"

"Who can show us on the map?"

Isabelle Purdy raised her hand, went to it and pointed to Colorado.

"Where would you say that is?" I asked her.

"Ma'am?"

"What part of the United States—North? South? West?"

While a couple of hands waved frantically, she stared at the map, then shrugged and gave me a smile.

"I know, Teacher, I know," Jimmy Carew shouted.

"Did you live in a big city?" Elvira Vaughn asked.

"No. My family always lived in coal-mining towns."

"Do they do that the same way as gold mining?"

"I don't think so," I said. "When you mine coal you have to tunnel deep down into the ground."

"They do that here too sometimes," Robert Merriweather said. "It's what they call drifting."

"Was the school you went to anything like this one?" Isabelle Purdy asked. She had the same kind of cheerfulness as Fred and her mother—always ready to break into an easy smile. And she was as immaculate as her mother, too. Her white middy blouse made her a standout. Most of the others had come to school in the same bib overalls and shirts they wore every day—even the girls. One of the Vaughn twins had a grimy shadow that came halfway up her neck. We'd have to start working on good health habits, I thought.

"Something like it," I said, "but we had different grades in each classroom."

"Can you drop your teeth out?" Jimmy's little brother Willard asked.

"No, I can't," I said. "Can you?"

"My father can," Willard said proudly. "He can hand 'em right out to you on his tongue." He illustrated for me.

"My father's got a goiter as big as a baseball," Eleanor Vaughn bragged, turning to her twin sister again.

"That's right," Evelyn said on cue. They were like two comics in a vaudeville show.

Before we broke for lunch I gave my six older children a diagnostic arithmetic test and while they were taking it I kept Willard and Joan busy making cut-outs and pasting.

After lunch we appointed monitors for taking care of the stove, cleaning the board erasers, sweeping the schoolroom and the outhouse and raising and lowering the flag.

Right in the middle of it we had an unexpected guest. Uncle Arthur walked in. Wearing a long gray coat that almost dragged the floor in front, he told us to just go ahead with what we were doing and pay him no mind. He stood by the door looking on, hands clasped in back of him while we went about our business.

"D'ya have an extra chair, missis?" he finally asked me.

The class seemed to take his being there for granted and I couldn't bring myself to ask him to leave, so I sent one of the kids into my quarters for one. He sat down, folded his arms under his beard and just looked on for a while.

He didn't say anything until after I'd tried a couple of the kids at oral reading, then he said, "When you gonna have penmanship drill, missis?"

"Maybe in a couple of days or so," I said.

"I could give ya plenty songs you could use for makin' circles 'n' straights if you like." He took a pad from his coat pocket. "Show ya right now if you want."

"Can he, Teacher?" Jimmy asked. "They're fun."

I'd never been much for penmanship, maybe because my own penmanship was so bad. If he had a way to make it fun I was all for it.

I told him to go ahead and he opened the pad. He wrote a capital N for us, chanting as he did it. "Ya make a loop and go down, climb a hill to the top, then go down to the bottom and there you stop." He recited a few more rhymes for other letters and the children were fascinated. "That teaches the kiddies how to write a good hand, ya see."

"We don't have time to do it right now," I said, "but I'd appreciate it if you'd teach me the rhymes."

He promised to write them all down for me, and then he left. I complimented the class on how well they'd behaved while he'd been there.

"Him and those other old-timers always drop by," Jimmy said. "They like to. *You* know—they're kinda lonely."

A little later I found out I was going to have to be careful how I explained things. Jimmy asked me why everybody had to come to school at the same time and eat lunch at the same time. "How come you can't do things when you feel like it?"

"If everybody did it would be like a three-ring circus," I said.

"What's a three-ring circus?" Elvira asked.

"Well," I said, "it's like a chautauqua, only it's bigger. It has elephants and clowns and—"

"What's a shuh-tawk–wa?" Jimmy asked hesitantly.

I explained that a chautauqua was a fair, only to have Elvira ask what a fair was. By the time I was finished nobody really had any idea of what a three-ring circus was like. They had never seen clowns, or jungle animals, or acrobats. They knew nothing about all the things that the children in Forest Grove knew about—radio programs and air shows, movies and automobiles. If I was going to cite examples I'd have to pick things they were familiar with—gold mining and trapping, dog teams and hunting. Talking about the future of air transportation or radio left them uninterested—until I told them that one day soon airplanes would probably be bringing the mail right here to Chicken, or that maybe in another year or two they'd be able to listen to all the radio shows that people Outside could tune in on.

One thing I could see was that I didn't have to worry about keeping their attention. Everything was new to them and they were hungry to learn.

Their big problem was reading. The only pupil who could read well was Isabelle Purdy. The rest of the class had trouble reading orally from a third-grade reader. The Vaughn twins were thirteen, but their sister Elvira, three years younger, could read better than they could. A few of the children could do fifth-grade and sixth-grade arithmetic—Robert Merriweather was good enough to do seventh-grade work—but their reading comprehension was terrible.

It had been almost a year and a half since there'd been a teacher here, and except for Isabelle and Robert, none of them knew anything about history or geography or social studies. I'd have to figure out some kind of a starting point—some way of getting them

90

interested enough in history and geography so that they wouldn't be bored by them. Before I could do that, though, I'd have to get them to feel like a class, not like just a bunch of kids that happened to be in the same room. They weren't used to talking with each other much—at least not about anything that didn't have to do with mining or trapping or local gossip. They needed something that would bring them together and let them show off what they could do.

When 3:30 came nobody wanted to go home, which was fine with me. I invited them all into my quarters for cookies and hot cocoa. I still wasn't used to the cookstove. Trying to put just enough wood in to keep the oven at the right temperature was driving me crazy, but the cookies I'd made weren't too bad.

"Oh, looka that," Elvira said, admiring my coat. It was wool suede with a mouflon fur collar and cuffs. She ran her fingers along the sleeve. "Feels nice," she said.

Her sister Evelyn pinched the fabric expertly and shook her head. "You won't be able to wear that around here too long."

"Why not?" I asked. It had cost me $35 and it was my prize possession.

"Come winter it won't be warm enough."

"That's right," Eleanor agreed.

"So what?" Elvira said. "It's still nice to look at."

The cocoa was just about ready and I'd started to pour it when Jimmy Carew called to me. "Is this yours, Teacher?"

I nearly had heart failure. He'd found the nickel-plated revolver and was showing it to Robert and little Willard.

Taking it from him, I put it on the highest shelf in the cache, shoving it back out of sight.

School was over for the day.

Fred popped in a little while after they left and asked me how I thought I did. I told him I'd been scared at first, but now I felt pretty optimistic.

"The only thing I'm not sure of, though, is how to make one class out of them."

"What do you mean?"

"Give them the feeling that they're all learning to-gether, find a project they could all work on. Back in the States it was easy. I could take them to a museum, or to the local dairy or cannery, then we would talk about it and write compositions about it. Besides that, everybody was in the same grade, so they had a lot in common to begin with. Here they're all in different grades. What I need is some kind of a project they can all work on, something local. I'm going to take them on field trips, but I need something else."

"You could take them to see some of the old sour-doughs."

"You think they'd like that?"

"The kids? They'd love it. So would the old men."

"That's not a bad idea. The only thing I'd have to do is make sure I don't wind up getting lost. I still don't know my way around here."

He laughed. "Make a map."

"Did you say a map?"

"Uh-huh."

I could have kissed him. "You just found my project for me."

I was just about to explain the idea to him when there was a knock at the door. It was Eleanor Vaughn. At least I thought it was. She and Evelyn looked so alike I couldn't tell them apart yet. "I'm sorry to bother you, Teacher," she said, "but I lost a mitten. I thought maybe I left it in the schoolroom."

We took a look around, but it wasn't there.

I didn't think anything about it until later, when I remembered how her father had dropped in the night before. Fred had been with me then too. It could have been a coincidence, but I had the uncomfortable feeling it wasn't. I tried to remember how the twins had been dressed when they came to school. They lived only right next door, and after I thought about it I realized that all they'd had on were sweaters. Neither of them had worn mittens.

VII

If there's one thing that fires up a class for the day's work, I'd found, it's some good rousing singing the first thing in the morning. And this class was no exception. Right after we went through *Yankee Doodle* and a few other songs, I started my two beginners out with some busywork, then gave reading-comprehension tests to a few of the older kids. While they were busy I worked with Isabelle and Elvira on long division.

In the middle of it Willard got bored with what he was doing and started scaring little Joan by telling her a bear was going to get her next time she went to the outhouse, so I had to separate them temporarily.

About mid-morning Merton Atwood showed up. He was even quieter than Uncle Arthur, glancing down shyly every time I happened to look his way. He watched Elvira do a long-division example at the board, then Isabelle, but when my oldest boy, Robert, did an example I saw him raise his hand.

"Mr. Atwood?"

"Mert." He shifted uncomfortably.

"Mert."

"How come that didn't come out even?" he asked me, pointing to the board.

"That's long division with a remainder," I said. "You come out with a fraction."

He stayed until lunchtime. The example was still on the board and he went up and stared at it. "That easy to learn?" he asked me.

"Long division? Easy as pie."

"Alwuz been in'risted in learnin' that. Alwuz wanned to, but never did."

"Come by after school some time and I'll show you."

"I might do that," he said. "I just might."

"You could do me a favor too."

"What's that?"

"Could you draw me a simple map of Chicken here on the board with a dot to show where everybody in the class lives?"

He did it for me. He drew in Chicken Creek and then drew lines for the two other creeks that Joan Simpson and Robert Merriweather lived on. After lunch I told the class about the project I had in mind. "It's something we can all work on together," I said. "We're going to make a map of Chicken, something like this one, but bigger. We're going to use one whole wall for it. Everybody can draw a little picture of their own cabin and we'll put it up in the right place."

They liked that idea, of having the place they lived in and their name right up where everybody could see them. "But that's only part of the project," I said. "What we'll do is find out all about Chicken—its history and geography, what grows here, what's produced here, everything. After that we'll find out about other places."

"But there's nothing to know about this place," Jimmy said. "There's nothing here."

"Oh, I can think of a dozen things I'd like to know about it. Just one, for instance—does anybody know how Chicken got its name?"

Nobody did, so I asked Robert Merriweather if he'd ask around and write a report on it. He said he would. Then we decided that the next day we'd go on our first field trip to collect leaves and rocks and any other interesting things we could find.

After school, as the children went out the door, there was a roly-poly Indian woman waiting on the porch. She was bundled up in a light blue flannel coat that was made out of a blanket, and she had a little girl with her. "How you do, Tisha," she said. "My name Rebekah Harrin'ton. I come see you."

"I'm glad to meet you," I said. "Come on in."

"This my kid," she said when we were in my quarters. "Lily. Lily, you say how you do."

94

Lily peered up at me from under a peaked hat of wolf fur. I could barely see her eyes under it. "How you do," she said. She was charming.

Mrs. Harrington put a paper sack down on the table. She took out a few pounds of dried salmon. "F'you. Present."

"Thank you. I was just about to have some tea. Would you like some?"

"I like. Yes." I took her coat. She sat down and made herself comfortable, hitching her skirt up a little. She had on a couple of other skirts underneath it. "You got nice place," she said.

"Thanks to Fred Purdy."

"Ah, Fred he good boy, you make bet on that. Whole Purdy family got good people. Everybody like."

It took her a few minutes to get around to why she'd come, and it was just what I was hoping for. She wanted to enroll Lily in school. "You not got too much lotsa kids now?"

"Not at all. I don't have enough. How old is Lily?"

"Fo'. He be fi' soon—Janawary."

When she said "he" I looked at Lily again to make sure she was a little girl. She was. "She's a little young," I said, "but I think it'll be all right."

"Oh, he be one smart kid my Lily," she assured me. "Learn like hell. Already he write A, B, F, P—many alphabets. My husbin Jake he teach." All of a sudden she became sad. "Only one bad thing, Tisha. Lily he scare come school all alone heself. Need Momma."

"You can sit with her till she gets used to it."

"You mean it?"

"Of course." With all the old-timers who'd been coming in I couldn't see any harm being done.

Her grin was as big as sunshine. "You one helluva good joe, Tisha. I come with Lily tomorrow."

The next morning they were almost the first ones to arrive. After the Pledge of Allegiance I told the class that Lily was going to be their new classmate. "She's a little shy," I said, "so I'd like you to be especially nice to her."

"How about *her?*" Jimmy Carew said, pointing to Rebekah. "She comin' too?"

"Until Lily gets used to school and can come on her own."

There were some snickers.

"Is anything wrong?" I asked. But nobody said anything.

I didn't think anything more about it, and once we got down to work the class didn't either, but the next day Evelyn Vaughn told me that her father said the school board wanted to have a meeting right after school.

The three of them came into my quarters looking solemn—Maggie Carew, Angela Barrett and Mr. Vaughn. I was surprised to see Angela on the board since she didn't have any children. I asked them if they'd like some coffee or tea, but they said no. The four of us sat around the table and Mr. Vaughn rapped his knuckles on it. "The meeting will come to order," he said.

They asked me a couple of questions about what I'd been doing, and I told them about the project. They didn't seem too impressed. Mr. Vaughn got right to it. "How come you're letting that Indian woman come to school?" he said.

"Mrs. Harrington? She's just sitting with Lily."

"Is that what she told you?"

"Yes. She said that Lily was a little scared to come by herself, so I said it would be all right if she sat with her until Lily was used to it."

"Well, we don't like it," Angela said.

"She's not bothering the class at all," I said. "She's quiet as a mouse."

"We want 'er kicked out," Angela said sharply.

"And the kid along with her," Mr. Vaughn added.

I was stunned. "Lily? But why?"

"She's under age. A kid has to be over five and under sixteen to go to this school. You know that."

"I know, but does it matter that much?"

"It matters to us," Mr. Vaughn said. "You have enough to do to teach our own kids properly without wasting time on some little siwash that doesn't belong here."

"I don't think it's doing any harm to let her come," I

96

said to Maggie Carew. She hadn't said anything up to now and I had the feeling she'd be more receptive than the other two. "She's a bright little girl, and besides that we don't even have a full enrollment. We're supposed to have ten and all we have is eight."

"The law is that this school is for kids from five to sixteen," Mr. Vaughn said before Maggie could answer, "and the law's the law. Let's take a vote on it. I vote that Lily Harrington, being too young to attend this school, be expelled. How do you two vote?"

"I vote the same way," Angela said.

"Maggie?"

"You got a majority already," Maggie said. "You don't need mine."

"We'd like to make it unanimous."

"I'm all for throwin' Rebekah out," she said, "but I don't care about the kid one way or the other."

"You abstain?"

"Yeah." She didn't seem too happy about the whole thing.

"You've got your orders," Mr. Vaughn said to me. "See that you carry them out."

After they left I sat thinking about it. I couldn't believe it—that people could act that way. Just because someone was an Indian. I was ashamed of them. And I was ashamed of myself too. If I'd had any guts I'd have told them off, let them know what I thought of them. But I didn't. I'd let them buffalo me because I was new and I'd been scared of them. Now I had to tell Mrs. Harrington her little girl couldn't come to school.

I asked her to stay after school the next day, then I told her. The look on her face made me wish I was a thousand miles away. She knew as well as I did why the school board didn't want Lily, but all she said was, "He sure like go school my Lily."

"I know. I'm going to write to the commissioner about it, Mrs. Harrington. I'm going to ask him if he can make an exception in Lily's case. I'm sure he will. In the meantime, if you want to, you could bring Lily over here after school a couple of times a week and I could tutor her."

"What tooda, Tisha?"

"Teach. I could teach her here in my quarters a couple of times every week."

"You do that?"

"I'll be glad to. Let's make it every Monday and Thursday right after school. You can learn at the same time."

She smiled. "Tisha, you make me too much happy. You bet we come!" She went out beaming.

That wasn't the end of it, though, because the next morning, right after we finished singing, Rebekah and Lily showed up again. With them was a big man, Rebekah's husband Jake, and all I needed was one look at him to know there was going to be a storm. He was as nice as could be to me, though. He took off his Stetson and said he was pleased to meet me. Then he asked me what swivel-eyed jackass said his little girl couldn't come to school.

I took him into my quarters and explained the whole thing to him.

"The school board, eh . . . Well, little lady, I gather *you* don't have any objections to my little girl gettin' educated."

"None at all."

"You sit tight then, while I have a little talk with the school board."

He slammed out of my quarters and went right next door to Mr. Vaughn. We could hear everything that happened from the schoolroom. He pounded on Mr. Vaughn's door and what followed after that was probably the finest and most eloquent cussing I'd heard since I was a little girl in Blazing Rag. It started off with him calling Mr. Vaughn a mangy, misbegotten, worm-eaten egg-sucker and went on improving with every sentence. Not one of us in that classroom said a word the whole time. All we could do was marvel at it. There were a couple of silences in between the cussing, but it went on gathering steam for about five minutes without one word being repeated. "Now, you potbellied, yelping, walleyed sonofabitch," Mr. Harrington finished off, "is my little girl goin' to school or ain't she?"

We couldn't hear what Mr. Vaughn said, but not ten seconds later Mr. Harrington strode back in as red as the smoked salmon Rebekah had brought me. "Little lady," he said, "Mr. Vaughn said that if it's all right with you, the school board would be pleased to have Lily attend your class." He even remembered to take off his hat.

"I'd be delighted, Mr. Harrington."

"How about you?" He asked Rebekah. "You want to give me a hand takin' out the sluice box or park here for a while?"

"I come help you, Jake," Rebekah said proudly.

"Well then let's go, woman. There's work to do."

I'd have kicked my heels together and jumped up and down if I'd been alone. The whole thing couldn't have worked out better if I'd planned it. Lily was in school, Mr. Vaughn got what was coming to him, and I was off the spot with the school board.

For the next few days everything went fine. The class really took to the idea of the map of Chicken. It started us talking about all the different kinds of maps there were, treasure maps and world maps, weather maps, and produce maps. We decided that since we had a whole wall to use we ought to show not only where everybody lived, but some of the things we'd found on our field trip. We'd come back loaded with treasures—birch and cottonwood leaves, samples of willow and alder, and rocks galore. Elvira Vaughn had even found a piece of black silicon with a shell fossil in it. After some discussion we decided to put some of them up on the map. The rest we'd make up books about—leaf books and fur-sample books, animal-picture books and food books. The project began to take on shape. When it was finished, we decided, we'd invite everybody in Chicken to come and see what we'd done. The class was so enthusiastic about it that I had trouble bringing them back to their regular lessons.

Robert Merriweather's report turned out to be excellent and I tacked it on the wall.

HOW CHICKEN GOT IT'S NAME

Chicken got it's name from the first prospecters who came here. There was a lot of Ptarmigans here and they thanked God for it because they were hungry. They were so grateful they wanted to name this place Ptarmigan, but they couldn't spell it. They named it good old American Chicken instead. This is what Uncle Arthur said.

Mert Atwood says this isn't true. Chicken got it's name because they found gold nuggets as big as chicken corn here.

No one can ever know the real truth, I guess.

Inside of a few days the schoolroom began to feel like one, with pictures and lesson papers all over the walls, our rock collection on one of the shelves, and a little herb garden sitting in tin cans on one of the window sills. Not that we didn't have our troubles. With everybody doing different things in one room there were bound to be arguments. When my three beginners were restless they'd get in everybody's hair. Willard would bother the older children or start scaring Joan and Lily by telling them about a wolf coming into their cabin some night to eat them up. They'd begin to cry, disturbing the others, so I'd have to find coloring work or something else for them all to do, or let Willard go home for a little while.

Aside from that the only other problem was interruptions. Everybody in and around the settlement seemed to feel the school was the one place open to the public any time. Mr. Strong had told everybody I had the key to his store, so every so often someone would come in wanting to buy something. A few times it was people like Angela, who lived in the settlement, and I was able to tell them to come back after school, but a couple of other times it was people who lived some distance away, like Joe, and I had to leave the class. I finally posted a notice on the school door saying no goods could be purchased at the store during school hours.

On Friday still a third old-timer wandered in. His name was Ben Norvall, a wrinkled old basset hound of a man with drooping moustaches. He was just about the most well-spoken individual I'd met here so far. He could quote Shakespeare by the yard and he offered to

100

lend us his whole set of Shakespeare's works if we promised to take care of it. He even told the class the story of Macbeth and they'd been spellbound by it. The only bad thing about him was that he looked and smelled something awful. I mentioned him to Maggie Carew and she told me not to let him in again.

"If you do," she said, "you're ruinin' it for the rest of us. No one's lettin' him in until he burns those clothes he's got on and takes a bath. As long as he's got a place to go he won't do it."

By the time the first week was over I felt pretty good. As far as I could tell the class was really interested in what they were doing and they liked coming to school. The only trouble I could see I might have was teaching Robert arithmetic. He was pretty good, and I'd have to do some studying to keep ahead of him. Aside from that I was pretty optimistic.

I shouldn't have been though, because on Monday I was in trouble with the school board again. This time it was over Chuck. He showed up Monday morning about fifteen minutes before school. Robert had already started the fire in the schoolroom stove, and I was inside my quarters making my bed. Outside, Jimmy Carew was tossing a ball against the porch base and talking with the Vaughn girls. All of a sudden he stopped and there was silence, until Jimmy said, "Where'd *you* come from?"

"From Louse Town," Evelyn Vaughn said.

"Who is he?" Jimmy asked her.

"Mary Angus' kid."

"You talk English?" Jimmy asked him.

"Yiss," Chuck said.

"Whattaya want here?"

"Come school."

"Like hell you are," Evelyn said. "This is a white school."

"I come here."

"Who says so?"

"Tisha, she say I come."

" 'Tisha'? Who the hell's Tisha?"

"He means Teacher."

"I know what he means."

I went outside. "Good morning, everybody," I said. "Hello, Chuck—nice to see you here finally. How are you feeling?"

He looked down at the ground and mumbled, "Good."

He looked anything but good, though. He was thinner than ever and his lips were all chapped. His clothes didn't help any. His mackinaw was so small his wrists stuck out and his pants were so big the bottoms were ragged from scraping the ground.

We had the Pledge of Allegiance inside because it was so cold out that ice bridges were forming all along the edges of the creek. After we sang I introduced Chuck, gave him a seat and started everybody working. When they were all busy I took him over in a corner and gave him a second-grade reader to read from for me. He didn't do well with it, but he did fine when I tried him with a first-grade reader. His arithmetic wasn't bad either.

The class was restless that morning, too many of them preoccupied with giving each other looks about him. A couple of times he got hit by a spitball, but I couldn't see who did it.

During recess the older kids wanted to play dodge ball. After we showed Chuck how to play I took my three young ones on the side to play with them. After just a few minutes had gone by, the dodge ball game got out of hand. I didn't see it until it was too late. By the time I stepped in Chuck's nose was bleeding, and he was crying. They'd made him "it." I took him into my quarters, and after the bleeding stopped and he was cleaned up, I called everybody back inside. "Who started the rough stuff?" I asked Robert.

"Nobody," he said. "We all just did it."

"I'm surprised at you. You should have stopped it."

"It wasn't my fault. They don't want him."

"Who's 'they'?"

He didn't answer.

"Well let me tell you something—all of you. Whoever 'they' are, if 'they' do anything like this again, 'they' are going to be in trouble."

During vocabulary with the older children I gave

Evelyn Vaughn the word "intelligent" to put into a sentence.

"Siwashes aren't very intelligent," she recited. A few of the older kids giggled.

"Can you tell me what the word siwash means?" I asked her.

"Sure. It's a dirty low-down black Injun."

More giggles. I felt like throttling her. "There are certain words," I said, "which I don't want to hear in this class room. One of them is siwash."

"What's wrong with it, Teacher?" Jimmy asked. "Everybody says it."

"It's a mean word—like hunkie or nigger or kike. Now," I asked Eleanor, "do you think you can find another sentence for me?"

"How about if I said *Indians* aren't very intelligent?"

"Do you really think that's true?"

"I sure do," she answered.

"All Indians?"

She nodded.

"How about people who are only part Indian?"

"You mean like half-breeds? I guess so," she said.

"I should tell you," I said, "that my own grandmother was an Indian. That makes me part Indian too. Do you think there's anything wrong with my intelligence?"

Eleanor shifted uncomfortably. "No."

"Is that really true, Teacher?" Jimmy said.

"Yes, it is."

"What kind of an Indian was she?" Elvira Vaughn said.

"Kentuck."

"I never heard of that kind."

"They're like any other kind—Comanche or Sioux, any kind of Indian."

"Oh, well," Jimmy said. "They're *American* Indians. They're different from the ones we got here."

"Why?"

"They just are."

"If they are it's not very much. Indians are Indians, and there are all kinds."

"Was your grandmother like these Indians?"

"I'll tell you the truth," I said. "If you saw her in the Indian village you'd think she was one of them."

"How come you don't look Indian then?"

"I guess I take after my grandfather. He was white."

"*That*'s why you're smart enough to be a teacher."

"Not necessarily. My grandmother was a pretty smart woman. A lot of people said she was smarter than my grandfather."

Robert Merriweather hadn't said anything up to then. He raised his hand. "If your grandmother was an Indian," he said logically, "then your father was a half-breed."

"I guess that's right. But you know something? Where I come from nobody cared about it. As a matter of fact whenever anybody found out I was part Indian they thought that was a pretty interesting thing to be. . . . Now we've got work to do, but just remember, what people are doesn't matter, whether they're Indian or Irish or Negro or anything else—they're just people."

When school was over for the day, Chuck hung around for a few minutes. "You tell truth, Tisha?" he asked me. "You Indian?"

"I'm part Indian, yes."

"You make moccasin?"

"No. I don't know how to do that."

"Cut fish?"

"Not too well."

"Trap?"

"I'm afraid not."

He thought it all over. "Funny Indian," he murmured.

Elvira Vaughn knocked at my door right after supper that night. She was all embarrassed. "My father said to tell you that me and my sisters won't be coming to school tomorrow," she said.

"How come?"

"My father said you'd know why."

I didn't sleep too well that night, and the next morning I was up at five. I did some washing just to keep busy, then I brought some wood in. By 8:30, when Robert arrived to start the fire, I was in the schoolroom putting some work on the board and listening for anybody who'd be coming. At a quarter to nine Isabelle Purdy and Joan Simpson arrived just as I went out to ring the hand bell for the first time. A few minutes later Rebekah brought Lily in, and right after that Chuck arrived. The Vaughn girls didn't show up at all. And neither did Willard and Jimmy. At nine I went out and rang the bell for late call, but there was nobody in sight. The settlement was quiet.

During recess I saw Willard and Jimmy playing up by the roadhouse. I decided to go over and talk to them, but as soon as I headed in their direction they ran indoors.

I tried to go on as if it was just a normal day, but every time I'd look at those five empty chairs I felt miserable. After school I must have sat for an hour drinking tea and trying to think what to do. Finally I threw on a sweater and went next door to the Vaughn cabin.

Mr. Vaughn opened the door.

"I wonder if I could talk with you for a few minutes?" I asked him.

"What about?"

"About the girls not being in school today."

"What about it?"

"Well, I know they're not sick. I wondered why they were absent."

"I kept them home."

"Will they be in school tomorrow?"

"We'll see," he said. Then he closed the door.

I stood there looking at the closed door, feeling like a little girl who'd done something awful. I started over to the roadhouse, then I changed my mind. I just didn't have the guts to stare into another face that might look at me as if I was a stone. So I went back to my quarters and stared at the walls for another hour.

I hadn't done anything wrong, but I still felt guilty. They were the ones who were wrong—Maggie and Angela and Mr. Vaughn. They were all wrong. They had no right to keep Chuck or Lily or any other little kid out of the school just because they thought they were dirt. There were plenty of people who'd thought

105

I was dirt when I was a kid. I could even remember one teacher who used to favor the kids who came to school dressed in nice clothes. She was always calling on them and smiling at them, while she looked at the ones like me as if we were trash. She'd even made me wear a sign one day when she found lice in my head during health inspection. I'd gotten them from playing with two kids next door and I'd never had them before, but she made me sit in the corner all day wearing a cardboard sign with "Dirty" printed on it. As long as I lived I'd never forget that. Or her. I'd hated her from then on.

I tried to think what I'd do if I was Miss Ivy, but it didn't help at all. She just wasn't the kind of person you fooled around with. She'd have gone right up to Mr. Vaughn and Maggie Carew and told them she expected to see their children in school the next day and no nonsense about it, and that would have been that. By suppertime I couldn't even think about eating. I decided that I'd wait till after supper, then I'd go over and talk to Maggie. The idea of going through another day, and maybe more, with less than half a class was unbearable.

Maggie saved me the trouble, though. Just before six Jimmy knocked at the door. "My mother says is it all right if the school board comes over after supper?"

"Sure. You can tell her 7:30 would be fine."

Before 7:30 came I went through a half a dozen conversations with them, and if I was able to say half the things I'd thought of I'd get a speech prize. I gave them quotes from the Declaration of Independence, the Bill of Rights and the Ten Commandments and ended with some beautiful phrases about how education was the birthright of all Americans. As soon as they trooped in, right on the dot, though, I felt just as tongue-tied as I'd been on the first day of school. They were grim. They turned me down when I offered them tea.

I had the stove going really hot so they'd be comfortable. Angela Barrett took off her sweater right away and my eyes nearly popped out. Her arms had so many tattoos they looked like an art gallery.

"I prepared the minutes of the last meeting," Mr.

Vaughn said, opening a composition book. "I'll read them."

"We can do without that," Maggie said.

"We're supposed to read the minutes," Mr. Vaughn said.

"What for?" Maggie said. "We know what we said."

"Are you making a motion that we waive them?"

"Wave 'em, fry 'em or boil 'em, I don't care. Let's get to what we come for."

Mr. Vaughn cleared his throat. "We'd like to know on what grounds you've taken Joe Temple's half-breed into the school."

"The same grounds on which I'd take any pupil in, Mr. Vaughn."

"He doesn't belong here. If you weren't a cheechako you'd know that. He belongs in the Indian village school."

"But he's not *in* the Indian village now."

"That has nothing to do with it. He shouldn't be in the same school with our children."

"I don't want to argue with you, but I don't see on what grounds you want to keep him out."

"According to the law," Mr. Vaughn said, "this school is open to, and I quote, 'white children and children of mixed blood who lead a civilized life.' You are aware of the law, I take it."

"Oh yes," I lied.

"Then there's your ground—'children of mixed blood *who lead a civilized life.*' That kid isn't civilized. None of those Indians from that village are."

Now that it came right down to it, faced with the three of them I wasn't feeling as brave as I thought I would.

"Well?" Mr. Vaughn said.

"Isn't that your interpretation, Mr. Vaughn? Chuck can read, he can write, as far as I can see he's like any other little boy who—"

Maggie cut me off. "My kid says he can't even talk civilized." This time she was in agreement with them.

"Besides that he's a bastard," Angela said.

"I hadn't even thought about that," Mr. Vaughn said.

"I don't see how I can do what you're asking," I said.

"Oh, you don't," Mr. Vaughn said.

"No. I just can't tell that little boy to get out of class for no good reason." And you wouldn't make me tell him either, I thought, if Chuck had a father who'd knock your block off.

"You've been given the reason. We're telling you the reason. We're not running a school for uncivilized siwashes and the law will back us up. Now are you going to tell him or do I have to do it myself?"

"I can't."

"Then I'll do it for you. We'd better take a vote on it to show we're doing it lawfully. I make a motion that the half-breed child known as Charles Temple be excluded from the school on the grounds that he does not lead a civilized life. How do you two vote?"

Maggie and Angela said aye.

"That settles it," Mr. Vaughn said.

Maybe it settled it for them, but it didn't for me. I was so mad I could have thrown the stove at them.

"We don't want you to have any hard feelin's, Annie," Maggie said. "We're just tryin'a show you what's best. You're still new here, ya know."

"I know."

"I'll take that tea if you're still offerin'."

I served her and Angela some. Mr. Vaughn didn't want any.

"Want you to know my kids think you're a good teacher, too." Maggie said, taking a sip.

"If there's no further business," Mr. Vaughn said, "we can close this meeting."

Not as far as I was concerned. Without my even having to think about it I heard myself say, "It's too bad I had to come all the way out here for nothing."

"How's that?" Mr. Vaughn said.

"I'm going to have to close the school."

About to take another sip, Maggie made a sound into her cup and put it down quickly. "You what?"

"I'll have to close the school," I repeated.

Mr. Vaughn's eyes narrowed. "What are you talking about?"

108

"I don't have enough of an enrollment," I said. I had to hold my hands tight in my lap, they were shaking so much.

"You got plenty enrollment," Maggie said.

"No I haven't," I said, trying to keep my voice even. It sounded to me as if I was squeaking. "Under the law there has to be ten pupils."

"You got my two boys, his three girls, the Merriweather kid, Simpson's little girl, and Isabelle and Lily."

"That only makes nine."

"I hear Nancy Prentiss is coming out. That'll make ten."

"*If* she comes out. Right now there's only nine."

"Well, so what?" Maggie said. "That's just a technicality. Plenty of schools don't make the enrollment." She snorted. "If you hadda rely on a full enrollment all the time there'd never be a school in the bush."

"I don't know anything about that," I said, "but this is my first teaching job in Alaska and I don't want to start out by breaking the law." My hands were sweating and my heart was pounding so loud I thought they could all hear it.

Maggie stared at me for a long moment as the point got home to her. Mad and disgusted, she pulled in one side of her mouth. "You telling us you'd pack up and git?"

"That's what I'd have to do, Mrs. Carew."

"You're bluffing," Mr. Vaughn said.

"No I'm not. You told me yourself—the law is the law."

He was so mad I was afraid he might smack me or something. "You dirty little snotnose," he snarled. "How dare you give us an ultimatum!"

"Simmer down, Arnold," Maggie said.

"Like hell I will." Even the veins on his goiter were standing out. "I never heard of anything like this in my life!"

"Will somebody please tell me what's going on?" Angela yelled.

"We're being blackmailed, that's what's going on," Mr. Vaughn said. "We've got a second Catherine Winters here—another Indian lover. I heard you're part siwash," he said to me, "now I believe it. For my part you can just pack up and get the hell out of here right now. As far as I'm concerned this meeting is adjourned." He walked out without saying another word.

Angela had her arms crossed in front of her. She didn't say anything, but her expression spoke worlds. It was pure hate.

"Angela, you go on back to the roadhouse," Maggie said. "I'll be there in a few minutes."

When she was gone Maggie said, "You're expectin' to teach in Eagle next year I take it."

"Yes."

"If I was you I wouldn't—not if you keep that little half-breed in the class. They got a school board there too. If they don't want you they don't have to take you. They're not gonna like it when they hear about this."

"There's not much I can do about that."

She got up. "You got gall, I'll say that much for ya —more gall than a Government mule. You're a good kid and I like ya, but I'm gonna tell ya something and I'll tell ya right to your face—don't go too far or you won't be teachin' in Eagle or anywhere else in Alaska next year. People are goin' to be writin' to the Commissioner about this, more people than you think. You're a little too interested in siwashes for your own good."

"I don't want any trouble, Mrs. Carew, but that little boy is entitled to—"

"Never mind what he's entitled to. Maybe you don't want trouble, but you got a peck of it right now."

"I didn't ask for it."

She buttoned up her coat. "You got it nevertheless. I'd advise you to watch your step. I'm willin' to look the other way on this. Other folks won't. You'll find that out."

She walked out without saying good-bye.

VIII

The next morning I couldn't wait for the class to arrive, wondering if they were all going to show up. If they didn't I didn't know what I was going to do. By the time it was a quarter to nine I was a nervous wreck, and I swore to God that if the whole class came, from then on I'd cause the least trouble to Him of anyone who was ever born. They all showed up though, even the Vaughn girls, and when we sang that morning you could have heard my voice clear over to Steel Creek I was so glad.

But I found out right away what Maggie meant about people not looking the other way. There was a couple named Dowles who lived in two separate cabins down near the end of the settlement. Even though they were married they hadn't talked to each other in years. The wife was a little bird-like woman and she'd loaned me a wash boiler. She scuttled in during the morning and said she needed it. I had some clothes simmering in it and I told her I'd give it to her after school if that was all right. Then about 11:30 an old sourdough who lived all alone on the other side of the creek came in and said would I mind letting him have the two chairs he'd loaned me. He was expecting company, he said. I gave him the chairs. My dishes went next, when Elvira came up to me before she went home to lunch. "My father says could you give us back the set of dishes we lent you? We need 'em for our own use." She was all red and blushing and I felt sorry for her. She was the nicest one in the whole family, but every time there was some kind of a dirty job to do she was the one who was sent to do it.

I tried not to let the way people felt bother me, but

it did. I wanted to get along with everybody and have them like me. But here I'd been in this place no more than ten days and already I'd made people antagonistic over what I'd thought would have been the last thing I'd find on a frontier—prejudice.

Not everybody, of course. Along with some others, Uncle Arthur and Mert Atwood were on my side. Uncle Arthur said it didn't matter that much one way or the other, but Mert was hopping mad. He was in the classroom when Elvira took the dishes home and right then and there he made me go over to Mr. Strong's store with him and bought me a whole new set. I didn't want him to because I knew he didn't have much money. None of those old-timers did. They pulled maybe five or six hundred dollars worth of gold out of the ground in a season, which just about got them by, but Mert insisted.

Joan Simpson's parents invited me over for supper a couple of nights after it happened and they thought it was funny. A young couple out of Idaho, they'd built themselves a sturdy little cabin on Forty-five Pup. A pup was just a little creek that branched off a bigger one, and Forty-Five was so named because it branched off of Chicken Creek at a forty-five degree angle. They'd made a nice life for themselves. Tom Simpson had been a carpenter and his wife Elizabeth had been a seamstress, so they were pretty self-sufficient. I spent a nice evening with them.

"Don't pay it any mind," Tom said. "That Vaughn gink is just a blowhard. I heard that when he lived up at Fort Yukon he was all for forming a branch of the Ku Klux Klan, but he couldn't get any takers."

The one person who surprised me was Mrs. Purdy. "I think you have make mush trouble for yourself, Ahnne," she said when I was over at the house one night. "Many people not like what you have done."

"That's not the half of it," Fred said, smiling. "I can tell you in one word what they think—ugh!"

Mrs. Purdy frowned. "I do not see the joke, Frayd. It is bad for this Indian boy to be in the school."

"Why, Mrs. Purdy?"

"Can you not see, Ahnne? He is dirty, ignorant.

112

What you call a . . . a . . ." Her hand fidgeted in the air as she tried to think of the word.

Fred leaned his cheek on his fist. "Bad example," he said.

"Yes. Thank you. It will be different, Ahnne, if Chuck is clean, neat. He is not. He is dirty and smells bad."

"That's simple," Fred said to me. "Tell him to take a bath."

"I've been thinking of it."

"Mary's got to pack water pretty far," Fred said, "but even if she didn't she wouldn't force him if he didn't want to. Indians are kind of easy on their kids."

"Think she'd mind if I gave him one?"

"Not at all. *He* would, though, I'd bet."

Mrs. Purdy shook her head. "It would be better, Ahnne, if you leave this boy Chuck alone. People look at him and think all native children are like him."

Fred groaned. "Ah, Ma . . ."

" 'Ah, Ma,' you say. *I* say I would like Mary Angus to go back to Indian village and take her children with her."

"Yeah," Fred said drily. "You want her to go back so bad you were the first one to say I ought to bring her over some wood. Tomorrow I'll go over and haul it all back."

Mrs. Purdy didn't think it was funny. "We must help those who need our help. We cannot let her freeze. But she does not belong here and the boy does not belong in this school. It was the same with Rebekah Harrington when she came to the school. That was not good," she said to me.

"How about the old-timers then? They drop in whenever they like. If they can do it, why can't Mrs. Harrington?"

"Rebekah is different," she said. "People do not respect her."

"If they don't, then what does it matter what she does—whether she comes to school or anything else? As far as I'm concerned, as long as she doesn't disturb the class she has as much right to sit down in that schoolroom as anyone else."

113

Mrs. Purdy shook her head. "Ahnne, you are young. You do not know what is in the heart of people here. *I* know. My children know. You must be careful."

She was really upset, and it made me realize something. She wanted to fit in, be like everyone else, and any native who didn't was a reflection on herself. And suddenly I realized too why Mr. Purdy acted the way he did, never saying anything when I was around and just going off by himself. He'd done the same thing tonight. He was ashamed of Mrs. Purdy, ashamed that she was Eskimo, and Mrs. Purdy knew it. It was hard to believe, but I knew down deep it was true, and I felt sorry for him.

Later on Fred walked me home. The ground was as hard as concrete and slippery with leaves. The trees were so bare now that during the day you could see the game trails running through the woods. I put the hood of my parka up right away.

"Your mother really worries about what people think of her, doesn't she?" I asked Fred.

"Well, it took her a long time to make friends around here."

"I kind of felt bad arguing with her."

"You didn't say anything wrong."

I slipped on some leaves and he grabbed me. When he let me go we were both a little self-conscious. We kept trying not to bump into each other all the rest of the way. When we reached the schoolhouse we were walking a couple of feet apart.

"Anything you need to have done in the classroom?" he asked me.

"You've done so much I don't like to ask you."

"I've got plenty of time till trapping season."

I told him I could use some cubbyholes for the kids to put their stuff in, and he said he'd come by some time in the next few days.

Chuck stayed.

How he was able to put up with the way the other kids treated him, I didn't know, but he stayed. They made life miserable for him. The only thing I couldn't blame them for was not wanting to sit near him in class. He smelled something awful. It was partly my

114

fault, because with everybody giving him such a bad time, I couldn't bring myself to tell him he smelled as bad as Ben Norvall.

If the kids talked to him at all it was just to make fun of him. They mimicked his accent and called him Ol' Man Yiss. "Are you half-baked or half-breed?" they'd ask him. "You got a siwash bitch for a mother and a father who don't even know your name." "Go back to Louse Town," they told him. "That's where you belong."

It wouldn't have been so bad if he could have held his own with them, but when they made him mad he couldn't think fast enough in English to talk back to them. He'd just stand there getting red in the face with fury and wind up stomping off.

No matter how many times I talked to them about it, it didn't do any good. Once they even waylaid him after school and threw rocks at him, chasing him all the way home to his shack. When I mentioned it to Mr. Vaughn and Maggie Carew they said they couldn't do anything about it. Mr. Vaughn hated him so much that sometimes I even thought he put the kids up to some of the things they did.

One afternoon, after Chuck had left the room, he dragged Chuck back in by the scruff of his neck. Chuck was terrified. His pants were open and he was trying to hold them up and keep from tripping at the same time.

"Here's your star pupil," Mr. Vaughn said. "He's so civilized he doesn't know enough to use the privy. I caught him squatting out in back."

He walked out leaving Chuck standing in front of the class, his own waste all over his pants and the class laughing. He looked so pathetic I didn't know whether to burst into tears or go out and tell Mr. Vaughn exactly what I thought of him. I took Chuck into my quarters and cleaned him up as best I could, but he smelled awful—worse than he had before. I told him to stay in my quarters and when school was over I did what I should have done when he first came. I got all my pots out, filled them with water and put them on the stove. Then I took him over to the store with me.

There we picked out a couple of good warm flannel shirts for him, two pairs of bib overalls and some socks. He loved them, but back in my quarters, when I told him he was going to have a bath before he could put them on his jaw dropped.

"Aw no, Tisha."

"You want those new clothes?"

"Yiss."

"You want to come to school?"

"Yiss."

"Then you're going to have to take a bath."

In he went, and while he was bathing I went over to the store and picked out a couple of pairs of long underwear. The pair he had on were shot.

When he was finished and all dressed up he looked like a different boy. I let him see himself in the big piece of mirror I had. "Like yourself?" I'd given him a shampoo and combed his hair.

He smiled. "Look too much good."

"We're going to do this once a week," I said. Even with scrubbing we hadn't been able to get all the dirt off him. Some of it was just too deep. The water in the washtub was black and scummy. After he helped me throw it out in back, we sat down and had something to eat.

"What bastid, Tisha?" he asked me.

"A bastard?"

"Yiss."

I tried to think of a way to explain it without hurting his feelings, but finally I just had to come out with it. "Well, a bastard is somebody whose mother isn't married. There's nothing bad about it. As a matter of fact a lot of famous people were bastards." That didn't come out the way I meant, but Chuck didn't care.

"Evelyn and Jimmy call me one bastid. Say I no got fodda."

"Sure you've got a father. Everybody's got a father."

"Why them kids they no like me?" he asked me.

"They don't know you yet, Chuck. That's the way kids are sometimes. You'll just have to give them time to get used to you. When they get to know you better and see what a fine boy you are they'll like you a lot."

"You know me?"

"I think so."

"I wait. Pretty soon them kids they know me too."

When the kids saw him the next day they almost didn't recognize him. It didn't make them any friendlier to him, though. When they found out I'd given him a bath and got him some new clothes they called him teacher's pet. But he kept coming. Whatever he had to put up with it was better than just hanging around that awful shack he lived in. I thought I'd been poor when I was a kid, but he didn't have anything. The lunches he brought were the worst I ever saw—stringy rabbit that was half-cooked, or fried bannocks that were little more than flour and water. After a couple of days I started making him sandwiches.

I had to admit that I was fond of him. I couldn't help it. There was just something about him that was so good and steady that it made me furious when the kids picked on him.

He dropped over to see me on Saturday and brought his little sister with him. She was a beautiful little thing, long black hair, delicate nose and big brown inquiring eyes.

"She name Et'el," Chuck said. He tried to get her to say hello to me, but she was too afraid. She hid in back of him. "She like too much you give brode."

I cut a slice of bread I'd baked that morning, smeared it with butter and honey and gave it to her. She gobbled it down so fast I was afraid she might throw it back up. She didn't though. Two more slices disappeared the same way.

Chuck brought her into the schoolroom and showed her some of his work, his leaf book, a couple of spelling papers and a picture of a moose he had drawn.

Before the two of them left I asked him where he liked it better—the Indian village or here.

"Indian village," he said. "Kids no play me here."

"I guess you'll just have to give it more time."

"I don' know, Tisha. I wait and wait and wait for them kids know me. They never know me."

"Sooner or later they will."

He sighed. "I hope maybe you be right. I wait too long I be old man like Uncle Arthur."

IX

"Is it time yet, Teacher?"

I looked at my watch. It was one minute to twelve. "Almost. Everybody's books and papers put away?"

They all answered yes, anxious to get out. The pack train was due in some time after lunch and this time I'd told them they could have the afternoon off. The first time Mr. Strong came in I'd kept school right up to the last minute, not wanting the school board to feel I was shirking my duty. But there'd been no point to it. All the class had done was waste time.

Mr. Strong hadn't been fooling when he said that the pack train coming in was a big day for the settlement. It was the only link we had with the outside world, with newspapers and magazines, mail from friends and relatives Outside, and supplies we'd ordered from the general store in Eagle. Everybody primped up a little, maybe not in Sunday clothes, but in the best and cleanest weekday ones, and the women put on a little rouge. Outside the schoolroom it was usually quiet during the day, with maybe just the sound of somebody sawing wood or doing some hammering, or a dog barking. But when the pack train was due in the miners for miles around drifted in starting about eleven o'clock, and the dogs all over the settlement had to take note of each arrival and try to out-howl each other about it. The whole settlement livened up and the class was too excited to work. Not that I blamed them. I was pretty excited myself. Today especially, because Nancy was coming in.

From now on I wouldn't have to eat supper all alone and I'd have somebody to talk to at night. I was getting lonely. She hadn't shown up the first time Mr. Strong came in and I was afraid that maybe she or her mother had changed her mind about her staying with me, but Mr. Strong had told me she'd be out with him on this trip.

"School's out for the day!" I yelled, and a minute later the classroom was empty.

The pack train didn't come in until late—almost three. By then it had started to snow again and it looked as though it might stick. Fred had come in to pick up his family's mail and he was playing softball with some of the kids, batting out easy flies to them. I was playing too, when all of a sudden the dogs all over the settlement began to bark and howl, raising a racket in their kennels. It meant that Mr. Strong was pretty near. We were having a good time, so we kept playing while everybody who'd come in from the creeks started emptying out of the roadhouse and others came straggling out of their cabins. I yelled for Fred to pop one over to me, and he hit one that went over my head. The ball hit the side of the Vaughn's storm entry just as Mr. Vaughn came out. He picked it up and the kids started yelling and waving for him to throw it to them, but he didn't. He walked over to me with it, his mackinaw collar turned up to hide his big goiter.

"What are all these kids doing out of school?" he asked me.

He knew as well as I did why they weren't in school, but he couldn't pass up the chance to let me have it.

"I gave them the afternoon off," I said.

"Who says it's up to you when they should have a holiday?"

"I'm sorry, Mr. Vaughn, I didn't think there was anything wrong in it."

"I suppose you don't see anything wrong in playing with them like a wild Indian either. I've seen you do it during recess." He turned to Angela Barrett and a few others who'd come up. "You ever see a teacher carry on that way?"

"Not in any school I ever went to," Angela said.

"Not in any I ever went to either," Mr. Vaughn said. "You'd better start watching your step."

I turned beet red, too embarrassed to say a word. He didn't like me and he didn't make any bones about it. Merton Atwood had come up, the black flap he'd made for his yachtsman's cap pulled down around his ears.

"What're you pickin' on the girl for?" he asked Mr. Vaughn.

"I'm trying to get her to act like a teacher."

Mert came to my defense. "What do you mean, act like? Girl's the best schoolmarm this place ever saw."

"The next time you want to take time off," Mr. Vaughn said, "you get permission from the school board."

Mert spoke right up again. "What're you talkin' about? Ever since I can remember, these kids been gettin' the afternoon off when the pack train's due in."

"You mind your own business. No little snotnose is going to decide how to run things here. We were here long before you arrived," he said, pointing a finger at me, "and we'll be here after you're gone. You're too damn smart for your own good."

"You don't have any right to speak to me that way, Mr. Vaughn."

"I'll speak to you any way I damn please." He pointed that finger at me again. "One more word out of you and I'll smack all that smartness right out of you . . . Go on," he challenged me, "let's see how fresh you can be now."

He was really working himself into a rage, and I began to feel weak in the legs. I was embarrassed too. Everybody was watching, and more and more people kept drifting over from the post office to see what was going on. I didn't know what to do. I didn't dare try to reason with him because he'd have slapped me as soon as I opened my mouth. I was even too scared to move.

Fred's hand touched my arm. "C'mon, Anne."

He started to lead me away and I went along willingly.

"Good thing your boyfriend has more brains than

120

you have," Mr. Vaughn sneered. "I was just getting ready to take you over my knee."

He kind of sniggered, and Angela Barrett laughed too.

That did it. Fred whirled around. "You won't lay a finger on her," he said.

Mr. Vaughn looked as if he'd just heard something he couldn't believe. "What did you say?"

He walked over to us with blood in his eye. Fred was still holding the baseball bat and he drew it back without saying a word. All of a sudden I knew he'd use it if he had to. I heard Mert say, "Good boy, Fred," and I didn't know whether I felt more proud of Fred or scared of Mr. Vaughn.

"Are you threatening me?" Mr. Vaughn said.

"You touch her or me and I'll let you have it," Fred said.

He looked Mr. Vaughn straight in the eye when he said it and Mr. Vaughn knew he meant it. It made him swell up so I thought he'd burst his goiter.

He had a cruel wide mouth and teeth like one of those fish that swim way down in the deeps. He was a full head taller than Fred and he'd have chewed Fred up right then and there if he could have. He was afraid of that bat, though.

"You black-assed half-breed sonofabitch," Mr. Vaughn said. "It seems to me I've seen your face around here an awful lot lately." He was still holding the ball, and suddenly he drew back and threw it. Fred ducked, but he didn't have to. It went wild.

Fred looked him straight in the eye. "You go to hell," he said.

My brain started working, and I found my tongue. "Mr. Vaughn, I didn't think anyone would think it was wrong for me to give the kids the afternoon off," I said. "I'll be glad to talk about it with the school board if you want me to."

That took the wind out of his sails. He gave Fred a contemptuous look just to show he was too puny to bother with, then he went on over to the post office. Fred and I drifted over along with everybody else and

121

I tried to act as if nothing had happened, but I was so upset that the whole time we waited for the pack train I could hardly say a word to anybody. Even if he didn't like me he had no call to say what he did to me, especially in front of the class and everybody else, and he certainly didn't have any call to say what he did to Fred.

I felt a little better as soon as I saw Nancy. She didn't act too enthusiastic, though. All she gave me was a curt "How do." She gave even less than that to the people who said hello to her. She just mumbled something and then looked away. I figured she felt strange. As soon as she was settled down, she'd probably be more friendly.

Inside my quarters, while Nancy put away her things I sat down and read a note from her mother that Mr. Strong had handed to me. Along with a few other things Mrs. Prentiss had to say, she wrote that Nancy was usually sensible, "but keep an eye on her. Don't let her go off to any of those miners' cabins by herself. She's inclined to be lazy and stubborn. You make her toe the mark. I've warned her to be obedient and help out all she can. Otherwise you'll send her home and I'll whip the daylights out of her. Don't be afraid to tell her that." She'd also had second thoughts about her offer to pay me. "I heard you don't have an outfit," the note ended. "Since it won't cost anything for Nancy's room maybe we can work out something where I send you some grub for her keep."

I put the note in the stove, not thinking one thing or the other about it. Once I had a little boy in my class whose father wrote me that the boy was a liar and a thief, and he turned out to be one of my smartest and best pupils. So I knew better than to judge somebody from what somebody else said.

She didn't have much with her, just a few pairs of bib overalls and a couple of washed-out old dresses that looked as old-fashioned as the ones in Mr. Strong's store. After we found a place for everything I told her how much I'd looked forward to having her with me. She didn't say anything to that. Aside from being so lonely, I went on, the school was taking up so much

122

time that I couldn't keep up with all the chores. "I guess it wouldn't be so bad," I said, "if there was running water. I never realized how much water a person used until I started packing it up from the creek— water for washing clothes, for washing yourself, for cooking, washing dishes. That's all I seem to do all day is pack water and then dump it out." I started to laugh when I told her about the first bath I took. It was a major undertaking. Besides a five-gallon pot I'd had to borrow from Maggie Carew, the top of the cookstove had been crammed with every pot I owned. But when I poured the water from them into the washtub, even with cramping myself down in it, it came up about five inches. After I was finished I felt as dirty as when I started. On top of that it was another major job to dump all the water out back. "Ever since then I've settled mostly for sponge baths."

She didn't find anything funny about that, so I asked her about her schooling. "What grade have you gone through?"

"Eighth."

"Without being able to read?"

"I can read somewhat."

I gave her the nearest book at hand, a fifth-grade reader. Opening it, she studied it for so long that I thought she wasn't going to read. When she finally did she spat the words out like pits, but she did well enough.

"You read fine," I said. "I don't see why you need me."

"I know most of the words," she answered.

"That's what I'm saying. You read pretty well."

"You don't understand," she said. "I know how to read this book 'cause my ma tutored me with it."

"How long ago was that?"

"Two years ago."

She saw that I still didn't understand what she was getting at.

"I can only read," she said, "if somebody reads it to me first and shows me the words. Don't you see? My ma read this to me."

"But that was two years ago. That's a long time."

"I studied with it for a whole year," she said. "Try me with another book."

I showed her a book of fairy tales. "Have you ever read this?"

She shook her head. I opened the book to the beginning of a story. She studied the page for almost a minute before she began to read. Later I realized that she had guessed at the first few words. " 'Once . . . upon a . . . time . . .' " She paused before she went on, and what came from her next was gibberish. ". . . Three . . . was . . . a . . . title . . . tar . . ." I looked over her shoulder. "There was a little tailor," the words read.

She went on, the rest of it just as senseless, until finally she gave up. "I don't know what I'm reading," she said. I had her try again, but it was the same. She even mistook one letter for another—an *l* for a *t*, a *b* for a *d*. When I questioned her I found out she didn't know what a consonant or a vowel was, nor had she ever memorized the alphabet. To her a word was just a bunch of letters written down in a certain order. She didn't know that the letters made up syllables and that each syllable had a sound.

Now I understood what she meant when she said she could read something only after somebody read it to her first. She was able to memorize the key words, and guess at the rest. I'd never seen anything like it.

Her teachers had pushed her through to the eighth grade, I guessed, figuring it wouldn't do any harm and would make her feel good. She couldn't go any further, though, because in order to get out of the eighth grade she had to pass the territorial examination. And she wasn't able to read it. After quizzing her for a while I found that she had learned her school work pretty well. She was smart, there wasn't any doubt about it.

"We'll enroll you tomorrow morning," I said.

"I don't want to be enrolled," she said tightly.

I had to prod her before she told me the reason: she felt she should have been out of the grades already and couldn't face the idea of failing again. She became so upset that I agreed not to enroll her even though she would attend classes like the other pupils. At night,

I promised her, I'd give her any extra help she might need.

For the first week I blessed Mr. Strong for advising me to take her. I'd fallen way behind in all my cleaning, washing and ironing, but Nancy pitched in with the chores so willingly that inside of a few days my quarters were spick-and-span. She did most of the cooking too, and even took the job of keeping the fire going. I didn't know what I'd have done without her, especially when it came to water. The snow that had started on the day she came kept up until it was two feet deep and the creek was running thick with slush ice. Then all of a sudden the temperature dropped to thirty below and the creek froze up. She was one step ahead, though, because she'd already piled snow high alongside the door, and there was our water supply. I didn't care much for the taste of it. It was flat, until Nancy dumped oatmeal in the barrel, and that improved it.

"We'll have to go easy on the water now," she told me.

"I thought I was going easy on it before," I said.

She said no, I'd have to go even easier. The trick, she showed me, was not to throw any water away until it was thoroughly used—first for personal washing, then for clothes. If necessary it could be used a third time to scrub floors. It didn't seem very sanitary to me at first, but after packing in snow and ice a few times I stopped worrying about hygiene. She also pointed out to me that Maggie Carew was not only shorting me on each cord of wood she had contracted to supply for the school, but that half of it was green instead of dry. "That's why the stove smokes so much."

After the first week or so problems began to come up between us. I'd told her that before she could learn to read she was going to have to learn how to recognize all her letters, printed and written, and learn the sounds they had. She buckled down at first, memorized the letters in no time, and even started to write simple three-letter words. But when a couple of the older kids saw what she was doing they made fun of her. That ended that. She told me she wasn't going to work in the classroom any more, at least not on her reading and writing. I let her work in my quarters on those two things, but I wanted her to join the class for discussions, arithmetic, field trips and everything else. She'd sit in class, but she wouldn't say anything unless I called on her. She was bored. Pretty soon she wasn't even completing her reading and writing assignments. Either they were done sloppily or not at all. When I asked her what the matter was she said that she didn't understand why she needed all the drills I was giving her in syllables and sounding out words. She wanted to learn to read and write, and she couldn't see that she was doing so. I told her that she'd have to start from the beginning. "I know you think you're not getting anywhere right now, but once you catch on you'll be reading in no time."

It didn't do any good. She just didn't seem to be interested in learning the way I could teach her. If I asked her why she hadn't finished something, she'd say she didn't understand it, and no amount of explaining could get her to.

I started to think that maybe she didn't like me, but she didn't seem to like anybody else either—especially the oldtimers. They'd been a big help to the class with our project, and had invited us over to their cabins when we went out on our field trips. We learned a lot from them about how they lived in the old days. Mert Atwood even showed us how they used to make butter. He brought over some caribou horns that he'd sawed up into lengths almost a foot long. We put them in a big pot and boiled them for almost three days, then we took them out and let the water cool. After a couple of hours, just as he said it would, a couple of inches of white butter formed at the top. It tasted good, too.

But Nancy didn't take to the old-timers. The only person she did like was Joe Temple. One time she went over to his cabin and stayed there for quite a while. I hadn't even known she'd been there until Uncle Arthur mentioned it to me. I spoke with her about it and asked her not to do it again. She said she wouldn't, but she was surly about it.

Mert came over after school one day, and after he'd

126

visited with us for a while he took off his yachtsman's cap and removed an envelope from it.

"Got this here letter th'other day," he said to me, "but I'm shipwrecked if I can find my glasses. Can't read a thing without 'em. Maybe you wouldn't mind readin' it for me."

I knew he couldn't read and didn't want to admit it, so I told him I'd be glad to. When I was finished Mert thanked me and put the letter back in the envelope.

Innocently, he asked Nancy how she was coming along with her reading.

"Hell of a lot better'n you ever did with yours," she said belligerently.

Stung by the remark, Mert smiled tolerantly. I tried to make conversation after that, but it didn't do any good. "Well," Mert said after a couple of minutes, "time to lift anchor and shove off."

"You really hurt that old man's feelings, Nancy," I said after he was gone.

"Well he hurt mine too."

"He was only trying to be sociable. He didn't mean anything."

"I didn't ask him to talk to me, didn't ask him to come here either."

"Nobody asked him. He just came because he's lonely and he likes to talk with us."

"Well let'm be lonely some place else. He's like all them other old windbags, dirty and smelly and always braggin' about how they're gonna get rich some day and the things they're gonna do when they are. They're not gonna do any of them things ever. They're just wastin' time jawin' and I'm not about to let'm waste my time."

She didn't like it either when I gave Chuck a bath, acting as if he was just about the lowest thing she ever saw. She didn't say anything the first time, but the second time she said that we ought to make him haul in the snow himself. "Unless you fancy waitin' on siwashes," she said.

I tried to kid her. "Ah, come on, he's only a little boy."

"You can't even turn around here without trippin' over 'im."

"He likes it here."

"Between him and all them other kids you'd think this was a roadhouse."

She didn't like the idea that the kids were always trooping in and out. Even after school they'd come over sometimes to work on something they hadn't finished in class or to play in the school room. I didn't mind it at all, but I could see how it would get on her nerves, so I tried to discourage them from coming into my quarters and get them to stay in the schoolroom instead.

But things kept going from bad to worse between us. I'd heard about some of the feuds that people who shared cabins sometimes got into and I'd always thought they were funny—like Harry Dowles and his wife moving into separate cabins and never talking to each other. I'd found out that even Uncle Arthur and Mert Atwood had been cabin-mates until one winter when they had an argument. They split everything up evenly and what they couldn't split they cut in half just for spite. They even cut their stove in half, Ben Norvall had told me, and the two of them nearly froze to death.

Now I could understand how that could happen. When you lived in close quarters with someone and you weren't getting along, everything that person did annoyed you. Sometimes it was all you could do to keep your temper. That's what was happening with Nancy and me. We finally got to the point where she wasn't even saying good morning unless I said it first.

A couple of weeks after she arrived Mary Angus came over one Saturday to bring me a pair of moccasins she'd made for me. She brought Chuck and Ethel with her. She didn't look well at all. Her cheeks were all flushed and there were dark circles under her eyes. I introduced her to Nancy, but Nancy just sat where she was at the kitchen table, sipping some hot cocoa, and hardly even looked up. Mary didn't want to, but I made her sit down and have some tea while I tried on the moccasins. As soon as she did Nancy got right up and went over to the couch.

128

The moccasins were beautiful. They were winter moccasins, with good sturdy moosehide below the ankle and caribou with the fur turned out up to the knee. She'd beaded them with dyed porcupine quills and trimmed the tops with rabbit fur. They fit perfectly too, but after I took a look at the beat-up moccasins on her own feet I didn't feel so good.

The three of them didn't stay long. While they were there, I gave Chuck his favorite—a slice of my "brode," as he called it, smeared with butter and honey. I gave one to Ethel too.

As soon as she bit into it Chuck started to bawl her out in Indian. She stopped with her mouth full, looking at him wide-eyed, while he pointed to me. Finally looking up at me she said something like "Oo." Chuck patted her. "Ver' good. She not got good manners, Tisha. I teach her say T'ank you."

"I'm proud of you, Chuck," I said. I was too. I'd been teaching him to say thank you when somebody handed him something or did something for him.

After they all left Nancy said, "You shouldn'ta done that, Teacher." I'd told her a couple of times she could call me Anne, but she wouldn't.

"Done what?" I asked her.

"Had 'er to the table."

"What was wrong with it?"

"People around here don't even let siwashes into the house much less sit down with 'em to the table."

"Then they ought to be ashamed of themselves."

She didn't say anything to that and I was glad she didn't. I was mad enough so that we'd have had a stemwinder, and things were bad enough between us already.

We both started to get petty. It was her job to see to it that we always had enough wood and water on hand. But when we ran low on them a couple of times, I had to remind her. After the second time she said it might be a good idea for us to take turns doing it.

"I've been leaving it to you," I told her, "because I figure you can do it better than I can." I also figured I was making up for it by tutoring her at night, but I didn't mention that.

129

She didn't say anything, but after I had to remind her a couple more times I got the hint. Finally we took turns washing the linens, sweeping, doing the dishes and everything else.

I hadn't planned it that way at all. I was in the schoolroom almost all day and I'd sometimes be working long after supper planning lessons and activities. I'd thought that Nancy would help me out the way I'd helped out Miss Ivy. But it wasn't working out that way. I had as much to do as I had before, and besides that I had to put up with someone I liked less every day. When I'd passed through her parents' roadhouse it was clean as a whistle, and so was Nancy at first. But after a while she was leaving her old dirty clothes hanging on nails or over a chair and didn't bother to wash them until they smelled as gamey as Ben Norvall's. If I mentioned it to her she'd put them all in a pile and keep them out of sight, but she didn't wash them any more often than she did before.

I mentioned the situation to Mr. Strong one day while we were going over the accounts in his store. "It's too bad," he said. "I was hoping that maybe getting away from her family would be of some help to her."

"What's the matter with her?"

"She's simply been worked too hard too long, madam. She's a good girl, but she's never had a chance. Her mother's been driving that girl ever since I can remember—made a slave out of her."

"If I could just get her to talk . . ."

"Can't get a word out of anyone in that family. All I can tell you is, she hasn't had it easy. You saw that roadhouse her folks run, the nice way they keep it. Well, they do it by making those kids of theirs hop. Nancy practically raised her two brothers by herself, and when she wasn't taking care of them she was working the garden or making beds or doing something else—but look, that's none of your affair. Send her on home if you can't take it."

I didn't want to do that if I could help it, especially after what he said. It made me understand why being able to read was so important to her, why even though she wasn't learning she still hung on. "I *gotta* learn, Teacher," she told me once. It was the only time she'd ever opened up. "I gotta pass that eighth-grade exam. If I do my mother promised I could go to high school in Fairbanks." It was the only chance she had to get away from her family.

But no matter how hard I worked with her it didn't do any good. I started to get surly myself. Everybody else in the class was working hard and having a good time, but Nancy couldn't seem to become interested in anything we were doing. She remained an outsider, never raising her hand to offer an answer, not wanting to answer even when I called on her. The class knew that I was tutoring her and they were jealous of the fact that she was living with me. They called her Miss Dumbbell and mimicked her by putting on sour faces when her back was turned. Once when I asked Jimmy Carew to read aloud, he did an imitation of her— slumping down in his seat and staring hard at his book, which he held upside down.

The situation came to a head one afternoon close to dismissal when Nancy rose from her seat, went over to Jimmy and smacked him hard across the ear. Then she walked into my quarters, slamming the door behind her. Stunned, Jimmy fanned his smarting ear and tried to hold back the tears. Then he put on a surly expression that made the other children laugh. Asking the class to be quiet, I went in to talk to Nancy, but she was already out the front door and didn't stop when I called her.

It was well after supper when she came back, leaving the door open a few more seconds than necessary while she wiped some mud off her shoes. I'd propped a piece of mirror on the table and was sitting by the stove marcelling my hair. There was going to be a dance in the schoolroom the next night and I wanted to look my best. I asked her where she'd been.

"Over to Joe Temple's."

"By yourself?"

"Uh-huh."

"You think that was a good idea?"

She shrugged and started to take off her parka.

"We're low on water," I said. Ordinarily I'd have gotten it myself, but I was feeling mean.

She made two trips, each time leaving the door ajar and letting the cold in. When she was done she sat down on the couch and stared into space, her eyes occasionally following the waving iron.

"I asked you once before, Nancy, not to go over to Joe's place alone."

"We just talked."

"I'm sure of that. But while you're here you're my responsibility. If I ask you not to do something there's a reason for it."

We were silent for a few moments, then Nancy said, "He's got Mary Angus for that, if *that's* what you're worried about."

"Why did you have to slap Jimmy?" I said, changing the subject.

" 'Cause he was taking me off, been taking me off for three days now."

"You could have told me. I'd've made him stop it."

"No need to now. He won't be making faces anymore."

I decided not to put the decision off any longer.

Finished with the iron, I started putting on a hair net, trying to think of a nice way to say what I was going to, but I couldn't. "Nancy, I think we've both tried as hard as we can and we're not getting anywhere."

She sat very still, her eyes meeting mine for a moment, then she stared down at the floor.

"Maybe it would be a good idea," I went on, "if you went home for ten days or so, give us both a rest. How would that be?"

She didn't answer. We both knew that if she left it would be permanent. An hour later I was studying my eighth-grade arithmetic, trying to figure out division of fractions, when she broke the silence. "You don't like me one bit, do you?"

"That's not true," I lied.

"Then why you sending me home?"

"I don't think we're doing each other any good."

"Just 'cause I slapped Jimmy Carew."

"No, that's not it."

"Well, then what is it? 'Cause I won't do all the scrubbin' and cleanin' you want?"

"Nancy—"

"Well, that's not what I come here for," she went on, deliberately using poor grammar. "I do enough a that at home. I come here so you could teach me to read and you sure ain't done it."

"No, I *ain't*," I said, beginning to lose my temper, "and the way you go around here I'll never be able to. Not the way you are. You're so busy being angry, you haven't got room for anything else inside of you." Nancy stared at me in surprise while the words poured out of me. "You've lived in this part of the country all your life, but when people stop by here to visit with us you won't say a word to them. You won't even look at them half the time. How do you think that makes them feel?"

"What'm I supposed to say to 'em?"

"Anything that comes into your head. It's better than glaring at them. And if you can't think of anything then just give 'em a smile. You've got a beautiful smile when you want to use it, you've got a beautiful face if you'd just wash it once in a while." I stopped, sorry I'd said as much as I did. I hadn't meant to. I calmed down. "When you came out here, Nancy, I was really glad to see you. I needed all the help you could give me, and you gave me a lot—at first. Now you won't do anything—you won't make the bed, you won't pack water, you won't even change your clothes unless I ask you. And when I do ask you to do something you look at me as though I'm being mean."

"My mother ain't payin' for me to cook and clean," she said stoically. "She's payin' for you to tutor me."

It was my turn to be surprised. "Nancy, your mother isn't paying me anything."

"What are you talkin' about? I heard 'er tell you when you first came through that she'd pay you for takin' me."

"Yes, she did. But I sent her a note back on the day you arrived. I told her she could forget about paying me."

She fought against believing me at first, but when I assured her it was true she went pale.

"Why'd you do that?" she said. Her voice seemed to come from far away.

"I was glad to have the company," I said honestly. "I was afraid being here all by myself." She looked so miserable that I wished I could think of something to console her. "I guess I should have told you," I said finally.

There was coffee in the coffeepot and I asked her if she wanted some. She shook her head. After I poured a cup for myself I sat down at the table again, feeling terrible.

"Nancy, if you'd like to stay, maybe we could try again."

She got up and went to the window. She slowly rubbed some moisture from a pane and stared out into the darkness.

Then she cried for a long time.

X

From then on Nancy changed. She hadn't been one to show her feelings much before we had the argument, and she didn't make any big display after it, but I could see the difference in her right away. Up to then I almost had to drag her out of bed in the morning. After that she was up when I was and sometimes even before. She was a dynamo, cleaning and washing, taking care of herself and doing so many chores that half a dozen times I had to tell her to slow down. She wouldn't, though. The way she acted towards me you'd have thought that my letting her stay with me without getting paid for it made me some kind of a heroine.

I kept complimenting her all over the place and she just glowed. She hardly ever looked me straight in the eye, and she wouldn't smile because of the cavities in her front teeth. I could tell she was pleased, though.

After a few days we sat down and had a good talk, something we'd never done before. I told her I appreciated everything she was doing, but I didn't want her wearing herself out. She said I wasn't to worry about that. "I just want to show you I appreciate what you did for me," she said, picking at some loose threads on her overalls. It was a habit she had that used to drive me crazy, always giving her attention to something else when you talked with her, as if she didn't really care what you were saying. She did, though. She just didn't know how to show it.

I tried to tell her I didn't do any more for her than Miss Ivy had done for me—a heck of a lot less, really, because I needed her help—but she wouldn't hear of it.

"You did more for me than anybody in my whole life," she insisted, "and I'm not forgetting it."

"If you really feel that way there's one way you *could* pay me back," I said.

"What's that?"

"Be a little more friendly with the kids in class."

"Won't do any good. They don't take to me."

"They would if you gave them the chance. They're a little afraid of you." I told her that she could act as sort of my assistant, like a helping teacher.

"Some helping teacher," she said, pulling out a thread she'd been worrying, "I can't even read."

"Nancy, you *can* read. All you have to do is give up that old crazy system you made up. Sit down and learn how to break words up into sounds and I guarantee you'll be reading inside of a month. Then you'll really be my assistant."

She didn't promise anything, and I didn't expect too much, so I was really surprised when she not only buckled down to work, but in her own way tried to be nicer to the other kids. Before, whenever she was in

135

class she wouldn't budge for anybody. Now she started getting up to close the stove door whenever the classroom became too hot, or open it when it was chilly. When a few of the "books" the children had made started falling apart, she fixed them. She took them over to the roadhouse and sewed the pages together on Maggie Carew's machine, then shoved them at the kids with a gruff, "Here, I fixed 'em for ya." She was tops in arithmetic too, so one morning I asked her if she'd help Jimmy with his multiplication tables. She and Jimmy hadn't said a word to each other since she'd slapped him and neither of them looked too keen about the idea. I sent them into my quarters to work, and when I glanced through the door a few minutes later she was tutoring him as if she'd done it all her life.

After she helped Jimmy the class was less leery of her. She even made up a game—a multiplication clock, she called it. It was a clock made out of cardboard with one hand on it, and she'd move the hand from one number to the next while the kids multiplied by two, or three, or five. After a while, we used a stopwatch to see how fast each of the children could do it.

She really blossomed. It didn't take more than a couple of weeks before some of the kids were taking a shine to her. During recess, when it was too cold for the little ones like Joan and Willard to go out, I let her supervise the older kids outside while the little ones played in the schoolroom. In private I told her that I'd appreciate it if she'd watch out for Chuck. The other kids didn't pick on him as much as they had when he first came, but once in a while they still reminded him he wasn't as good as they were, especially the Vaughn twins.

She watched out for him better than I could. During one recess I heard him start to cry outside and I went to the door. I opened it just in time to see Nancy give Eleanor Vaughn a shove that made her sit down on her behind fast. She'd have done the same with Evelyn if Evelyn hadn't danced out of the way. They must have washed Chuck's face with snow because it was all red and wet. None of them saw me, so I figured I'd

136

let Nancy handle it. She was tougher than the two of them put together.

"You keep your hands off this kid from here on," Nancy said to Evelyn, putting a mitten on Chuck's shoulder.

"Since when you sticking up for siwashes?" Eleanor said, getting up.

"I'm not stickin' up for 'em anymore 'n I'd stick up for you," Nancy answered. "The teacher says you keep your hands off, so keep your hands off."

"You don't have any right to tell us what do do," Eleanor sneered.

"That's right," Evelyn said.

"I'm not tellin' you what to do. I'm just tellin' you that if you lay your hands on this kid again I'm gonna bash your head in."

They left Chuck alone from then on.

I guessed I was never so happy in my life as around that time. Everything just seemed the way I'd dreamed it would be—the settlement and all the country around hushed under a thick white blanket, the snow dry enough so you could walk around in moccasins and never get wet. Now I realized what the North was really like. It was made for winter, because winter was when everything went on. You could ski any place you wanted to and get there twice as fast and twice as easily as you could before there was snow. People went out and brought in the trees they'd cut for firewood and left lying until they could use sleds to haul them. The whole country just opened right up. You could hear somebody talking on the trail half a mile away, or dropping a pan on the stove a mile from the settlement. It was so quiet and open and free that it was like being let out of prison. It put everybody in good spirits and they went around looking the way the country did —clean and fresh.

Came lunchtime, the class was usually out of the room like a shot, and fifteen minutes later, after bolting their lunch, the kids were outside with sleds and skis. I learned how to ski in no time at all. I'd done a little when I was a kid, but that was just with barrel staves. It wasn't anything like real skiing. Once I

137

learned I was as anxious as the class to get out and slide the hills.

The one thing I would have liked to learn was ski-joring—holding onto a string of dogs and letting them pull you—but I wasn't any good at it. Fred was expert at it and he tried to teach me a couple of times, but the dogs kept pulling me off balance. Finally, on the second try, he told me he was going to work something out where that wouldn't happen. "You be ready next Saturday morning," he said when I asked him what it was. "I'll be by around ten."

Almost on the dot I heard him call my name, and when I opened the door he was out there on his own skis, waiting. He'd brought his favorite lead dog, Pancake, and two others. "You ready?"

It wasn't that cold out, so I threw on a canvas parka with a warm sweater underneath. Outside on the porch I started to take my skis, but he said leave them. Then I saw what he'd done. He'd fitted an extra pair of straps on his own skis so I could stand behind him.

"You think it'll work?" I asked him.

"I don't know," he said. "I never tried it."

Nancy watched from the doorway while I got on, and I had the barest second to wave to her before he yelled "Mush!" and we were off.

We didn't go too fast at first because the dogs weren't able to dig into the packed-down snow of the settlement. Once we were on the trail, though, we speeded up. Then Fred began to sing *Sweet Rosie O'Grady* to them and they began to pull like sixty. Everybody had a different way of making sled dogs pull. Some used a whip. Others, like Angela Barrett, yelled and cursed at them all the time. Her dogs were so used to it that they wouldn't pull unless she swore at them, so you could hear her coming from a half-mile away. Fred sang to his and they loved it.

"No singing!" I yelled.

"Why not?"

"We're going too fast."

"We haven't even started."

"Fred, we'll fall!"

"No we won't!"

138

I held onto his parka as tight as I could, his skis crunching under us. The dogs were thirty feet ahead, the full length of the lead rope. If they geed or hawed all of a sudden I knew I was going to be dumped.

But I hung on. Skiing was fun, but it wasn't anywhere near as exciting as this.

After a while I started to congratulate myself. I was doing pretty well. I leaned into turns easily and could key my movements to Fred's, as if we were on a bicycle built for two. We must have gone half a mile before I got so cocky I didn't look where we were going.

The trail took a sharp turn. Fred leaned to the left, I dragged him off to the right, and we went flying.

Luckily we ended up in a drift, laughing. We didn't bother to get up right away, just lay back where we fell. "You all right?" Fred asked.

"Perfect. Maybe I'll take a nap." I propped myself up on my elbows, watching the dogs. They'd taken a spill too, and a couple of them were tangled in the lead lines. They were well trained, though, and didn't get excited about it. Pancake was a beauty, brown mask over a gray wolf face and slanted ice-blue eyes. Panting, he went to Fred as though he'd done something wrong, his tail down and his rear end moving from side to side.

"Look at that. He thinks it was his fault," Fred said. He sat up and started untangling the rope.

"Well, whose fault was it?"

"Yours."

"I knew I'd be blamed."

"Better than blaming Pancake." He rubbed the dog's head. "He'll feel bad."

"How about me?"

"You can take it."

I picked up a gob of snow and tossed it at him. He blocked it easily and it went to powder, then shoveling up a bigger gob, he hefted it high in the air. It plopped down on the hood of my parka and most of it stayed there.

"You look like a tree," he said.

"Nicest thing you ever said to me."

I looked up at the blue sky. It was still early, but

the sun was low, skimming the distant mountain tops and sending out long blue shadows from the trees.

I watched Fred while he straightened out the harness. He'd been out on the traplines the week before and he was brown as a coffee bean. I'd really liked being so close to him on the skis and I wondered if he felt the same thing about me. I had a feeling he did. Even if he did, though, he didn't show it. It was the way he always acted with me. Careful. So far all he'd done was hold my hand once when we were alone. We never talked about it, but I knew full well why he was being so careful. He'd swallowed a lot of that half-breed baloney people around here were always slicing and it made him keep his distance from me, as if he wasn't as good as the next boy and I was something special. If he'd been pure white he'd have acted a whole lot different.

I wished there was some way I could show him how much I liked him, but I didn't know how. I'd tried just about everything.

The last time I was over at his house I'd let him beat me at carom checkers, and when we talked politics lately I let him convince me he was right even though he was a Democrat and I was for the Republicans. I'd even told him all about the junky places I'd grown up in, and how one summer I'd worked as a hired girl on a ranch, just so he wouldn't think my being a teacher made me a member of the aristocracy, but he still kept his distance.

I didn't know what more I could do. When I used to live with Miss Ivy she told me that boys didn't like it when a girl ran after them. There were ways to show a boy that you favored him, she said, ways you could encourage him—only she never told me what those ways were. I figured I'd given him all the encouragement I could, short of coming right out and being bold about it.

Fred got up now, brushed himself off and gave me a hand. Then we were off again.

A couple of minutes later we were in sight of Mary Angus' place.

There was smoke coming from the stovepipe, which

meant she was all right. A couple of weeks ago when I'd seen her on the trail near Fred's house, I'd been scared she might die. She'd been pretty far away and it was almost dark. She was pulling a hand sled, and her little girl was with her. They were probably heading out for her trap line. We waved to each other, but before she went on she doubled over, coughing. A minute later when I crossed the place where she'd stopped I saw there was blood spattered all over the snow. Every time I thought about it I felt as sick as I did then. I'd written to the minister in Eagle to ask him if he could collect some food for her from the people there and he'd said he would. The Purdys saw to it that she had enough wood too, but there wasn't much else anybody could do. For a second I wondered if we should stop and see how she and her little girl were, but I decided against it. I'd just be bothering her.

A little later Fred and I were close to Lost Chicken when we started back for home. It was getting dark already, so we took a short cut across some fresh snow, figuring we'd pick up the trail again just past Uncle Arthur's place. The dogs had to break trail, leaping forward like fish breaking water, and it slowed them down, so we walked.

We found Uncle Arthur doing some "drifting" a little distance from his cabin. It was back-breaking work, especially for an old man like him, and he'd taken his parka off. He was all gnarled and twisted up from rheumatism and he must have been about seventy, but it didn't stop him from working with a pick and shovel. They were lying beside the prospect hole he'd dug, along with his coat.

Inside the hole, which was about two feet deep now, he'd piled kindling and logs. He'd put a match to them and was climbing out of the hole just as we got there. The fire would thaw the frozen ground so he'd be able to dig down a little further. Eventually he'd dig down to paydirt—anywhere from twenty to forty feet—and if he got some good pans out of it he'd spend the summer mining the surrounding ground. If the hole didn't pan out he'd prospect somewhere else.

"How you be, Missis?" he asked me.

141

"Fine, Uncle Arthur. You enjoying your cornflakes?"

"Hate cornflakes," he said. "Gave'm to Mert Atwood. That dumb bunny'll eat anything."

I knew he'd say that, but I couldn't resist asking him. Now that Mr. Strong was able to use his big sled he'd finally brought out the corn flakes Uncle Arthur had ordered—six cartons of them. But Uncle Arthur hadn't really wanted them. Like a lot of other people in Chicken, Uncle Arthur felt that Mr. Strong was making too much money on his mail contract, so they ordered as many bulky things by parcel post as they could. The more space Mr. Strong had to give to parcel post, the less he had to use for freighting in the more profitable items that he sold in his store or that people ordered from Eagle. Uncle Arthur had hit on the perfect item to annoy him—cheap, bulky, and light enough so that the parcel-post rate was cheap, too. Now he had all the other old-timers ordering them. But Mr. Strong got back at them by not bringing them out until after the freeze-up, when he had plenty of room on his sled.

Uncle Arthur picked up his coat from the snow and put it on, throwing his head back so his beard wouldn't get caught as he buttoned up.

"Gonna have penmanship drill tomorrow?"

"Sure."

He never seemed to get tired of it, and if I didn't have it on the day he showed up he sulked and complained.

"That the way the two of you come out," he asked Fred, "on one pair of skis?"

"Yes."

"Makes it pretty cozy, I guess, but I don't know if it's somethin' the kiddies ought to see. Doesn't set a good example, if you know what I mean."

I wished he hadn't said that. It made Fred and me uncomfortable. It was hard for me to figure him out. Sometimes I thought he liked me. Other times, like now, he'd be cantankerous.

Fred talked mining with him for a couple of minutes, then we left. I knew he was still bothered by what Uncle Arthur had said. Instead of the two of us ski-joring out, he slung the skis over his shoulder and held the dogs on the lead.

Once we were out of sight I took his arm.

"When are you going to take me on that snow picnic?" He'd promised to a couple of times already.

"I was thinking we'd go in a couple of weeks."

"Why so long?"

"Have to go out on the trap line in a few days."

I was disappointed. He'd be gone for about a week. What was worse was that he hated everything about trapping. Most of the time the animal was still alive when he got to it. Hissing and snarling with fear, it had to be clubbed to death, then skinned before the carcass froze. He'd told me all about it. The only reason he did it was because his family needed the money.

"I wish you didn't have to go," I said.

"Me too. I'm going to miss you."

"Will you?"

"Yes I will."

"I feel the same way. I'll miss you too."

If that didn't let him know how much I liked him, then nothing would. He dropped the skis on the snow and I got all tensed up wondering if he was going to kiss me. I could tell he wanted to because he looked very serious. Suddenly I thought of what he'd said about going out on the trap line. "Fred, you're not going to miss the dance, are you?" The Friday night dance was only a few days away.

"Don't you worry, I won't."

"Wouldn't it be nice if we could have midnight supper together this time?"

Uncle Arthur always brought his ancient gramophone to the dances and along about eleven o'clock the square dancing stopped and everybody danced to the scratchy records he put on. He always saved the *Home Sweet Home* waltz for last and nobody knew when he was going to play it. When he did, it was the signal for each man to run and grab the woman he wanted to take to the roadhouse for a midnight supper. I'd ended up with Mert Atwood one time and Joe Temple the other, but never with Fred. Uncle Arthur

143

always made sure we were too far apart to get to each other.

"I'll keep an eye out," Fred said, "but I think the odds are against it. Wouldn't do for you to end up with a half-breed."

It was the first time he'd ever said anything like that.

"I know, but will you try anyway?"

"I have. I even know what color the label on that record is, but Uncle Arthur's pretty cagey."

"What color is it?"

"Green."

"You're really smart. I never thought of that."

I'd stayed as close to him as I could without stepping on his feet, so if he wanted to kiss me he had all the chance in the world. He looked at me in that serious way again and even before his arms went around me I knew he was going to. He was still holding onto the dogs' lead line, and I thought to myself that if one of those dogs pulled on the line now I'd kill it. But they all stayed quiet. And then Fred's mouth was on mine. I felt gawky and nervous at first and my heart was pumping like a steam engine, then all of a sudden I was feeling warm and wonderful, as if this was where I'd always been headed. After he kissed me he held me away from him a little and the way he looked at me I knew he'd always cared for me more than he'd let on. A lot more. Then his mouth was on mine again.

His parka was open at the neck and when I laid my head against his shoulder I could feel the heat coming from his body. He smelled of wood smoke. I wished we could go somewhere where we could be alone and sit and talk and hold each other.

"I shouldn't have done that, Anne."

"Why not?"

"You know why. There's a lot of difference between us."

"Does that mean you want me to become a Democrat?"

I don't know what made me say it. Usually I was the serious one between the two of us, but it made him

144

laugh, and he took me in his arms and kissed me again.

We found a place to sit down on a small shelf of rock right over a creek bottom. Fred cut some spruce boughs for us to sit on and we leaned back, me in the crook of his arm. There was some scraggly brush right in front of us, so unless somebody knew we were there we couldn't be seen from the trail. It was a cozy spot and we snuggled together for warmth. After a while I said, "You still think you shouldn't be kissing me?"

"Uh-huh."

"How come?"

"Anybody sees us you'll be in for trouble."

"How about you?"

"There's nothing anybody can do to me."

I wasn't as sure as he was. "That day Mr. Vaughn picked on me I think he ended up more mad at you than at me."

"Probably," Fred said.

"Doesn't that bother you, people feeling that way?"

"No."

"It bothers me, makes me feel as if I'm in prison."

"Oh, maybe it bothers me once in a while," he admitted, "with people like Strong, or the Carews, but not with the likes of Vaughn. If somebody doesn't know me, what do I care what they think about me?"

"I was afraid he was going to beat you up that day."

"Not while I had that baseball bat he wouldn't."

"Would you have used it?"

He smiled. "Not if I could have run."

"You mean you *would* have used it?"

"If he'd really tried to hit you, I guess so . . . I don't know."

We started talking about what he wanted to do in the future. He'd worked for wages a few times and he hadn't liked it. What he wanted more than anything was to be on his own. He and his father had plans to buy a tractor. With it, he said, he'd be able to do ten times the mining they were doing with pick and shovel now.

"How would you get it in here?" I asked him.

"By airplane, have it shipped in piece by piece. It'd

be expensive, but it would be worth it." Eventually he wanted to have his own airplane too, he said. There were a million things he wanted to do. He wanted to travel and he was thinking that if everything worked out the way he wanted he might even try farming. He felt it could be done, that anything that was done in the States could be done here. He loved it here.

"You just look out there," he said. "It's so big and beautiful it makes you feel wonderful just to be alive. I couldn't even think of living any place else."

I'd never heard a boy his age talk that way. The boys I'd known were all interested in going to work for some big company or other, getting an automobile and maybe buying a house one day.

We were still talking when all of a sudden a gust of cold air hit me. It was as if a giant box of dry ice had dropped on us. It took my breath away.

"We'd better get back," Fred said. "Temperature's starting to drop."

I couldn't understand what his hurry was. We weren't more than half an hour away from the settlement. Ten minutes later I realized what he meant, though. Ice fog was swirling around us and I could feel the cold nipping at my body, almost like teeth, trying to pull the heat out of me. It made me realize what it must be like for Fred to be caught in that kind of freeze when he was out trapping in the middle of nowhere. The ice fog became so thick that we had to depend on the dogs to stay on the trail. If I'd been alone I'd have been scared, but as long as I was with Fred I wasn't. All the way back I felt as if I were part of him, his body pressing against mine, lean and strong.

By the time we reached my quarters the thermometer outside the window read thirty-five below zero. When he'd called for me it had been zero.

Nancy had a roaring fire going in the stove, but even so there was frost along the far walls. Fred stayed long enough to warm up, then headed for home. "See you Friday," he said.

I felt so good I wanted to sing out and dance around the room. I had more energy than I knew what to do with, so I washed some clothes. I sang *Row, Row, Row*

Your Boat, scrubbing up and down on the washboard to keep time.

"Boy, are *you* happy," Nancy said.

"Happy? Of course I'm happy. I'm always happy."

"Not like you are right now."

"Fred and I had a nice time."

Fred was a kind of a taboo subject with her, so she didn't say anything. I could tell something was on her mind, though.

She waited until after supper to bring it up.

"You mind if I tell you something, Anne?" she asked me while we were doing the dishes.

"Go ahead."

"Sure you won't mind?"

"Is it that bad?"

She shrugged. "Well . . . There's a lot of talk goin' around about you and Fred."

"What kind of talk?"

"You know. That you and him are hangin' around each other too much."

"Let 'em talk."

"Some of it's pretty salty."

"For instance."

"Ah . . . you know what I mean."

"Who's doing the talking?"

"Mr. Vaughn, Angela, Harry Dowles—all of 'em."

"I don't care about them."

"They're not the only ones. A lot of other people don't like it either. A couple of 'em have already written to Juneau about you."

"I guess there's not much I can do about it."

She'd been washing the same plate for the past minute. Finally she dipped it in the cold water and handed it to me to dry.

"If he was any kind of a man," she said, "he'd stay away from you. He oughtta know how people around here feel."

"He does."

"Then why does he keep comin'?"

"Because we like each other."

She rested her hands on the rim of the washtub. "Anne," she said, turning to me, "you're so good you

147

don't even realize what you're doing. That man's a breed. The way you act towards 'im is, well . . . *you* know, like somebody who's more than a friend."

"Is that the only way you think about him, Nancy—that he's a half-breed?"

"Well he is."

"Does that mean he's less of a person?"

"I never thought about it much."

"I'm pretty fond of him—and more than just as a friend."

She picked up a cup and started washing it. I couldn't read her expression, but she was unhappy.

"We could talk about it if you like," I said.

"No, that's all right," she said quietly.

For the next couple of days it stayed so cold that Nancy and I warmed up the bed with hot rocks before we got in. Even then we tossed a coin to see who was going to get in first, and when we woke up in the morning the blankets were stuck to the wall. On Thursday it dropped to forty below, and even though we moved all the tables in the schoolroom close to the stove, Willard, Joan and Lily couldn't work for their feet being so cold. We finally had to move the whole class into my quarters and let the little ones sit in the bed.

When Uncle Arthur showed up for school he said that if it was this cold and here it was only November, we were probably in for a three-dog winter. I asked him what that was and he said that a one-dog winter was nothing. You stay warm at night with just one dog in bed with you. A two-dog winter, now that was tough, but a three-dog, "Well, missis," he said, "it gets so cold the smoke freezes in the stovepipe."

That was an exaggeration about the smoke, but it was close. Up until the cold weather hit that week I never understood why Mr. Strong kept such a big supply of laxative pills in his store. I knew after it did, though: nobody wanted to go to the outhouse until it was absolutely necessary, so by the time you went you needed all the help you could get.

It was the outhouse that almost caused a tragedy of sorts at the end of the week. Ten minutes after I excused little Willard Friday morning he still hadn't come back to the classroom, so Nancy went out to see what was keeping him. Ordinarily I wouldn't have bothered because he was in the habit of running home sometimes and staying there a while, but this time I just thought I'd check. I was sure glad I did, because Nancy came back right away, trying not to laugh and looking worried at the same time. Willard was stuck to the seat.

Getting him off turned out to be a major undertaking. We tried pouring warm water around him, but it froze almost as soon as it hit the boards, so finally Mr. Carew had to bring a crowbar and pry the boards off. The outhouse was a two-holer, so when we carried Willard into my quarters the boards were long enough so that he looked for all the world like a prince on a litter. It didn't seem to bother him, though. We propped one end of the boards on the stove and the other over a chair and he sat as calm as you please until he thawed off.

After that Mr. Vaughn loaned us a ten-gallon kerosene can with the top cut off. We put a toilet seat on it and put it in the cache. Since it was almost as cold in the cache as it was outside, somebody lined the seat with caribou fur to make sure nobody got stuck again.

The weather didn't keep anybody from coming to the dance, though. Just about everybody showed up. They were really something, those dances. Before everybody arrived the old-timers would sit around playing cribbage or rummy, and Fred would take out his banjo so that the rest of us could play musical chairs. By the time it was 8:30 the schoolroom and my quarters were jam-packed and we were ready. Then with Fred on banjo, his mother on accordion and Ben Norvall playing the fiddle and calling, everybody stomped and swung their partners so hard the dirt kept jumping up between the floorboards. And that Friday was no exception. It got so hot we didn't even need the stove after a while.

I had as much fun watching as dancing, especially when Rebekah Harrington was on the floor. She was almost as heavy as Angela Barrett, but she swung around and do-se-do'd like a young girl. Now that it was colder she wore about half a dozen skirts, and as

149

the dance wore on she worked herself into such a sweat that she kept taking them off, one after the other.

She'd started showing up at school every so often again, but if the school board objected to it they didn't say anything to me, so I let her come. They didn't want to tangle with her husband Jake again. She must have been studying with Lily at home because she knew her letters. Whenever I gave my beginners drill with flash cards I could see her lips moving, naming the letters as I held them up. She wanted to learn to read, I knew that, but so far I hadn't tried to work with her. I intended to, though, as soon as I felt I could do it without getting into trouble over it. She was just about the happiest person in all of Chicken. It didn't seem to bother her in the least that the women in the settlement snubbed her. It didn't bother Jake either. "Goddammit, boys," he told a bunch of miners in the roadhouse one night, "if you had the brains God gave you, you'd mush out to that Indian village and bring yourself back a squaw." Rebekah and his little girl Lily had been with him. Picking up Lily, he'd stood her on the table. "Take a look at that beauty, will ya—black as the ace of spades, but I love her! And that goes for my woman too. You want to look down your nose at me, you go on ahead. She ain't the Rose of Sharon, but goddammit, I got myself the fattest, cleanest, hardworkingest woman any man here ever warmed up to on a cold winter's night!"

"Got biggest mouth in whole No'th country too," Rebekah had murmured. She hadn't looked too happy, I didn't blame her, but Jake just laughed, crooked an elbow around her neck and gave her a fat kiss on the cheek.

She plumped herself down alongside of me and Maggie Carew right after the square dancing was over and Uncle Arthur was winding up his gramophone.

"How you doin', Tisha?" she asked me.

"Fine, Rebekah. How about you?"

She let out a long sigh of satisfaction. "Ah, I have lotsa fun me. Like dance too damn much. How you doin', Miz Carew?"

"Gettin' by," Maggie said.

150

"You make plenty money tonight," Rebekah said. "Everybody they too hungry when dance over, they maybe eat table and chair. What you think?"

"Whatever money I make you can be a damn sight sure I'll earn it."

"By golly," Rebekah said, sympathetically, "you tell truth. Not easy make cook for so much people."

Maggie got up. "I better get along. Gotta start preparin'."

Rebekah fanned herself with her hand. "Whew— too damn hot, I think."

I had to smile. "Too much dancing, I think."

"Ah, I like have good times. Life short. Today you here, laugh, tomorrow you go in ground, everybody shovel dirt on you."

Uncle Arthur had put on a waltz and the kids who were still awake were the first ones out on the floor. Two or three of them were already asleep on my bed along with Rebekah's Lily. Jimmy Carew was dancing with Joan Simpson, while one of the Vaughn twins was trying to wrestle Mert Atwood around the floor. As usual Fred danced the first waltz with his mother. They were so graceful that most people just stood on the side and watched them. He glanced over at me and we gave each other a quick smile. I'd looked over Uncle Arthur's records and made sure about the label on *Home Sweet Home*. It was green, all right.

As the evening wore on I kept looking over at Uncle Arthur whenever I could, hoping I'd spot that label. I saw him start to put it on once and so did Fred, but he took it off again when he saw the two of us head for each other.

It was almost two o'clock before he slipped it on. I was talking with Nancy and the next thing I knew Joe Temple was tapping me on the shoulder and grinning down at me. Except for the way he treated Mary Angus, I didn't have anything against Joe, but I was so annoyed I felt like going over to Fred and saying, "Why don't we let them all go over to the roadhouse and you and I stay here together?" It must have showed, too.

"Don't look so peevish," Joe said when we were

151

waltzing. "You could have ended up with old man Vaughn."

That would have been something. Ever since the school-board meeting he hardly nodded to me.

"And you could have ended up with Angela Barrett."

When the waltz ended, I went to get my coat. I caught Fred's eye and we both kind of shrugged as if to say that's the way we knew it would be.

The roadhouse was so crowded it took almost an hour before everybody was served. Even Willard was carrying plates back and forth.

Joe had taken out a pipe and was smoking and I was almost finished eating when Maggie came over. "How's the grub?" she asked.

I told her the truth. It was delicious. Nancy and I had cooked up some salmon bellies and sauerkraut a couple of times, but Maggie's was the best I'd tasted. She'd saved Joe and me the little table against the wall, and had even put a candle on it.

"Good to see you two together," Maggie said. "You make a nice couple."

"That's a coincidence," Joe said, "we were just talking about getting married."

"Wouldn't hurt either of ya," Maggie said. "Keep you both out of trouble. 'Specially her," she added before she walked off.

I felt like telling her that if he married anybody he ought to marry Mary Angus. Back in Evansville once there'd been a boy who'd gotten a girl into trouble and there wasn't one woman in town who didn't think that the right thing for him to do was marry her. And he did, too. If Mary hadn't been an Indian everybody here would have felt the same, but because she was they didn't give a hoot. They even took Joe's side, which was worse. Maybe she wasn't right in doing what she did, but she wasn't the first woman who'd ever made a mistake like that and she wouldn't be the last.

I looked over to where Fred was sitting with his mother and I wished I was there with them. Everybody at the table was having a good time exchanging tall stories, and Ben Norvall's turn was next. He sat combing his moustaches with his fingers while people kept suggesting stories they wanted to hear him tell again.

The second time he'd showed up at school I'd had to take Maggie's advice and tell him that he couldn't come in unless he took a bath. Face black, hair matted, filthy pants held up by wire and string, he looked like he'd come out of a cave. Even so, not wanting to hurt his feelings, I weaseled around a little, saying that I didn't personally find the way he looked and smelled offensive, but that I had to protect the health of the children. The truth was that, even keeping as much distance as possible between us, I still came near the edge of a dead faint a couple of times.

I'd brought him into my quarters to tell him in private, and he'd been very understanding. He'd had no idea, he'd said, that the children's health was endangered. Now that he did, he would take steps to remedy the situation. The next time he showed up he was a different man. Bathed, and dressed in clean clothes, he fairly glowed. He'd even bought a new pair of heavy duty suspenders to hold up his pants. The only drawback was that now his face was washed you could see all his blackheads sprouting like potato eyes.

He was a good storyteller though. The one he told this time was about a partner of his who'd died on him in the middle of winter.

"I didn't know what to do with that sucker," Ben was saying. "I couldn't tell when the marshal'd be out to pick up the body and he was beginning to smell worse than a siwash fish stew. I couldn't leave 'im outside because there was a blizzard blowin' and he'd a been covered by drifts so high I wouldn't be able to find 'im till spring. Had an outside cache, but he was too damn heavy for me to lift him up to it."

"What'd you finally do?"

"Well, you're not gonna believe this, but it's God's truth. I just took 'im out and propped him against the side of the cabin, left him there for about two hours till he was frozen stiff, then I stored him up in the cache."

"I thought you said he was too hard to lift."

"Too hard to lift in one piece, I meant. But stiff like

153

he was all I had to do was snap off his arms and legs, then throw 'im in the cache piece by piece. The marshal was a little peeved when he had to collect him, wanted to file charges against me for desecratin' a corpse, but I explained the situation to him and he was as decent as you please. I heard later that after the undertaker got through with that sucker not a soul was the wiser."

Ben's story was followed by a few more from others, each one wilder than the one before. When they were ended I asked Joe if he'd seen Mary lately. He said no.

"I don't mean to stick my nose in, Joe, but she really needs some help. She goes out trapping and she shouldn't."

"I thought you said you don't mean to stick your nose in."

"I don't, but I just can't understand why you treat her the way you do."

"I don't treat her any way at all. I haven't even seen her in over a month."

"That's what I mean. Don't you care anything about her at all?"

"Why should I?"

"Because she's a human being." Because she had two children by you was what I wanted to say.

"Hey, are you a social worker or a teacher?" he asked sarcastically.

We didn't have much to say after that, and in a way I was sorry I'd said anything about it at all. He wasn't a bad guy. He'd made a pass at me once, but when he saw I wasn't interested he hadn't made a fuss about it.

We left a few minutes later. He was quiet all the way back to my quarters, so I knew he was irritated with me. I didn't realize how mad he really was, though, until we reached the porch and I thanked him for taking me to supper.

"Forget it," he said. "You taught me a lesson. I tried to help you out tonight by keeping you and that Purdy kid away from each other. Well from now on I'll mind my own goddamn business and you mind yours." Then he turned away from me and walked off.

XI

"Fred!"

"Hi, Anne."

"Come on in, it's freezing."

Nancy and I had just finished going over a math problem when he'd knocked. I'd heard he'd been back from the trap line for a couple of days and I was wondering when he'd be over. If Nancy hadn't been there I'd have given him a hug, I was so glad to see him. He'd lost a little weight from being on trail and eating and sleeping in rest cabins, but he looked wonderful.

He didn't stay long. I walked out with him on the porch before he went home.

"You ready for a snow picnic?" he asked me.

"Sure."

"How about Saturday?"

"That's swell. Where do you want to go?"

"We'll go over to West Fork," he said. "It'll take about two hours to get there, so I'll pick you up around nine."

He was going to kiss me, but he glanced over at the Vaughn cabin and changed his mind. "I'll see you Saturday," he said.

Before that Saturday came Mrs. Purdy paid me a visit after school. When I opened the door I couldn't have been more surprised to see her. She smiled up at me from under a beautiful hat of otter fur that made her look as chic as a Paris model. She needed something from Mr. Strong's store, she said, but I had the feeling she wanted to talk with me in private.

Inside the store it was cold enough so that you couldn't smell the usual collection of musty odors. All she wanted, she said, was a can of peppercorns. She was going to make a pepper-pot stew and had just run out. She stuffed the pepper in the pocket of her fur coat, and as I was writing it down, she said, "You are going on snow picnic with my Frayd he tell me."

"On Saturday."

"He like you very mush, Ahnne," she said.

"I feel the same way about him."

"I understand why he likes you. You are attractive. Wear nice clothes. Yet I do not understand why you like *him* so much. He is only boy. He make no money, have no house, have nothing. Is that not so?"

"I never thought about that."

"Not wise. You are pretty, Ahnne. Many men like marry you. Some day you marry man who have mush money, give you *big* house, many things . . . Frayd, he give you nothing." She said it as if he were a dismal failure, and I almost had to smile.

"Mrs. Purdy, why don't you tell me what's really on your mind?"

She laughed, a lilting laugh full of good humor. "I see why you teasher, Ahnne. You are . . ." She stopped and tapped a mittened hand on the counter, searching for the word she was thinking of. She shook her other hand in frustration. ". . . Intelligent," she said, sighing with relief. "Someday," she added, exasperated, "I get new tongue. This one—agh." We both laughed at the face she made. Then she was serious.

"Please, Ahnne," she said slowly, "do not like him. It is not good . . . You savvy what I say?"

"Mrs. Purdy, do you think that Fred and I have done anything wrong?"

"No. I not say this. I say only that now there is mush trouble. Three days ago Mr. Strong come see me. He tell me of you and Frayd. Tell me Frayd like you too mush. People know, and it is very bad. I am shocked he tell me this, Ahnne. I not know. When Frayd he come home I talk with him. He say it is true, and I weep. I am afraid, Ahnne. People will not talk with Frayd like before. Not talk with me, with my husband, and my Isabelle."

"Then maybe they're not your real friends, Mrs. Purdy."

156

She shook her head impatiently. "Ahnne. You are young, not understand. People here not like see white man, dark woman. Mush worse they not like see white woman, dark man. You like my Frayd too mush, Ahnne. Better to close book on that. Too many tears come your eyes, too many pains in your heart . . . I ask you—I tell Frayd you not like him anymore. Yes?"

I didn't want to hurt her for anything in the world. "Mrs. Purdy . . ."

"Ahnne, I beg of you."

"I'm sorry . . ."

She was angry, but it only lasted a few seconds, then she collected herself.

"I say good night to you, Ahnne," she said, "but first I tell you something make me sad almost to cry. You must come my house no more."

She started to say something else. Instead she turned and went to the door.

"Mrs. Purdy!"

She went out. I turned off the oil lamp I'd lit and went after her, locking the door as quickly as possible. By the time I caught sight of her she'd gone around the back of the store and was moving toward the shortcut home.

I called to her, but she didn't turn around. And as her tiny figure kept moving away I felt almost the same way I had years before when my Grandmother Hobbs had stood in the road and waved good-bye to me.

For the rest of the week I was afraid that when Isabelle came to school she'd tell me that Fred wouldn't be able to make it on Saturday. Knowing how much he loved his mother, I knew he'd want to hurt her even less than I did.

When Saturday morning came, though, he was outside with his sled almost on the dot of nine. It was still dark out—the sun wouldn't be up for a couple of hours yet—but it looked as if it was going to be clear.

As soon as I came out I saw that Pancake wasn't his lead dog this time. He'd put Pancake at wheel instead, directly in front of the sled, and harnessed all the malamutes up front with Shakespeare in the lead. Fred had taught me enough about sled dogs so I knew why.

It had snowed again a few days before and the dogs would have to break trail part of the way. The heavier dogs like Pancake would be more likely to break through the snow and have tough going. The lighter malamutes would pack it down.

Shakespeare was really anxious to show what he could do, or maybe he knew Pancake was back there watching him, because as soon as I was tucked in the sled and Fred yelled "Mush!" that whole team took off as if it was their picnic they were going on.

Once we were out of the settlement, Fred launched into a chorus of *Oh, Susanna* and they really pushed into their collars. For the first hour we moved along at such a good pace and it looked so easy that I asked Fred to let me try driving.

"Might be a little hard for you," he yelled.

"No it won't."

"We'll be hitting some hummock ice soon, so maybe you better wait."

"I'll bet you I can do it."

"You sure now?"

"Positive."

We changed places and it seemed so easy at first I wondered why he'd hesitated. I started to sing *Ta-ra-ra-boom-dee-ay* and all the dogs worked so hard that for the first time Shakespeare wasn't setting the pace. But between having to jump off to keep the sled from tipping and trying to manipulate the lead lines, I found out that it took a lot more strength than I thought to keep the sled on trail. I finally decided to give up when we hit the hummock ice. It was like going over slippery rocks. Sweating and hardly able to breathe after a while, I said, "Fred, maybe you ought to take it."

"You sure you want me to? You're not doing bad at all."

"I'm getting a little tired." It was all I could do to hold onto the handles.

"There's only about another quarter mile before we'll hit the ridge, then it'll be downhill." He didn't turn around and I didn't realize he was trying not to break out laughing.

"I don't think I can make it."

"Sure you can."

"Fred, I mean it. My hands are killing me . . . Whoa!" I yelled to the dogs. It came out like a whisper and they didn't pay any attention. "Fred—"

He was trying to keep a straight face, but he couldn't.

I didn't see anything funny about it. "If you don't take this right now I'm gonna let it go."

He was laughing so hard he could barely yell whoa to the dogs. He stumbled out of the sled, trying to stop, but every time he looked at me he'd start all over again. Finally I started to smile in spite of myself. He took me in his arms and gave me a big hug, then he held me away from him. I couldn't think of anybody who ever looked at me the way he did then, unless it was Granny Hobbs. Only it was a lot different, and it made me feel a lot different. I had all I could do not to tell him I loved him right then and there. Because I did. Maybe I hadn't had that much experience with boys, but that didn't matter. I knew I'd never felt this way about anybody and that I never would again about anybody else. And I saw in his eyes that it was that way with him too.

Once the hummock ice was behind us we moved along fast, and finally we reached the crest of a hill from where we could see West Fork joining the Forty Mile River. Ahead of us stretched endlessness.

Months before the river below had been running, rushing along so fast that there didn't seem to be any force on earth powerful enough to stop it. But now something had. Something held it in a mighty grip, freezing it solid, freezing West Fork all the fifteen miles back to where it began, freezing the Forty Mile all the way to Steel Creek and beyond to the Yukon. The sun was just coming up over the mountains—blood-red and cold. I felt as if I was standing in the mightiest cathedral that had ever been built. There was no end to it, and no beginning. All I could do was look at it and worship.

We found a picnic spot at the base of a soaring face of rock, and Fred tied the dogs. They were pretty well-trained, but they still had enough wildness in them so that if they spotted a rabbit or some other small animal they'd take off after it. In a little while, what with the fire and the bright ball of sun, it was warm enough for us to take off our parkas. I made some tea and we sat drinking out of tin cups.

"You think we'll ever get to go to the roadhouse with each other after the dance?" I asked him.

"No." He took my hand and held it in his own. There were cuts all over his from where the skin had been torn by the cold steel of the traps. My own hands were chapped and rough, but compared to his they were slender and soft. Most of his fingernails were broken off.

"Look at the difference," he said.

"Next time you come over I'm giving you a manicure."

"I meant look how light yours are—how dark mine are."

"I like your hands."

"You know what I'm talking about. We shouldn't even be here, together like this."

"What can anybody do to me, take back more pots and pans?"

"It's no joke. They can be a hard set, some of these people. When I told my mother we were going on this picnic . . . Well, I guess you know how she felt. She told me she went to see you. She's really upset."

"How about you?"

"I'm worried. About you and about my mother."

"You don't have to worry about me."

"Well, I do. If I had any sense I wouldn't have taken you out here all alone."

"Do you want to go back?"

"No."

He put some more wood on the fire and then I moved into his arms. After a while I didn't feel too well.

"What's the matter?" Fred asked me.

"I don't know," I said. "I think I'm dizzy from holding my breath every time you kiss me."

"Then what are you holding it for?"

"Aren't you supposed to?"

"I never heard of that."

"That's what I always thought."

"If you breathe through your nose a little it'll be easier. Try it."

I tried it and it made all the difference in the world. Up to then I'd been wondering why kissing someone had been so much trouble but now I saw how much fun it really was. You learn something all the time, I thought. I could have kept on all day after that, except that my lips started to burn after a while. "I just learned something else," I said.

"What?"

"Why Eskimos rub noses. Their lips are always chapped."

"I don't rub noses."

"You're only half-Eskimo."

He smiled at that, then a moment later his eyes flicked to someplace in back of me. "We're being watched."

I tried to sit up, but he held me tight. "Don't move too fast," he said. "Just turn your head slowly."

I did what he said, but I didn't see anything.

"There," Fred said, "standing by that rotted spruce."

I finally saw him—a shaggy-coated moose. He'd been feeding on some willow, but now he was still, looking our way. He was tremendous, the racks on him wider than I was tall—maybe six feet and covered with white winter fuzz. He didn't seem to see us.

The sled was only about ten feet away, Fred's rifle slung across the handles. He started to ease away from me.

"Let him go, Fred."

"Anne, that's fresh meat—eight hundred pounds of it. Think of it," he said, "pickled tongue, braised kidneys, liver, heart, steak. You'll have enough for the whole winter."

"But we won't have a picnic." He'd have to butcher it right then and there and it'd be a mess of blood and entrails. He thought about it, then waved a hand toward the moose. "Have a good dinner," he said. The moose saw the movement, dipped his head and shambled off.

After we ate we took a walk out onto the river. It had frozen smooth in the center, but near the banks it was a mass of twisted shapes that looked like a sculptor had gone crazy. On our way back to the sled we were moving through a thick tangle of buckbrush when all of a sudden the whole brush came alive and exploded. I thought it was some big white animal jumping up and I screamed. The air churned with the flapping of wings —a whole flock of ptarmigan I'd flushed. In a moment they were gone.

When we got back to the sled I was all for building up the fire and staying there, but it was dark already and Fred said we should get back.

We hadn't seen another person the whole day, and on the way back I kept imagining we never would again, that we'd just go on and on through the moonlit night until we came to some magic place that we'd never have to leave. I leaned back in the sled and stared up at the heavens, imagining that we were on our way up to them, gliding into the stars on a trip to the Milky Way.

I came back to earth with a jolt, because suddenly there was an ominous crack from under the sled. Right after that the bottom dropped out from the right runner, the sled tipped over, and the next thing I knew I was tossed out like water from a dipper.

I thought I was going to land soft, but I didn't. There was a crust of ice under the snow. I crashed through it and landed with a jolt on bare ground about a foot below. Fred went tumbling too, but he got to his feet right away, waded across snow that cracked and gave under him like pie crust and charged into the dogs. They were on solid ground, but they'd been jerked off their feet. As soon as they got up they started snarling and fighting with each other and tangling themselves up in the lines. Fred had to kick a few of them before they settled down and we were able to take stock.

We'd been lucky. We were shaken up, but aside from a few bruises we were all right. It could have been far worse. We'd gone through some "shell ice" that had formed over a shallow basin. Rain had probably filled up the basin, then frozen on the surface while the water below had seeped into the ground. It was one of the hazards of the trail.

The sled was on its side, but it wasn't damaged. The dogs' momentum had carried it to the edge of the basin and it hadn't gone through. We were able to right it fairly easily without even unharnessing the dogs, and then we were on our way again.

It was after six when we reached the settlement. Fred said good night to me on the porch. "See you at the dance Friday night," he said.

A few minutes later I'd changed into some slipper moccasins and Nancy and I were preparing supper when she told me we were going to have a visitor later on.

"Who?"

"I'll give you one guess." She acted as if I should have known who it was. "He's from Eagle."

"I can't imagine."

"Really? From the way he talked you'd think you were engaged to marry him."

"Now I have to know who it is."

"Cabaret Jackson."

XII

A little later on Cab stomped in, all dolled up in his Saturday-night cowboy clothes. He'd taken a bath at the roadhouse and pomaded his hair so that he smelled like a barber shop. He brought me a big heart-shaped box of candy, and just as Nancy had said, he acted for all the world as if the two of us were just one step away from the preacher if I'd just say the word. He was as loud and brassy as when I'd seen him in Eagle last, but he was such a good-natured grinning fool that I just had to like him.

He was leaving in the morning, he said, and he wanted to take me over to the roadhouse for some dancing. I told him that I had a headache and wasn't feeling too good, so he said in that case he'd stay over and take me for a sled ride the next day and supper the next night. I got out of the sled ride, but he wouldn't take no for an answer on the supper, so I said if he'd take Nancy too I'd go, and he settled for that.

I'd offered him coffee, but he said he was drunk on love already and didn't want to sober up. "Cab, I can smell what you're drunk on and it isn't love, I can tell you that," I said.

That made him whoop up a storm. "Ain't she somethin'?" he said to Nancy. "Ain't she really somethin'? Come on, Teacher, you gotta come over the roadhouse —just for a little while. I got all this money a-jinglin' in my belt, and if I can't spend it on the most beautiful gal in the Forty Mile what's it good for?"

"You must have struck it rich."

"I sure did," he said craftily. "What I got on that sled a mine's more precious than gold, grub or fire."

"What have you got?"

"Never you mind," he said. "Those delicate ears weren't meant to hear things they shouldn't."

He was running liquor, Nancy told me after he left. "He runs it all over the Forty Mile."

"Isn't he afraid of getting caught?"

"Not him. He's got the fastest dog team around, which is about all he's got. The deputy marshal went after him once when he started selling it in the Indian village, but that didn't stop him. He was so cocky he left notes for the marshal wherever he went, even told him where he was heading for next. The marshal kept on his trail for two weeks, then finally gave up. Cab's team was just too good."

I saw his team the next day, kenneled in back of the roadhouse. They were a mean bunch, but they looked fast: lean in the flanks and heavy in the shoulders. If Cab had wanted to make money honestly with them he could have. There were always people who were willing to pay top dollar for a man who knew the country and had a good team of dogs—metallurgists or businessmen who wanted to be mushed into the interior for one reason or another. It made me feel kind of sorry for him. He just didn't want to do things the right way, or maybe he didn't know how. All he was interested in was wasting his time drinking and bragging about how he'd been in every cabaret and honky-tonk from Dawson to the Bering Sea. I more or less told him that when he took Nancy and me over to the roadhouse the next night.

"Teacher," he said, "no truer words have ever been spoken. What I need is a good woman to keep me followin' my star. Somebody like you."

"Not me, Cab."

"I'd take a vow that nary a drop would I touch, and I'd build you a cabin that'd be a palace."

I told him thanks, but I intended to stay single.

"I tell you, Teacher, if you'd say yes, you wouldn't be sorry."

When he took Nancy and me back to my quarters he said he still wasn't going to give up. It was a game to him now and he was enjoying it. He was heading down toward Tanacross the next day, he said, and he'd be coming back through Chicken in time for the next Friday-night dance. He'd try again then.

We told him to come on ahead because that was going to be the Thanksgiving dance. We'd be having a party and everybody was welcome. It was due to start in the afternoon with the Thanksgiving pageant the class was putting on, then there'd be games and supper and finally the dance itself. Cab said he'd be there, "and if the answer is still no by then, Teacher, I'm gonna mush up to the Arctic and never come back."

"You better get an outfit together then," Nancy told him, " 'cause your prospects don't look too good."

The Friday-night dances were fun, but the Thanksgiving party was the biggest blow-out we'd ever had. We'd planned it for weeks and by the time Friday rolled around we were ready. The schoolroom really looked festive. The class had cut turkeys and pumpkins out of colored paper and pasted them on all the windowpanes. Streamers and paper chains hung from the ceiling. "B'Gawd, missis," Uncle Arthur said when he saw it, "you can hang me if this isn't the most Thanksgivin'est lookin' place I ever saw in my whole life!"

By four o'clock there were so many people in the

165

schoolroom that even though an icy mist rolled in every time someone opened the door, we hardly needed the stove. Except for Fred's mother, who was down with a cold, and his father, just about everybody showed up.

Nancy was the hit of the whole party, but before it started she didn't even want anybody to look at her. She and I had cut her hair short the night before, then marcelled it the next morning. She'd put on the dress we'd made for her and I'd helped her put on lipstick and rouge, just about the smallest amount you could wear and still have it show, but as soon as she looked in the mirror it was all I could do to stop her from washing it off and jumping back into her bib overalls.

"Anne, I look like a flapper! Everybody's gonna laugh at me."

"You look beautiful," I told her. And it was the truth.

"The dress is so short," she complained.

"Nancy, you've seen the pictures in the catalog yourself. It's no shorter than any girl your age is wearing now."

She was scared and happy at the same time and I couldn't blame her. I'd felt the same way when I wore my graduation dress. She was even more scared because compared to how she'd been dressing up to then she looked racy. Her old dresses had come down below her calf. This one had a sloping hemline that was about an inch below the knee. The only way I could finally get her to keep it on was to threaten to take off my own dress and wear bib overalls. It was one threat I didn't want to keep, especially since Fred's mother had made the dress for me and it was my favorite. A chemise with a flowered print, it had soft fur along the cowl neckline and insets of tatted lace along the bodice and the flounce. Mrs. Purdy had told me it was an old Eskimo design, but it looked smarter and more modern than anything I'd ever bought in a store.

When the first few people came in Nancy pretended to be busy at the stove and wouldn't even turn around. She couldn't get away with it when some of the children swept in, though. Jimmy Carew was in the lead and he stopped short. "Who are you?" he asked. He didn't even recognize her.

"Who do you think I am?" Nancy said grimly.

"Holy cow!" He stared at her, his mouth gaping. "Nancy, you look beyootiful!"

She was a hit all right. When Ben Norvall took a look at her, he rubbed his eyes in astonishment and started quoting Shakespeare. " 'But soft!' " he said, gesturing grandly, " 'What light through yonder window breaks? It is the east, and Juliet is the sun.' "

Nancy blushed beet-red, loving it. "Oh, now you get outta here," she said, slapping his arm.

The only one who didn't say something nice was Mr. Vaughn. Sure enough, he said she looked like a flapper. Nobody paid any attention to him, though. He was so old-fashioned that he wouldn't let his daughters dance the foxtrot.

As soon as we counted heads and found everybody was there the class put on the pageant. It was about the landing of the Pilgrims at Plymouth Rock and what they went through during their first winter.

After that we had early supper, and everybody dug in. We'd all saved our appetites, and with Maggie Carew's bear soup simmering on the stove to tantalize everybody, we were starved. Along with a whole load of oranges and apples, we'd had corn on the cob freighted in from Fairbanks, and everybody helped themselves to dozens of succulent moose spareribs, pickled caribou and dried king salmon. Willard Carew was sitting alongside me. He'd never seen whole corn before and was eating the cob and all.

"I sure don't think much of this," he whispered to me. "It's makin' me sick."

"Try eating just the yellow part," I told him. "Most people don't bother with the rest of it." He liked it a lot better after that.

We topped it all off with dried-apple pie and ice cream, but the best part of the whole meal were the apples and oranges. They'd cost us a lot—two bits apiece to have them shipped in, but they were well worth it. We hadn't seen a piece of fruit in a couple of months, and even though the apples were mealy and the oranges weren't the best, everybody sat around biting into them and making faces at each other as though they were in heaven. I'd almost forgotten how sweet fresh fruit tasted.

Once the supper was over we cleared the tables out of the schoolroom, and after the women did all the dishes Fred struck up his banjo and the square dancing was on. Filled up as everybody was it took a little time for them to get going, but inside of an hour Rebekah had three skirts off and the lanterns all over the schoolroom were shaking as though there was an earthquake.

Cab didn't breeze in until about nine, stomping in with a bottle of whiskey in one hand and gin in the other. I asked him to please take them out again because besides its being against the law, I didn't think it was right to have drinking going on in the schoolroom. There were still plenty of people who you could tell were nipping from flasks on the sly, but at least they didn't come out in the open with it.

Cab laughed and took the bottles out, but he must have hidden them outside somewhere and wrapped them up in furs so they wouldn't freeze, because as the night wore on half the men in the place, and Angela Barrett too, kept making jokes about how they didn't know why, but they just seemed to have to go to the outhouse more than usual that night. The whole bunch of them smelled like a brewery after a while and started reeling all over the place when they danced, hardly listening to the calls.

Cab was the worst, bragging and carrying on about his dog team without a stop. He went over to Joe Temple and said he'd heard Joe had a good team of dogs and he challenged Joe to a race. But Joe saw right away how drunk he was and said he'd heard about Cab's team and wouldn't go a two-mile heat with him even if Cab gave him a mile-and-a-half lead.

"Good thing you wouldn't," Cab said. "That bunch you got wouldn't be no more match for my dogs then a string of asthmatic poodles."

After a while I didn't even want to dance with him, he was getting so wild.

The square dancing ended about ten o'clock, a little earlier than usual because it had been a long day. Everybody was hungry again, though, so we were still going to have midnight supper over at the roadhouse. I should have known something was going to happen when Uncle Arthur and a few other men started talking with Cab about how fast Fred's team was. Everybody knew Fred's dogs were not only good, but the best-trained of anybody's around here, so I didn't realize that they were trying to start something. Cab button-holed Fred and was all for having a race with him right then and there. "I just mushed 'em fifty miles to here and I'll put 'em up against yours right now."

Fred said no, he'd heard that Cab had come in second in the Annual Dog Derby at Fairbanks last year and he wasn't in that class. That should have settled it, but it didn't. Later on I found out from Nancy that Uncle Arthur and a few others had kept bending Cab's ear about Fred's dogs, leading Cab on and getting him steamed up. She said she thought they were telling him things about Fred and me as well, but she didn't know for sure. Whatever they said to him, Cab cornered Fred again just before the dance was over, but Fred wasn't having any of it.

"I'll make it over any distance you want," Cab said, "over any country you want."

"Thanks, Cab, but I'm not a racing man."

Cab had that stubborn look that said there was just one thing in his mind and he wasn't going to be talked out of it. "If you're scared you'll look too bad we can make it a fifty-mile mush and I'll give you an hour head start."

"Cab, I just don't want to race you."

"Hell, I hear them's all Indian dogs you got anyway. Ain't worth the fish ya feed'm."

Fred walked away from him, but Cab was back to the same song again right after Fred and I danced a fox-trot. By this time his eyes were all bloodshot and he was getting mean. I was hoping that even if I didn't end up with Fred when the *Home Sweet Home* waltz went on, at least I wouldn't end up with Cab. He was willful when he was sober, drunk he was impossible.

169

But when the *Home Sweet Home* waltz did go on I was flabbergasted: for the first time Fred was right beside me.

That was the loveliest waltz I'd ever danced with anyone. For the first time in my life I really felt beautiful. Just having Fred look at me the way he did made me whirl around that floor as if we weren't in a dinky little schoolroom somewhere out in the wilds, but in the grand ballroom of a palace.

Before the waltz was over a whole bunch of people had already left so that they could get to the roadhouse and be served before the crowd. Nancy had ended up with Cab and as the rest of us were leaving they came over to Fred and me. "You're pretty lucky there, boy," Cab said. "How about tradin' off partners? No offense, Nancy."

"No thanks, Cab."

Cab wasn't too happy about it.

In the roadhouse Fred and I sat at the end of one of the long tables. I wished we could have had the table for two, but I didn't care. Just having midnight supper with Fred was enough. We could hear Cab yelling all the way over on the other side of the room, still challenging anybody in the house to a dog race. Then I heard somebody say something about Fred and a few men laughed.

I didn't pay any attention to what was going on after that because Fred and I were talking, but when we were almost finished eating Nancy came over. She leaned down close to me. "Anne," she whispered, "if I were you and Fred I'd dog it outta here fast. Somethin's goin' on."

"What is it?"

"Trouble. You better go as soon as you can."

I told Fred what she'd said. We looked over at the other table. Angela Barrett was just about as drunk as Cab and she was staring over at Fred and me with hate in her eyes. There wasn't too much talk coming from where Cab was, just some murmuring, but there was something in the air, all right. Fred and I got up and he went to pay for our supper.

"Hey now, Teacher, you ain't leavin' so early, are ya?" Cab yelled out.

"Sure am, Cab. I'm dead tired."

He got up from the table and made his way towards us. "Hell, you don't have to go yet," he said. I said I did, but he had something in his mind and didn't even listen to me, just asked me the same thing over again. Fred brought my coat over and Cab tried to take it from him. "You just give that coat to me and I'll take care of 'er. She can't go home yet. It's too early."

"Cab, I do want to go home," I said.

He understood, but he didn't care. Fred hadn't let go of my coat, and Cab tried to take it from him again. "Lemme have that," he said.

"It's all right, Cab," Fred told him. "I'll take her home."

"You will like hell," Cab said. "Let it go." Fred looked at me, but before he could decide what to do Cab shoved him. Fred let my coat go and fell against the counter. "I said I'll take 'er home, goddammit, 'n' I mean what I say!"

I was scared now. The whole place had gotten quiet, and everybody was watching to see what was going to happen. They weren't only watching, either. They were waiting, waiting like a pack of wolves for Cab to do their dirty work. They'd been wanting it to happen, planning for it to happen, and now they were licking their chops. Now I knew why Uncle Arthur had finally put the *Home Sweet Home* waltz on when Fred and I were close. Anything to get Cab riled up more. And Fred knew it. I could see by the way he was looking at everybody. He was cornered, being forced into a fight with Cab.

"Now you hightail it outta here, half-breed," Cab said to him. He was wound up like a spring. He wanted to fight bad, you could see it in the way his shoulders moved, as if he was going to shake himself apart any second if he didn't start lashing out. I felt sick to my stomach.

"I don't want any fightin' in here," Maggie Carew said. "The two of you want to settle it, go on outside."

"That's fine with me," Cab said.

"Cab, I don't want to fight with you," Fred told him.

"Thought so," Mr. Vaughn said. "He's going to crawfish."

"Sure is," Angela said. "Even an Arkansas Jew'd be fighting by now."

Cab wasn't listening to anybody anymore. He had blood in his eye and he kept moving his shoulders the way a kid does when he's excited about something and wants to get to it.

Fred moved away from the counter. He'd gone dead white around his mouth and he was all tightened up, so I was surprised he could walk so easily. He went over to get his parka where it was hanging on a hook, and took it down. Cab rushed over to him and gave him another shove that sent him flying into a whole bunch of men. They pushed him right back and he went bang up against Cab. Cab must have thought Fred was coming after him because his fist went out and he hit Fred in the mouth. It was just a glancing punch, but Fred's lip started to bleed and it kind of stunned him. That did it for everybody. Mr. Carew and another man grabbed Cab, two others grabbed Fred, and they hustled them both out the door. I kept trying to get them to stop, and I yelled out to Cab that if he wanted to he could take me home, but nobody was listening to me.

So there Fred was, out in the middle of the snow, his parka still hanging over his arm and Cab staring at him wild-eyed, going into a slight crouch, telling Fred to get ready. And everybody was really having a good time now. "Slam'im in the mush, Cab." "Chew'im up!" "Paste 'im under the tab!" Not one of them was rooting for Fred.

I went over to Joe Temple. "Joe, get them to stop, please."

"And get myself slugged? No thanks."

Fred was still trying to get out of it, not raising his hands or doing anything but watching Cab. "Come on, boy," Cab said, "get 'em up."

"I told you, Cab. I don't want to fight with you."

Then Cab started to move in, all crouched up like an animal, his fists going as if he was winding up yarn, his eyes all wild. I was scared, really scared. I thought Fred would be too and I wouldn't have blamed him, but he wasn't. I almost didn't recognize him for the expression on his face. It was the strangest expression I'd ever seen on anyone, the look he might have had on trail when he was all alone and in trouble and it was only him against an enemy. At that moment I didn't know him at all.

I tried to go over to him, but Angela Barrett grabbed me. She was as strong as a wrestler.

"Let me go, Mrs. Barrett."

"You just settle down," she said thickly, "or he won't be the only one to get the shit knocked out of 'im."

What happened next made everybody jump. There was a big explosion and I caught a flash of flame out of the corner of my eye and smelled the sharp odor of burnt powder. It was Rebekah's husband, Jake Harrington, standing there holding Mr. Carew's thirty-aught-six over'n'under. Everybody froze and my ears were ringing so I could hardly hear what he was saying. He'd fired into the air, but now he was pointing that shotgun straight at Cab. "Go on back inside, Cab," he told him quietly.

Cab was drunk, but he wasn't so drunk that those two barrels staring him in the face didn't sober him a little.

"This is none a your business," he said to Jake.

"Only tryin' to do you a favor, Cab," Jake said.

"It's not him you're doing any favors," Mr. Vaughn said. "It's the breed." He was standing in back of Cab.

"It's him," Jake said. " 'Cause if he tries to hit that boy I'm gonna kill 'im. So maybe you better move outta the way."

You can bet Mr. Vaughn moved, all right. And he wasn't the only one. Everybody standing near Cab moved away too.

"What do you say, Cab? It's cold out here."

Cab said something he ordinarily wouldn't have said with ladies present, but he could be excused for it.

Then he slouched back into the roadhouse and everybody else started moving back in too. I pulled away from Angela.

"C'mon, Fred." I took his arm.

"Anne," Nancy called after me, "I'll stay here a while."

All the way back to my quarters Fred was trembling so hard I thought he was going to fall down. Inside, he slumped into a chair. I built up the fire.

"Did he hurt you?"

"No. I'm trying to hold my supper down."

After a little while he picked his head up. "I could use an aspirin."

I gave it to him along with some water. His chin was smeared with blood and his lip was a little puffy. I got a wet cloth and gave it to him. He went over to the mirror and dabbed the cut. I felt it was partly my fault. If he'd been badly hurt I'd never have forgiven myself. The thing that bothered me the most, though, was how everybody had really wanted to see him beat up.

"I'm glad you're not hurt too bad."

He almost smiled. "Me too. I just wish there was some way I could keep my mother from finding out about it."

"All she has to do is take one look at you."

"Well, at least she won't have to know what it was all about."

"What'll you tell her?"

"Oh, that Cab just got drunk and took a poke at me. This is a mess," he said. "Anne . . ." He started to say something else, but just then Nancy came in carrying my coat.

I went outside with him when he was ready to leave.

"I'm sorry, Fred."

"It's not your fault."

"I kind of feel it is."

I waited for him to say something, but he didn't.

"Why are you looking at me like that?" I asked him.

"No reason."

"Fred . . ."

"What?"

I wanted to say, I love you. Instead I said, "Can you

174

kiss me good night or does your mouth hurt too much?"

He leaned down and his lips just barely touched mine. Then he hugged me so tightly it took the breath out of me. Before he walked off the porch, he stared at me in a way that gave me the most awful feeling, as if he'd pushed me away or shut me out. I wanted to call him back, ask him to stay a little longer. But I didn't. I just stood there, looking at all the cabins strung along the snow.

Far off to the northwest a flickering yellow glow appeared in the distance. Fred had told me it came from a peat fire that had been smoldering in the tundra ever since last summer. The snow had partly smothered it, but once in a while it burst into flame anew. It blazed up now, as if somebody had just lit a big collection of candles. Then it went out. I started to feel chilly and went inside.

Nancy was just slipping her nightie on.

"Thanks for trying to warn us," I said.

She murmured something, then pulled back the blankets and got into bed with her socks on. A little later when I climbed in beside her, her head was underneath the blankets. She poked it out while I was still curled up in a ball, trying to get warm.

"Anne?"

"Mm . . ."

"Jimmy told me that Mr. Vaughn told his father you're gonna have a baby by Fred. He said that come spring you'll be swoll' up like a poisoned dog. I told him it was a damn lie."

I wondered why she was bringing it up now—then I realized she must have heard me ask Fred if he was able to kiss me goodnight. She'd probably been shocked. As good friends as she and I were, she still couldn't see how I could like Fred so much. She was waiting for me to deny what Mr. Vaughn had said. All of a sudden a picture came into my mind that made me smile—a little quarter-Eskimo baby toddling around the room looking exactly like Fred. It was so vivid I had trouble keeping my voice even. I said, "If it'll make you feel any better, Nancy—no, I'm not going to have a baby. I'll tell you the truth, though. If I was I'd want it to be Fred's."

Right after I said it I was sorry. I had no right to shock her like that on purpose. The silence was so thick you could have cut it with a knife.

"Nancy . . . try to understand. Will you?"

Her answer was a long time coming.

"I'm trying, Anne," she said, her voice troubled. "I'm trying. But it sure is hard."

XIII

"Fred went over to Steel Creek," Isabelle told me Monday morning. As soon as she'd showed up for school I'd asked her about him. Every time I thought of the look on his face when he left Friday night, I'd had a sinking feeling. I had the same feeling now.

"When did he leave?"

"Early yesterday morning. Did you know he was in a fight?" she asked me, wide eyed.

"Yes, I did. When is he coming back?"

"As soon as he can, I guess."

I asked her what he'd gone for, but she said she didn't know. I asked Nancy if she had any idea why he might have gone to Steel Creek, but she said there was nothing she could think of.

His father showed up for the mail when Mr. Strong came into the settlement a few days later.

"How's everybody in the family?" I asked him while we were standing on line outside the post office.

"Fine," he said. "They all say hello."

"What did Fred go to Steel Creek for?" I asked him.

"See some people over there. He ought to be back in a few days."

I had the feeling he was holding something back and

I wanted to ask him more about it, but I couldn't bring myself to pry any more.

There was a letter for me from Lester Henderson. He wrote me that he'd received the first monthly report I'd sent him at the beginning of October, and he was very satisfied with it. Then he went on to say that he'd received letters from a few people in Chicken.

> ... The general tone of them is that you are a good teacher and have high moral standards. I've received two letters from parents, however, who object to your association with an Indian woman living there. One of them also mentioned that you have been teaching the children about the Indians and that you seem to be fond of a young man of mixed blood, Fred Purdy. (I've heard of the Purdys, by the way, and by all accounts they are a fine family.)
>
> I want you to know that I have the utmost faith in you and your abilities, and your personal life is your own. I do wish to advise you, however, to be as diplomatic as possible, especially if you wish to teach in Eagle next year ...

His letter was dated November 6th, three weeks before, and it sounded as if he'd heard from plenty of people. They must have started writing him around the end of September, just about the time Mr. Vaughn and the school board came down on me. I could imagine what they must have written him since then about Rebekah, and about Fred too.

I wrote him back that I was going to do the best I could. More than anything else, I told him, I wanted to justify the faith he had in me. I told him all about Rebekah too, why I'd taken her into the school and what had happened because of it. If he felt she shouldn't be sitting in, I said, I'd tell her she couldn't come.

There was a letter from Cathy Winters too, inviting me up to the Indian village for a few days during Christmas vacation. She'd written to me right after the whole business about Chuck coming to school had happened and since then we'd written to each other a few more times. I wrote her that I'd love to come if I could arrange transportation. "If I can, I'll be there around

Christmas day. That way I can come back with Mr. Strong when he comes through there on the 27th."

Those next five or six days just seemed to drag by. By the time Fred was due back, every time I'd hear footsteps outside I'd think it was him, and if anyone came up on the porch I'd feel that little jolt of expectancy. But it was always somebody else.

Uncle Arthur came over right after dark one afternoon. He wasn't his usual flinty self, and at first I thought it was because he knew I still wasn't feeling any too friendly towards him after what happened. "Mert Atwood asked me if you'd mind comin' over to see him," he said.

"Do you know what for?"

"He needs to see you, missis. He's feelin' poorly." From the way he said it and the hang-dog look he had I knew right away something was wrong. Mert had been sick for the last few days.

"You want me to go with you?" Nancy said.

"I think Mert wants to see 'er alone," Uncle Arthur said.

I got my parka, put on a couple of pairs of wool socks under my moccasins and we started out. "Is it very bad?" I asked him.

"It isn't good." He'd gone over to Mert's cabin a few days ago, he told me, when he hadn't seen smoke coming from the stovepipe. If he hadn't found him, Mert would have frozen to death.

"Damn fool," Uncle Arthur said crossly, "I alluz told him he don't eat right. Fries himself up them bannocks all the time. What good's bannocks do ya? Nothin' but flour and water. He don't eat right, don't do nothin' right. Don't even know enough to close 'is own door. Every damn summer he leaves it open when he goes out and lets some bear wander in. Then you know what he does? Stands around cussin' and swearin' at that bear until the poor dumb animal's too scared to come out. So he comes over to my place and tells me to come on and bring my gun. An' I have to shoot it. Now isn't that just cockeyed dumb?"

"It's pretty careless," I said. He was feeling so bad about Mert that he had to get his anger out some way.

178

"Careless," Uncle Arthur scoffed. "He ain't careless. He's crazy as a bedbug, that's what. Ever see all them ships in his cabin? Ships all over the place. If he likes ships so much why didn't he go to sea?"

He was talking about the pictures on Mert's wall—prints and engravings of everything from full-rigged schooners to the Queen Mary.

He kept on complaining so much all the way over that I knew he was scared Mert was going to die. They'd known each other almost forty years. At the roadhouse they'd sit and play checkers by the hour, arguing over which one of them knew more about mining or where the best fishing was, or how to cook a porcupine or dress a hen.

The ground around Mert's cabin was a junkyard of rotting sluice boxes and unused lumber. Like all the old-timers, Mert never liked to part with anything even though it was useless to him. Gear shafts and broken wagon wheels littered the ground along with a couple of pumps and an old steam engine, all of them covered with snow. And stacked in neat tiers was some heavy-gauge pipe that Uncle Arthur was always trying to get Mert to sell to him. Mert wouldn't do it, though. It didn't matter that the pipe was useless to him. It was part of his life.

"I'll get that pipe, you just wait and see," Uncle Arthur had told me once. "The day he dies it's mine. We made a deal when we split up—first one of us that dies, the other gets his outfit. And missis, I can't wait for the old fool to go."

"You don't mean that, Uncle Arthur," I told him.

"I don't, eh?"

He showed me how much he meant it when I was over at his cabin for dinner once. In a corner of the room was a coffin. "Cut the boards myself," he told me proudly.

"How long have you been working on it?" I asked him. There were carvings all over it, of spades and mattocks, gold pans and sluice boxes. The work must have taken him years.

"Too long," he said. "Every day the first thing I do when I go out the door is look to see if there's smoke

179

comin' from his chimney, but the ol' fool just won't die."

Now that Mert was sick, he was heartbroken. He left me a short distance from the door. Before he walked away he said, "Missis, I'm sorry about what happened t'other night. Don't blame it on Mert. He didn't have aught to do with it." I knew that without his telling me. Mert was just about the kindest and most harmless person in the area.

I had to knock a few times before Mert called out for me to come in. When I did I felt terrible. He lay on his cot, a couple of dirty pillows under his head. The stove was going full blast, and he was only a couple of feet away from it. When I said hello to him he shook his head, fighting off an attack of pain. I asked him if I could do anything for him but he shook his head again. His face under a few days' growth of beard was pasty, and his waist-long hair, usually tied with a string, flowed over the pillow and all around him. The blue yachtsman's cap that I'd never seen him without lay on the floor under his cot. His mouth kept falling open, and I could see by the way he'd clamp it shut that he was losing control over his jaw muscles.

The pain spasms finally passed, and after he took a couple of deep breaths, he said, "Like you to do me a favor—write somethin' for me if you will. There's pencil and pad in that top drawer . . . I'd write it myself," he said as I went to the bureau, "but my eyes are a-goin' bad."

Even though he was dying, he was still ashamed to admit that he couldn't read or write. I saw the letter he'd brought me to read a few months ago. It was tacked to the wall above the bureau along with some others he'd received in his lifetime. Some of them were so old the writing on them was yellow and the paper was shredding.

I got the pad and he told me to look inside of it. Opening it, I leafed through page after page of long division examples, some of them a whole page long. It's what he'd come to school for—to learn long division. All his life, he'd told me, that was the only thing he ever really wanted to learn, how to divide big numbers.

"I proved every one of 'em and they're correct," he said. "What do you think of that?" He was as proud as he could be.

"I think you really did it, Mert." I sat down at the foot of the cot and found an empty page. "What do you want me to write?"

"My funeral service," he said.

That hit me right between the eyes. Flustered, I said, "What for?"

"Cuz I'm gonna die." He waved away any argument. "I'm gonna die an' there's no gettin' away from it. Maybe tomorrow, maybe next week, I don't know. But it'll be soon."

He was telling the truth, trying to be offhand about it, even a little tough, so I wouldn't start pitying him.

"If you want to shed some tears you better go outside."

"I'm not going to cry," I said, "but if you don't mind my asking, why do you want it done now?"

"Cuz it makes me sick the way everybody carries on when they plant ya—sayin' all kinda lies, 'n' the poor sap they're plantin' can't say a word back."

"I'll tell you the truth, Mert. I don't really know anything about writing a funeral service."

"It's simple," he said. "I'll be a'lyin' in here, up on that there table. All you gotta do is write down some things about me an' Uncle Arthur'll say 'em. That's all there is to it."

"What kind of service do you want?"

"Good one. Want some honest things said."

"I meant religious, like a special psalm that you might—"

"Hell, no! Don't want any of that organ music junk. Don't believe in it. But you got the idea. I knew you were the one to do it."

"But I don't know what you want, Mert."

"You say some things an' I'll tell you if it sounds right to me."

"I wouldn't know what to say. It seems to me that

181

if you really want an honest service you might know what's best to say. You know yourself better than anybody else does."

He thought about it. "That's a good idea," he said finally. "That's a humdinger of an idea." He paused, thinking. I kept pad and pencil ready.

"Say something like this," he said. "Say I been a good miner . . . Say that all the time I been here in the Forty Mile I liked it here. Say everything's been A-one and that I didn't have no kicks at all."

He stopped and I scribbled it all down, then he thought again. "Say I wanted to mine an' I mined. Say the only thing I wished was I'd struck some rich pay 'stead of just makin' a livin'."

After I got it all down I asked him if there was anything else. He shook his head.

"We should have some particulars," I said. "When were you born?"

"Why you wanna know that?"

"I don't know. We'll have to put it on your gravestone . . . Or maybe for legal reasons," I added lamely.

"We don't need that. I won't be havin' no gravestone. Say this instead. Say when I come into this country—'97 I think . . ." His eyes lit up as he remembered. "Say that there was gold everywhere you looked in those days—poor man's gold, gold in the water you washed with, gold in the mud on your boots . . ."

By the time I finished putting it down he was staring past me vacantly, still thinking about the past. His mouth hung slack.

"Mert . . ."

His jaw clamped shut and he saw me again. "If you want to," he said, "you can put in what I done while I was here—minin', fishin', an' huntin'."

"Don't you think there ought to be *something* religious?"

"Fine with me," he said. "We'll take care of it right now. You put in there that I don't believe in church or ministers nohow. Don't believe nothin' about 'em. Say that."

"That's the way you want it?"

"That's the way . . . When I meet my Maker, I'll

meet 'im the way I always did. By myself. Them church busybodies been gettin' in the way too long."

He was hit by pain again and when it was over he looked as if all the blood in his veins had turned to dust. "Say one more thing." He spoke so softly that I could hardly hear him. "Say that everything I got goes to Art—Arthur Spratt—my friend these many years . . . He's to take charge of my funeral. He knows what I want."

I wrote it down and he scrawled his mark under it.

On the way back I couldn't help thinking how brave Mert was. He had next to nothing, a dirty old cabin out in the wilds someplace and nobody to take care of him in his old age. But he never complained, just kept on going year after year.

When I got back to my place, I almost missed seeing the skis leaning up against the wall on the porch. I had to look at them twice before I realized whose they were, saw the holes for the extra straps Fred had put on them for me. For just a second I couldn't believe it, but when I opened the door there he was, sitting on the couch having a cup of coffee.

He'd come back from Steel Creek a few hours ago, he said.

"Why'd you have to come over now?" I said. "I look terrible."

"You look pretty as ever to me."

"Can you stay for supper?" I asked him.

"No, I haven't been home yet," he said.

The three of us talked a while longer, and then he asked me if I'd like to go for a walk.

"Sure."

"If anybody's gonna take a walk it'll be me." Nancy said to me. "You already had your walk. I'll go on over to the roadhouse."

"Sure."

I almost asked her to stay. Even before she went out I could tell something was coming, something I didn't want to hear. "Feels like I haven't seen you for years," I said after she was gone.

"Feels that way to me too," he said. He was all tensed up and nervous.

183

"Want some more coffee?"

"Thanks."

"Since when did you get so polite?" I said it as a joke, but it didn't sound funny. It sounded stupid.

He got up from the couch and went over to the pot-bellied stove while I poured his coffee I heard him open it up, then take a couple of pieces of wood from the woodbox and heft them in.

"Anne . . ."

I put his cup down on the edge of the cookstove. Somehow I had a good idea what he was going to say, and I didn't turn around. I braced myself, waiting for it.

"I'm going away," he said.

"Where to?"

"Steel Creek. There's some guys doing some winter mining there and they can use another hand."

"How long will you be there?"

"Till June."

Till June. I'd be gone then.

I still didn't want to turn around, but I picked up his cup from the stove and put it down on the table. I was as numb as if somebody had grabbed the back of my neck and was shaking me.

"When are you going?"

"Tomorrow."

That hand on the back of my neck felt tighter than ever. The gas lamp threw our shadows on the wall I was almost surprised to see mine there. I felt as if I'd faded away to nothing.

"I don't want to go, Anne. I don't want to go at all. But I have to."

"Why?"

"I don't want to see you hurt."

"I can take care of myself."

"Not once these people turn against you, and that's what they're doing. Come spring you won't have a job in Eagle or maybe anywhere else in Alaska. They can write letters to the commissioner that'd curl your hair."

"They already have. I'm not scared of them."

"I am. Not for me. For you. For you, for my mother and my sister."

I think I must have groaned then, I felt so awful. "Oh Fred . . ."

He was as miserable as I was. "Don't you see, Anne? There's nothing else I can do. I've thought it over and over. I can't do you anything but harm. I don't have a thing right now. I can't give you anything, I can't take care of you."

"That's what your mother said to me."

"There was a nurse up at Fort Yukon. About a year ago. She was white. She fell in love with an Indian minister, a really fine man. Everybody liked him, but once they found out that he and that nurse were in love with each other they made life so unbearable for the two of them that she finally went Outside and the Bishop had to transfer him to another parish. You see what I'm trying to say?"

"No." I knew he was doing it for me and that he thought it was the right thing, but he was wrong. And yet I didn't know how to make him see it.

"I'd better go," he said finally.

I moved over to him and my arms went around him. "Please, Fred. Don't."

"I have to."

"You don't have to."

I knew he'd made up his mind and I kept trying to think of a way I could change it. Maybe he didn't know how much I loved him, I thought. Maybe if he did—if he really knew—he wouldn't be able to leave.

"Hold me . . . ?" My mouth searched for his and I pressed myself against him, hoping it would tell him how much I loved him, hoping he'd realize there wasn't anything I wouldn't do to make him stay. At first I thought he was responding, reaching for me. Then he gripped my arms and held me away from him. "Anne, will you try to understand . . . !"

"You don't have to go right now," I said desperately. "We can talk a while. Just stay until Nancy gets back."

He hesitated. He didn't want to leave, and for a moment I thought maybe he wouldn't. But then he let my arms go and he was moving to the door. I didn't want to beg him, and I guess I should have had more pride than to do it, but right then I didn't care about pride or anything else. I didn't care what Miss Ivy or anybody else had ever told me about what was right for a self-respecting girl to do and what was wrong. All I cared about was him, holding him and having him close to me. If I could just keep him close to me now, I thought, he'd stay.

"Please, Fred," I asked him, "don't go. I love you so much. It isn't fair."

"Anne, don't let's do it like this," he said, his voice hard. "I'm going."

That stopped me almost as if he'd slapped me. I was acting cheap. I let him go. He said something else before he went out and closed the door behind him, but I didn't listen. I heard him walk off the porch and move off around the back and I kept thinking it wasn't fair. I'd never loved anybody as much in my entire life as I loved him and now he was going away from me for the stupidest reason in the whole world.

"It isn't fair," I said, starting to cry. "It isn't fair at all."

It wasn't until later on, long after Nancy came home and the two of us went to bed, that I realized what he'd said before he went out. He'd said, *I love you.*

When I remembered it I almost started crying all over again. He thought he was doing something noble and good, when all he was doing was showing he didn't think he was as worthwhile as anybody else. And that made it even more unfair.

XIV

The next morning I was so bleary-eyed when I woke up it seemed as if I'd slept only a few minutes. The blankets were frozen to the wall, as usual. I tugged them free and lay back, glancing at the clock. 7:30.

I dived back under the covers and tried to go back to sleep, but it was no use.

Wearing a couple of heavy sweaters, Nancy was sitting alongside the stove, a book open in front of her, studying some arithmetic. So as not to wake me she had lighted the oil lamp instead of the Coleman lantern. As soon as I pulled the blankets off I felt the cold. The stove had a roaring fire in it, but there were dots of white all over the walls from where the nails were frost-covered. Nancy called them frost buttons. When my feet touched the floor, I jerked them back. It felt icy, even through my socks. Nancy got up and pumped the Coleman lantern, then lit it and the room became bright.

"Morning, Anne," she said.

"Morning. What's it down to?"

"Fifty-four."

Fifty-four below zero. Getting some bib overalls and a shirt, I hung them over the stove to warm them, then dressed quickly and brushed my teeth. Pouring a cup of coffee, I went to see the temperature for myself. Nancy had already rubbed a hole in the thick layer of frost that covered the window. I rubbed again and peered through. It was dark outside, but I could read the thermometer.

"It *was* fifty-four. It's fifty-six now."

I washed in silence, thought about breakfast, but had no appetite.

Pouring another cup of coffee, I sat down for a minute on the unmade bed, trying to think what I should do next. Instead I thought of Fred, thinking that maybe he would come over and tell me that he had changed his mind, that no matter what anybody said or did he loved me. Over and over again I imagined all kinds of romantic scenes, but deep down inside I knew he wouldn't be coming. He'd made up his mind and I knew him well enough to know he wasn't going to change it.

I did some washing just to keep busy, but I couldn't shake off the feeling of being trapped. I kept wanting to go somewhere, anywhere, just to get out, and every fifteen minutes I'd look at the time, hoping that somehow another hour had gone by. In a couple of days I'd be leaving for the Indian village, and it helped a little to think about it. I'd be catching a ride with a freighter who'd passed through the day before with two big rowboats and a load of pipe on his huge double-ender sled. He was headed over to West Fork with them and wouldn't be back for two more days. After I hung the wash in the schoolroom I did some ironing. Then finally I couldn't stand being cooped up any longer. I started to get dressed.

"Where you going?" Nancy asked me.

"For a walk."

"Want me to go with you?" She knew how I was feeling. I'd told her last night that Fred was leaving. Even though she was glad for my sake, she was still trying to be sympathetic.

"No."

"It's pretty cold out there."

"I won't go far."

I started to walk without even thinking about where I was going. A couple of times it crossed my mind that maybe I could go far enough so that I wouldn't be able to get back and I'd freeze. Or maybe I could get caught in a blizzard. It was mean enough out so that it wouldn't take long to freeze to death if I did. Gray and still, it was so cold that my parka was white with the frost from my own breath.

After a while I found myself near Mary Angus' shack. It looked so lonely and forlorn I almost started to cry. For the first time I really understood why she was staying here, how even though she was sick she could keep on living in a place like that. If you loved somebody enough you could live anywhere.

From there I went towards the Purdy cabin. I stayed far enough away so nobody inside could see me, wishing I had the courage to go and knock at the door. I hung around hoping that if Fred hadn't left yet I might see him and talk to him, but after an hour my feet began to sting and I headed back home.

The next day I took a long walk over to the Forty Mile River. I was feeling so sorry for myself that I went out on the ice hoping I'd find a spot thin enough to break through. All I managed to do was stay out so long that I wound up with frostbite. I didn't even know it until I got back and realized my toes were numb. Nancy had to help me bathe my feet in snow and then warm water. They were so badly frostbitten that the pain was agonizing before circulation came back, and I knew I'd never do anything like that again.

Finally the freighter came back from West Fork and it was time to leave for the Indian village. Nancy came along. She was going to visit her family. She wasn't anxious to, but she didn't want to stay in Chicken all alone.

It was a nice trip, easier than going by dogsled. The double-ender was fourteen feet long and built for carrying heavy cargo. Compared to a dogsled it was a luxury liner. We piled hay inside of it, and when it was too cold to sit up front with the driver Nancy and I scooted down under the tarpaulin cover and bundled up in fur robes. We followed the same route Mr. Strong took down the Forty Mile River, and we made it to the Indian village in a day and a half.

It was dark when the sled pulled in, dark and windy. The cabins strung along the frozen river banks were black silhouettes against a bleak gray landscape. Cache doors banged in the wind and empty fish-drying racks stood like trembling skeletons.

Cathy was as glad to see me as I was to see her. Neither of us had talked with a girl near our own age since the last time we saw each other. The first night we stayed up until almost three in the morning and she told me why she had come here. She was writing a thesis on the Athapascan Indians of the Forty Mile for her doctorate. She was on her second year here and would have liked to stay on for another. But a lot of white people had written letters to the Alaska Native Service about her, saying that she was "spoiling" the Indians, so she had a feeling this was going to be her last winter.

She was from upstate New York, a graduate of Columbia University. I felt like a hick next to her. Not that she put on the dog, she was as natural as could be, but she'd seen plays on Broadway, read everything Sinclair Lewis wrote and had even met people like John Barrymore and Katherine Cornell.

That first night turned out to be practically the only chance we had for a really good talk. A flu epidemic had started a week before, and from the next morning on, Cathy didn't have too much time to herself. She'd taken in two little girls whose parents were down with it. Caring for them and keeping up with all the other things she had to do didn't leave her much time.

I didn't think I'd be affected by the village the way I'd been the first time, but I was wrong. When I made the rounds with Cathy the next morning I was horrified. In one cabin after another families huddled around small stoves that smoked and sputtered with green wood, or else they lay in tiered bunks, shivering under thin blankets. And everywhere there was coughing, eyes that watered, cheeks flushed crimson.

In one cabin there were seven children, the oldest about eleven. Every one of them was hollow-eyed and needed a bath and a good meal. Cathy went in to change the bandages on a little boy who'd burned himself. I flinched when I saw the burn: his whole forearm was raw. It happened to kids a lot, Cathy said. They huddled too close to the stove in their sleep, and sometimes they'd let a hand or arm fall against it. In the same cabin she changed the dressings on a little girl's neck. The ones she had on were filthy, and her long hair clung to running sores.

Cathy really gave it to the father, Arthur Jack. He was sitting on the bottom tier of a bunk, glassy-eyed and smelling of whiskey even though it was only about eleven o'clock. She asked him in English what he was going to do about getting some grub and some wood. "Soon. Soon I get," he said thickly.

"When?" Cathy asked him. "After all your kids are dead?"

"Tired now. Sick."

"Drunk you mean."

"You no mind business," he warned, making a fist, "get good beating."

His wife, a little hunched-up woman, sat in a corner

mending a snowshoe. She had a black eye and one side of her mouth was all puffed up.

Cathy didn't bat an eye. "You touch me and Titus Paul will hit you so hard you'll never lay a finger on a woman again."

He glowered at her, but that was all. Back at her place I told her that for a few seconds I was afraid he might have hit her.

"He wouldn't dare. He knows what Titus would do to him if he tried anything."

Titus had lunch with us that afternoon, and from the way Cathy acted around him I could see she was pretty fond of him. I couldn't understand why, though. He was a tough customer. With that tight-skinned face of his and eyes that bored right through you, he reminded me of a lizard. The scars all over his neck didn't help either. He hardly said a word the whole time he was there. He didn't speak English very well, and when he did speak it you'd have thought he was Moses the way he made pronouncements. About halfway through lunch Cathy asked him if he was going out trapping soon and he barely nodded. "I asked him what kind of dogs he had.

"McKenzie River Husky," he said.

The McKenzie River Husky was supposed to be the true Northern dog. It had a strong wolf strain. You could see it in the long slanting eyes, the muzzle, and the coarse short hair. I told him that Fred favored the Siberian husky and the malamute.

"McKenzie River Husky better," he said flatly. "More smart. On trail, take harness off McKenzie River dog, he run for timber, not come back till feeding time. Good strong dog. You have dogs?"

I said no and he didn't bother to look at me again. Cathy told him about her visit to Arthur Jack. "He's beating up Minnie again and drinking too much. Will you talk to him?"

"Why?"

"Because if you don't those kids of his are going to die."

He didn't say he would and he didn't say he wouldn't.

After he left I asked her if he was the chief and she said no. "He swings a lot of weight, though. I used to go to the Council about people like Arthur Jack. All they did was have a meeting and tell them to change their ways and then they'd do whatever they wanted. Titus Paul'll tell him he'll break his neck if he doesn't get out and do some work. He'll listen to Titus, for a while, anyway."

Titus was sort of the unofficial head of the village, she told me, one of the few Indians the whites couldn't boss around. When he was little he'd gone to a boarding school for Indians at Carcross, in Canada. The school had been run by whites and was finally closed when the authorities found out that the kids were starving. Some of them had even been beaten to death. Titus was lucky to be alive. The scars on his neck were from glandular TB, the running sores that so many children in the village had. His were especially bad because the way the people at the school had treated the sores was to plaster them over with plain adhesive tape. "By all rights he should hate whites," Cathy said, "but he doesn't. He's not fond of them, but he doesn't hate them."

"Honest to God, Cathy," I told her. "I don't know how you can bear to stay here."

"Somebody has to do it."

"I wouldn't."

"Oh yes you would. From what I hear you've stuck your neck out a few times already."

"That's different. What I can't see is doing things for people when they won't do anything for themselves."

"Anne, I told you when you first came through here," she said sharply, "that you couldn't judge these people by white standards."

That got my Irish up.

"Cathy, you have to have *some* kind of standards. Can't they go out and just cut enough wood to keep warm, or put up meat for the winter?"

"They're doing the best they can. They just don't think about the future the way white people do. They did fine before the white man came along. Look at this." She took a stone ax down from a shelf. "This is what they used before the whites came—stone, stone tools, stone weapons. And they survived. So don't try to tell me they can't do things for themselves."

"That's what I'm trying to say. Now they've got more—axes and hatchets, knives and rifles. They have everything you can think of, so how come they just sit around and starve?"

"Because they're weak. Before the whites came these people were hunters. Their diet was almost all meat and that practically raw. They had the strength to go out and take some game. Now they eat the white man's grub—flour, sugar, canned goods, junk. And they drink his liquor . . ."

I dropped the subject, but I still didn't understand. When I'd gone out with Cathy in the morning the first thing I'd noticed was the empty space alongside so many cabins—an empty space that should have been filled with cords of wood. Alongside Cathy's place and the church and a few other places the wood was neatly ricked up, but at least half the rest had almost none. Yet nobody stole wood from anybody else. I could remember how, when I was a kid, my brothers and I used to slip down to the railroad tracks at night with burlap sacks and pick up whatever coal had fallen off the cars. It was stealing, but everybody did it. And I knew that if I were living here—or any other white person for that matter—and my kids and I were freezing to death, *I'd* sure have stolen wood from somebody. Yet nobody did. As far as I could see they were practically committing suicide. It just didn't make sense; if these people made out all right before the whites came, how come they couldn't do it now when things should have been easier for them?

I didn't find out until the next night, after the dance in the church.

It was the last night I was there and I wasn't looking forward to the dance. I figured that with all the hunger and sickness around, it wouldn't amount to much. I couldn't have been more wrong, though. The church was packed, with pews pushed back against the walls and a huge oil drum heater that sent out enough heat to bake everybody twice over. The Indians cured their leather with urine, so what with all the parkas and the moccasins, the air took getting used to at first. Once the dancing started, though, there was so much noise and fun I forgot all about it. Most of the men wore bib overalls and a shirt, but the girls were really gotten up, bright combs in their hair, plenty of bracelets and colorful kerchiefs around their necks.

Cathy looked lovely. She had on a dress that I wouldn't have dared to wear, but on her it was exquisite. Made of caribou skin that was as soft as chamois, it had a fox collar that showed part of her back. It was almost like a long parka, except that it was split to the thigh, and the hem, trimmed with beadwork and fur, came to a point in front and back.

The dance itself was less rackety than the ones at Chicken because hardly anyone wore boots or shoes. The men were better dancers, too. In Chicken the men used to get so rough at times that I'd be scared of getting knocked out by an elbow. Here, even though there was plenty of whooping and floor-stomping, there wasn't anything rowdy about it. I didn't see any of the men ask a woman to dance. They'd just go over and lead her out on the floor and that was that. The people who weren't square dancing stood on the sidelines tapping their feet and clapping in time to the music, some of them chanting *Little Brown Jug* or *Turkey in the Straw* in their own tongue.

I danced the first couple of sets with Ben Norvall. He'd left Chicken a couple of weeks ago to come here, where he was living with Mary Magdalene. Face flat as a pie, and a lump of snuff always tucked inside her lower lip, Mary was strong as a football player. When she didn't have a lip full of snuff she smoked a smelly old pipe. Ben wasn't any prize package either, so they were about even. Besides beginning to smell bad again, he was full of mischief and was always stirring up trouble. Once I sold him a gallon of kerosene and he went around to everybody asking how much they'd paid me for a gallon; then he said I'd charged him ten cents less. It wasn't true, but it brought three or four customers down on my neck before I straightened it out. Ben was always doing things like that. He especially enjoyed getting people mad at each other by telling them what other people had said about them. In every place that he'd lived he'd eventually get on people's nerves so much that they'd finally threaten to burn down his cabin if he didn't get out.

Between sets he told me that he was going back to Chicken when I went back. "These people just don't appreciate me," he said, "so I'm gonna siwash it back to my own people." It was the exact same thing he'd said when he left Chicken, which probably meant he'd worn out his welcome here fast.

After the second set was over I was sitting down for a rest when someone came over and stood in front of me, his moccasin tapping the floor in time to the warm-up music. I looked up. It was Titus Paul. He didn't say a word, just held out his hands and kept that one foot tapping. Up until then I wondered what Cathy saw in him, although when he walked in earlier all dressed up in beaded leather vest and broad-brimmed leather hat he looked kind of dashing in an ugly way. The way he was looking at me now, though, I automatically gave him my hand and let him lead me out on the floor. He was as good a dancer as Fred, maybe even a little better.

After I danced with him, no sooner did I sit down than there was another Indian standing over me, smiling and tapping his foot. It was that way for the rest of the night.

The dance didn't break up until after two. Ben Norvall and Titus came back with Cathy and me to her house, the four of us fighting a wind that blew down the frozen river so hard we had trouble keeping our feet. The moon was out, bouncing off the parts of the ice that the wind had polished. We sat around with our parkas on until the fire that Titus built up in the stove was going strong.

"How'd you enjoy the dance?" Cathy asked me.

"I liked it . . . You're a good dancer, Titus."

He didn't say anything, just glanced at me with those lizard's eyes of his.

Ben was sitting back in an overstuffed chair that was leaking cotton padding, his feet in front of the open stove door. "That all you can do is grunt when a lady pays you a compliment?" he asked Titus.

There was a long pause, then Titus said slowly, "Thank you."

"That's the trouble with you Indians," Ben said, needling him, "you don't talk. If you did you wouldn't be in the fix you're in."

"What's talking got to do with it?" Cathy said.

"White people like a man to talk, say what's on his mind. That's the way they get to know him. With Indians it's the other way round. They get the feel of you by just sitting quiet. If they don't like what they feel they walk away. Isn't that right, Titus?"

Titus nodded.

"What's wrong with that?" Cathy asked.

"Nothing at all if this was an Indian world, but it isn't. It's a white one. The trouble with these people is they don't understand that. That's one reason they're goin' under."

"They're going under, as you say, because they've been used."

"Used! Aw now, Cathy, where do you get that stuff from? Only person who ever used an Indian is another Indian. You don't use these suckers. Bulldoze 'em maybe, but you don't use 'em. What do you say, Titus?"

"I listen what *you* say," Titus said gruffly.

"See what I mean?" Ben said.

"I'd like to hear it too," Cathy said. "What do you mean 'bulldoze'?"

"What I mean is that if it was the other way around, if the white man hadn't bulldozed these people, they'd've bulldozed the whites."

"That's some way to look at things," Cathy said.

"It's not the best, but what are you gonna do when there's no cop on the corner and it's every man for himself? Hell, when I came into this country you didn't mess around with the Kutchins—none of them—the Vunta, the Natche, the Tutchone. They were tough as they come. They'd walk right up to your cabin and tell you they wanted to make a trade with you, give you so much for so much. Nine times out of ten you got the worst of the bargain, especially if you were all alone.

196

They didn't threaten you if you didn't trade their way, but when there's just you, or maybe you and a partner, you weren't about to tempt Providence. No sir, I'm telling you, they were tough. They didn't steal—still don't. If they wanted something they went and took it. That was their way." He looked at Titus. "You tell me if I'm lyin'."

"You tell truth," Titus said.

"You betcha it's the truth," Ben went on. "They were a strong bunch. Why you couldn't hammer a nail through the muscles of some of those braves."

"Then what happened?" I asked.

"I don't know," Ben said. "They got soft, I guess, lazy. Never thought much about it. *You* know?" he asked Titus.

Titus thought it over, then he said, "Nothing."

"What does that mean—'nothing'?" Cathy said.

"Nothing. We are same as always."

"But you're not," Cathy said, "that's just what we're talking about."

"We are same," Titus insisted. "We think same as before. Before white men came."

"What kinda thinkin' is that?" Ben asked him.

"Like hunter. Something turn up. Today hungry. Tomorrow big cook."

Cathy didn't understand and neither did I, but Ben seemed to. "Huh!" he said. "I never thought of it that way. 'Something'll turn up.' Damned if it isn't the truth."

"How about letting us in on it?" Cathy said.

"Think of it this way," Ben said. "Before *we* came these people lived in sweathouses. They're like igloos," he said to me, "a wood frame with snow built up around it. The Indians weren't any more sociable than they are now, so there was just maybe two or three families traveling together—one family to a sweathouse. They just drifted from place to place. Well, imagine living out there in all that wind and ice and the only thing between you and starvation whatever game you can take. Half the time they starved. Sometimes they'd go so long without eating they'd chew the rawhide off their snowshoes. They had a tough time of it even before the white man came—the women in particular. These people never did think too much of women. The squaws had it so miserable that sometimes if they had a little girl-baby they'd kill it so it wouldn't have to suffer like them."

"They really did that?" I asked Cathy. She nodded.

"They sure did," Ben went on. "Now you ask yourself something—if them suckers had it so hard there must have been *some*thing kept 'em going, something that kept 'em alive. And they did. They had faith."

"You mean like faith in God?"

"*Their* gods, the Spirits. Same thing, I guess. Anyway, they had faith, real strong faith—kind of faith the wolf has."

"What do you mean?" Cathy asked. "*Animal* faith?"

"I mean hunter's faith," Ben said, "any kind of hunter, man or beast. Wolf's got it. No matter how much his ribs are stickin' out, he's got the courage to go on, the faith that somethin's gonna turn up. White men, they don't think that way. They think like the beaver, put somethin' away for tomorrow. The real hunter, and again I'm talking about man or beast, he doesn't do that. That's what the Kutchins were—hunters. They were born to it. Why they hunted moose by runnin' 'em down on snowshoes. They could run all day, most of 'em. Try to put people like that to workin' for wages, doing manual labor and they're no good at it. That's why white people think they're lazy."

"What does all this have to do with faith?" Cathy asked.

"Everything," Ben said. "You've heard that faith moves mountains. Well, it does. Gives people strength. And it gave those Kutchins strength too. Faith. 'Today I'm going to bed so hungry I could eat my dog,' they'd think, 'but tomorrow I'm gonna come across a nice fat caribou and the whole bunch of us'll have a big cook and eat till we're sick. Something'll turn up.' Something always did, too. And one day something else turned up—the *unjyit,* the white man. Yep, the white man. And by God, here was the answer to a hunter's prayer. 'Behold!' that Indian said, 'Just look at that white critter, will you? Comes into this country out of

198

nowhere and before you know it he's building himself cabins ten times bigger than a sweathouse. And grub? Great Spirit, look at it all! He's got it stacked in tin cans, in sacks, in boxes, shoots it without the least trouble.'

"So the Indian went to this white man and he said, 'Bud, I like your style. Want to live the way you do. How do I do it?'

" 'Bring me furs,' the white man says, 'all kinds—lynx, muskrat and marten, black fox, red fox and wolf. I'll take 'em all.' 'Easy,' says the Indian. And he did it—stopped hunting food and started hunting fur, started trading for axes and traps and guns, flour and tea.

"He stopped traveling from place to place and settled down where the white man was. For a while he didn't do too bad. Missionaries came around and taught 'im all about Jesus Christ, which was fine with him, because the one thing he wanted to know more about was the God that had made this white critter so rich and powerful.

"Well, I tell you, for a good many years that Indian was like a bear in a blueberry patch. He did real fine, kept them furs comin' and lived better than ever he did before. Until the day came when it all went bad. The price of fur went down. Where maybe it took a stack of fur halfway up a man's shin to buy a sack of flour, one day it took a stack up to his waist, then up to his shoulder. Then for a while the white man hardly wanted any furs at all. That Indian was stuck. From living in one place and eating the white man's food, he'd gotten weak. Flour, sugar, biscuits—none of that stuff can keep you going for long. You need meat in the winter, good fresh meat with plenty of fat on it. But there wasn't any meat around, at least not nearby. The white man had chased it away and the Indian, not being a hunter anymore, didn't have the strength to go any long distance for it.

"He was stuck all right. Every winter things got worse for 'im. Weak as he was, he picked up all the white man's diseases—influenza, whooping cough, TB. The only thing that made him feel good for awhile was liquor, so he drank that whenever he could get enough

199

money to pay for it. He got weaker and weaker, sicker and sicker. But no matter how weak or sick he got, he still held onto the faith that'd kept him going when he was a hunter—'Something'll turn up. Somehow I'll make it through the winter.' And that's what keeps all these people in this village going even today—the faith that something's bound to turn up. And that's the awful part of it. This time it looks like it's not going to. These people are on their way to the big El Dorado up in the sky. They've hit the sunset trail and they're dying. All because of faith."

When he finished we were quiet. Even Cathy was moved.

Titus reached over and touched Ben's arm. "You tell story good," he said, and when Ben remained silent he pointed a finger at him. "Why you no say thank you?" He broke into a big smile and it made us all laugh.

I couldn't get over what Ben had said, though. "Does it have to be that way?" I asked him. "Isn't there anything that can be done about it?"

Ben shrugged. "I don't know. Schoolin', I guess."

"It's not doing it so far," Cathy said, "at least not here. The only reason most of these kids come to school at all is because it's the warmest place in the village and I give them a hot lunch."

"Well then what *can* be done?" I said.

"Raze this place to the ground," Cathy said. "Burn it and move everybody up to the Chandalar country."

"Where's that?" I asked.

"Northwest of here," Ben said. "There's a tribe up there won't even let white men come near 'em except to trade once a year. They mushed up there to get away from the white man. Doin' pretty well too."

We all looked at Titus. He shook his head.

"No. We live here. We stay here."

"And die here," Cathy said. "Maybe I'm pessimistic, maybe I'm wrong, but I don't see how this village is going to make it. We've got two children and a new-born babe dead so far, and the worst part of the winter is yet to come. And when it's over, when spring is here again, what'll happen? The old people and the women and children will go to the fish camp and some of the men will go to Eagle to find jobs. They'll cut wood for the riverboats, work on the boats as deckhands, then they'll all come back here and go through another winter. What you said is true," she said to Ben. "Almost everybody here is living in the past."

"Not everybody, Cathy," Titus said. "Some, they learn. Little children get educate, every year learn more. Read. Write. We *learn*," he said emphatically. He went on to say that the Indians had never had it easy, that for them to go north and try to live the old way wouldn't accomplish anything. Their life was here.

Listening to him talk, slowly, confidently, and thinking about what Ben had said, I finally realized what Cathy meant when she'd told me I couldn't judge these people by white standards. They were doing the best they knew how, and the last thing in the world they needed was to have people look down their noses at them. They had guts.

The next day, when Mr. Strong and Nancy came through to pick me up I was almost looking forward to being back in Chicken. I'd left there hoping I'd never see the place again, but staying with Cathy made me realize that my troubles just weren't that big. When the two of us said goodbye and I thanked her for letting me stay with her I meant it. I'd learned a lot.

XV

We arrived back in Chicken on New Year's Eve, and Maggie invited us to a party at the roadhouse. I didn't feel like going. Instead I stayed home and wrote a letter to Fred. I told him exactly how I felt. I missed him badly, I wrote him. I never knew it was possible to miss somebody so much, and all I did was think about him. I told him that I was mad, too—mad because he was wrong. "You may say you did it for me," I wrote, "but I wonder. I wonder if maybe you just didn't really care about me that much. Maybe you were just trifling with my affections, and when it really came down to it you just took the easy way. If you did then I want you to write and tell me. I can take anything as long as it's the truth . . ."

When I finished the letter I felt better. I put it in an envelope and stamped and addressed it before I could change my mind about sending it.

I sat and read for a while after that. Occasionally I'd hear whoops and hollers and square-dance music from the roadhouse. I didn't have any desire to go over there, though. Nancy had tried to get me to come, but I'd told her there wasn't anybody there I wanted to see. It wasn't that I hated them, because I didn't. Not now, anyway. For a few days I had hated them with all my might. Now I didn't know how I felt towards them—indifferent, probably. All I wanted was for school to open so I could get busy again and not have time to think.

I was still up when twelve o'clock came and everybody started hoorraying and whistling and banging on pots. Then they started singing *Auld Lang Syne* and that almost started me bawling, it made me feel so lonely. Someone came running towards the schoolhouse just as they got towards the end. It was Nancy. She burst in and there were tears in her eyes. "Anne," she said, "I just wanted to come over and wish you . . . wish you a—" That was a far as she got before she rushed over and threw her arms around me and then we both started bawling. She kept saying over and over how bad she felt for me and I kept saying she shouldn't, the two of us crying so hard I couldn't tell whether I was consoling her or she was consoling me. We had such a wonderful cry that when it was over we almost smiled. "Please come on over, Anne," she said. "Everybody wants you to—Uncle Arthur and Joe and Maggie Carew, everybody."

I said no, I was too tired. And I was—all kind of cried out and empty. "You go on and have a good time," I said. "You deserve it." She did, too. She'd been looking tired lately and I was worried that she was pushing herself too hard at school.

After she left I took out the letter I'd written to Fred and thought about whether to send it or throw it in the stove. I almost threw it in before I made up my mind I'd send it. After that I made a New Year's resolution that from now on I wasn't going to think about anything but teaching school and doing my duty, and I was going to do the best job I knew how. It made me feel better right away.

When school opened again I could feel almost from the first day that something was different about me. I wasn't short with the children or anything like that—we still sang in the morning and had as much fun as before—but I made them work harder. They only had till June to get all the schooling they could, I figured, and they were going to get it. And that went for Rebekah too. I'd been kind of pussyfooting around with her, scared to come right out and teach her for fear of what people might say. Knowing it, she never asked any questions and just picked up what she could, but she was dying to learn. From then on I treated her like everybody else, called on her for answers, gave her assignments and let her know she was expected to learn as much as she possibly could. It was just what she'd been waiting for and she loved it.

Not one person said a word about it to me either.

People must have noticed I'd changed, because they acted differently towards me, as if I wasn't a kid anymore—or a cheechako either for that matter. They stopped asking me things like whether it was cold enough for me or not and what I wanted to be when I grew up. When Uncle Arthur and Ben Norvall came into class a couple of days after school opened they started kidding around right away. I usually let them get away with it, but this time I told them that I'd appreciate it if they'd calm down until recess when we could all have fun. They did it too, without even looking at me cross-eyed. I felt a little bad about it when it came to Uncle Arthur because Mert Atwood had died the day before and he wasn't feeling too good. They both stayed, though, and just to please Uncle Arthur I gave penmanship drill.

I couldn't put my finger on what it was, but I felt different, all right—as if all my life I'd been trying to be what other people like my parents or Mr. Strong or all the people here in Chicken wanted me to be. Now I was going to be myself. I wasn't going to be hard to get along with, or go out of my way to say anything mean, but from now on people were going to have to take me for what I was. It was the way Cathy Winters felt, I realized. I knew now why she'd answered Mr. Strong the way she had. I still wouldn't have answered him like that myself, but I'd care just as little as she did about what he thought of me personally. It was as if I'd grown up all of a sudden, as if up to then I'd been a girl and now I wasn't anymore.

A couple of weeks after school started I got a letter from Fred. He hadn't been trifling with my affections at all, he wrote. He cared for me more than he'd ever cared for anybody in his life.

I did what I thought was right, Anne. I didn't do it because I was scared of anybody. I can't tell you how much it turned me inside out to come here, but I did it because I love you so much that there was nothing else I *could* do.

God, how I wish I was on my own and could do just what I want! That's the thing that really hurts—that I love you so much and there's nothing I can do about it. I keep thinking that some day maybe I'll be able to, and then I also think that when that day comes you'll probably be married to somebody who loves you as dearly as I do.

If I can take it, I'll be staying here until summer, so I won't be seeing you for a long time. Maybe never again. I don't know. I just want you to know that I love you deeply, but I am not going to take up any more of your time. Come the summer you'll be going to Eagle to teach and then you'll probably forget all about me. And maybe that's the best thing.

I read the letter over and over, and every time I saw the words *if I can take it* I winced. On the way back

204

from the Indian village I'd asked Nancy how Fred was doing at Steel Creek and she'd told me he was lonely. "The other miners aren't too friendly to 'im," she'd said. "They don't like to work alongside natives or halfbreeds. They won't even let him bunk with 'em."

"Where is he staying?"

"Ma and pa rented him the workshed back of the roadhouse." She was embarrassed. "It's not too bad, Anne. It's a pretty good place. I mean it's nothing like Mary Angus' place. It's got a wood floor and it's clean."

Every time I'd thought about it I wanted to kill somebody. Fred lived in a workshed all by himself when here he had the most beautiful home of anybody and a family that loved him. And it was all my fault. He hated working for wages, and on top of it he had to work with men who didn't even want him. He must have been miserable, but all he'd said about it was *if I can take it.*

I wrote him a letter telling him I thought he should come back. "We don't have to see each other at all," I ended it.

I promise you that. I won't even say hello to you if I should see you. I'll act as if I don't even know you. I know how you feel now and I'll respect your feelings, so please don't stay there just because of me.

I signed it "Your friend (and I mean just that), Anne."

In a way that was the most peculiar time I ever went through. I'd never felt more alone in my life, and yet at the same time I felt more whole than I ever did. I didn't seem to need anybody, as if there was a protective shell around me that made me so sure of myself I couldn't say or do anything wrong. I didn't know what it was, but I took everything in stride. Not that I didn't feel things. I did. I just felt them in a different way. The night that Nancy finally accomplished what she'd set her heart on, for instance, I was so composed I hardly recognized myself.

We were just sitting around not doing much of anything that night. Nancy was looking through a Third Reader and I was practicing on the harmonica. As long as I didn't have a piano I figured I ought to have a musical instrument to play when we needed music for songs and games, so I'd taken it up at the same time Jimmy had. When Nancy and I had been feuding she'd always asked me to stop while she was studying. Now nothing seemed to bother her. I was playing *Home on the Range* and not doing bad at all when I heard her say, "Anne?"

I looked over at her and there was just no way to describe the wonderful smile on her face. Even before she said a word I knew what had happened.

"I can read," she said.

"You sure?"

She nodded.

"Go ahead."

" 'Once upon-ay-time,' " she read, " 'ay-crab-left-thee-sea-and-went-out-upon-thee-beach-to-warm-him-self-in-thee-sunshine . . .' " She went on, sounding out each word the way a little kid would. Once or twice she almost got stuck, but she kept going. It was the first time she'd ever read anything without my help, and she read it perfectly. I didn't know anything about psychological blocks. I did know that if that was what had been holding her back up to now, it was all gone. When she finished she was glowing.

"Was that reading?"

"That was reading."

We tried her with a newspaper just to be sure, and she read some headlines from the Fairbanks *Daily News—Miner*. She didn't do too badly with a few paragraphs from *Collier's* either. She was so happy about it she almost started to cry. A couple of months before I'd not only have joined her, but I'd have wanted to run out and yell the news up and down the length of the settlement. Not that I wasn't as happy as she was. I felt wonderful for her, and we stayed up late talking about plans for her future. I just wasn't surprised. It was as if I'd known all along it was going to happen and accepted it that way—as something I'd expected.

Too excited to sleep, she sat up reading long after I

turned in. The next morning she told me she'd been up till two. She wasn't the least bit tired either. She could barely wait for the class to show up to tell them all, and before the day was over everybody in Chicken knew she was able to read.

Maggie Carew invited us both over to supper to celebrate. It was the first time she'd had me over in quite a while, and it meant she wanted to bury the hatchet. Now that Fred was gone she felt more kindly towards me, or maybe she was even feeling sorry for what had happened. I didn't know and I didn't care. I liked her. At least she was honest and straightforward. She'd been about the only one in the settlement that really said what she thought and she hadn't made any bones about it.

After supper she asked me if I was looking forward to teaching in Eagle next year.

"I don't know," I said.

"Whattaya mean ya don't know," she said. "You got a contract, ain't ya?"

"Yes, but I hear the school board has some doubts about me."

"Well, I oughtta have something to say about that," she said. "End of next spring we're movin' there. I bought the roadhouse right alongside the dock. I'll put in a good word for you—unless a course you got other plans."

"No, I don't," I said.

I didn't have any at all.

I'd always kept a scrapbook of poems that I liked to read over and over. My favorite was "Waiting" by John Burroughs. When I reread it it seemed as though it was almost written for me.

> Serene, I fold my hands and wait,
>   Nor care for wind, nor tide, nor sea;
> I rave no more 'gainst time or fate,
>   For lo! my own shall come to me.

It was exactly the way I felt. I was just waiting—for what I didn't know. Something. There was an empty space inside of me, but what was going to fill it up I couldn't say.

Came February I almost wondered if I wanted to teach anywhere in Alaska at all because suddenly the weather turned so mean it felt as if God had gone away from this part of the world. Day after day the sky stayed so dark you couldn't tell whether it was day or night. For almost a week the temperature dropped to fifty and lower and stayed there. Even if there'd been no thermometer we'd have known how cold it was: all the moisture was sucked out of the air, leaving everybody thirsty all the time—no matter how much tea or water we drank we still felt dry.

People began to get as mean as the weather. With the holidays over everybody had cabin fever—aggravation from staying indoors day after day—and they started quarrels with each other over everything. Uncle Arthur swore Ben Norvall had stolen a pick from him and just for spite went out and sprang all of Ben's traps. Then, in a drunken rage one day, Angela Barrett threw a pot of scalding water over one of her dogs when he barked too long. Maggie Carew's husband had to put it out of its agony by shooting it.

Maybe if I hadn't had the class to keep me busy I'd have felt the same kind of aggravation. Sometimes I'd find myself getting annoyed over small things, but most of the time I was calm—not hard or cold or anything like that—just kind of detached, as if I was still waiting for something to happen.

When it did finally, it was a day I'd never forget.

It was just after the class came back from lunch. It was sixty below that day and the little children were using my bed again. I was beginning to think the bed was the most important article of furniture I had. Besides the kids using it when the floor was too cold, Nancy and I had had to put our sack of potatoes in it because it was the only place we could be sure they wouldn't freeze.

We were tidying up in my quarters when I heard Evelyn Vaughn start up with Rebekah in the schoolroom. "Hey, Rebekah—how much two and two?"

"Fo'."

"How much one and two?"

"T'ree."

"How much t'ree and two?" she mimicked.

"Fi.'"

"Rebekah, me think you one damn smart woman," Evelyn said, "right Eleanor?"

"That's right."

At first I used to interfere when anybody made fun of her, but by now she could take care of herself.

"Oh no," she said to Evelyn as I walked into the room. "You not think Rebekah smart, little lady. You think *you* too much smart. Think you not speak good English and Rebekah not know."

Evelyn looked as though she was sorry she'd started, but Rebekah wasn't going to have any mercy on her. She was as tough as Evelyn anytime, and a lot smarter. She opened her eyes wide and pointed a finger at her. "You not be nice I make bad medicine. Send Brush Man get you at night."

"Who's the Brush Man?" Evelyn asked, uncertainly. Rebekah's expression was so horrible the whole class was spellbound.

"You not know Brush Man?"

"No."

"He live all over—in tree, in hole, anyplace—only come out when dark."

"I don't believe it," Evelyn said. She was afraid of the dark and everyone knew it.

"Aagh!" Rebekah cried. The sound was as terrible as her expression. "You say this, Brush Man get you for sure! You know how when too much cold you see little blue light in bushes?" I'd seen it myself once in a while—static electricity. "That tell you Brush Man near. But you never see him till he grab you—*then* you see him, ha ha."

"What's he look like?" Evelyn asked. She was trying to make out that she didn't care, but she was worried.

Not taking her eyes off Evelyn, Rebekah raised her hands over her head and bared her teeth. "Ten feet big," she growled, "maybe more. Much hair. Face all black from cold and long teeth like grizzly. Yellow eyes like punkin. My father big medicine man, tell me how bring him. You make more fun me," she warned Evelyn, "I send Brush Man for *you!*"

In the silence that followed we heard three distant rifle shots, one right after the other. We all knew what that meant. Someone was calling for help. I asked the class to sit quietly while Nancy put on her coat and went outside to see if anyone knew where they'd come from. She came back a few minutes later. "The Carews think they came from somewhere over towards the Purdys," she said. "Your mother and father's goin' over," she told Jimmy. "They said you and Willard could go along."

After that there was no keeping the rest of the class in, so I let them all go, with the exception of Joan Simpson. Three more shots came as they all ran out.

"I think maybe come from Mary Angus, Tisha," Rebekah said.

"You feel like going over?" I asked Nancy.

"If you want."

Outside, even though I had a scarf over my face the first breath I took caught in my throat. Before we could head over to Mary's we had to take Joan Simpson home. She was too young to let her go alone. For the first few steps our warm moccasins slipped on the snow, but then the bottoms coated up and we were able to walk. Joan lived in the opposite direction. It took us fifteen minutes to get to her cabin, and then we started back for Mary Angus' place. A gray-black mist hung over everything, and the cold made it impossible to talk, so we trudged all the way in silence, moving fast enough to stay warm, slow enough to avoid perspiring.

The kids were playing outside the shack when we got there. A couple of them were riding in Mary's hand sled while Robert Merriweather pulled it and Jimmy pushed from behind yelling, "Mush!" As soon as they saw Nancy and me they came running over.

"Mary's dead, Teacher!" Jimmy yelled.

"Dead as a doornail," Willard chimed in.

"And there's blood all over the place. They won't even let us come in. Ask 'em if they will, Teacher? We wanna see."

Jake Harrington was standing outside the door with Rebekah.

210

"Is it true?" I asked them.

Jake nodded. I pushed the door open. There were a lot of people inside, but only a sputtering candle for light so at first I could only make out Angela, the Carews and Joe Temple. "Close that goddamn door before this candle goes out!" I heard Angela yell.

I closed it.

"Well, it's our little teacher," she said sarcastically. She was drunk, smiling at me in a way that made it plain she didn't have any use for me. She'd been drinking more than ever the past few weeks and getting worse every day. A few days ago in the roadhouse Ben Norvall had said something she didn't like and she went after him and gave him a couple of good wallops before anybody could stop her. He was in a corner with Chuck, the two of them bending down over what must have been Mary's body. Ben was covering her up with a wolf robe.

"What happened?" I asked Maggie.

"She musta hemorrhaged," Maggie said. "When they get as far gone as she was they go fast."

Mr. Vaughn was there too. "Take a slant at her," he said, jerking a thumb towards the corner. "See what a good klooch looks like."

"There's no need for that kinda talk, Arnold," Maggie said. "We're tryin' a decide what to do," she said to me. "Joe here's gonna get his sled and mush the body over to our place. We'll keep it in the extra cache till Strong can tote it up to the Indian village, but we ain't figgered out what to do with the kids yet."

Now that my eyes had adjusted to the darkness I saw Ethel. She was sitting on a box, with nobody paying attention to her. She was wide-eyed and scared from all the commotion. I went over to her.

"How about it, Joe," Angela said. "You gonna take the kids?"

"What am I supposed to do with them?"

"All you gotta do is keep 'em a week or so," Maggie said. "Then Strong'll mush 'em outta here."

"I don't know anything about taking care of kids," he said.

"That's what they all say," Angela said. "They can

211

make 'em, but they don't know how to take care of 'em."

Ben and Chuck got up from Mary's body. I was glad Ben had covered it with the wolf robe. I didn't want to see it. There was blood on the edge of the mattress and a big pool of it on the dirt floor that was all frozen and blackened. Chuck was in shock. I put an arm around him and he just let me hold him without making a sound. "This one had it the worst," Ben said, putting a hand on Ethel's head. "I was going by and didn't see any smoke coming from the chimney. Came in and she was sitting alongside Mary there." He patted her head. "If ol' Ben hadn't happened by," he said to her, "you'd liable to have froze to death."

"Maybe she'd of been better off," Maggie said.

"That's sure as hell true," Angela said. "She certainly ain't got nothin' to look for'ard to in that Indian village." She took out a flask and drank a couple of mouthfuls.

Mr. Carew spoke up. "Unless we're gonna stand around here jawin' all day, let's decide what we do with the kids."

Chuck was limp against me. I put a hand on his shoulder.

Angela said, "I vote Joe takes 'em. Teach 'im a good lesson."

"That's not funny. I told you before I wouldn't know what to do with them."

"How about you, Maggie?" Angela asked. "You got the bunkhouse."

"I got my own to look after."

"I'll take them," I said to Joe.

"*You*'ll take 'em!" Angela said.

"Yes."

"How are you going to take care of them and teach school too?" Mr. Vaughn asked.

"I can manage it."

"That's fine with me," Joe said, relieved. "Thanks, Anne."

"I don't think it's right," Mr. Vaughn said.

"I agree with 'im," Maggie said. "She's just a kid."

"Then why don't you take them?" Joe snapped at her.

She looked as if she was considering it and for a few seconds I held my breath. I wanted them. I wanted them badly.

"I got my own," she repeated.

"They're all yours," Joe said to me.

I picked up Ethel. "You take Chuck," I said to Nancy.

"Sure." She was a little surprised.

Nobody made a move to get out of the way. They just stared at me as if I was some kind of a circus freak.

"Anybody else want them?" I said.

Nobody answered.

"Then if nobody minds, we'll take these children home."

XVI

Ethel was quiet until we reached the door. Then she realized that I was taking her away and she began to scream. By the time we were outside she was fighting me tooth and nail and I had to let her down. Even then I could barely stop her from running back inside the shack. She was just too young to realize her mother was dead.

If it hadn't been for Ben Norvall I don't know how we'd have gotten her home. He went and got Mary's hand sled from the kids, then helped me tuck a blanket around Ethel and tie her into the sled. It was the only way we could get her out of there. She wouldn't even pay any attention to Chuck when he tried to talk to her.

Harnessing myself to the sled, I started pulling, but

I hadn't gone twenty yards before my lungs felt as though I were breathing fire. I was so rattled I'd forgotten to put a scarf over my mouth.

It was hard going, the snow so dry that it tugged at the runners like sand. After ten minutes Nancy took over, and all the way back to the house Ethel kept screaming and struggling. When she threw her head back the first time and I saw her face I thought for a second something terrible had happened to her—until I realized it was her tears. They'd frozen all around her eyes.

By the time we were inside the house, Nancy's cheeks and nose had turned white, and from the numbness I felt I knew mine had too. Ethel ran straight under the table and sat there crying. And no sooner was Chuck inside than he started crying too.

Nancy put the kettle on for tea while I tried to console him. It took a while before he was able to stop, and then he wanted to know when his mother was going to wake up. I had to tell him that she wasn't going to, that she was dead. Even though he knew what the word meant he couldn't accept it as meaning he'd never see her again. "Who take care me now?" he asked me.

"I'm going to take care of you."

"When my mudda come?"

"She's not going to. You're going to stay here with me and Nancy. Chuck—" He looked as though he was going to start crying again. "I need your help. Can you help me? The first thing we have to do is explain to Ethel that she has nothing to be afraid of here. She doesn't understand what's happened. You're going to have to tell her. Can you do that?"

He went over to the table and kneeled down beside his sister. She was still sniffling, but she listened to him. She almost started crying again at one point, but he made her stop. They exchanged some words, and when they were done she looked kind of lost. She let Chuck lead her out from under the table. My sense of smell had been frozen up to then, but it came back just as Ethel stood up. The worst odor in the world hit me. Her parka was covered with grease and old food, but that wasn't what it was coming from.

214

Nancy wrinkled her nose. "She must have done something in her pants."

"We'll have to give her a bath."

"The sooner the better," Nancy said. "Pee-yew."

While the water was simmering on the stove there was a knock at the door. It was Maggie and her husband with Chuck's and Ethel's things, some moccasins and clothing, a .22 rifle and a couple of pairs of children's snowshoes.

After we had enough hot water in the washtub I took off Ethel's parka, but when I tried to take off her clothes she pulled away and began to cry. I asked Chuck what was wrong.

"She not like take off clothes," he said. "Nevuh take off."

"She has to have a bath."

Chuck explained to her in Indian, pointing to the washtub. She shook her head. It was no.

"You better tell her she's going to have to," I said. "There's no two ways about it."

That did it. He explained, she took one look at Nancy and me and the next moment she dived under the bed. There was nothing else for it but to go after her, which we did. I got a bite on the hand and Nancy a good healthy kick before we dragged her out screaming to high heaven. Chuck put his fingers in his ears, and while Nancy held onto her I took off her clothes—knee-length moccasins, a light jacket, and a calico dress with another cotton dress underneath. Her undergarment had me stumped when I got to it. It was tight-fitting, like a union suit. It even had a drop seat, but there were no buttons up the front.

"What is it?" I asked Nancy.

"Indian-style underwear. The mothers sew 'em up in it around October and it stays on till April."

"How do you get it off?"

"Cut it off."

I got a pair of scissors and Nancy held her still, but as soon as I started to cut Ethel panicked. She struggled and screamed so loud it made my eardrums ache. It scared Chuck, and he began to cry in sympathy. I stopped, not knowing what to do.

215

"She's gotta have a bath, Anne," Nancy said.

I knew that, but I couldn't help feeling like a villain. The best thing to do, I thought, was get Chuck out so he wouldn't have to watch.

"Ugh," Nancy said, trying to hold Ethel away from her. I didn't blame her. The drop seat was brown, soggy and foul. Some of the stuff was on me too.

"Chuck, are you hungry?"

He said he was, and as soon as he stopped crying I got him into his parka and brought him over to the roadhouse. After I explained what was going on to Maggie, she said she'd give him something to eat and keep him until I came over for him.

When I got back, Ethel and Nancy were just as I'd left them. Ethel was still in tears. As soon as I came near her with the scissors again she was so terrified she tried to climb Nancy.

"Maybe if we gave her something to eat first she'd calm down," I said. "She loves bread and butter and honey."

"C'mon, Anne," Nancy said, "we gotta do it. Give 'er somethin' to eat now, she'll throw it right up."

"But suppose she gets a heart attack or something?"

"If anybody's gonna get a heart attack, it's gonna be us," Nancy said. "You ready?"

"Would you rather I held her?"

"If I thought you could I'd let ya. She's a wildcat, this one. I'll hold, you cut." She got Ethel in a good strong grip. "Start cutting," she yelled.

I started, shearing both sleeves up to the neck, then cutting and ripping down to her ankles, peeling the garment as I went. Finally it was all off. Naked and screaming, she looked more animal than human, her hair matted, her whole body just one mass of caked dirt and excrement.

Nancy picked her up, and together we brought her over to the tub. I tested the water. It was just right. We lowered her into it. As soon as we did, all hell broke loose. If she was frightened before, she was horrified now. I'd never have believed that a little child could have had as much strength as she did, but she went into a rage. As if we'd dumped her into a tub of ice cold water, she let out a shriek, started striking out and clawing at the two of us, and before we could stop her, water was flying in all directions and she was out of the tub. I managed to grab her wrist and the next thing I knew she was trying to bite me. If anybody had walked in just then they would have thought Nancy and I were a couple of white savages bent on killing and cooking a little Indian girl. Ethel must have thought just that, because she dodged around the room as we went after her, overturning chairs and screeching horribly. Before we were able to grab her finally, I nearly fell in the washtub and Nancy almost got a black eye.

In she went finally, fighting and clawing in a berserk rage. We didn't dare try to wash her. It was enough just to hold on to her. There wasn't but half the water left in the tub. What wasn't on Nancy and me was all over the floor, and some of it near the wall was already frozen. Ethel kept struggling to get out, thrashing around and fighting so hard that I was almost ready to give up. Until suddenly Ethel just sat back, choking out sobs, all the fight gone out of her. Nancy and I looked at each other in relief. I didn't know anything about the way I looked, but if I looked half as bad as Nancy I was a mess.

We started to wash Ethel and she let us do it. She'd done all she could and now the battle was over. She whimpered and talked to herself in Indian, even tried to tell us a couple of things, but she didn't lift a hand to stop us when we used the washcloth. She was a little scared when I added some hot water after about ten minutes, but it was only to look at me with soft liquid eyes, silently pleading with me not to hurt her.

She'd looked pretty bad when we started washing her, but once we'd shampooed her hair and washed her face even Nancy was taken with her. "Gee, Anne, if you didn't know she couldn't speak English, you'd think she was like any other kid. She's a beauty."

She was too, with skin like a dusky rose and shining black hair. By the time we were ready to take her out she was playing with the water, trying to poke holes through the layer of scum on the surface. When we stood her up and started to dry her she looked so frail

217

and helpless I'd have given anything to be able to tell her she was safe and that we weren't trying to hurt her.

We put her in bed to keep her warm, then rummaged through the stuff Maggie had brought, but there were no clothes for her. Whatever she owned she'd had on.

"I'll have to go over to the store and see what I can dig up," I told Nancy. Ethel had disappeared under the blankets and crawled down to the foot of the bed right alongside our sack of potatoes. I went over and listened.

"Sounds like we have a gopher," I said to Nancy. "Can you eat potatoes raw?"

"I don't know. I never tried 'em."

Not wanting to take any chances I pulled the blankets back. Sure enough, she'd gotten into the sack and was munching away on one. I took it away from her and she cursed me roundly before she dived back under the blankets.

I couldn't find too much in the store to fit her, a pair of bib overalls that were a little big, some long underwear, socks and a corduroy shirt, but at least she had clean clothes.

On the way back I picked up Chuck. He watched without saying anything while Nancy and I dressed Ethel. We had to roll up the bottom of the overalls and she looked lost in the shirt I'd bought, but she really looked cute. Even Chuck thought so. "Jesus Chris', Tisha," he said. "She one pretty girl, I t'ink." He went over to her and examined her carefully, then sniffed her. "Smell good, too," he added approvingly.

"Maybe you ought to introduce us," I said.

"Dis Tisha," he said pointing to me. "Tisha. An' dis Nancy." He said something to her in Indian, then pointed to us again, but Ethel didn't say anything. Chuck nudged her impatiently. "Tisha . . . Nancy," he said warningly.

"She's a little scared, Chuck. Give her time."

"No no. She say." He said something to her in Indian again and stabbed a finger at me. "Tisha."

"Tisha," she said.

"An' Nancy."

"Nassy," she mimicked.

Nancy and I applauded. "That's wonderful. She's very smart, Chuck."

"You bet," Chuck said. "I tell her she no say I give one big smack."

One thing we didn't have trouble with was getting her to eat. She wolfed down two thick slices of bread for supper and a good helping of moose roast and beans. She didn't like having her face and hands wiped, though. That made her cry.

Maggie Carew came by right after supper. "Joe brought the mother over," she said. She looked at Ethel admiringly. "Kid doesn't look half bad now. Havin' any trouble with 'em?"

"None at all."

She put a paper sack down on the table. "Some of Willard's old clothes. They might fit the girl."

I thanked her and before she went out she said, "If the two of 'em are too much of a handful maybe I could put the girl up in the bunkhouse."

"They're no trouble at all, Mrs. Carew."

"Nice of you to keep 'em here."

"I don't mind a bit."

The clothes came in handy. There was a small flannel nightie in the sack and even some diapers and rubber pants. When it came time to put Ethel to bed, though, she raised a howl and wouldn't let us. We asked Chuck to explain to her about pajamas, but he didn't understand the idea himself. He and Ethel had always slept in their clothes. She had to have the diapers, though, because she'd be sleeping between Nancy and me.

"Maybe if Ethel saw you change your clothes she wouldn't mind so much," I told Chuck. He said it was all right with him, so back I went to the store for a pair of pajamas to fit him. He was fascinated by them, liked them "too much," but Ethel was still suspicious, so we made a compromise for her—diapers under outer clothing. Before we put the diapers on her we had her go to the toilet in the cache. She was afraid of the toilet seat, though, and we finally had to settle for letting her do her business on newspaper.

We put them both in the big bed so that Ethel

219

wouldn't be scared. When Nancy and I were ready for bed a little later we'd transfer Chuck to the couch. We'd built the fire up in the schoolroom so we could work in there and let them sleep, but as soon as we went inside and started to close the door Chuck wanted to know where we were going. I told him we'd be in the schoolroom, but he said he'd be scared if we went, so we stayed. Nancy worked away on a reading comprehension test I gave her while I drew some outlines for hand puppets the kids wanted to make. Chuck and Ethel tossed and turned for a while, murmuring to each other, then they were quiet. I thought they were both asleep, but Chuck wasn't. He called to me, and I went over to him. He was still trying to understand what had happened.

"My mudda, she catch die," he said.

"Yes."

"She all by herselfs in cabin. Priddy lonely, I t'ink."

"They've taken her out."

"Where they take?"

"They put her in the cache—in back of the roadhouse." I tried not to get choked up, but it was hard.

"Still priddy lonely." He started to get up. "Maybe I go see. She not be lonely."

"She's not lonely, Chuck. She's sleeping. And she's very happy."

"You ti'nk so?"

"I know it. She'll sleep forever now. And she'll never again be cold, or hungry, or sad."

"You no tell lie? She never be hungry, be cold?"

"Never. That's the truth. Her spirit is up in Heaven now. She's very happy."

"She have big cook?"

"What's big cook?"

"Kill big fat moose. Have big cook. Eat."

"Oh yes. She has everything there."

"I like dat. She one good mudda me. You good mudda me too, Tisha. You take care me like real mudda."

"You're a fine boy, that's why. Now you go to sleep. Good night."

"Night."

220

My eyes were so wet that I could hardly see when I sat down. I looked over at Nancy. Her face was all twisted up and she was trying her best to hold back her tears. Finally she got up and went into the schoolroom. I went in right after her and the two of us stood like fools, crying silently so that Chuck wouldn't hear us.

Later on we transferred him to the couch, then we both got in on each side of Ethel. We'd left the oil lamp on so they wouldn't be scared if they woke in the middle of the night. Ethel was in a deep sleep, a lock of long black hair curled across her cheek. I pushed it back. She was lovely.

Outside a wind rose and little drafts of freezing air nipped in. I thought of Mary lying cold and alone in the dark cache. There was nobody to take care of Chuck and Ethel now, nobody at all. They were all by themselves. Back in the shack, when everybody had been standing around trying to decide what to do with them I'd wanted them right away. The longer I'd stood there listening to the whole bunch of them talking about Chuck and Ethel as if they were dirt, the more I wanted them. Maybe it was because nobody had ever wanted me either when I was a little kid—nobody except Granny. They needed somebody to take care of them, and I could do it.

"You awake, Nancy?"

"Uh-huh."

"What do you think about keeping Chuck and Ethel here?"

"For how long?"

"I don't know. But I don't want to send them back to the Indian village. Not now anyway."

"How long do you want to keep 'em?"

"As long as I can."

"Yeah, but I mean how long?"

"I'll give you one guess."

When what I was getting at finally dawned on her, she still couldn't bring herself to believe it.

"Anne—you saying you want them for your *own?*"

"Yes." Up to then I'd had doubts about it myself,

221

but saying it out loud made them all disappear. "What do you think?"

"I don't know . . . That's up to you," she said.

XVII

I asked Nancy not to tell anybody about it. Besides the fact that it was going to start a ruckus, they were still Joe Temple's children and I'd have to talk to him before I could go ahead and keep them. If he said no, there wasn't anything I could do. I wanted them, though, I knew that for sure.

For the first few days Ethel never let Chuck out of her sight. Everything was new to her and she was scared, but you wouldn't have known it from the way she acted. Not that she didn't cry. It took hardly anything to set her off. She'd start crying as soon as Chuck left the room, or when school was over and the kids left, things like that. But otherwise she was about the most self-possessed little girl there ever was. She was timid, but she had every right to be. She couldn't understand a word of all the English flying around her head.

One thing that helped was that the kids in class were nice to her—much nicer than they were to Chuck. It was partly because she wasn't any competition for them and partly because they knew she was an orphan. They didn't make fun of her or try any of the nasty things they'd tried with Chuck. In fact they all went out of their way to get her interested in something.

She and Willard took to each other from the beginning. The first morning she came in he wanted her to sit at his table. She sat down alongside of him and he started babbling to her right away, until I finally had to tell him to be quiet. By afternoon he had her coloring with crayons and making paper chains. He also had her eating the flour paste and licking the window. The first one I didn't mind too much, but the second was dangerous. It was his favorite sport, getting his tongue to stick to the window just enough so he could still pull it away easily. He'd lost a sliver of tongue doing it once and there'd been blood all over the place. I stopped it fast.

Ethel wandered around so calm and quiet most of the time you'd have thought nothing in the world bothered her, but it wasn't so. After a couple of days we started finding bits of food hidden all around. One time I found a piece of bread in my sock. Chuck explained to her that there would always be plenty of grub, but it didn't stop her. She kept stashing bits of meat and everything else here and there.

I'd always heard that mothers had a lot of trouble getting their kids to eat, but with Chuck and Ethel there wasn't a problem in the world. The only time Ethel didn't have an appetite was at supper the first day. She just stared at her plate until the rest of us finished, then right after that she threw up chunks of every color in the rainbow—all the crayons she'd been coloring with.

Having the kids around all day helped her a lot, and in a few days she was repeating words all over the place—book, sandwich, eat, dish. She was as fastidious as they come, too. Chuck always gulped his food so fast I had to keep telling him to slow down, but Ethel ate like a little princess. After we finished supper one night she put her hands out and said, "Hello?"

"Well, hello," I answered. It was the first time she'd ever said a word by herself.

She looked at Nancy and repeated it, so Nancy said hello to her too. She shook her head, got down from her chair and went over and pointed to the cupboard. "Hello?" she piped.

I went to it and looked inside. She wanted jello, I finally realized.

The fourth night she woke up screaming, throwing her arms around my neck and holding on as if there was a devil after her. Even after Nancy lit the gas lamp she was still too terrified to go back to sleep and she wouldn't let me go, so I got up and sat in the rocker with her, until an hour later her eyes closed.

I had almost a full week to go before I'd have to talk with Joe Temple about my keeping her and Chuck, and I kept putting it off. I was shy about doing it. But finally, a couple of days before Mr. Strong was due in, something Chuck did forced me to.

He'd been trouble that whole day, knocking into the other boys on the sliding pond, talking out of turn and even deliberately tearing a drawing of Isabelle's. It wasn't like him. Yet when I tried to get him to tell me what was wrong he said it was nothing. Then, just before dismissal, he threw a pencil at Evelyn Vaughn. I told him to go into my quarters and he stomped through the door and started kicking chairs around. By the time I went in after him they were all over the place. As soon as he saw me he ran out minus hat and coat and headed for the outhouse.

I left him alone, figuring he'd be back as soon as it got too cold for him, but when ten minutes went by and he was still gone I threw on a jacket and went out after him. It was dark outside. A kind of sinister gray pall hung in the air, erasing even the near hills. I pushed on the door, but Chuck had braced a foot against it. He was crying.

"Chuck?"

He didn't answer. Mr. Carew called to me from the roadhouse.

"Somebody stuck again?" He was holding an armful of wood.

"No. It's all right, thanks," I called back, then I lowered my voice. "Chuck, I wish you'd come out of there."

He didn't answer me, and I waited to hear the roadhouse door slam before I said, "Chuck?"

"Go 'way."

"It must be terribly cold in there . . . Won't you come out?"

"I never come out. I catch die, you no see me no more."

"I'd feel terrible if that happened."

224

"Oh, no. You no care. You be happy." I could hear his teeth chattering.

"Chuck, if anything happened to you I don't know what I'd do. I love you very much."

He was furious. "You lie. You one sumbitch white woman tell big lie!"

"You must be awfully mad at me . . . What did I lie about?"

"You say you take care me. You no take care me. You make me go 'way Indian village." He could hardly talk for shivering.

"Chuck, I didn't lie to you. I want you to stay with me. Don't you know that?"

"Ev'lyn, he say when Mr. St'ong come he take me 'way."

"Can I come in, Chuck? Please?"

There was a long silence, then the door moved. I pushed on it and it bumped against him. He was huddled on the floor, in the corner. I sat down between the holes. All I could see was the top of his head in the dimness, his breath misting up around it.

"Could you come up here and sit with me?"

He stayed put.

"Please, Chuck. I want to tell you something."

He had trouble standing up, his legs were so cramped. He sat down beside me, trembling, and I put an arm around him. What a place to talk with somebody you cared about, I thought, sitting and freezing in an outhouse. The only consolation was that it was too cold to smell.

"What Evelyn told you wasn't true. I'm not going to send you away—not if I can help it. I want to keep you and Ethel with me, but I have to talk to your father first."

He relaxed a little. "Why you talk with my fodda?"

"Because it's going to be up to him."

He looked up at me and he almost smiled. "My fodda no care, Tisha. He say yes. I know he say yes."

"Whether he cares or not I still have to talk to him. I'm going to tell him what a fine boy you are and that

225

I want you to stay with me. I want it very badly. You believe me?"

His arms went around me and he hugged me with all his might. "I believe, Tisha. Oh, I believe too much." He straightened up, happy. "I gonna tell that Ev'lyn he lie."

"Don't tell her anything. Not yet. Let me talk to your father first, all right? Not a word. Now for God's sake let's get out of here."

After supper I skied over to see Joe. I'd never been over to his place, but I didn't have any trouble finding it. He lived about a mile from the settlement on Stonehouse Creek. All I had to do was follow a sled trail till I reached the creek, then follow the creek up the hill to his cabin.

As many times as I had gone out at night alone it still scared me a little. There was no wind, and a bright crescent moon shone down. Everything was so still it was like being alone in a big wax museum. Nothing moved. Every twig, every bush that pushed up through the whiteness stood out in the pale moonlight. By the time I reached Stonehouse Creek, slung my skis over my shoulder and started up the hill I felt almost like two people, one of them breathing hard and making all kinds of noise, the other out there watching me moving along, a tiny speck in a big white sea. The hill was steeper than it looked, and before I was halfway up I was sorry I'd brought the skis. They weighed a ton.

Joe's dogs began to howl and act up before I reached the top. He came out to see what was going on and I waved to him.

"Tea or coffee?" he called.

"Tea!"

He disappeared inside and came out again just as I reached the top. The racket from the kennel made it impossible to hear, so he didn't say anything until we were inside.

"No chaperone?"

"I couldn't get her to climb that hill."

He held out his hands. "I'll take your duds."

I slipped off my parka and plopped down into a

chair. He had a nice place, just the kind I'd have expected. There were a few guns on the wall—a high-powered rifle with a telescopic sight, a shotgun and a revolver—and they all were clean and gleaming with oil. He took as good care of his things as he did himself. He'd made a built-in basin for the kitchen counter, and on the shelf over it all his toilet articles were lined up neatly—hairbrush and comb, shaving brush and mug, shaving lotion and straight razor. The whole place was so neat and clean compared to mine I felt like a slob. With all the kids trooping in and out, my place was always a mess.

He had a good library too. Some painted boxes nailed to the wall were filled with books: Dickens, Sinclair Lewis, Fitzgerald, Milton. A can of tobacco and a rack of pipes sat on a crate beside a rocking chair. His cot was made army-fashion and was pushed against the wall. There were some nice furs he'd hung on wooden hoops. I couldn't tell what they all were, but I recognized the silky rust-gray, almost topaz color of lynx, and two soft, shining pelts of silver and black fox.

The only thing I didn't like was the odor of all the furs that were piled on newspapers. They smelled rank. It was only too bad that the women who were going to wear them couldn't see the whole sickening process of trapping, killing and skinning the animals they came from. They'd never wear them again.

A few burlap sacks already crammed with furs were piled by the door.

"That's some catch," I said.

"Half of it's last season's." He handed me a steaming cup of tea. "The price wasn't that good, so I held on-to them."

"That was smart."

"Same thing anybody would do if they could afford it, but most of these old-timers can't. That's how you make money in this country—have enough money so you can hold out for your price."

The cup felt nice and warm. Joe poured himself some coffee, then took a bottle of Canadian whiskey down from the shelf.

"Mind?"

"No, go ahead."

Just to be courteous he offered me some. I said no and he poured some into his cup. "Skoal," he said, taking a sip.

"Joe—"

"Don't say a word. I want to see if I can guess what this visit is all about. You didn't come for my company, I'm sure of that. Or for supper—it's too late. I guess I give up."

"It's about Chuck and Ethel."

"What about them?"

"Can I have them?"

"Are you serious?"

"Of course I am."

He laughed. "What do you want them for?"

"What's the difference?"

"You're asking me to give you something. I want to know why you want it."

"Joe, I just want them."

"Good enough. Take them."

I'd expected him to say no and I had a dozen arguments all ready. Now I hardly knew what to say. "You mean it?"

"Sure. You know you're going to get people all riled up, though, don't you?"

"I guess so."

"Doesn't that suggest anything to you?"

"Like what?"

"Like the fact that ever since you've been here you've been getting them riled up."

"Is that my fault?"

"Whose else is it? You're a genuine card, let me tell you."

"I don't know what you're talking about."

"You mean it doesn't seem peculiar to you when a young single girl decides all of a sudden that she's going to play mother, especially when she knows that everybody isn't exactly fond of the offspring she'll be playing it with."

"I'm not playing anything."

"Then why not avoid a whole mess and let those kids go to the Indian village where they belong?"

"Joe, you know what that Indian village is like. It's not a place for a dog, much less for children. Don't they mean anything to you at all?"

"No."

"How about Mary—did she?"

"What's she got to do with this?"

"You're asking me questions. Why can't I ask you?"

"Mary and I were finished over a year ago. I didn't ask her to come out here. She came on her own. I tried to get her to go back a half a dozen times. I told her I'd give her enough money to tide her over the winter if she would, but she wouldn't."

"She must have loved you an awful lot."

"That was her hard luck."

He knew how cruel that sounded, but he didn't apologize. He took a long swallow of coffee, finishing it. Then he got up. "Why'd you come into this country?" he asked me while he poured himself some more.

"To see it."

"No wonder you go around like Little Miss Muffet. Everybody took bets the day you arrived. Half of them bet you'd last about a month after freeze-up and the other half bet you'd stay and freeze to death."

"Sorry to disappoint everyone." I started to get up.

"Don't get so insulted." He made a motion for me to sit down and poured some more whiskey into his coffee. "It's about time somebody told you a couple of things. The first is that it wouldn't be a bad idea for you to get your nose out of the air and stop judging people so much. Maybe you came here for the fun of it, but nobody else did. They came to make a strike, get rich and move on, because that's all this country's good for."

"You sound as though you don't like it here," I said.

"You're beginning to get the idea."

"Then why do you stay?"

"For the same reason everybody else does," he answered. "I can't afford to go. Two kinds of people live here—the ones that have investments, like me, and the ones that don't have enough money to pack up and get out, like these old-timers who have it in the back of their mind that they're gonna hit a big pay streak one of these days. That's why they hang on even though their bones ache and they'd like nothing better than to hightail it for California and forget this place ever existed."

The whiskey had relaxed him, or maybe he simply needed to talk. He stopped long enough to take a deep breath.

"Maybe you don't like the way I treated Mary, but what do you know about her and me? She knew what she was doing. I never told her I was gonna marry her, even though there were times when I thought about it. But all I'd have to do was think to myself, what happens when I go Outside—when the two of us go Outside? What could I say to people when I introduced her? 'Here y'are folks, meet the wife. She knows everything there is to know about curing fur, making jerky, drying fish, chopping wood or sewing mittens. Just don't talk to her about politics, literature, current events, art, mortgages, or anything else like that.' "

I tried to interrupt him, but he wouldn't let me. "Well, the problem never came up, because we broke up. I didn't want her to come out here, but she made up her mind she was gonna do it and that was that. I gave her just enough grub to keep going, hoping she'd go back to the Indian village. She wouldn't. So I thought if I simply didn't give her anything she'd be forced to go back. Well, it didn't work. She made up her mind she was gonna stay, and when an Indian gets it in their head to do something, nothing gets it out."

I got up and asked him to let me have my parka.

"I've got a couple more things to say," he went on, "then if you want I'll walk you back to your place."

"I can make it on my own," I said.

He took my parka down from the rack and handed it to me. "Have it your way," he said. "You stepped on a lot of toes since you've been here and if you weren't as nice a kid as you are you wouldn't have gotten away with it. Or maybe it's just that you're a kid and so everybody looked the other way. If people don't like Indians they don't like Indians and that's their business. I've got nothing against Indians myself, but I'm not about to

230

start lecturing other people on how to feel toward 'em, and that goes for half-breeds too. Fred Purdy did you the biggest favor in the world when he pulled out of here, only you don't have enough sense to see that. This is his home. He has to live in this country. He's not about to make it tough on himself by messing around with a white girl. He did the right thing by you. You ought to be grateful. Instead you have to go ahead and stick your foot right smack in people's faces again and take these kids. Well I'm telling you you're making a mistake."

"You all done?"

"All done."

"You asked me before why I came into this country. I'll tell you the truth. I thought I was going to find something wonderful here—everything I ever dreamed about. Maybe that's stupid, but that's what I thought. Well, I found out one thing. People here aren't much different from the ones back in the States. The only difference is that here they can do anything they want, which means acting just about as mean and selfish as they can."

"You want a soapbox?"

"I'm just telling you how I feel."

"Oh, for Christ's sake, Anne, put on some rouge and lipstick, have some fun, and stop worrying about the underprivileged."

He looked so smug and superior I felt like gnashing my teeth. "Joe, honestly, I'd really like to give you a punch. All you've told me so far is that you don't like the country and people around here don't like Indians. Well, if I want to like both of them that's my right—and I'm getting sick and tired of people looking at me as if I'm a nut because of it."

He smiled. "It hasn't stopped you so far. Go ahead, take the kids. Do what you like with them. Just remember they're still part savage."

"If they are it's probably the part they got from you."

I thought he'd get mad at that, but he didn't. "I'm sorry," I said.

"Forget it."

I started to go. "I can still have them?"

"They're all yours . . . Wait a minute."

He walked over to one of the burlap sacks and ripped it open. Peering inside, he pulled out first one, then another black fox pelt. They were perfectly matched and worth a lot of money. He fluffed them out, then clamped the snouts together and draped them around my neck.

"Peace offering," he said.

The way he was smiling made me feel sorry for him. His cabin was neat, and he was pretty well off, but when it came right down to it, all he had was a comfortable place to be lonely in.

"Thanks, Joe." I said. "Will you do me one more favor? Don't say anything to anybody. There's no use in anybody knowing until Mr. Strong comes in."

He said he wouldn't.

Outside, when I got to the edge of the hill and looked down, I couldn't bring myself to push off. I was scared I'd run into a tree.

"What's the matter?" Joe asked.

"It's pretty steep."

"That it is."

I put the skis together and sat down on them. "Don't laugh," I said. "Give me a push."

He pushed me off. Halfway down the skis separated and I went tumbling. The skis went on down without me.

I could hear Joe laughing. "Still in one piece?" he called. He didn't have to raise his voice. It carried clearly.

"Just divine." I did a quick dance step that made him laugh even more, then I collected the ski poles and the furs and walked and slid down the rest of the way. He was still in a good mood when I reached bottom and started strapping on my skis.

"So you think we're all mean, eh?"

"Sometimes. Not most of the time." It felt strange to be talking with him as if we were in the same living room and not a quarter of a mile apart. "How about you? You really think this is such an awful place?"

"Sometimes. Not most of the time . . . Sometimes I

stand up here and I look out over everything, and then I think, it's all mine. All of it. I don't have to buy it, pay taxes on it or worry about it. It's mine." He was quiet a fêw seconds and I thought he was going to go on. Instead he just said, "Well, goodnight, kid."

"Goodnight, Joe."

I felt good all the way home.

Ethel was asleep, but Chuck was still up. When I told him the news he let out a yell and hugged me. "I know you make him say yes, Tisha, I know you make him say yes!" He was so excited he didn't fall asleep until after ten.

"What do you think Mr. Strong will say?" I asked Nancy later on. He'd be expecting to take Chuck and Ethel back to the Indian village along with Mary's body.

"He'll be speechless," Nancy said.

"Be nice if everybody else was too."

"Don't you worry, they won't be."

XVIII

On the days Mr. Strong came into the settlement I always let the class out about fifteen minutes before he arrived. On those days there were always at least one or two visiting dog teams tied up by the roadhouse. They belonged to miners and trappers who'd mushed in either to pick up goods or to send stuff out. One minute they'd be lying in the snow all quiet, maybe sleeping, the next they'd be lifting their heads, then getting up and stretching. After that, between them and the local dogs it was pure pandemonium—barking and howling that kept getting louder and louder until owners and drivers put a stop to it. Sure enough, if it didn't happen to be a stray animal or a stranger that had started them off, fifteen minutes later Mr. Strong's horse-drawn sled would come rumbling into the settlement. How they could tell he was on the way nobody knew, but they could.

This time they started barking right after lunch. As soon as the class heard them everybody stopped work and listened, waiting to make sure it wasn't something else. Even though it was just about the right time there was no guarantee it was Mr. Strong. There wasn't even a guarantee he'd come in at all on the day he was supposed to. Too many things could hold him up: heavy drifts, a sudden storm or an accident. Now that it was February the weather was especially freakish. The past few days you couldn't even hang out wash. No sooner would you get it on the line than it froze, and then the wind would bang it up against you hard enough to hurt.

So we were quiet, listening as the barking became more and more excited. And finally someone down by the roadhouse yelled out exactly what we wanted to hear: "Wahoo-o-o-o! The dogs say he's a-comin'!"

After I let the class go I threw a sweater around my shoulders and went out. The air was flying white and it was colder than it usually was when it snowed. I ran across the road to check the fire in the stable. I always started it in the morning when Mr. Strong was due in, then kept it going all day. After the long, miserable trip his horses had, the least they were entitled to was a warm stable. After I put another log in the stove I filled the feed bags, then ran back to my quarters. There were a lot more dog teams tied up near the roadhouse than usual, I saw. The word was out that prices at the Seattle Fur Exchange were at their highest now and everybody was shipping their catch out.

Fifteen minutes later everybody including me was waiting outside the post office, stomping around to keep warm.

Jimmy and the rest of the kids were busy piling up snow at the edge of the settlement. They did it every time Mr. Strong was due in, built a barrier a few feet high just so they could watch Mr. Strong's horses kick it to pieces when they went through it. Chuck and

Ethel were with them, making their contribution. As soon as we heard the jangle of the bells in the distance the kids came running over to the crowd. Ben Norvall leaned down over Chuck. "Been happy staying with the teacher, have ya?"

Chuck said, "Yiss. Tisha make good grub me."

"That's the way to a man's heart," Ben said. His moustache was peppered with snowflakes. "Bet you'll sure be sorry to go back to that Indian village now."

"I no go back," Chuck said. "I stay here."

"Is that so?" Ben looked at me inquiringly, but I pretended not to be paying attention.

Uncle Arthur was on the other side of me.

"B'gawd, missis, it was good of ya to take care of the little tykes. I ain't the marryin' kind, but if I wuz I'd ask for your hand and take these two to boot."

"Then they could all go up to the Indian village and live happily ever after," I heard Angela say to somebody.

Jake Harrington came over with Rebekah and Lily. "Howdy, Teacher."

"Hello, Mr. Harrington."

"How's my woman doing in school?"

"Fine."

"Hope so." He smiled. "I can't get a lick of work out of 'er these days with all the studyin' she's doing. Next thing you know she'll want to go to college."

We heard the bells and everybody got quiet. A few minutes later the sled materialized, rocking and tinkling and crunching its way toward us.

Mr. Strong was standing up looking like a big bear, furred from head to toe, cracking his whip and urging the two horses on. He didn't have to, they wanted to get here as bad as he did, but it made a good impression on everybody and showed he was on the job. As soon as the horses smashed through the snow barrier the kids had built, they tried to head over to the stable, but Jake Harrington and a couple of other men ran out and shied them back towards the post office. They'd had a rough trip, you could see that. The corners of their mouths dripped blood from where the frozen bit

235

had torn them up and their blankets were hung with icicles. The two of them were just one big cloud of steam.

There was somebody sitting up front alongside Mr. Strong. As soon as the sled stopped he jumped down and yelled at the men who were crowding forward. "Just hold on, all a you! Lemme get my wife and baby out."

It was Elmer, Maggie Carew's son-in-law. He moved to the back of the sled where somebody was already pushing up the covering canvas from underneath. When he pulled it back, there was Jeannette, swaddled in a cocoon of furs. She started to hand Elmer a little bundle wrapped in blankets, but Maggie was already alongside of him and said, "Give 'er to me!"

While he helped Jeannette down all the women crowded around Maggie to have a look at the baby. She wouldn't let them see it though. She headed right over to the roadhouse with it, not even taking a peek herself. If they wanted to see it, they could come over later, she said. She wasn't about to let it catch its death out there in the cold.

I got all my mail, then went back to my quarters with Nancy and the children. There was a letter from Lester Henderson, and he didn't have very cheering news. It wasn't that he didn't like my work or think I wasn't doing a good job. "Your reports are thorough and your pupils seem to be making excellent progress," he wrote. "Personally, I'm more than satisfied with your work, especially since this is your first year."

> However, there may be some difficulty in my placing you in Eagle next year. At this point I can't say for certain, but please don't let it concern you. I have any number of other schools I can place you in, and you may rest assured that I'll do so with pride . . .

I knew what that meant. People had written to him about me, and the chances were that the school board in Eagle wouldn't want me teaching there. I tried not to let it bother me too much, but it did. I wanted to teach in Eagle. It was close by and I knew what it would be like. On top of that Maggie Carew was moving there, and even if she wasn't crazy about me, she was somebody I knew. I didn't relish the idea of going to some strange place where I'd have to start all over again.

After supper, Nancy started to get dressed up to go over to the roadhouse. What with everybody coming in from all over to send out their furs it was kind of an occasion and there was going to be a dance and partying. I had to go over to Mr. Strong's store to go over all the accounts with him and give him the cash I'd taken in, but I kept putting it off until Nancy was all dressed, then I couldn't put it off any longer. "I'll be back soon," I told her.

Joe Temple was banging away at the piano when I went by the roadhouse and everybody was singing *Yes, Sir! That's My Baby*. I was hoping the store would be empty, but Mr. Vaughn, Harry Dowles and a couple of other men were sitting around the oil-drum stove when I walked in. The place was suffocating with heat and tobacco smoke. Harry Dowles shifted his quid of chewing tobacco and asked me if I was coming over to the roadhouse.

"I don't think so," I said. I didn't want to drag Chuck and Ethel over there, tonight of all nights.

"Too bad." He spat into the big tin can sitting by the stove. "Fred Purdy's liable to show up." Harry's wife was the one who'd taken back the washboiler from me when I threatened to quit if Chuck didn't stay in the school. Because he and his wife weren't on speaking terms, they were always asking other people to relay what they wanted to say to each other. Once they trapped me between them, and for over fifteen minutes they drove me crazy repeating to the two of them what they could have told each other in a third of the time. They were both peculiar people, and it made me nervous to be around them. Him more than her. With a pale pudgy face, some missing front teeth, and eyes like little pieces of black coal, he looked like an evil snowman. He was always acting as if he knew something you didn't, and I thought he was just being smart now, so I didn't pay him any attention. But then he said, "I'm givin' you the straight goods, Teacher—ain't I, Walt?"

Mr. Strong was leaning over the counter going over some figures. He nailed one of them with his pencil and looked up at me over his glasses. "Fred came in with me," he said.

"How come I didn't see him?"

"He jumped off at Stonehouse Creek and siwashed it from there."

Harry Dowles chuckled. While I went over the accounts with Mr. Strong I knew they were all giving each other know-it-all looks in back of me, but I just pretended I wasn't any more affected than if I'd just been told it was snowing outside. I wouldn't give them the satisfaction. I kept hoping they'd leave before I talked with Mr. Strong about Chuck and Ethel, but they stayed put. After we finished tallying up I was about to mention it, but Mr. Strong beat me to it.

"Too bad about Mary Angus," he said.

"Yes, it was."

"We all have to take the sunset trail sometime or other," somebody said.

"That's the truth," Harry Dowles said.

"I'll be bringing the body back to the Indian village," Mr. Strong said. "I won't be paid for it, but it's my duty. It was commendable of you to look after the two youngsters."

"I didn't mind at all."

"You may bring them over here tonight if you wish. I can give them a couple of sleeping bags. Or if you don't mind I can pick them up before I leave tomorrow."

"You won't have to do either," I said. "They're going to stay with me."

He peered at me over his glasses again. "I don't understand."

"I'm going to keep them for a while. I don't think they ought to go back to the Indian village just yet."

Mr. Vaughn made a snorting noise and Harry Dowles spat. He must have missed the tin can because I heard

238

the squirt sizzle against the stove. "Kinda got your hands full as it is, don't ya, Teacher?" he asked.

Mr. Strong frowned at him. "I'm having a conversation with this lady, Mr. Dowles. I'd be pleased if you wouldn't interrupt." He turned back to me. "Madam, I'm sure your intentions are good, but those children belong among their own people."

"I want to keep them with me, Mr. Strong."

"I believe that you are all of nineteen years old—"

"No, I'm twenty now."

"Since you have not reached the age of consent, I don't see how you are entitled to take charge of children that do not belong to you."

"I already spoke with Joe Temple about it. He said it's all right with him."

"For how long do you intend to keep them?"

"I don't know."

"I asked you a simple question because I am afraid you are on the verge of making a grievous error. How long do you intend to keep them?"

"For quite some time."

"Quite some time," Mr. Vaughn mimicked. "Jesus Christ." He got up without another word, took his parka from the wall and walked out. He'd be headed for the roadhouse to tell everybody. The others stayed put.

"I'd suggest, madam, that you bring those two children here tonight."

"I've pretty well made up my mind."

"I would be doing you a service if I were to go over to your quarters right now and take them forcibly."

"And I'll help you out," Harry Dowles said.

"I don't think you'd do something like that, Mr. Strong," I said. I was pretty upset by now, scared he'd do it. He shook his head a little and his mouth tightened up. "Goodnight, madam," he said finally.

I walked out shaking. I'd wanted to stop at the roadhouse and see Maggie's granddaughter, but with Mr. Vaughn inside spreading the good news about Chuck and Ethel, I wasn't about to.

Nancy asked me right away how it had gone and I told her what Mr. Strong had said.

239

"Well, if he did come over for 'em he'd have plenty of help. You want me to stay?"

"No. You go on and have a good time. I'm not worried," I lied. I didn't mention the news about Fred.

After she left I played tic-tac-toe with Chuck for a while, then after he and Ethel were in bed I sat down to write to Mr. Henderson. I told him that if he could manage it I'd prefer to teach in Eagle, but that if he couldn't I'd take another school. I also wrote him about Chuck and Ethel, explaining who they were. "I'll be keeping them with me at least until June," I wrote, "and I have the feeling you'll be getting some letters about them from people." I tried to kid about it to take the edge off a little.

> Ethel, the little girl, sleeps with Nancy and me, so between the three of us and the potatoes you might say I have about the most crowded bed in the Forty Mile. It will be emptying out a little pretty soon, though. We're getting low on potatoes.

While I was addressing the envelope there were quick footsteps on the porch and the door was flung open. I was scared out of my wits, thinking it was a bunch from the roadhouse come to take the kids, but it was Nancy. She had tears in her eyes and a big red welt on her cheek. Maggie Carew was right in back of her, fuming mad. She hadn't even bothered to put on a shawl. "Just what the hell are you up to now!" she yelled before I had a chance to say anything.

"What happened?"

"What does it look like?" Maggie said. "She nearly got her head knocked off on account a you."

"The kids are asleep, Mrs. Carew."

I brought the lamp into the schoolroom and we closed the door behind us. "Are you crazy?" Maggie hissed at me.

"What happened?"

"She sassed Angela and Angela walloped her one and it's all your goddamned fault."

"It isn't her fault," Nancy said. "Nobody asked Angela to hit me and if you'd of just let me alone—"

"She'd of really given it to ya, so shut up." She turned to me. "Are you keepin' those kids?"

"Yes, Mrs. Carew—"

"I don't want to hear any blabber. All I wanna hear is that those kids are goin' outta here. Otherwise there's gonna be hell to pay."

"Mrs. Carew—"

She wouldn't let me talk. "Do you have any idea what you're doing? You got half the people in this place thinkin' you're nuts and the other half ready to lynch ya."

This time she let me talk. "Mrs. Carew, I'm doing what I think is right. If those two kids were white nobody would think twice about my keeping them here."

"If they were white they wouldn't *be* here! Look, I'm try'na tell you somethin' for your own good. You keep those kids and you're askin' for it. Goin' daffy over that half-breed was bad enough, but this takes the cake. Do you realize you're lousin' up your whole future?"

"I'm not worried about it."

"Well you better. You better worry about a lot of things from here on in. There's talk over to the roadhouse about some a them comin' over here and takin' those kids whether you like it or not."

That did it. I saw red. I was so mad that if I'd had a lightning bolt I'd have thrown it at that roadhouse and everybody in it. "I'll be right back," I said.

I went into the cache and put a box by the wall. Getting up on it, I felt around for the nickel-plated revolver, my hand finally closing around the holster. It was freezing cold, and if I hadn't been so mad I'd have realized I was in for a shock.

"What are you gonna do with that?" Maggie said when I marched back into the schoolroom.

"If I have to I'm going to use it." I took the revolver out of its holster. "I'm going to keep this out until I go to sleep tonight, and when I go to sleep I'm going to put it under my pillow. Please do me a favor. You tell anybody at that roadhouse who has a mind to set foot in here and take those children from me that if they try to, so help me God I'll shoot 'em. I will shoot them dead."

"You'd be crazy enough, wouldn't you"?

"You are absolutely right."

"I'll tell 'em. But I'll tell you one thing too. Maybe you don't know it, but I been stickin' my neck out for you. Come spring I'm leavin' here for Eagle as you well know and buyin' the Adkins's roadhouse there. That Adkins woman is on the school board and she wrote me to find out if you were as crazy as she's been hearin'. Well, I wrote her back, sayin' you were just a chee-chako and didn't know the ropes, but that you were a damn good teacher and if she could swing it, to see that the school board didn't turn you down. She came back to me and said she'd do it. Well, I'm gonna tell you here and now that I'm about to change my mind and tell her you're as crazy as a bedbug and that compared to you that Mrs. Rooney is a patron saint. Now are those kids leavin' here tomorrow or ain't they?"

"They're staying with me."

"Then that's the blow that killed Father. I wash my hands of the whole thing. I'll tell you one more thing, young lady. This ain't over yet—not by a long shot. As for you, dummox," she said to Nancy before she left, "you stay out of Angela's way."

As soon as she was out the door I let out the yelp I'd been holding in and rushed over to the stove. Throwing open the door, I shoved the revolver in as far as I could without burning my hand.

Nancy was wide-eyed. "What's wrong!"

"It's stuck to my hand."

I kept hopping around in front of that stove as if I had to go to the outhouse. A few seconds later the metal warmed up enough. I dropped the revolver on the table with a sigh of relief and started blowing on my hand.

"What'd you hold onto it for?" Nancy said.

"Just to make a point."

My hand was all right. A couple of blisters, that

242

was all. I asked Nancy what happened between her and Angela.

"Aah," she sneered, "Angela was saying things about you, about how you and Fred carried on and that he'd probably lived with you a couple of times. She said she had a good mind to come over here and wipe the floor with you and feed Chuck and Ethel to her dogs. I told 'er she oughtta mind her own business and she walloped me."

"We better stay out of her way."

"I'm not afraid of 'er.

"I am."

"You heard about Fred bein' back, I guess," Nancy said a little later.

"Yeah."

"I guess they musta given him a real bad time."

"I'll bet they did."

We didn't sleep too well that night. Every time I heard somebody go by I expected them to come charging in. But nobody bothered us.

XIX

"Cargo," I said to the children I was giving a spelling test to the next morning. "The riverboat carried a cargo of provisions and supplies."

"Willard's licking the window again, Teacher," Joan Simpson said.

"Willard," I called, "I've told you for the last time to cut that out." Yesterday under his expert guidance Ethel had finally left part of her tongue on the window. She'd literally gushed blood for a while and it had frightened her into a screaming fit. It almost did the same for me.

"If you were busy doing your own work," I snapped at Joan, "you wouldn't care what Willard was doing." Joan gave me a hurt look and went back to doing the simple sums I'd given her. I shouldn't have snapped at her but I was nervous. I could hear Mr. Strong swinging open the doors to his stable across the road. He'd be leaving in a few minutes, and even though I didn't think he'd try to take Chuck and Ethel by force I was still a little worried. I hadn't slept much last night. I'd kept having weird dreams that I was a little girl again, sleeping on a cot in the kitchen, and I'd kept waking up all night, thinking that any minute Angela and the other vigilantes might come charging in.

Rebekah was aggravating me too. For some reason she was in a bad mood when she came in this morning, especially with Chuck and Ethel. Ethel had sidled up to her while she and Lily were copying letters together out of the alphabet book. Putting her finger on the open page Ethel said, "Book?" Rebekah shoved her away. She gave her such a hard push that Ethel started crying and Nancy had had to take her into my quarters. A little later when I asked Rebekah to let Chuck work with her and Lily at their table she said there was no room for him. I let it go and sat him alongside of Joan, but it had irritated me.

"Through," I went on. "The train went through the tunnel."

"That's a hard one," Isabelle said.

"Nah, it's easy," Jimmy Carew said happily. He started to write and Evelyn Vaughn tried to peek at what he was doing, but he cupped a hand around his work.

"Yah!" I heard Mr. Strong yell to the horses. Everybody looked up as the jangle of bells sounded outside and the sled was on its way. I sat back and relaxed. I looked at my watch. It was 10:30. Nancy was taking the test also, so I asked Rebekah to take the littles ones out for recess.

When the test was over nobody else wanted to go out, so I left Nancy in charge and went outside myself. Chuck and Willard were busy terrorizing the girls by throwing snowballs at them and Rebekah was shouting

244

at Chuck in Indian. *"Awnee!"* she yelled to him: Come over here!

He didn't listen. Instead he threw some snow at Joan. Rebekah stalked over to him, grabbed a handful of his parka and shook him viciously.

"Rebekah!"

She let him go and he fell on his behind. He got up and was about to kick her when I grabbed him. "Stop it!"

"She hurt me. I not like her one goddamn bit," he said. "Sumbitch dirty black Injun!"

"You will not use that kind of language!"

"She call me same, say me dirty black Injun I say same her."

"Go inside. I'll talk with you later."

He stomped in, slamming the door behind him. The other kids were watching and I told them to go ahead and play, we'd be going inside in a few minutes. "Rebekah, why are you picking on him?" I asked her.

"He one dirty mean kid, that kid. Him and sister. Dirty and ugly them both."

"They're not dirty and they're certainly not ugly."

"You not tell me!" she huffed. "I see lotsa Indian kids and I tell you you make one big mistake not send Indian village. Chuck, he no damn good and Ethel same thing."

"You still haven't told me why you're picking on them."

"I *tell* you, no? Kids no damn good. Both ugly like Uncle Arthur."

"From now on keep your hands off them."

I walked away from her and started the kids playing *Ring Around the Rosie*. Ethel didn't know what it was all about, but she joined in anyway and they had a good time. Rebekah came up behind me.

"Tisha . . ."

"What is it?" I didn't bother to turn around.

"I no like you be *sahnik* me," she said.

I'd heard Chuck use the word, so I knew that it meant angry. "I'm not *sahnik* with you," I lied.

"You *sahnik*."

"All right, I'm mad," I said, turning. "It just seems to me that you're going out of your way to be nasty to Chuck and Ethel and I don't like it. I don't like it at all."

She looked so contrite I felt bad.

"You A-number-one fine lady, Tisha, I have good feel in my heart for you. Like you too much. Want you be happy."

"What has that got to do with Chuck and Ethel?"

"You no savvy lotsa things in No'th country. You catch big troubles you keep this kids. Everybody hate— not like see Tisha-no-husband be motha for dirty Injun kids. I try help you. Be mean. Tell you kids no good, maybe you send Indian village. You see?"

"Yes."

"You not be *sahnik* no more?"

"No, but try to be nice to them, will you? They need it badly."

"You keep for sure?"

"For sure."

"You no worry." She patted me on the shoulder. "I treat nice."

Before we went back in she said, "I make one big lie, Tisha. They good little children. Smart. Ethel, she pretty like Mary. Chuck, he pretty like Joe Temple. I tell you truth now."

"Thanks, Rebekah."

"You welcome."

After lunch the weather turned so cold I had to put the little children in my bed again, and at dismissal time I kept Isabelle and Joan in. They were both too young to let them go home alone in this cold.

Joan's mother picked her up a few minutes after school was over, but no one came for Isabelle until a half hour later. Somehow I had a feeling it was going to be Fred, and sure enough, it was. I'd kept preparing myself for when I'd be seeing him again, and I'd made up my mind to be level-headed and poised. The last thing I was going to do, I'd said to myself, was act as if the world had come to an end just because things had worked out the way they had. As soon as he walked in, though, I felt the kind of lurch you get when you walk

246

downstairs in the dark and think there's one more step where there isn't. He came in, bringing the sharp tang of cold air with him, and any poise I thought I'd have turned to mush.

Not that he did much better. No sooner did he say hello to me and Nancy than he let Chuck buttonhole him and show him a couple of things he'd made in school. He looked through the book of minerals Chuck had made as if every page had a special message for him. Finally Nancy took the kids into the schoolroom so we could talk by ourselves, and at first we just sat there like two blocks of ice.

"I guess you're glad to be back," I said.

"I sure am," he answered.

"You back to stay?"

"Uh-huh."

We both started to say something at the same time, then like Pierre and Gaston we told each other to go ahead and talk first. We were so polite you'd have thought we were the king and queen of England. "I was just going to say," I said, "that I guess you heard about my taking Chuck and Ethel."

"Me and everybody else in the Forty Mile," he said.

"What did you think?"

"That it was just the kind of thing I'd expect you'd do."

He meant it as a compliment, but I couldn't help kidding him. "Oh you would, would you?"

"Yes, I would. That's the way you are." The way he said it made me feel like glowing, but then I had to go and put my foot in it.

"Why'd you come over?" I blurted out, and as soon as I did I was sorry. I should have kept things light. Instead I had to open my big mouth and force things.

"I wanted to see you one more time," he said.

"You going away again?"

"No."

"Oh."

"I just came over to say good-bye."

"That's stupid." There I go again, I thought, saying exactly the wrong thing. "I mean I told you in my let-

247

ter that I wouldn't act any way around you but like a friend. Didn't you believe me?"

"Yes I did, but—"

"Well, then why do we have to say good-bye? Can't we even be around each other, be friends?"

He shook his head as if he was tired. "I shouldn't even have come over," he said. "I just can't make you understand."

"No, you can't," I said, trying to get angry. If I didn't I was afraid I'd start crying and I wasn't going to do that. I'd cried enough already. "I can't understand why two people who like each other aren't even entitled to look at each other . . . Fred, you're the one person around here who really means something to me . . . I love you. I love you very much. I don't want you or anybody in your family to be hurt, and I swear that none of you will be because of me. Can't you believe that?"

His elbow was resting on the table. Impulsively I put my hand on his. "Oops, wrong thing," I said, pulling it back. "See, I'm learning already."

He almost smiled, but not quite. "Do you know why I left Steel Creek?"

"Because they treated you lousy there."

"That was part of it, but not the whole thing. I knew when I went that the men wouldn't be too friendly. The only reason I was hired in the first place was because the foreman is a friend of my father, so I got what I expected. But I finally realized that there wasn't any point in staying there. The reason I went was to take the pressure off you and my mother, but after a while I realized that I could do the same thing even if I came back. All I had to do was make sure that you and I stayed away from each other. That way everybody'd be happy."

"Except you and me."

He shrugged, then he got up.

"I guess you won't be at the next dance, then."

"I'll be out on the trap line."

I got up too. "How about the one after?"

"Same thing."

248

He hadn't taken off his parka. It was untied at the throat and his neck was the color of coffee and cream, his face darker. I remembered how he'd smelled of wood smoke every time he held me.

Inside the schoolroom we could hear Nancy and the children tossing rope rings onto the wooden post. Chuck must have made a ringer because he shouted excitedly.

Fred said, "Anne, if you ever need me, if you ever need me for anything at all, I'll be here. That's what I came over to tell you."

"Thanks. Should we shake hands now or something?"

He just stared at me without saying anything for the longest time. "I didn't mean that," I said finally.

"I know. But I meant what I said."

He went past me to the schoolroom door. Opening it, he told Isabelle it was time to go. A couple of minutes later they left.

"What did he say?" Nancy asked me.

"Good-bye."

A few days later, when it rained, Mr. Purdy showed up for Isabelle. The following week Mrs. Purdy came over for her. Like Fred, it just wasn't in her nature to stay mad at someone. We had a cup of tea before she took Isabelle home. She didn't pay any attention to Chuck and Ethel at all except to glance at them once in a while, then her eyes would go right past them as if they didn't exist. But she knew they were there. Chuck was working on a spear and doing a beautiful job on it. He'd found a piece of metal somewhere, cut a groove in the end of the spear and fitted it in and tied it with rawhide, then he'd painted it and added some ptarmigan feathers. It was turning out to be a work of art. When he showed it to Mrs. Purdy, she managed a grudging compliment.

"How long you take care them, Ahnne?" she asked me.

"They're with me to stay. I wouldn't give them up for the world."

She shook her head disapprovingly. "You are foolish. There are many people who do not like this, a fine white girl who is teacher ruin reputation with such children."

"Frankly, I think they've finally stopped caring one way or the other."

"This is not so. Here in bush we all live together—like people in one house with many rooms. You have most important room in whole house. If people have argument with you they cannot come here. They do not wish this to happen."

"They don't come here anyway. I don't have anything to do with most of the people here."

"Ah, but you are wrong. I tell you long time ago, Ahnne, you are verree important person in settlement." She waved a hand around the room. "Here children come school—my Isabelle, Vaughn girls, Carew children, others. All these people must be friendly with you—talk with you. People come here for dance. They must talk with you or not come. You have keys Mr. Strong's store. People come store must talk with you. If they tell you truth, no more can they come. Better not to tell truth, be friendly, talk. Yet inside"—she tapped her heart—"they very angry."

I'd never thought of it that way, but Mrs. Purdy was right.

"I don't think there's anything I can do about it, Mrs. Purdy."

"Indeed, Ahnne, there is something make you happy, make everybody happy." She looked over at Chuck and Ethel, picked up a handful of air and threw it towards the door.

"She pretty little girl," Chuck said after she and Isabelle left.

"She's not a little girl, Chuck. She's Isabelle's mother."

"She mudda? No fool?"

"No fooling."

At the next dance I couldn't help thinking about what she'd said. Maggie Carew was the only person who'd said anything directly to me, but when I looked around the room I realized that there were a lot of others who felt the way she did.

The schoolroom was as crowded as it had been for

the Thanksgiving dance. Even though the weather outside was foul, now that it was February people wouldn't pass up the slightest opportunity to get out and go somewhere. With the wind howling outside most of the time and the days still dark, you needed to be around people more than ever, especially if you lived alone.

Elmer and Jeannette Terwilliger had come with the Carews and they brought the baby along. I didn't think I'd ever seen anything so tiny in my life as that baby. It was about two months old and just about perfect in every way, but blanket and all I bet it didn't weigh more than nine or ten pounds.

"Nine and a half," Maggie said, holding it while her daughter and Elmer were dancing. Everybody'd been standing around it oohing and ahing and carrying on and you couldn't blame them. There was something about a baby that just made you feel good, especially here. Her name was Patricia.

"Can I hold her?" I asked her.

Maggie handed her over to me. She was sleeping and I rocked her a little. "Like to have one like that?"

"I sure would."

"You won't as long as you got those two," she said.

The music stopped and the sets broke up. Jeannette came over with her husband. She smiled and put her hands out for the baby. I handed her over.

"How's my perfect gem?" she cooed to her. "Huh? How is she?"

"Same way she was a minute ago," Maggie said drily.

"Think she's pretty?" Jeannette asked me.

"She's beautiful."

"I wish she'd eat more," Jeannette said.

"She's doin' fine," Maggie said.

"No, she's not, Ma. She don't eat enough."

" 'Cause you hold 'er too much. Everytime she cries or makes a whimper," Maggie said to me, "there she is holdin' 'er and rockin' 'er and not givin' 'er a chance to get up an appetite."

"Oh, Ma," Jeannette sighed.

Robert Merriweather came over. "Teacher, the kids want to know if you'll get a square together with us."

"Sure."

I collected Jimmy Carew, Joan Simpson, Elvira, Lily and Chuck, which made seven with Robert and myself. Then Uncle Arthur joined our square and took Lily as his partner. Jimmy paired off with Joan, Robert Merriweather took me, and Elvira paired off with Chuck. I should have had better sense than to let Elvira and Chuck be partners, but I wasn't thinking. No sooner did the two of them join hands than Mr. Vaughn called out loud enough so everybody looked his way. "Elvira, come over here!"

I knew right away what he was mad about, but it was too late to do anything about it. Elvira went to where he was sitting alongside Angela Barrett.

"Don't you know any better?" he yelled at her. "How many times have I told you not to have anything to do with that kid? How many times?" He didn't wait for her to answer. He just slapped her. "Go on home," he said to her. She ran out, tears streaming down her cheeks. I wanted to go after her, but it would just have made things worse.

The whole room was quiet, everybody either looking over at our square or at Mr. Vaughn. If I'd had Angela Barrett's muscles I'd have gone over and told him exactly what I thought of him, and what I thought of him would have made what Jake Harrington said to him sound like a Sunday-school lecture. As it was though, I just stood there blushing with embarrassment and wishing one of the women still sitting down would take the empty space alongside Chuck.

Mrs. Purdy played a few notes on the accordion and that broke the silence. Ben Norvall, who was standing up on a box, pointed to our square. "One more lady over here," he called, "one more lady."

Jeannette handed her baby to Maggie, came over and took Chuck's hand, and the dance was on again.

I didn't have too good a time after that. I kept thinking of Elvira back in the cabin all by herself and blaming myself for it.

When the *Home Sweet Home* waltz was played I ended up with Joe Temple. By that time Chuck and Ethel were fast asleep so, leaving Robert Merriweather to watch them, I went over to the roadhouse with him. Maggie gave us the table by ourselves again.

I wasn't very good company. Joe tried to cheer me up, telling me not to blame myself for what happened. "I shouldn't have let you have those two in the first place," he said.

"Why not?"

"It's not doing you or anybody else any good."

"It's keeping them out of that village."

"And you in the dog house. I'm even getting the cold shoulder for giving them to you."

"You worried about it?"

"Not me. I would if I were you. Everybody's getting crankier and crankier. There's no telling what they're liable to do."

I didn't think anything more would happen, but I was wrong. The next time Mr. Strong came in he brought me a letter from Nancy's mother. Mrs. Prentiss didn't mince any words:

. . . I want you to send Nancy home with Mr. Strong right now. I don't want her staying with you any more. You ought to be ashamed of yourself. First you take a halfbreed lover then you go ahead and adopt two siwash brats you got no business to. You aren't decent company for self-respecting white people. I wouldn't be surprised if you end up having a siwash of your own by that lover of yours. You do what I say and send Nancy home to me.

I didn't show Nancy the note, but I told her some of what her mother had said. When we sat down for supper that night she burst out crying right after we started to eat. I was hit pretty hard myself. She'd become almost like a sister to me.

She begged me to go over and talk to Mr. Strong, ask him if he wouldn't talk to her mother and try to convince her to let her stay for at least a while longer. "Please, Anne," she said. "If anybody can do it, he can. My mother respects him, and if he was to tell her how much I'm learning and how my being with you isn't doing me anything but good, she'd let me stay."

253

Finally I did. He was alone in the store when I went over and he listened to everything I had to say, then shook his head. "Her mother wants her home," he said.

"Nancy thinks if you'd talk to her she might change her mind."

"In all good conscience, madam, I cannot do that."

"She deserves the break, Mr. Strong. She's been working so hard."

"Be honest with me. Do you think she could pass the eighth-grade exam if she were to take it today?"

"She'd have a better chance if she could stay a little longer."

"Would she pass or not?"

". . . I think so."

"In that case I believe she is better off at home. She can continue studying on her own."

"You really think I'm a bad influence on her."

"I am under the impression, madam, that you do not care one way or the other what I think."

"I admire you very much, Mr. Strong. I always have and I always will."

He cleared his throat. "There is nothing I can do," he said, "and that is the plain truth."

Before I went out he said, "Generally the school board in Eagle would have made up their mind by this time whether or not to retain your services next year. We have not done so as yet, but we will do so by the end of next month, then we shall telegraph our decision to the commissioner in Juneau. I'm sure you realize what I am trying to say."

"Yes, I do." I had until the end of March to change my ways.

"I hope, madam, you will not disappoint me."

The next morning, after I told the class that Nancy was leaving, we didn't even pretend to work. None of us wanted to see her go, and until about eleven o'clock, when we heard the stable door across the way bang open, we had a little party for her.

We all went out to see her off. The sun had been up for more than a half hour, but the sky was so overcast it was almost like night. "You make sure you study

254

everything I gave you," I said to her. I'd given her a couple of books to take along and marked the pages for her.

"I will," she said.

We'd filled a pillowcase with all her stuff. She handed it to Mr. Strong and he shoved it under the tarpaulin covering the sled.

When she said good-bye to Chuck she told him to be a good boy. "With me gone," she said, "you're gonna have to help out more—do the dishes and things like that."

He stuck out his lower lip. "I no do dishes," he said proudly. "Womans do dishes."

"Just the same, Anne's gonna need all the help you can give her, you savvy?"

"I help plenty."

She picked Ethel up. " 'Bye, sweetheart," she said, giving her a hug before she put her down. It was time to go.

"You keep studying hard," I said to her.

"I hate to go," she said.

"You'll be back to take the exam before you know it."

She swallowed hard so she wouldn't cry, then we hugged each other good-bye. "Thanks, Anne," she whispered. "Thanks for everything." She hugged me tighter. "You were right to take those two," she said. "They're good kids. I hope it works out."

It was a big thing for her to say, a real big thing, and I appreciated it. We'd both have started to cry if we said anything more, so we didn't.

Then she was clambering up on the sled and the children were all shouting good-bye to her. As soon as Ethel realized Nancy was going she started to cry.

The sled pulled out. Nancy turned around a couple of times to wave, and then she was gone. We all went back into the schoolhouse.

Right from the start the place seemed emptier without her, and came suppertime I really missed her.

Over the next couple of days, especially after school, I missed her more and more. Besides not having her company anymore, and her help with the chores, I started having trouble with Chuck and Ethel. I didn't know which one was worse. Ethel always seemed to be under my feet, clinging to me and putting her arms out to be picked up, and Chuck didn't take to it at all. He was always pushing her away from me, wanting to be close to me himself. I tried to explain to him why Ethel was doing it, but it didn't do too much good. With Nancy gone there was only me, and Chuck wanted to make sure Ethel wasn't going to take first place. So they carried on their little war, he giving her a pinch or a sock when he thought I wasn't looking, she holding on to me every chance she had.

Even with the jealousy and the rows, though, I loved having them. Ever since I could remember I'd always wanted children of my own to take care of. Once when I was a little girl there were two little kids that lived next door to me that my mother never let me play with. She said that they were dirty and had lice. One day while I was talking with them over the fence—the two of them scratching and whimpering—I felt so sorry for them that I brought them into our yard and filled an old washtub full of water. I figured that if I cleaned them up my mother wouldn't mind if I played with them. They loved it and so did I—until my mother caught me. She was furious, and so was my father. He gave me a good whipping and sent me to bed without my supper, saying that would teach me not to play with trash. I didn't know what I'd done wrong, so I guessed there was just something wrong with me. If there was then the same thing was still wrong with me, because I could no more have parted with Chuck and Ethel than if they'd been my own little brother and sister. I even went to sleep when they did. It was easier than trying to get them to bed by themselves now that Nancy was gone, and it turned out to be fun. With Chuck on one side of me and Ethel on the other, I sat up in bed with a book of fairy tales and read until they dropped off. Ethel didn't have the least idea of what the story was about, but she seemed to enjoy it as much as Chuck did. In the morning I'd just get up earlier to get my work done.

A few days after Nancy left, Jeannette and her husband started for Eagle, with Jeannette and the baby tucked into the Carews' sled. They stopped by the schoolhouse before they left so Jeannette could say good-bye to Jimmy and Willard and let them have one last look at their niece. The Carews had a fairly good string of dogs, but there was an awful lot on the sled for them to pull. Since Maggie would be closing the roadhouse, she was trying to move as many things to Eagle as she could. All told there must have been about seven or eight hundred pounds there.

Ben Norvall said they oughtn't to go with so much packed on the sled. "There's a storm comin' down," Ben said, "and you're liable to run right into it."

Maggie came out of the roadhouse while they were still talking about it. She'd had second thoughts too. She came on over and looked the sled over pretty carefully. "Maybe you oughtta leave off some a them things," she said to Jeannette's husband. "You're liable to take a spill and get hurt." They argued about it for a while, then decided to take off a couple of picture frames, a whole bunch of iron pots and a small Yukon stove. Some more discussion followed, until finally they took off a couple of hundred pounds before they left.

A few hours later Ben was proved right. A really mean freeze came in so fast you could hear the nails in the walls snapping as they contracted. Even after we built up the fire, till the sides of the stove were red hot the schoolroom was hardly bearable. It was the wind that did it, sweeping down from the north and bringing sleet that drove against the windows so hard I thought they'd break. It wasn't any kind of weather you wanted to be out in and for a while I thought I'd have to keep Isabelle and Joan Simpson overnight. But Mr. Purdy showed up for Isabelle about seven and Joan's father came about a half hour later.

When I was putting Chuck and Ethel to bed that night somebody knocked at the door. I yelled come in, but nobody did. After another knock I went to it. It was still sleeting out and I could hardly see beyond the edge of the porch. Right in front of the threshold was a fancy little box all done up with gleaming ribbon and cellophane. My heart gave a jump. I thought right away that it was from Fred and I poked my head out around the jamb with a smile I hadn't felt like showing in weeks. I should have known better, though, because there, hugging the wall so tight his Stetson was tipped down to his nose, was Cab Jackson. He tipped it back up and gave me that big dumb grin of his, then he picked up the fancy box and held it out to me. "Howdy, Teacher."

It was too cold to do anything but invite him in and have him get the children all awake again. Chuck was right out of bed, of course, wanting to see the present. Ethel was up too and they wouldn't go back to bed until I'd let Chuck open the box and take out the bottle of perfume that was in it. I gave them each a smell, then hustled them off to sleep, with Chuck getting the cellophane wrapping and Ethel the ribbon. Then I gave Cab a cup of coffee and made a cup of tea for myself. "I'm sorry 'bout what happened last time," he said. "I don't hardly remember any of it, but I sure wish you wouldn't be mad at me."

"I got over it."

"You wouldn't maybe want to splash a little of that perfume on and come over t'the roadhouse a spell, would ya?"

"I can't leave the kids alone, Cab."

He looked over at them and I could feel a sermon coming, so I changed the subject. "D'you come in from Eagle?"

"Nulato. Did a little business there. I'll be mushing over to Eagle when I leave here—tomorrow mornin' I reckon. Teacher," he said, "you mind if I tell you somethin'?"

"I'll have to hear it first."

"There's some mighty loose talk bein' spread about you."

"Nothing I can do about that."

"You're roonin' your whole career, people are sayin', an' they're right."

"I'll make you a deal, Cab. I won't say anything to you about whiskey running if you won't say anything to me about what I do."

"I got to," he said. "You are just too fine a person
258

to have people talkin' the way they are. I got a good mind to let that Joe Temple have it for givin' them kids to you."

"I hope you won't," I said. "I asked him for them."

"But don't you see you're throwin' away your whole future? The only thing stoppin' that school board in Eagle from givin' you your walkin' papers right now is old Strong. He's a-tellin' 'em to wait 'n see . . . And Teacher, I don't want you to lose that job. Shucks, I was bankin' on you bein' there. I got some pretty deep feelings about ya, as you do know by now."

"I appreciate it, Cab. I appreciate everything you're trying to tell me, but I know what I'm doing and I want to do it."

"No you don't, Teacher. You got a heart big as all outdoors and you're lettin' it rule out your good sense. I'm askin' you as one who is truly interested in your welfare and your good name—you just let me mush them two kids outta here and you'll wind up the happiest female in the Forty Mile. You will."

"It's getting kinda late. I've still got some work to do."

He got up and took his mackinaw down from the drying rack. He looked at me as if he was really worried. "You sure you feelin' good, Teacher? You know—not sick or anything? Sometimes that can happen . . ."

"I'm not tetched, if that's what you mean."

He smiled. Then he said something I thought was really touching. "I guess you think I'm kinda wild and not smart. And maybe I'm *not* too smart either. But I got deep feelin's, Teacher, deep and good feelin's. About you 'specially. I wanta do somethin' for you, in the worst way. I wanna be a help to you. You know what I mean?"

"I think so . . . I appreciate it."

"Good night."

"Good night."

When I went to sleep the wind was raging, blowing so hard that if the windows hadn't been frozen in place they'd have been rattling loud enough to keep us all awake. I woke in the middle of the night. It was warmer and it wasn't sleeting. Getting up, I turned the stove

259

damper down, then I went into the schoolroom and did the same thing. It was so quiet outside that I went to the window. Snow was falling softly. I didn't look at the clock, but I had a feeling it was about three. If it kept falling this thickly there'd be two feet on the ground before morning.

It must have stopped soon after because the next morning there were just a few more inches on the ground. It was gloomy and foggy out all that day, though, so we didn't even go outside for recess.

A little after school was over Harry Dowles knocked at the door and said he needed a couple of things from the store. Joan's mother hadn't come to pick her up yet and I didn't like the idea of leaving the children alone, so I offered to give him the key.

He said no thanks. "Wouldn't want to be accused of shoplifting. Only take a minute," he said.

I peeked into the schoolroom. The three of them were playing line cabin. Chuck had stretched a blanket over a few boxes and Joan and Ethel were inside the "cabin," while Chuck was out "trapping." They were playing so well that I didn't see any harm in leaving them for a few minutes. I told Chuck to make sure the three of them stayed in the schoolroom, then I went out.

In Mr. Strong's store, Harry said he needed some blue thread. The color he wanted wasn't on the rack with all the other thread so I had to hunt through some boxes before I found it. Then he asked for a tin of tea and five pounds of sugar. After I weighed out the sugar, he looked around, scratching his head. "Somep'n else I wanted," he said.

"Maybe you'll think of it later," I told him. I'd been gone over five minutes and wanted to get back.

"No," he said. "It's somep'n I need bad." He kept looking around making a big show of trying to think, and I should have realized then and there something was wrong, but I didn't. I reeled off a bunch of things and he kept saying no, none of them was it until I mentioned matches and he said he could use a few boxes, but that still wasn't it. Finally I told him I had to get back and that made him all kinds of nervous.

Just then from outside I heard Cab yell out "Yah-h-h-h—mush!" I didn't take particular note of it except to wonder why he was leaving so late. Last night he'd told me he'd be leaving early in the morning.

"Well," Harry Dowles said then, "I guess I can't think of it. You go ahead and tally up." He put a hand on the counter and it was shaking. I looked at him and his eyes shifted away.

And then it came to me. My first instinct was to say I was wrong, that nobody would do a thing like that. But then I knew I was right. I knew it. It was written all over Harry's face, and I felt sick.

I ran for the door, and then I was outside, running along the path to the schoolhouse and seeing Angela Barrett just ducking into the roadhouse storm entry. Cab's sled was already well out of the settlement, speeding up the trail beside Chicken Creek, and he was cursing his dogs a blue streak, yelling for them to move faster. He was running in back of it, so I couldn't really see the sled at first. But then the dogs swung to the left where the creek jogged and the sled was in full view for a few moments.

Chuck and Ethel were in it.

XX

"Cab, come back!" I yelled. "Come back!"

I started to run after him, but it was useless. The dogs were fresh and the sled was moving too fast. I'd never be able to catch him.

I kept yelling and calling, but he didn't so much as turn around. In a minute the sled veered to the left to avoid a big patch of scrub, then disappeared. I stood there dazed, hearing Cab urge the dogs on, and then I didn't even hear that anymore. I turned back.

Except for little Joan, who was standing on the porch of the schoolhouse shivering, no one was out. The whole settlement could have been deserted. Inside my quarters I asked her what happened.

She was almost too bewildered to tell me. And frightened. "They just came in here, Teacher," she stammered, "a whole bunch of 'em. They came in and took Ethel and Chuck away—just took 'em. I was scared they were gonna take me away too."

She broke into tears. It took a few minutes before she could tell me who had done it.

"Mr. Vaughn. And Mrs. Barrett. And that man whose sled it is . . . Why did they do that, Teacher?"

She looked as though she was going to cry again. "There's nothing to be scared of," I told her. "They won't be back."

I gave her a cookie to munch on and I looked around. The bureau drawers were open. At least they'd taken some of the children's clothes. Ethel's dresses were gone from the wall too. Chuck's spear was still where he'd left it, though.

I couldn't think. I tried to, but everything had happened so fast that I couldn't get my thoughts together. The room looked empty, as if nobody lived in it. Dead.

I heard Joan's mother come up on the porch and knock. The sound seemed to come from another world. I must have told her to come in. When she did she saw right away that something was wrong. Joan ran over to her and told her that Chuck and Ethel had been taken away. She looked at me and asked me if it were true, but something was sticking in my throat and I couldn't answer her.

"Who took them away?" I heard her ask Joan.

"Mrs. Barrett," Joan said. "And Mr. Vaughn, and another man too."

"Oh, that's terrible," her mother said. "Anne, that's terrible." I saw her hand come over and felt it touch my shoulder. "When did it happen?" she asked me.

I said, "Just now."

She wanted to know if she could do anything for me. I said, "No. Thanks. Thanks very much. You take Joan home. I'll be all right."

After she left I sat listening to how quiet it was.

My feet began to get cold, so I got up and looked around for something to do. I started to straighten things. If I could just keep busy straightening things up, I thought, I might be able to start thinking again, figure out what to do. I shut the bureau drawers, arranged the chairs around the table neatly and then went into the schoolroom to see what I could do there. The kids had left it in pretty good order so there wasn't much to keep me occupied.

The funny thing was that I couldn't cry. I wanted to, I even tried to, but I couldn't. If I cried I wouldn't be able to think, and I had to do that. I had to think, figure out how to get Chuck and Ethel back. When I thought that, my mind started working again. That's what I had to do, I realized—get them back.

Tomorrow was Friday, then the weekend. I'd get someone to take me up to the Indian village then. Maybe Joe Temple would do it. Or Fred. I'd start out right after school. I'd miss a couple of days, since I probably wouldn't be back until Tuesday or Wednesday, but I'd get them back.

Somebody came up on the porch and knocked.

It was Maggie Carew. She came in and stood in front of the closed door in her long blue coat, with her arms crossed. She made some kind of sound that could have meant anything from sympathy to "That's that."

"Did you know they were going to do this?" I asked her.

"I heard about it," she said. "It wasn't my idea, if that's what you're thinkin'."

"Whose was it?"

"What's it matter?"

"You can tell them there won't be any school on Monday. Tuesday either."

"Oh. . . ?"

"I'm going up to the Indian village. I'm bringing Chuck and Ethel back."

"The hell you will."

"The hell I won't. I'm going right after school tomorrow."

"You can save yourself the trip. Those kids are there to stay, thank God."

"Not if I have anything to say about it."

"You won't. When Cab gets through tellin' those Injuns what'll happen to 'em if they let you have those kids they'll scalp you before they let you so much as touch 'em."

"What can he tell them?"

"That if they so much as let you *look* at those kids that's the end of 'em. There's a few of 'em work on the riverboat in season. A couple of 'em get work at the Prentiss roadhouse and some more at Eagle. He'll tell 'em if they let you have those kids they won't ever work for anybody around here again. He's also gonna tell 'em that Strong won't tote a goddamn thing in or out of that village either. Nobody will. If that ain't enough he'll tell 'em he'll get the marshal after them. And believe me they'll listen. So like I say, save yourself the trip."

"Is that the truth?"

"You're darn tootin' it's the truth. Don't believe me if you don't want. Go on up there, but you'll be goin' on a fool's errand."

I felt weak.

"Good riddance to bad rubbish, if you ask me," she said. Then she softened a little. "They did you a favor, Annie. I know you liked them kids, but one day you'll see how much better off you are without 'em. You'll be teachin' at Eagle next year now, at least if I have anything to say about it, and I do. You'll see, Annie. You'll see it was all for the best."

"I will, will I? I'll tell you something, Mrs. Carew. You know what I feel like doing? I feel like leaving this place right now and never coming back."

"Don't talk so. You don't mean that and you know it."

"Oh I mean it all right. Do you realize what you've all done? Just because you're mad about something, because you're feeling mean about something, you're taking it out on those kids."

"I don't even know what you're talkin' about. Nobody's takin' anything out on anybody."

264

"You know what I'm talking about, all right. Those kids weren't hurting a soul. All they wanted was a warm place to stay and some decent food. And maybe a little kindness from people. Instead all they got was meanness."

"Not from me, they didn't. Anyway it's all water over the dam now. No use cryin' over spilt milk."

"Is that all you have to say?"

"Now looka here, I just come over to be nice. I don't know what you're blamin' *me* for. I didn't have anything to do with this."

"You could have stopped it. They're children, Mrs. Carew—just little kids. What were they doing that was so terrible? Who did they hurt? Don't you realize what that Indian village is like? Don't you realize that you might as well have sent them to the electric chair?"

"I mind my own business."

"Is that what you'll tell Jimmy and Willard if they ask—that you let two kids be taken away to starve or freeze to death because it was none of your business? I'm ashamed of you."

She walked out. If she thought anything at all about what I said, she kept it to herself.

My hands were sweating and cold. I went over to the stove to warm them. I hadn't felt so bad since Fred had walked out on me. My mind was going a mile a minute. I tried to think where Cab was now. He'd probable gotten to Stonehouse Creek already. From there . . .

An idea hit me and I tried to put it out of my mind, but it kept coming back so strong that finally I knew I had to try it. There wasn't anything else I could do.

I put on a few pairs of socks under my moccasins, got my parka and went out.

There were some thin snow flurries in the air. Dry as sand, they swept in veils along the ground. I made pretty good time. It only took me twenty minutes to get to Fred's house.

Isabelle answered the door, surprised to see me.

"Is Fred home?" I asked her.

"Out in back, Miss Hobbs. Come on in, I'll go get 'im for you."

"I'll talk to him there."

I went around the back to the stable. I could hear him using the grindstone. He was sitting down, working the treadle, sparks flying from the ax he was holding. He looked up, and as soon as I saw him I could feel everything I'd kept bottled up inside me start to spill over. I was able to blurt out, "Fred, they took Chuck and Ethel away from me," and then I was in his arms blubbering and carrying on. He kept trying to get me to tell him what happened, but I couldn't. Everytime I tried I'd start crying all over again. Finally when I was able to control myself I hiccupped it all out. Mrs. Purdy came in right in the middle of it and wanted me to come into the house, but Fred said maybe it'd be better if I stayed there with him.

"We'll be in in a couple of minutes. Go on back in the house, Ma," he said gently.

She left and I finished telling him the whole story, including what Maggie Carew said about my not ever getting Chuck and Ethel back once they were in the Indian village.

"They didn't have any right to do that," he said. "They didn't have any right at all."

"Fred, will you help me?"

"How?"

"Go after Cab with me."

"Now?"

"Right now. Right this minute. Please, Fred. If we can get to Cab before he reaches the Indian village I'll be able to talk to him, reason with him. I know he'll let me have them back if I can just talk to him."

He didn't say anything. "Fred, please. Please help me, otherwise I'll never get them back."

"How long ago did Cab leave?"

"About an hour."

I was asking a lot, I knew that, and I made up my mind that if he said no I wouldn't ask him again.

"You sure you want to go after him?" he said.

"I do."

"Is he toting anything else on the sled?"

"Whiskey."

266

He thought about it. Then he said, "Go on home. Put on your warmest clothes and pack some spares—spare parka, moccasins, socks, underclothes. I'll be by as soon as I can."

I nearly knocked him over I hugged him so tight.

"Get going," he said.

I flew getting home, and I was ready in twenty minutes. I didn't know whether he wanted me to pack food, so I put together some frozen beans, tea and some meat. Then I sat down to wait. I wondered what his father and mother would say to him. They'd try to keep him from going and I couldn't blame them. After a half hour I wondered if they'd convinced him.

A few minutes later I heard a shout and the sound of a sled approaching. I ran to the door, but it was someone else, someone carrying a passenger. The sled pulled up at the roadhouse. I shut the door.

I was ready to give up after another half hour went by. And then suddenly there he was.

I told him what food I'd packed, but he said leave it. He had everything we'd need for a week, he said.

"A week!"

"I don't know how long it'll take us to catch up with Cab or what we're liable to run into. If the trail is bad we may need everything we have."

"Somebody just mushed in to the roadhouse. Maybe you can ask him."

We went over together. The man who'd come in was a freighter, carrying a passenger to Fairbanks. The two of them were eating when we walked in. The passenger was a Dawson banker and the driver was trying to wolf down a steak and answer Maggie Carew's questions at the same time. She was worried and so was her husband. Angela Barrett was there too.

"You didn't see a sign of them at all?" Maggie was asking the freighter. She was badly upset.

"Only sled I seen was Cabaret Jackson's, 'n' that was about two hours ago," the driver said.

Her husband was trying to calm her down. "Now, Maggie, they coulda hit some bad weather and holed up in any number of places."

"You bet your boots they did," the driver said. "There was a stretch back there day before yesterday where I didn't make more'n a mile the whole day."

"How about when you passed Jamison's," Maggie asked him, "d'you see any smoke?"

"Didn't get that near," the driver said. "I stayed on the river all the way from Bonanza Bar till I hit here."

"What's the trail like through Franklin?" Fred asked him.

"Drifted in," the driver answered. "Unless you got somethin' won't wait I'd advise you to stay put."

"You're goin' after Cab," Maggie said to Fred.

Fred nodded and Angela Barrett said, "I hope he kills ya."

"Shut up!" Maggie snapped at her. Maybe she'd have felt the same way as Angela if she wasn't so worried about Jeannette and Elmer, but she didn't give a hoot right now about anything or anyone but them. "Be on the lookout, will you, Fred?"

"I will," he said. "But I wouldn't be worried if I were you. Elmer knows this country. He wouldn't do anything foolish."

"I know he wouldn't,'" Maggie said, "but they should've at least been at Steel Creek when this man went through there. He says they weren't. Last time anybody saw 'em was at O'Shaughnessy's."

"They told me at Steel Creek nobody had been through for two days," the man said.

"Maybe Elmer didn't stop there," Fred said. "Maybe he stayed on the river and then cut across to Liberty."

"You keep a sharp eye out," Maggie said.

Fred said he would, and a few minutes later we were by the sled. The runners had frozen in.

"Gee!" Fred yelled.

The dogs dug in, then swung to the right, and with a crack the sled was free.

He told me to get in, but I suggested that I run along with him for as long as I could hold out to save the dogs work.

"You'll be doing plenty of that," he said. "We better save you as much as possible."

"Mush!" he yelled once I was in. And we were off.

For the first few miles we moved along fast. The dogs were eager and the hills were gentle. Then the trail toughened, and I got out to trot alongside or help push and shove the sled through scrubby spruce, down and up sharp banks and across hummock-littered tundra. I kept watch for anything that might make the sled tip or get caught, and for a while I congratulated myself. I was pulling my own weight on a tough trail. Then I became careless and didn't see a rock slick with ice. One of the runners ran over it, the sled tipped and before I could stop it it nosed off the trail and into a drift. The two of us struggled to get it out, but a runner was caught on something. We couldn't budge it.

"We'll have to unpack some of the load," Fred said.

"But we'll waste so much time!"

"Nothing else we can do," he said.

We worked at unpacking slowly—too slowly, I felt. Mad at myself for being so careless, I tried to work fast. Fred kept stopping me. "Slow down," he said.

"He'll get away."

"You're not in the schoolroom now. You're on the trail. Slow down and keep that scarf over your face."

I knew he was right. You had to pace yourself, not move fast enough so that you started breathing through your mouth, taking freezing air into your lungs. It was the first rule of the trail—don't exhaust yourself. We had to take off half the load before we could free the runner, then reload, again working at the same maddening slow pace.

"Couldn't we have gone around all this?" I grumbled, tossing a package of raw meat into the sled.

Fred pulled his scarf down. "Take a look over there." He pointed to the distance. "See that saddle between those two hills?"

I could see it through the grayness—a dip stretching between two crags that rose up above the timber line.

"We're heading for that," Fred said. "It'll be a long trip. You won't make it if you don't take it easy. We'll go as fast as we can."

I felt small. "I'm sorry," I said.

"Forget it. We'll catch up with him, don't worry."

Once we left the tundra behind it was like moving

269

along in a slow-motion dream, following a trail that wound ahead without any end, dipping across a creek, narrowing around a hill, then around still another hill when that was left behind. The dogs never let up, trotting along at a fast willing pace when we hit the flats, digging in almost as if they enjoyed it when the going was rough. Night came on fast and black and the Northern lights billowed like curtains across the starlit sky. We didn't talk. There was no need to, even if we weren't using all our strength to keep up a steady pace. We were on the trail, stumbling along, snowshoeing across snow ten feet deep, plodding through drifts and sometimes sailing when the trail was smooth enough.

We reached the base of the saddle three hours later, a long slope of white with nothing to mark it but the twin lines of Cab's sled running up as far as we could see. And alongside of it were the small footprints of Chuck and Ethel. I wondered how they were making out, whether Cab was pushing them too hard or being impatient with them. Halfway up, Ethel's footprints stopped and I could see where she'd sat down. She'd been too tired to go any further. Cab had gone on a short distance beyond, then come back, picked her up and brought her to the sled.

I thought that when we got to the top of the pass, maybe by some miracle we'd be able to spot Cab's sled, but we didn't. It was too dark to see anything but endless stretches of black forest and the dark winding outline of the Forty Mile River.

The ride down was worth the climb. For two miles straight Fred rode the runners, the only sound the squeaking of the sled and the *plop plop plop* of the white clods the dogs threw up behind them. I wondered how they could do it, go on like that for hours taking that burning cold air into their lungs. But they did. They even gave each other a playful nip once in a while when they didn't have to pull too hard.

We rode down a long slough to the river, then once we were on it we went like an express train, swinging around big drifts and patches of rough ice. Again Fred was able to ride the runners for long stretches and I hardly had to get out. If we hadn't been chasing Cab I'd have been in heaven. The moon came out after a while. The river widened, and we began to pass little islands. We were sailing along so smoothly that even Fred must have let his guard down, because without any warning Pancake suddenly veered off to the right and Fred lost his balance. He fell off the runners, fought to stay on his feet, then jumped back on. Pancake was still moving to the right, making a wide sweep. "Haw!" Fred yelled at him, but he kept moving until Fred had to stop the team.

Fred went up to him and he was really mad. "What the hell is the matter with you?" he yelled. "Don't you have any better sense than that? You nearly killed me, you blasted fool!" He said a couple of other things that weren't very complimentary. Pancake hung his head and took it all. "Now you damn well better go where you're supposed to," Fred warned him. Once in back of the sled he yelled haw, but sure enough Pancake veered off to the right again.

Fred stopped the sled again and this time I thought he was really going to give it to Pancake, but he didn't. Instead he looked over the area that Pancake had been so stubborn about avoiding, scanning it carefully. He'd told me long ago how many times a man had to depend on his dogs to stay alive and as it turned out this was one of them. "Well I'll be damned," he finally muttered.

He went to Pancake then, got down on his knees and put his arms around his neck, then he rubbed his cheek against Pancake's head, telling him what a good dog he was. I didn't realize what it was all about until Fred showed me. "See that over there—where the snow's a little darker, almost a little yellow?" I saw it finally. It was like a shadow. "It's a warm spot," Fred said. "Water. At the least we'd have wound up with wet gear. Probably worse. Pancake smelled it."

It was three weary hours later that we pulled up by a small cabin buried up to the eaves. The owner had dug a path from the door and uncovered the window, but otherwise you'd have hardly known there was a cabin there at all. "You stay here," Fred said. "I hear this man isn't too friendly."

There was smoke coming from the stovepipe and a faint yellow light coming through the window. Inside, a dog growled threateningly when Fred knocked.

"Who's there?" a gruff voice asked.

"Fred Purdy."

"I heard of you. You live up to Chicken."

"That's right," Fred said.

"Keep on a-goin'," the voice said. "Don' know you an' don' wanna know you."

"I have a lady with me. We've been on the trail over six hours and we'd like to stop a few minutes."

"This ain't a roadhouse."

"We don't want any of your grub. All we want is to get warm."

"Build yourself a fire. Keep a-goin', bud."

Fred muttered something I couldn't hear and I said, "Fred, let's go. We don't have to stop here."

"Listen to the lady, bud," the voice said. "She's makin' sense. I got a thirty-aught-six pointed at that door and it'll blow your ass clear to White Horse you try to come in here."

Fred jumped away from the door fast. "Did another sled mush by here in the last few hours?" There was no answer. "Did you hear me?"

"I heard you."

"Well, did it?"

"I ain't sayin' it did and I ain't sayin' it didn't."

Fred was mad. He walked back to the sled, took out his rifle and unsheathed it. Then he went over to the cabin door and threw the bolt. "Did you hear that?" he said.

"I heard it," the voice answered with a little less gruffness.

"Now, you inhospitable sonofabitch," Fred said. "I'm gonna ask you the same question again. If I don't get an answer I'm gonna knock out every damn pane in the window. Did another sled mush by here recently?"

". . . Yeah."

"How long ago?"

"Maybe three hours. Cab Jackson it was. He wanted to come in and I told'm the same as I told you."

"You sure it was that long?"

There was a pause. "Three hours and fourteen minutes. I got a book here I wrote it down in. I always write it down when anybody mushes by."

"Thanks." He came over to the sled. "He'd go on to the O'Shaughnessy roadhouse. Probably stay there overnight. It's eight miles. We can build a fire and rest a while or we can push on. I'm for pushing on if you can make it."

"I can make it," I said meekly. He looked so mad I'd have said I could do double cartwheels on the sled if he wanted me to. I'd never seen him like that before. In a way I kind of admired him for how tough and hard he could be, but it upset me too. Up to then I hadn't thought about what might happen when we caught up with Cab, figuring that somehow I'd be able to reason with him and talk him into letting me have Chuck and Ethel back. But suppose I couldn't? Cab could be pretty unpredictable. He could get mean about it and start saying some nasty things. Fred just wouldn't stand by and let him. I began to conjure up all kinds of things happening, maybe even shooting.

"Fred, will you promise me something?"

"What?"

"When we reach O'Shaughnessy's, you'll let me handle Cab."

"Promise."

"Cross your heart? I don't want you getting into a fight with him."

He smiled. "That makes two of us."

Those eight miles to the roadhouse must have taken us almost four hours. Even though Cab was following the trail the freighter had broken for him coming in, and he was breaking it even more for us, it was still hard going. And I was holding us up. You needed stamina for the trail—the kind of stamina you don't have unless you're used to it. All I had to do was trot alongside the sled most of the time, but I was still a drag. Fred never said a word about it, never told me to move faster. He just kept going.

The wind didn't help any. It started coming at us right after we left the cabin and beat at us so hard for a while that we were pinching ice off our eyelashes

273

every few minutes. Then one of the lead lines broke and we had to spell each other mending it, each of us working till our fingers were too cold, then the other taking over.

When the O'Shaughnessy roadhouse came into view I felt I'd never seen anything so warm and inviting as the yellow lights in its windows. We pulled up to the welcome yips of dogs tied up in the barn and no sooner did we stop than a bundled up figure came out of the roadhouse door. It was Mr. O'Shaughnessy.

"Inside with ye," he yelled over the wind when he saw I was a girl. "Oi'll help yer man put up the dogs."

I didn't need any urging. I went to the door so sure Cab would be on the other side of it that my stomach started doing flip-flops. When I opened it the wind shoved me in and nearly tore the door out of my hand. A man who'd been sitting down jumped up and closed it behind me. The heat of the place hit me with a lovely warm sting and the quiet almost made me reel. Mr. O'Shaughnessy's Indian wife had already pushed the table close to the oil-drum heater. She took me by the arm and led me over to it. "You sit down quick, Teacher. Get warm," she said comfortingly, then bustled over to the stove to pour a cup of hot tea. I was surprised she remembered me. I hadn't seen her in over five months, when I'd stopped with Chuck and Mr. Strong.

I plopped down and looked around. There was no sign of Cab. Some blankets were strung across part of the room to shield the bunk beds and I wondered if he and the kids were behind them. Mrs. O'Shaughnessy put the cup of steaming tea down on the table and helped me off with my parka. The man cleared his throat.

"Some night to be out on the trail," he said to Mrs. O'Shaughnessy. He was really talking to me, but he was being courteous. When people came in off the trail they were cold and tired and you didn't talk to them until they talked to you first. A snore came from behind the blanket.

I kept my voice low. "Is Cab Jackson here?"

Mrs. O'Shaughnessy shook her head. "No."

"You looking for him?" the man asked me. From the

274

way he asked it I had the feeling he already knew the answer. He was tall and pale, and he wore glasses. One of the lenses was cracked and ringed with adhesive tape.

"Yes."

"That's too bad," he said. "He's been here and gone. Left about a half hour ago."

XXI

"No, ye'll not catch oop with *that* bludy rascal bafore he's ta the Indian village," Mr. O'Shaughnessy said in his thick accent. A friendly pixie of a man with sauerkraut eyebrows and a veined nose, he was trying to convince Fred and me it wouldn't be any use for us to try and catch Cab. "Stay an' have yersilves a good noight's sleep. It's too foine a sthring of dogs the man has. *Too* foine fa the loikes uv him. Not that yer own sthring ain't a dandy," he said quickly to Fred, "but thim a his are greased loightnin'. An' Jaysus, man," he exclaimed, "he's an hour'n a half hid start on ye already!"

Cab had stayed only long enough to warm up and eat, he'd told us after we'd changed clothes. He'd made up his mind not to stop for sleep until he reached the Indian village.

"You're sure that maybe he won't stop anywhere else?" I asked him.

"An' where would he be stoppin'?" He seemed surprised I'd even ask such a thing. "There ain't nahthin' 'twixt here 'n the Injin village but one lone cabin."

The steak his wife had pan fried for us was thick and delicious, but I could hardly finish half of it. Once I found out that Cab had pushed on I didn't have much of an appetite.

"What made him go on?" I asked. "What's his hurry?"

Mr. O'Shaughnessy looked over at the man with the broken glasses as if asking him, then answered the question himself. "Because he's daft! Oi told'm he wuz daft, too. 'It's an outra-a-a-geous hardship for the little tykes,' I sez to 'im. Wud he listen? He wud not. 'Oi've made up me moind,' sez he. 'Oi has a mission Oi'm on, 'n' Oi shall not sleep until Oi've finished with it. Oi makes no stop till Oi've done whut Oi've set out ta do.' Did he say that or shall Oi be kicked inta Hell seven toimes for loyin'?" he asked the man.

The man nodded. He was a neighbor named Joshua Potter and he'd just dropped by for a visit. "That's just about what he said," he agreed.

"Oi'm sorry, lass," Mr. O'Shaughnessy said to me.

Mrs. O'Shaughnessy came over to the table. "You not eat," she said.

"I'm not hungry," I said.

The man sleeping in the bunk started snoring again and kept it up until Mr. O'Shaughnessy went behind the blanket and poked him. He hadn't waked up the whole time we were there.

I looked over at Fred. There were dark circles under his eyes. He'd hardly spoken a word since we'd come in. "Suppose we went over The Drop," he asked Mr. O'Shaughnessy. "You think we'd have a chance of catching him then?"

"The Dhrop?" He crooked his head and made a grudging sound. "It's a bad toime for takin' that trail. Bad indeed."

"It would save us two hours."

Mr. O'Shaughnessy looked at the other man. "Phwat do you think, Josh?"

"You might catch him," he said to Fred, "if your sled holds together."

"You have some chain I can borrow?" Fred asked.

"All ye need," Mr. O'Shaughnessy said.

Fred glanced at me. He was tired. We both were. He looked away quickly. "If you'll tell me where it is I'll go get it," he said, standing.

"I'll go with ye."

Fred collected his clothes. As he was about to go out, I said, "Hey, you're forgetting something."

"What's that?" he said.

"My duds," I said, getting up. I'd used the term to make him smile and he did.

"Oh. Yeah . . ."

I collected my own clothes and gave them to him.

"What's The Drop?" I asked Josh after they went out.

"Ptarmigan Drop. A pass. Bad one." He raised one hand and held it flat. Then he tilted it steeply. "Drops like this," he said. "This time of year it's half ice."

I thought about Chuck and Ethel. "Is there any chance Cab would take it?"

"Probably would if he weren't carrying whiskey."

"How about children?"

"Be glad he's got the whiskey," he said.

I heard the dogs yipping as Fred and Mr. O'Shaughnessy led them out of the barn. I sat back and closed my eyes, enjoying the last few moments of warmth and thinking how nice it would be to sleep before going out again. It was almost two in the morning and we'd been on trail for over eight hours. Suddenly I thought of something that made my eyes pop right open—the way Fred had almost walked out with my clothes. I was up like a shot.

I slipped and almost fell before my moccasins held onto the caked-down snow. The dogs were all harnessed and Fred was bending down in front of the sled. He was checking the spring fastening that held the main towline to be sure it was holding. It had given us trouble. As soon as I reached the sled I knew I had been right in coming out when I did. The tarp was lashed down over the load and Mr. O'Shaughnessy had my clothes bundled under his arm.

"You were going without me," I said to Fred.

"Cab's got a big head start," he said. "I'll have a better chance of catching him if I'm alone."

"I'm going."

"Anne—"

"You're not going alone. I mean that."

"It's going to be tougher from here on, and you're tired . . ."

277

"You're not going to catch up with him all by your-self."

I stood my ground and he gave in. We had to re-pack the load to make room for me to ride when it was possible, then we went back in and said good-bye to everyone.

I was able to ride for about a mile, and every time I thought about what he'd intended to do I'd get a lump in my throat. When we came to the bank of a slough we had to cross I got out. I put a hand on his arm.

"Fred." I pulled my scarf down. "I'm so proud of you."

He put his arms around me and held me for a few moments. "I feel the same way about you," he said. Then he let me go and we went on. I felt as if I could take on anything after that.

For as long as I lived I'd never forget those next six hours. Old-timers like Ben and Uncle Arthur had told me dozens of stories of forced mushes they'd made, and of how more often than they wanted to remember they'd almost frozen to death, but on that trip I found out I hadn't had the least idea of what they meant.

Compared to the trail we now took, traveling on the river had been a breeze. We sidled up hills that grudged us the narrow paths that bordered them and kept trying to edge the sled off. Twice, for stretches of a quarter of a mile, Fred had to put on snowshoes and break trail across snow that would have swallowed us up to the waist, while I stayed at the handle bars inching the sled forward. Time and again we both had to push from behind as the dogs labored to pull the sled up a steep bluff or the sharp bank of a creek. Half-buried bushes caught in the runners and tore at our moccasins.

Aggravated from lack of sleep, exhausted from push-ing and falling and being whipped by the wind, I sat down once and cried, telling Fred to go on and leave me, that I couldn't go any farther.

It wasn't all bad, though. Rounding a sharp turn in the trail once while I was on the runners and Fred trotted alongside, the dogs decided to speed up sudden-ly and I lost my grip on the handles. I went flying off down an embankment, and braced myself for a sickening jolt. Instead I did a flip, landed on my back and sank down in a soft fleecy bed, with my legs straight up in the air. I stared up at the sky, while Fred ran after the sled. I was still in the same position when he slipped down the embankment and his face loomed over me. "Anne, are you hurt?"

I knew how ridiculous I had to look, like a bug on its back. "Hurt my eye." I wiggled my legs for him. It was just what we needed. The two of us started to laugh hysterically. Even after we were on the way again all we had to do was glance at each other to make us giggle.

It was almost as if it was a turning point, because in a little while the trail eased and we pushed ahead up a winding creek. Even the wind started to help us, blowing at our back and giving us an extra nudge to speed us up.

"There it is!" Fred yelled finally, "Ptarmigan Drop!"

I looked for it, but I didn't see anything that resembled a drop. "Where?"

"The other side of that hill."

It looked pretty steep from where we were, but not half as steep as it did when we reached the base of it. The top was half a mile away, and it seemed impossible that the dogs would be able to pull the sled up. It was an obstacle course of ledges and clefts, boulders and stunted spruce. Even with the wind in back of us, it would be a tough climb.

"Isn't there another way up?"

"There is, but we'd lose too much time," Fred yelled. "We'll make it. Let's go!"

I got behind the sled with him and we both started pushing to help the dogs. After a few minutes I had to stop and rest. It was like trying to roll a boulder uphill, shoulders behind the handlebars, struggling upward a few hundred feet, then rest. I could feel every stab of willow, every rock, through my moccasins. It was as hard on the dogs as on us. They panted and clawed for purchase where there wasn't any, panted and strained where there was.

And finally we were at the top, all of us flopping down limply as if we were parts of one big body. My feet were bruised and I knew a couple of my toes were bleeding. I lay on my side, taking in huge gulps of air. Fred lay beside me.

"If you feel like crying," he said between deep breaths, "go ahead. I'll join in."

A couple of minutes later I sat up and looked out over the country that lay behind us. We were at the top of the world, and even as played out as I was my spirits lifted. The gray wide line of the river wound northeast through mountains whose sides were shrouded in mist. Above the mist loomed white pinnacles that stood out sharp against a midnight blue sky spangled with stars. Stretching directly below us was a long sweep of slope that was as inviting as a magic carpet, a carpet that led into a wonderland of dark green distant forests. It was dizzying.

I wondered how far down the slope went. After the climb we'd just had it looked like a dog musher's dream. The dogs would be able to take it at an effortless trot while Fred and I rode in style.

"That couldn't be The Drop," I said.

"No. It's down below."

"How far?"

"Couple of miles."

We took them as easily as I thought we would, leaving the wind on the other side of the hill. It was like traveling through a stage setting, the air clear and tingling, the moonlight sparkling off bushes laced with frost. The slope ended in a plateau and we veered to the right, skirting a sheer drop until the ground dipped and we rode down a wide trough for a short distance. The left side of the trough gradually lowered, the curved bottom flattened out and we came out onto a narrow ledge. There below was The Drop. I thought of how scared I'd been to ski down the hill at Joe Temple's cabin. This one made Joe's seem level. I didn't have to ask how it had gotten its name. It was obvious: you needed wings to climb it and wings to go down. It was just one long cascade of snow and ice-covered rock that ended half a mile below at Ptarmigan Creek. Even on foot you'd have to slide down most of it.

"Fred, we can't go down that in the sled—it's suicide!"

He was already untying the dogs.

"We're not. I am."

Now I saw what Mr. O'Shaughnessy's friend had meant when he said it could be done if the sled held together. If it got out of control and went too fast it would be smashed to pieces. The driver could be badly hurt, even killed.

I kept trying to talk Fred out of it, but he wouldn't listen to me. He'd done it before, he said, although not this late in the year when there was crusty snow and ice. "I'll make it," he insisted. He kept unharnessing the dogs, so I couldn't get him to look me in the eye to see if he was as sure as he sounded. Then he swung the sled around to face The Drop.

We were almost finished rough-locking the runners with chain when Fred pointed to something way off. "Look."

All I saw was the long flat sweep of the river.

"It's Cab," he said. My heart skipped a beat. "There on the river, all the way to our right. See?"

Then I saw it—a faint long speck darker than the gray around it. From this distance it looked as if it was barely moving.

"You sure it's him?" I began to feel excited.

"It's him," Fred said. "He may be a little ahead of us when we hit the river, but not much."

We finished chaining the runners quickly, then Fred told me to start down with the dogs. "I'll catch up with you."

"Fred . . ." I was torn between the excitement of catching up with Cab and the fear that Fred might be hurt.

"Go on," he said, "I'll make it, don't worry."

I started down with all the dogs except Pancake. Fred needed him to keep the sled pointed. I didn't have to walk. All I had to do was keep my balance and practically slide down, the dogs nipping at each other

281

and frisking around. I was halfway down when Fred let out a yell. I made the dogs whoa and sat down fast, bracing one moccasin against a rock.

By the time I looked up the sled was moving. Pancake was on a long lead, and the line was taut. Whether he'd be able to keep it taut once the sled picked up speed was another thing. Chains jingling, Fred on the runners, the sled nosed down in a straight line. Underneath the soft surface snow was hard crust, so Pancake had no trouble running, but the same crust was greasing the way for the sled. It picked up speed fast, even rough-locked as it was. A shower of sparks flew out from under the right runner as the chains scraped across a slab of rock. It didn't slow the sled down, though. Once over the rock the sled jumped forward and a spray of white flew out from behind as Fred rode the brake. Pancake had to run like sixty to keep the line from going slack. It was either that or get out of the way.

"Mush Pancake!" Fred yelled. "Yah-h-h—mush!"

By the time it was close to passing me the sled was rocking from side to side and Fred had to lean hard to keep it from tipping. Once abreast of me it hit a bump that sent the front of it two feet in the air. It came down with a punishing whump that I felt in the soles of my feet and Fred was bounced off the runners. I screamed, sure he wouldn't be able to get back on, that he'd end up tumbling like a rag doll, neck broken. But somehow he got one foot back on. In a kneeling position, he grabbed at the lashings and pulled himself up. Then he was standing, foot on the brake again, yelling to Pancake.

Once he was past the sled disappeared in its own boiling mist. In the next moment I thought my arm was going to be pulled from its socket. I was jerked forward by the dogs and went tumbling down the hill after them. Too excited to stand still, they were running after the sled, dragging me with them. It happened so fast I didn't have time to think or try to free the line from around my mitten. All I saw was a violent white world flying around me. Then my mitten was pulled off and I slid to a stop.

By the time the world stopped spinning and I got my

wits back the dogs were a snarling, yipping mass of confusion. Tangled up in the lines, they rolled and fought their way down towards the bottom of the hill. I didn't give one hoot about them, though, because there, all the way at the bottom was Fred. He'd made it and was already scrambling up towards the dogs.

Twenty minutes later we were on our way again, mushing down Ptarmigan Creek. I had a sore right arm and a couple of the dogs sported a red slash or two from the fight they'd had, but we were all in one piece. When we spilled down a cleft and onto the river I was disappointed. Cab was nowhere in sight.

"How far ahead is he, Fred?"

"Maybe half a mile."

"How far is it to the Indian village?"

"Another ten maybe."

"Fred, we've got to catch him!"

"We will—don't you worry. Pancake!" he yelled, "Domino! Samson—mush!"

"Mush!" I yelled right along with him. "C'mon, the whole bunch of you—mush!"

They mushed, too. They must have picked up the scent of the dogs ahead because they dug into their collars and surged as though they knew they were in a race and they had to win. We sped down the river like the wind.

We caught our first glimpse of Cab's sled when it was going around a bend in the river. That was all it was— just a glimpse before it disappeared around what must have been a gravel bar. A few minutes later when we rounded it ourselves there he was no more than a quarter of a mile away. We kept narrowing his lead until Fred called out to him. "Cab!" The hills picked it up and echoed it: *Cab. Cab. Cab.*

He stopped his team and waited. I couldn't see Chuck or Ethel behind him. I saw him take off a mitten and rub his eyes, trying to see who we were. As soon as he recognized us back went the mitten and he was off again.

"Cab—wait up!" I yelled. *'Ait up. 'Ait up. 'Ait up . . .*

But he wasn't trying to get away. He was letting us catch up to him gradually.

"Howdy there!" he called when we pulled alongside of him. His scarf muffled his voice. Between that and his furred hood I could only see his eyes, but I knew he was grinning. Chuck and Ethel were all bundled up. Chuck looked at us as if we were ghosts. "Tisha!" he called out. Ethel waved. The two of them were all right.

"Cab," Fred called over, "hold up a minute, will you?"

For answer Cab speeded his dogs up. "Cab, please stop," I called.

"You got a hundred dollars, Fred?" he called back. "A hundred spondulicks says I make it to Cross Creek before ya!"

"No!"

"No race, no stop."

"Take the kids off."

"No race, no stop," he repeated. "C'mon, boy, it's an easy mile, nary a bump nor a bang. How about it?"

I waited, wondering what Fred would decide. Ahead, the river looked fairly safe. Here and there were a few humps and some gnarled jags of ice, but they could be avoided.

"You're on!" Fred called back.

Cab let out a blood-curdling screech. "Mush, you buzzards," he roared. "Yah-h-h!" At almost the same time Fred let out a yell of his own and our sled jumped forward. We'd gone fast a few times on trail, but it was nothing like the way we went then. We flew across that snow with the wind behind us and the sled rocking like a cradle.

"Down!" Fred yelled at me.

He didn't have to tell me. That sled was a bare two feet wide and with someone sitting up it was no trouble at all to tip it over from the slightest bump. I slid down until I could just barely see ahead.

I looked over to Cab. We were running almost neck and neck, with him a few feet ahead. "Yah, Pepper!" Cab called to his lead dog. "Move that butt! Pull, you damn crow-bait, or I'll skin your hide! Yah!"

The teams knew they were in a race and they were pulling their hearts out. A few seconds later both sleds separated to avoid a jag of rough ice. Cab came

284

around his side too wide and he lost a few feet. Once we were straightened out we were a little ahead of him. The dogs were going so fast they were peppering me all over. One gob got me in the eye and I couldn't see for a couple of minutes.

Before I came to Alaska I'd always thought river ice froze the way it did on Christmas cards, smooth and even. But it didn't, at least not as far as a sled was concerned. If this was what Cab thought was without a bump or a bang I wondered what he'd consider rough. A couple of times I thought we'd turn over, but Fred held the sled steady. I looked over at Cab to see how Chuck and Ethel were making out. They'd both scrunched down as far as they could and were probably enjoying the ride.

A half-mile later Cab was a little ahead, but then his dogs had to veer off from some branches that had been blown onto the river and we were two team-lengths ahead of him. He and Fred were yelling up a storm, the echoes bouncing off the hills and yelling it all back to us.

Neither of us was going in a straight line. We veered all over the river, trying to keep to the smooth. One minute Fred and I would be in the lead, the next it would be Cab. When we both hit a stretch of soft snow at the same time and slowed down, Fred and Cab were off the runners and pushing. Cab moved ahead of us.

Once we were through it, both men on the runners again, Cab was still ahead. We were off to his left by this time, closer to shore and gaining on him when all of a sudden a rabbit appeared out of nowhere dead ahead. Pancake saw it, broke stride for just a moment as if he was going for it, and stumbled. It could have been a disaster. As it was it lost us the race. The dogs piled into each other and we ran into the wheel dog. He went down with a yowl and we plowed into three more of them before we could stop. None of them was hurt, but by the time Fred got all the harness straightened out Cab was too far ahead to catch.

He was waiting for us a quarter of a mile away. He let us come pretty close before he mushed on, but we never caught up with him again. We'd gain a little every now and then, but Cab reached Cross Creek a full two minutes before us.

Fred stopped the sled far enough away from him so the dogs couldn't get to each other, then he just stood for a couple of minutes trying to get his breath back. Cab was out of breath too. I got out of the sled and went over to Chuck and Ethel. They weren't any the worse for wear, but they were scared. Ethel put her arms out to me and I started to lift her out.

"Leave 'er be, Teacher," Cab said. "Sorry you came all this way, but I can't let you have 'em."

"Why are you doing this?"

"I ain't gonna let you roon your life."

I tried to convince him that he was wrong. No matter what I said he shook his head. He was doing it for my good.

"Let her have them, Cab," Fred said.

"I wouldn't butt in if I was you," Cab said.

"If Anne wants those kids it's her right to keep them."

"I'm takin' them where they belong," Cab said. He took off his mittens. "That's the way it's gonna be." He spoke so softly that if you didn't see his eyes you'd have thought he was being friendly.

"Fred . . ." I tried to take his arm, but he shook me off. He went to the sled and made as if to lift Ethel out. He never got to touch her. Cab charged right into him and gave him a hefty shove that almost made him lose his balance. "That's the way you want it, that's the way you got it," Cab said.

I wanted to stop it there and then. It wasn't fair. Fred wasn't a fighter like Cab. You could see just by the way he stood that he'd probably never had a fight in his life. He just stood there with his mittens bunched up in front of him as if he wasn't sure how you went about the whole thing. But not Cab. He knew what to do. He circled around Fred, his fists bobbing, while he moved in a little closer with each turn. Then all of sudden his left fist streaked out. Fred tilted his head back, but it didn't do him any good. Cab hit him on the side of the jaw with his other fist and it made such an awful sound I thought I was going to be sick. Fred fell right down, stunned. He didn't even know what had happened for a few seconds. He just sat there shaking his head, his legs spread open. He spat a chunk of blood out and there was a tooth in it. I started to go over to him, but Cab said, "Leave 'im be, Teacher."

I thanked God he wasn't drunk, because if he had been he'd have been all over Fred, trying to tear him to pieces. Instead he just stood over him, his fists holding invisible ski poles. "You get up, boy, and you're crazy," he warned. "You just say uncle now and we'll call it quits. Hey?"

Fred looked terrible. He wiped his mouth and smeared blood all over his chin, then he looked down at his tooth. When he looked up again I hardly recognized him. It wasn't only the blood, it was something else, that same expression he'd had when he'd almost fought Cab back in Chicken. I'd seen him get it on the trail when we had tough going. There wasn't any fear in it. It was calculating and deadly. His face was as gray as death and as cruel as numbing cold. All of a sudden I knew that the last thing he was going to do was call it quits.

"What do you say?" Cab asked him again.

Chuck and Ethel were on each side of me, Ethel holding on to me for protection. Scared, they'd clambered out of the sled and come right over to me.

Fred didn't get up fast, but when he did it wasn't like a man getting up, it was like an animal that was using every muscle in its body even before it was on its feet. As he did it a sound came from deep inside him that I didn't know a human being could make. When I heard it I felt that something terrible was about to happen, felt it even before Cab got hit the first time. Cab didn't have a chance. One second he was standing there with his fists weaving in front of him and the next there was blood spurting out of his nose and he was backing off with Fred wanting to kill him. I don't know how many times Fred hit him before he just toppled over backwards and his head hit the ice with an awful sound. Then Fred pounced on him, his knee landing on the side of Cab's neck. He wanted to get at him so bad that he sprawled past him only to scramble right back and

287

start pounding him as if he'd gone insane and Cab wasn't a man, but something to be beaten down into the ground. Cab kept trying to protect himself, but it didn't do him any good. Fred didn't care where he hit him, just as long as he could hit him. He pounded him in the ribs and there was a snap, then he pounded his face.

I kept trying to grab him and pull him off, but he didn't stop until Cab's head was lolling like a dead chicken's, his face smeared so heavy with blood it looked like a messed-up jelly apple.

We sat him up against his sled and put his mittens on him, then Fred set about trying to wake him up. We bathed his face with snow. Even after we got most of the blood off, he still looked terrible. His nose was broken and one eye was almost closed. Even after he healed, he wouldn't be looking the way he had before the fight.

He didn't come to for almost ten minutes, and at first he couldn't remember what had happened. One thing you had to say for him, though, was that once it all came back to him he didn't hold any grudge. In fact he acted just the opposite. As soon as he could stand up he told Fred he truly admired him, that he hadn't any idea Fred could handle himself that way. Fred said that Cab was pretty good himself and that he hoped he hadn't hurt him too much. Cab said Hell, he'd gotten beat up worse than that one time in Redman's Hall at Eagle.

He had to stuff some cotton in one of his nostrils and he didn't make a whimper. I was really worried about his being able to make it as far as the Indian village and so was Fred, but Cab said he'd be all right. In a way it was almost funny, Fred worrying over him and asking him if he was sure he was fit to travel and Cab telling him not to worry at all, he'd make it. A little while before they'd been trying to bash each other's brains out. Now they were carrying on like buddies.

Cab even got out a bottle of whiskey and offered Fred some. "Half-breed or not," he said, "you're a white man."

Fred turned the drink down and Cab took a few

288

swallows while Fred and I started putting Chuck and Ethel into our sled.

"I could go back with you as far as O'Shaughnessy's if you want," he said. "Looks like you might run into some bad weather." He pointed way far off to the southwest where the mountains were disappearing in a darkening sky. Fred told him we'd make out all right, so Cab just leaned back and watched us. We had Chuck and Ethel all bedded down and were about ready to go when Cab's dogs started sniffing the air and getting to their feet, a couple of them growling and bearing their teeth. Ours started to do the same thing and I thought that maybe they were going to start something between them, but they weren't. They were all looking back up the river.

Something was coming our way. All there was at first was a tiny patch of white fog moving toward us, then a dotted black line that turned into a string of maybe a dozen dogs. There was a man riding the sled behind them, another one trotting alongside. They were still too far away to make out who they were, but Cab's dogs turned so mean that they wouldn't settle down until Cab got a length of chain out and waded into them with it.

"Indians," he said, after he'd calmed them down. "My dogs don't take to 'em."

They were Indians, and one was Titus Paul. They must have been on their way back from their trapline because their sled was loaded. They stopped some distance away, their dogs as ready for a fight as Cab's. The other man stayed with them while Titus walked over.

It's funny how things strike you all of a sudden. I'd never thought about why Indians and Eskimos always ornamented their parkas with bright beadwork and plenty of color. I'd just figured that was their way. Until I watched Titus walking toward us. His caribou parka was a real beauty, white fur speckled with brown, topped by a wolf-fur hood, but as he came nearer I suddenly realized that after being on trail all this time I'd become tired and bored of seeing green and white. Looking at Titus was like seeing the whole world suddenly take on color, the slash of it at the hem of his parka, even the braided leather mitten-string that was attached to his collar. He looked like a Northern prince. Even the way he walked was kind of prince-like, long-legged and slow, chest out, and that small head of his above it all, making him seem taller than he was.

"Howdy, Titus," Cab called, "you make good catch? Take plenty fur?"

Titus nodded so you'd hardly notice, taking in Cab's condition without changing expression, then his eyes went flick-flick-flick, taking in me and Chuck and Ethel and dismissing us. Then they flicked to Fred and the dogs, and finally settled on Fred. Fred took off a mitten and offered his hand. "Fred Purdy," he said.

Titus took off his own lynx paw mitten. "Titus Paul," he said. Like his partner, he was all dressed in skins. His moosehide breeches were tucked into knee-high "husky" boots—moccasins made from the leg skin of the wolf above the ankle and moose leather below.

Cab took another swallow from the bottle and offered it to him. He took a couple of swallows, then handed it back. "You go Indian village?" he asked.

"Sure am," Cab said.

"You come see Cathy?" he asked me.

"No, Fred and I are going back to Chicken."

"We just had a little difference of opinion before you showed up, Titus," Cab said. The whiskey had already gotten to him, you could see. He was getting a mulish look to him that said he was thinking about something hard and coming to a conclusion about it. I smelled trouble and I wished Fred and I were gone. No doubt Titus had seen Cab's sled trail farther up the river and then seen where ours joined it. He looked at Chuck and Ethel, then asked them something in Indian.

Chuck pointed to Cab, explaining, then to me.

"You take kids from *skooltrai?*" Titus asked Cab.

"Yeah, I take 'em," Cab said, glancing at Fred and me. "I bring 'em back to Indian village where they belong," Cab answered. "People in Chicken no like they live there."

Titus looked at Fred. "Why *you* take from *him?*"

"Anne wants them."

I said, "Titus, they belong to me, their father gave them to me."

"They Indian kids. Indian kids belong Indian village."

"Glad you say that, Titus," Cab said. "Them two kids make this little lady lotsa trouble. Lotsa trouble. White people in Chicken no like *skooltrai* keep them. Make too much damn angry with her she keep them. Make angry with whole Indian village too!"

"Cab, you're a louse," I said.

Cab didn't pay me any mind. "You take these kids, Titus. Take to Indian village an' white people be lotsa happy."

Fred spoke up. "Titus, those two kids belong with Anne. She's been taking care of them. She wants them and they want her."

"Why you want?" Titus asked me.

"Because I love them."

The minute I said it I felt tears coming up and I was furious with myself. The last thing I needed right then was tears. I needed to be tough. Titus, he didn't know anything about tears, so I screwed my face up, and I gave him the meanest look I could manage. "What's wrong with that?" I said. "Is that a crime?" Somehow it didn't come out tough.

"Teacher," Cab said, grinning that dumb fool grin again, "you are the cat's whiskers."

"Cab, if you don't shut up—"

"Hold on a minute, Teacher. Titus, I ask you question. You have law in village—no brave go 'way from village without Council say yes. You savvy me?" Titus didn't say anything. "This little boy belong in village until Council say he can go. Am I right?"

Titus nodded.

"Well then I think you better take him and the little girl too."

He came over to where I was standing beside the sled and started to undo the ties. I don't know what happened to me then. As soon as Cab put his hands on Ethel I saw red. "No!" I yelled, and it was the strongest no I'd ever given to anyone. I didn't think and I didn't care. I just gave him the hardest push I could and he went sprawling. He looked as surprised as he had when Fred had hit him.

"These children are mine!" I yelled at him. "They're mine and nobody is going to take them away from me."

Cab stayed lying where he fell. One leg up in the air, he played the clown, looking up at me as if he were seeing me for the first time. Then Fred came over and stood beside me. "Calm down, Anne," he said.

"I'm *not* going to calm down. Ever since I came here everybody's been telling me what I'm supposed to do and what I'm not supposed to do. Now I'm going to do what *I* want to do!"

Titus' dogs weren't any friendlier than Cab's, so the Indian who'd stayed by the sled found a jag of ice he could chain them to. Then he came over and joined Titus. It was Arthur Jack. He looked over at Chuck, then said something and Titus nodded. I got in front of Chuck.

"Better let 'em have 'em, Teacher," Cab said. "They can get pretty mean."

I stayed put. "Titus, please, let me keep them," I pleaded. "Don't take them away from me. What chance are they going to have there in that place? What chance will Chuck have—the chance to grow up speaking broken English and maybe get a job sweeping up at a roadhouse? Or going to work on the riverboats? What chance will Ethel have except maybe to wind up living with some white miner the way her mother did?"

"They belong Indian village," Titus said grimly.

"They belong with me! Their father gave them to me."

He thought a moment. "You take girl," he said. "We take Chuck."

"Take him to what? What are you taking him to? Lame Sarah, who can't even feed herself?"

"You come talk Council. Not my business. Chuck Indian boy. You take him you make him white boy."

"I'll make you a promise. Let me keep him and Ethel and I swear I won't let them forget their own people. I'll never let them forget where they came from."

He was softening. I could feel it. "Titus," I said, "don't take them. I can make them strong, I can help them to be proud and stay proud. Let me do it."

He stared at me for the longest time, then his eyes flicked to Chuck and Ethel. Before he could say anything, Cab spoke up.

"Titus," he warned, "you no take these kids, them people in Chicken are gonna be mighty *sahnik* with ya. You gonna have Mr. Strong to deal with an' everybody else here in the Forty Mile. Now you be smart an' do the right thing, you hear? I'm warnin' you."

A wind came up, sending swirls of snow across the frozen surface of the river while Titus mulled the warning over. Then he asked Chuck a question in Indian.

"Aha," Chuck answered. Yes.

Then, just like that, Titus turned on his heel and headed back for his sled, Arthur Jack following. It happened so fast I didn't realize for a few seconds that Chuck and Ethel were mine. Cab did, though. "You know what the hell you're doin'?" he called after Titus.

Titus didn't pay him any mind and Cab took a few steps after him. "Titus! Damn it, are you deef?"

Titus finally turned around when he reached his sled. Cab stood with his back to me and Fred. I thought Cab was going to start more trouble, but he was as unpredictable as he was stubborn. "You wanna race to the village?" he called to Titus.

"You give me start," Titus called back.

"Hell, I ain't gonna give you no start," Cab said. "I got half a load of whiskey."

"I got full load fur."

"Give you a quarter mile 'n' betcha fifty dollars."

"Bet," Titus answered. "I fire two shot."

Titus' sled drove off and Cab came back. "Teacher," Cab said, "don't be mad at me. I was doin' what I thought was right."

I didn't pay any attention to him because I'd made up my mind I'd never say another word to him again.

"If it means anything," he went on, "I ain't gonna say anything to anybody about Titus lettin' you have those two kids."

"You really mean that?"

"I truly do. Shoot, I'm no snitch. I did my best an' that ugly weasel called my bluff. So how about lettin' bygones be bygones."

"All right."

He still looked in bad shape. I didn't see how he could have the energy left over to run another race. He did, though. He smiled at me. "Teacher, I'll tell you somethin' and I mean it from the bottom of my heart. You're an Alaskan."

"Thanks, Cab."

Fred released the brake on the sled and I got on the runners.

"See ya soon," Cab called.

"See you soon," I called back.

And that's the way we parted.

XXII

Fred found a place off the river that was out of the wind, then after we fed the dogs and built a fire we had some beans and jerky washed down with tea. Dead tired, Ethel fell asleep practically in the middle of eating, but Chuck was wide awake.

I'd asked him if Cab had treated him and Ethel all right and he said he had. He was confused, though. Too many things had happened too fast. "Where we go now?" he asked me.

"Back to Chicken."

"I not like that," he said.

"Why not?"

"Want go Indian village."

"You *want* to go to the Indian village?"

"Yiss. You come too there."

"I could take you there, Chuck, if that's what you

want, but I couldn't stay." I was disappointed. It was the last thing I'd expected him to say.

"We go other place maybe. You know other place?"

Then I realized what was on his mind. He wanted to be with me, but he was scared to go back to Chicken, scared of being grabbed again by Mr. Vaughn and the others.

I pulled him close to me. "Nobody'll take you away like that again," I said. "Don't you worry. I promise you, they'll be too scared to do anything like that. Isn't that right, Fred?"

"It sure is," Fred answered. His jaw was swollen, and it was all black and blue. "They try anything like that we'll beat 'em all up."

"You do that?"

"Sure will," Fred said.

Chuck smiled. He liked that. His head pressed into my shoulder, the fur around his hood tickling my nose.

Starting out, we piled Chuck and Ethel into the sled and Fred and I took turns riding the runners and trotting alongside. We'd take the route Mr. Strong followed, Fred said, along the river. If the weather held we could make the O'Shaughnessy roadhouse in seven hours, stop there to sleep, then push on for Chicken. He didn't say what we'd do if the weather didn't hold and I didn't ask. It never occurred to me it might not.

It would have been an easy trip if it hadn't been for the wind and the fact that we'd been up for almost twenty-four hours. The longer we kept going the more I couldn't help but wonder at the courage of men like Uncle Arthur and Ben. They'd come into this frozen land as newcomers, before it had hardly even been mapped, and they'd built cabins and made a go of it without any help from anyone. Uncle Arthur had told me he'd never even used a thermometer for the first ten years he'd been here. In the winter he'd just leave a vial of quicksilver out on the windowsill. "And if the quick froze, you knew it was too cold to go out," he'd told me.

Even now, thirty years after they'd settled here, the land was just as raw as it had ever been. Maybe it was settled a little more and had more people, but it was still a long lonely distance from one bleak outpost to another.

We'd been traveling for almost an hour. It must have been around nine o'clock and the sun should have been coming up. Instead it was growing darker and the wind was getting worse, lifting drifted snow and hurling it at us like balls of smoke. I was trotting alongside the sled when all of a sudden a blast came along that banged at us so hard I was nearly bowled over. Even the sled rocked. Fred stopped it and the dogs immediately dropped on all fours and started curling up.

"We're in for it!" he yelled.

The snow drove at us like a wall. We couldn't even talk. The two of us got down behind the sled and sat, waiting the blast out.

"Is it over?" I said after it died down.

"It hasn't started," Fred said, getting up. "This is just a lull."

"What'll we do?"

"Keep our fingers crossed. There's a cabin we can head for. A couple of miles farther up. We can hole up there."

A few minutes later the wind was at us again. It wasn't strong enough to keep us from going on, but it was meaner and colder than ever. I began to feel thirsty, and I had to stop myself from eating some snow. In this kind of cold it would be the worst thing to do, sucking precious body heat and giving nothing in return. The temperature was dropping fast and evaporating every bit of moisture. Even when we hit smooth ice the sled was balky and Fred had to trot behind it. The wind kept snapping at us like an icy whip, teasing us, then whacking at us hard. My mouth felt dry as dust.

We swung around a small delta, and Fred headed the sled for a big cleft in the bank, a slough. "Cabin's about a quarter mile up!" he yelled.

It was a long quarter mile. No sooner had we started up the slough than the lead dogs almost disappeared. Too deep and soft, the snow swallowed them up. Fred had to get out his and Chuck's snowshoes and the two of them moved ahead of us breaking trail while I drove the sled after them at a snail's pace. We moved up the side of the slough after a while and traveled along its bank, but even there the snow was piled too deep for the dogs.

The land leveled off a little, and finally Fred stopped. He and Chuck went off to look around. There was wood around us and it helped against the wind. I leaned an elbow on the handlebar and tapped the back of Ethel's hood. She turned around, brown expectant eyes staring at me over the mask of her scarf.

I smiled, then I remembered she couldn't see my mouth. I pulled my scarf down. "Where's the monkey?" I asked her. She thrust it out from the fur robe around her. It was her favorite toy, a fuzzy red monkey with brown button eyes. She'd held onto it even when they'd dragged her out.

"Monkey," she said.

"A happy monkey?"

"Monkey," she repeated, offering it to me. I made as if to grab for it, and she pulled it back under the robe. When it appeared again I made another grab and it went right back under.

Fred and Chuck came back.

"I can't find that cabin," he said.

"You sure it's here?" For a second I had the awful feeling we might be lost, but Fred nodded.

"Somewhere. It's probably drifted in." He put a hand on Chuck's shoulder, pointed. "Take a look over towards that rise," he told him.

Chuck went off in one direction, Fred in another, and I had to marvel at how fast they could move on snowshoes. Using them exhausted me, but Fred and Chuck swept around on them without the slightest effort. Fred kept moving farther and farther away, looking for landmarks, anything that would give him a bearing on where we were.

The dogs had been lying down quietly, muzzles flocked white. Now, one after the other, they got to their feet, sniffing the air. Either the wind had shifted and they smelled something they hadn't smelled before, or something was around that hadn't been up to now.

Pancake uttered a low growl, the ruff around his neck bristling. The other dogs were doing the same thing, and some of them began to whine. I called to Fred and he snowshoed over.

"What is it, boy?" he asked Pancake.

Pancake hung his head and kept growling. He was scared.

"Whatever it is, we can't worry about it," Fred said as Chuck joined us. "We'll head over that way." He pointed to where a double line of straggling willow and birch marked the path of a creek. "It's got to be around here somewhere."

He and Chuck started off, and I mushed the sled after them. A few minutes later we came to a clearing where the snow wasn't that deep and Fred and Chuck were able to take off their snowshoes. Fred took the sled from me. We mushed around the clearing, then down a sidling trail. We ended up beside the slough again, a little above where we'd left it. Below us were our own trail marks.

"It must be above us. We didn't come up far enough," Fred said. "Mush!" he yelled at the dogs. They started to move up the slough, then stopped dead, and no matter how much Fred yelled at them they wouldn't move. Pancake's hair was really up now. Fred moved up to him, grabbed his collar and jerked him forward with a curse, but Pancake braced his forelegs and wouldn't budge. When Fred tried to pull him forward again he snarled and bared his fangs. He meant business. I could feel the hair on my own neck start to rise.

"Fred, maybe there's a good reason why he won't go."

"He has to. We can't stay here. We've got to find that cabin!" His face above his scarf was dotted with pinpoints of blood from the driving wind.

He dragged Pancake forward a few feet and then that was the end of it. Pancake simply lay down and whimpered. *Do what you want to me,* he was saying, *I'm not going.* The other dogs did the same. It was eerie. Whatever was a little farther on had them too frightened to move.

"Stay here," Fred said to me and Chuck. He moved along the edge of the slough, then when he was almost out of sight I saw him stoop down and pick something up. He came back with it—a length of dog harness. It had been chewed. "There's what's left of a dog over there, just the skull, a few bones and some hair."

"Bear?" I asked him.

"Wolf," Chuck said.

Whatever Fred was thinking he kept to himself. He chained the dogs to a tree, then took his rifle out of the sled. "You stay here with the kids," he said to me. "I'm going to take a look around."

"Oh no. We're going with you." Nothing in the world was going to keep me there with him gone. I took Ethel out of the sled.

We slogged after him. I knew that wolves didn't attack people—at least not people who were alive—but I still felt nervous. Any minute I expected something to come running out at us from behind a bush or a tree. I held Ethel's hand tightly. Instead of going straight up the edge of the slough, Fred made a wide circle, then started working back towards it. Before we reached it we found the remains of another dog. Again it was only a skull, the wind had swept the rest away. There was something else too. Chuck found it snagged in a bush— a small length of polished hardwood with some webbing attached. It was part of a sled.

We went on a little farther until we all stopped at almost the same time. There a little above us was some kind of a ledge where there shouldn't have been one. It was right smack in the path of the slough, almost as though someone had built a curved platform across its banks. But it wasn't seeing the ledge that made us stop. It was what was on it: a pack of wolves circled around something. We were downwind from them, so they hadn't caught our scent, and with the wind blowing they hadn't heard us approach.

I counted seven of them. The smallest wasn't under a hundred and fifty pounds. They looked like ghosts through the flying drift, all of them staring at something, milling around as if they didn't know how to get to it. And that was the weird part. There was nothing there, at least nothing I could see.

Two of them were more restless than the others. Long-legged, with a gait like a cat's, they kept loping around the perimeter of something, stopping every so often to peer down. I didn't know what it was about wolves that made people think of them as enemies, but people did. Maybe it was because they were so smart, working together to bring down what they were after. Or maybe there was just something in the human mind that couldn't help itself, like the way fishermen hate sharks. But after I'd just seen what was left of the two sled dogs they'd taken, I didn't feel too friendly to them myself.

They saw us a few seconds later. Whatever it was that interested them, they didn't want to leave it, so they waited to see what we were going to do. The way they sized us up made my skin crawl. I'd always thought of wolves as smart dogs. This close they didn't resemble dogs at all. No dog had the huge head and powerful jaws these animals had, and no dog had their cold, shrewd gaze either. They were almost human. Or inhuman.

Fred went down on one knee, took aim, and his rifle cracked. The biggest of them, which must have weighed close to two hundred pounds, went right down. He rolled down to the end of the ledge, then just disappeared into a bed of soft snow below it. The rest of them took right off.

Fred told us to stay where we were and made his way up along the border of the slough. He glanced over to where the wolf had disappeared below, then moved out onto the ledge. I still couldn't figure out what it was, an ice bridge across the banks or what.

Fred went down on his hands and knees and inched forward. He stopped at right about the place where one of the wolves had been peering down and I thought I heard him call out, say something to somebody. I couldn't stand the waiting any longer.

"Fred, what is it?" I called to him.

He turned and waved me over. "Leave the kids there," he said.

I followed the same path he took, stepping in his tracks. I didn't know what I expected to see when I got there, but something told me it wasn't going to be pleasant. The ledge was bigger than I'd thought, bulging up a little towards the center. It wasn't solid either. There was a jagged hole almost in the middle of it. It was big, maybe four feet wide and three times as long. The whine of a dog was coming from it.

Fred pushed himself back from the hole before I reached him. He stood up, the front of him painted with snow. He pulled his scarf down, and his expression was awful. "Take a look," he said, "but be careful . . . It's Jeannette and Elmer."

I crawled up to the edge of the hole and peered in. My first thought was that whatever I was seeing couldn't be real. It was like a scene from another world. Underneath me was a huge domed ice cavern, and there in the darkness a dozen feet below, her face partially covered with a fur robe, her eyes boring into mine, lay Jeannette Terwilliger. I thought she was dead until her eyes blinked, and I saw the glint of tears in them. I heard myself say, "Oh dear God."

She was lying on her side among the rocks of the slough bed, a fur robe wrapped around her. Beside her was the smashed sled. She pulled the robe down a little, but her face was still hidden by her scarf. Elmer was a short distance away from her. All I could see were his legs. He'd crawled up the side of the slough, where he lay now, not moving. I couldn't tell if he was alive or dead.

In a split second I saw it all as it must have happened: the loaded sled moving across the innocent-looking snow, the domed roof of ice under it giving, shattering like an egg and the sled falling, crashing to the ravine below. It must have happened so fast that they were falling before they heard the hollow sound of the shell ice breaking under them.

Two dogs had been pulled down with them. One of them had already clambered onto the over-turned sled and was making motions as if to jump up at me, whining in eagerness. But the distance was too great. The other dog lay among the rocks, its neck broken. Jeannette hadn't taken her eyes from me.

"Jeannie?" I managed to croak out her name.

She made some sounds. That was all.

"We'll get you out," I said. Then, knowing I'd burst

into tears if I stayed a moment longer, I inched back and the scene disappeared.

"You're not going to cry," Fred said harshly. "We don't have time for crying. We've got to get her out of there."

I bit my lip. "What'll we do?"

Chuck and Ethel had come up on the ledge and Chuck started to edge forward. "Stay away from there," Fred said.

"Want see," Chuck said.

"You'll see later. I need you with me."

We followed him to a big fallen spruce where he started scooping snow out on the side of the trunk that was out of the wind.

"You'll stay here with Ethel," Fred said when there was a hole big enough for Ethel and me to huddle in. "I'll take Chuck with me." He gave me his rifle. "Hold onto this. You probably won't need it, but keep it anyway."

"Where are you going?"

"To find that cabin. I know where it is now."

He and Chuck went off to get the sled. From where Ethel and I were we could see the whole ledge. Ethel pointed to it and asked me something in Indian.

"It's a hole," I said. "There was an accident there. A bad accident."

"Hole?"

I thought about the baby. I hadn't seen her. I'd been afraid to ask Jennie about her, afraid she was dead. Now a whole bunch of terrible images crept into my mind. She could be under the sled, crushed, or she could have been thrown out. I kept seeing her flying out of Jennie's arms as dogs and sled crashed through the ice, kept seeing her lying in the snow and the wolves moving toward her. . . . Finally I couldn't stand it anymore.

"Stay here, Ethel," I said. I crawled back to the edge of the hole and looked down. Elmer was in exactly the same position as before. He must have been dead.

"Jennie . . . Jennie?"

She turned her head a little, but her hood still hid her face.

"Can you answer me?"

She groaned.

"Patricia—where is she?"

Her arm moved under the robe that covered her, then her mittened hand pulled down her scarf and I saw why she couldn't talk. Half of her face was white as snow, dead-looking. It was frozen.

"Ee-e-e-uh-h-h," she groaned.

"Here? Is that what you're saying? She's with you? Nod your head if you can and I'll know it's yes."

Her head moved slightly and I thought, thank God. Then I wondered if she was alive, but I couldn't ask Jennie that. "Hang on, Jennie," I said, knowing how stupid it sounded, but not knowing what else to say.

I went back to Ethel and while the two of us huddled together, I kept thinking about the accident and how it had happened. Jennie and Elmer had probably done exactly what Fred and I had—hit bad weather and come up here looking for the same cabin. Like us, they'd had trouble finding it, so they'd searched around blindly. Maybe they'd been caught in ice fog, or blizzard, but for some reason they hadn't seen that the ledge was false, a covering for a huge hollow blister. It had probably formed when water came rushing down the slough in a flash flood. The water must have gotten dammed up in some way and been held fast. By the time it drained out the surface of it had frozen, leaving just a shell. And Elmer hadn't seen it until it was too late. The same thing could have happened to anybody—to me and Fred. I'd heard of it before. I wondered how long Jennie had been down there. It could have been as much as three days, three days of lying in a frozen dungeon with hardly the barest chance of being found, and the wolves circling around above. If it hadn't been for the wolves we'd never have gone to the spot at all. She and Elmer probably wouldn't have been found until spring, maybe not even then, for then water would have come rushing down the slough, tons of it, washing everything before it into the river.

Over an hour must have passed before Fred came back with the sled. "We've found it!" he said. It was drifted in, just as he'd thought. He'd left Chuck to finish

303

the job of clearing the door. He'd brought a strong slender birch trunk with him that he'd chopped down. Tying a rope around the center of it he went over to the ledge and placed it across the narrowest width of the hole. After he made sure the ice on each side would hold, he let himself down the rope. I watched from above.

The dog that was uninjured was overjoyed. Fred had to cuff it a few times before it would stop jumping all over him. Then he lifted the sled off of Jennie. Half of the load was still in it, the rest of it—picture frames, a gold scale, mining tools, traps—was scattered all over the ravine bed.

He made Jennie as comfortable as possible and put another robe over her before he looked around. The slough was flat at the bottom, the banks sloping up gently to where the ice met them. He picked up a mattock that had spilled from the sled and chopped a good-sized rock loose from the frozen ground. "Anne, move over that way about ten feet." He pointed to where the ceiling arched down to meet the top of the bank. "Tell me if you can hear this rock hitting." His voice sounded hollow, as if it came from a tomb.

I did as he told me, listening. *Thump. Thump. Thump.* I scrambled back to the hole.

"I heard it."

"I'm going to try to dig out of here."

"You want us to come down?"

"No. Somebody's got to stay up there just in case."

"Fred, what about the baby?"

"I think it's all right. It's under her parka."

"Can you hand it up to me?"

"Jennie's arm is broken. I don't want to touch her until we can get her out . . . You're going to have to make out as best you can. I don't know how long it's gonna take to chop through this ice."

He moved out of sight and I heard him start chopping.

I went back to Ethel and we waited. She fell asleep again before Chuck came back. When he did I told him what Fred was doing and he went over to the hole to see if Fred needed him. He must have, because

304

Chuck swung himself over the birch trunk and disappeared.

It began to snow.

I got up once or twice to stamp around and keep the circulation going in my legs. The dogs had all curled up, still in harness. Nothing bothered them, not the wind or the driving snow. Noses tucked into tails, they lay as contentedly as if they were in a warm living room, letting the white pile up around them.

I kept looking towards the spot where I thought Chuck and Fred would come out for so long my eyes started doing tricks on me. Then finally I saw a small hole appear. After that the snow began caving in like quicksand, and I roused Ethel. Chuck's head popped up and he levered himself out of the hole as Ethel and I headed over towards him. "We digged out!" he yelled excitedly. The uninjured dog scrambled out right after him, yelping and frisking around Ethel and me, almost knocking us over.

I lowered myself into the hole slowly. My feet touched the solid bank and I felt Fred grab me. Then I was below the ice and Fred helped me down the bank.

It was like a gloomy world where time had stood still. Overhead was a dome of ice that stretched across from one bank to the other and maybe thirty feet up and down the slough. Outside the wind was howling, but it was quiet in here, snow flakes drifting down through the opening above. Elmer was stretched out on the bank opposite, his head almost touching the ice above him. He was frozen, one hand still upraised. There was a hunting knife in it, and above him you could see where he'd tried to chop away at the ice. One of his legs was horribly twisted, bent at a sharp angle where there was no joint. He'd managed to crawl up the bank, and he'd died there.

I went over to Jennie.

"Jennie . . ."

She opened her eyes.

"Jennie, do you want me to take the baby?" My voice bounced off the ice above.

She nodded. I pulled away the furs that Fred had covered her with, and lifted up her parka. The baby was lying against her stomach. Somehow, even with a broken arm, she'd managed to protect her. She was still wrapped in her blanket. When I lifted the blanket from her face my heart sank. At first I thought she was dead. Her face was a sickly blue, her little body still. She wasn't dead, though. The barest wisp of vapor curled from her mouth. I put her inside my own parka and she felt cold next to me, a cold little thing that didn't move.

"S-s-s-e-e-e," Jennie said. "S-s-e-e-e." Her eyes pleaded.

"Let her get warm first, Jennie," I said. "She's cold." I didn't want her to see the baby the way she was. She had enough misery already. Her eyes closed.

Ethel and Chuck had come down through the hole. Fred set Chuck to work making the hole wider, then he knelt beside Jennie. "She's out," he said. "Thank God." He picked up a man's shirt that lay in a pile of other clothes. "Rip that up," he said. "I'm going to set her arm."

He went after the sled with an ax until he had two lengths of wood for splints. After that he rolled Jennie on her back and eased the broken arm out of her parka. Even under the sleeve of her long underwear, the break was clear. He sat down and braced one foot against her armpit, then pulled on her wrist slowly. I turned away until I heard the bone snap into place. While he set her arm in the splint I walked up and down the slough bed, hoping I could jostle the baby into making even the smallest move. It didn't do any good, though. She lay still.

Fred kept working methodically and I marveled at how he could act so coolly. If everything had been on my shoulders I'd have broken down long ago. When he was finished he climbed up the bank alongside Chuck, took the mattock from him and chopped some more ice away. When he was done he tossed the mattock down and looked over at me wearily.

"How's the baby?" he asked.

"She's not moving." *She's going to die* was what I thought, but I didn't want to say it.

"You'd better give her to Chuck," he said. "I'll need your help with Jennie."

I handed the baby over. "Hold her tight," I said. I could have saved my breath. He was eight years old, but if ever I'd seen a boy act twice his age it had been him.

Fred lifted Jennie's shoulders and I took her legs. Halfway up the bank one of them slipped out of my grasp. Her foot dropped onto a rock, making a horrible sound—as if it was a rock itself. I glanced up at Fred, cringing inside. His mouth set itself in a tight line. Only one thing could have made a sound like that —a foot that was frozen solid.

XXIII

Somehow we managed to get Jennie up through the hole and into the sled.

We made a few trips back in to bring out food and things for the baby. Then Fred dragged out the dead dog and left it some distance away. There'd been some traps on the sled, and before we left, he brought five of them out and set them around the hole. We hoped they'd keep the wolves away from Elmer's body.

When we reached the cabin I wondered how Fred had found it at all. It squatted so low against a hill that I didn't even see it until we were practically on top of it.

Inside, the sloping ceiling was too low for Fred or me to stand up straight except by one wall, and there wasn't too much room to move around. It was shelter, though, and it was all we needed. There was oil in a dusty lamp. After Fred lit it we brought Jennie in and laid her on a rickety canvas cot, then Fred started a fire in the small Yukon stove.

I took Patricia out from under my parka. When I

307

looked at her I almost groaned. Her face and hands were a sickly violet in the light of the oil lamp, and there wasn't anything I could do for her except sit by the stove and hold her close to me.

After we stored our gear and filled some pots with snow, I started some stew thawing while Fred and Chuck went to work on Jennie. Fred filled a small washtub with snow, then took the moccasin and socks off her frozen leg. It was hard as marble, white up to the knee. He put it into the washtub and began to bathe the leg with snow while Chuck bathed her face. She hadn't regained consciousness and I hoped for her sake that she'd sleep for as long as possible. Once feeling came back to her she'd be in terrible pain.

It took a long time to boil water for tea. The stove had to be coddled, since the sheet-metal sides were too rusted and flaky to chance a big fire. Someone had laid a piece of sheet metal across the top to reinforce it, otherwise we wouldn't have been able to cook on it at all. Even so, it didn't throw out much heat.

I handed some tea over to Fred and Chuck, then poured some for Ethel and me. None of us had said a word since we'd come in. We were all played out, just going on nervous energy. Jennie moaned softly and moved her head. Some snow fell away from her face.

"How bad is she," Fred?"

He didn't have to say anything. His look was enough. He shook his head. "How about the baby?" he asked me.

"She hasn't moved."

"We have to decide what to do," Fred said. "Jennie's foot's frozen to the bone. The leg may be too, I can't tell."

"What can we do?"

"Get her to a doctor."

Outside the wind was blowing hard as ever, making the stovepipe hum. "How can we?"

"We have to. *I'll* have to . . . Even if she does get to a doctor she's going to lose her foot, maybe the whole leg."

"Where's the nearest one?"

"Dawson."

That was over a hundred and fifty miles.

"I could take her as far as Forty Mile," he said. "There's bound to be someone who could take her to Dawson from there."

Forty Mile was the first town across the Canadian border, but it was still ninety miles. I didn't see how he could make it, not as tired as he was. The weather outside was as mean as ever. "That's a long trip, Fred."

"I know," he said. "I'd have to get some sleep first, a few hours anyway, but I could do it. There are places I could stop at on the way. I've traveled in worse weather."

"When would you start out?" I asked him.

"After we eat and I get a few hours sleep. You'd have to manage here alone."

It was a grim meal. I hardly tasted the food. When Chuck and Ethel finished they sat stupefied. They couldn't stay awake anymore. They used a pail to relieve themselves, then they bundled up together in a sleeping bag we'd taken from the Terwilligers' sled. They were asleep before we buttoned the bag up.

Fred and I had another cup of tea.

"I hate to leave you all alone here," he said.

"How long do you think it might be?"

"Mr. Strong's due up the river in a day or two. I'll leave word at Steel Creek that you're here. With the weather like this, well, you'll be here a couple of days. Maybe more."

"You better get to sleep," I said.

"You think you can stay awake?"

"I'll have to." Somebody had to wake him up.

I took Patricia out of my parka to look at her again. She was losing the blue color. Her little hands were pink. If she woke up she'd have to be fed, so I had another reason for staying awake.

Fred laid out another sleeping bag and told me to wake him in three hours. He fell asleep almost as fast as the kids had. My watch had stopped, so I set it at twelve, then sat down on the edge of the cot. Jennie's face had begun to blister. Her foot was still in the washtub, the skin on her leg beginning to wrinkle. I leaned over, picked up some snow and bathed her leg with it.

When my hand touched the flesh it made me shudder.

After a few minutes I felt sleepy and got up. The dog that had been in the slough was lying between the stove and the wall. He lifted his head. We'd chained him up outside with the other dogs, but they'd attacked him, so we'd brought him in. I stood by the high wall for a few minutes, then I sat down on a stool by the stove. I took the baby out and rocked her. I brushed her cheek with my lips. It was warm, soft as a flower petal. She looked like Elmer around the cheeks and eyes, but she had Jennie's mouth, kind of pouty and nice. "Patricia?"

I'd changed her diapers and gone over her carefully to see if there was anything wrong with her. She had a black and blue mark on her thigh and it had swelled a little, but she didn't have any broken bones. Outside of some chafing from wet diapers she seemed all right. I rocked her some more and talked to her. She squirmed a little and there was a flash of pink tongue before she sucked it back in her mouth. Then she yawned. Excited, I walked back and forth with her. I had a bottle filled with diluted condensed milk, all set to be plunked in a saucepan if she woke. "Come on, Patricia. That's it," I said. "Just wake up and start yelling. You can do it . . ."

She stopped and was still.

There was a small fruit crate lying by the stove with some kindling in it. I emptied it out, laid some newspapers on the bottom, then wrapped a blanket around Patricia and placed her in the crate. After that I put some more wood in the stove. The sides of it were so thin that the fire gleamed through in places.

I sat down on the edge of the cot again and bathed Jennie's leg. I fell asleep right in the middle of it. I caught myself falling forward and my knees almost touched the floor before I woke with a start. For the next couple of hours I kept putting snow on my face and neck to stay awake.

A half hour before I was supposed to wake Fred, Jennie began to scream.

She kicked away the washtub and I had to grab her to keep her from falling off the cot. It happened so suddenly that I was terrified. One moment everything was still and the next I was wrestling with Jennie and sobbing hysterically for Fred. She thrashed around, screaming in pain. And finally Fred was on the other side of the cot, holding her in a firm grip, talking to her while she stared at us wild-eyed. She kept trying to talk, but her mouth was twisted in an ugly sneer and her words were just a babble of sound.

"Jennie, you're here with Anne and me," Fred kept repeating. "You're safe. You're safe, Jennie. Try to understand."

The wild look went out of her eyes. She stopped struggling and fell back in exhaustion. She realized where she was. Her eyes closed and tears of pain welled up from them. "Eshuh," she said quietly. "Ee-shuh."

"Patricia's here, Jennie," I said. ". . . She's sleeping. Do you want to hold her?"

She nodded.

I brought the baby and laid her in the crook of Jennie's arm. She raised her head to look at the baby a moment, then slumped back and closed her eyes. The pain she was suffering must have been excruciating, but she lay still. She had her baby.

"Jennie," Fred said, "I have to get you to a doctor . . . you understand?" She nodded without opening her eyes. "Anne'll stay here with the baby and take care of her." She only made the barest movement. She understood.

Chuck and Ethel hadn't waked up. They'd lived in close quarters all their life. They were used to all the noise that went with it.

While Fred made preparations to leave I warmed up a chunk of vegetable soup and fed the broth to Jennie. She was able to drink only a little of it. Once in a while she moaned softly, but from the moment I'd given her the baby she'd hardly made a sound. The only way I knew what she was going through was when I looked into her eyes. The pain was there, the pain of losing her husband and leaving her baby, and the pain in her tortured body. I could hardly imagine the suffering she was going through.

When Fred was ready we carried her out. The cabin

and the hill in back of it gave us little protection from the wind as we lashed her into the sled. Gray sleet drove at us, the cold pressing like water. When the lashings were secure I leaned over Jennie to say a hurried good-bye. "I'll take care of the baby, Jennie. I'll take good care of her."

She moved one mittened hand feebly and pulled the scarf from her mouth. One side of her mouth twisted up before her hand dropped. She had tried to smile.

Fred was ready to go.

There were so many things I wanted to say to him—how much I admired him, how much I needed him and wanted him, how deeply I loved him. But there was no time. Instead I said, "Please be careful, Fred."

"I will. Just don't you get scared."

"I've got the easy part."

I didn't wait for him to kiss me. If I did, I'd have waited till Kingdom come. I kissed him hard enough so that maybe it would keep him warm and safe and alive all the way he had to go.

Then he was gone, the sled disappearing in a gray swirl. I turned back into the cabin.

After a while I knew I couldn't stay awake any longer. I'd kept walking back and forth with Patricia as long as I could, coaxing her to wake up. It wasn't doing any good. She'd move a little, open and close a tiny fist, and that was all. She was a perfect little thing and inside of her there was a struggle for life going on, but there was no way I could help her. I felt myself caving in. I put some more wood in the stove, then crawled into Fred's sleeping bag with her. Even if the stove went out we'd all be warm enough.

I didn't know how much later it was that I started to wake up, thinking there was an alarm ringing somewhere. Groggy, at first I thought it was my father's alarm clock and I wondered why he didn't turn it off. It seemed to keep ringing for hours and it made me angry until I realized it wasn't an alarm at all. It was a baby crying.

Then I was awake. Beside me, Patricia was spluttering in rage—the most wonderful sound I'd ever heard.

I was out of the sleeping bag in a moment. I stood

up too fast and bumped my head on the ceiling. The fire in the stove was just embers. Shaking the ashes down, I heaped up some paper and kindling, then wood on top of that. It caught right away and I plunked the bottle I'd prepared into the saucepan. Then I turned up the oil lamp.

Chuck and Ethel were still asleep, the top of Chuck's head poking out of the bag. I rocked Patricia in my arms, talking to her, telling her she'd be eating soon, filling up on all she needed. I looked at my watch. It said 8:30. That meant I'd slept almost five hours since Fred had gone. I wondered what the real time was, whether it was day or night. I'd lost track and there was no way to tell. Sleet was needling at the window. It was iced over and it looked to be night outside. I couldn't be sure, though. I kept going over to the stove to check the bottle, but it always seemed as cold as ever and Patricia kept yelling. Her fingers found her mouth and she shoved them into it, gums clamping down on them. They satisfied her for a couple of minutes before she realized nothing was happening, then she bawled again for the real thing.

The bottle was tepid when I gave it to her. I just couldn't wait for it to get any warmer. She grabbed at the nipple, struggled with it, then pushed it out. I tried again and the same thing happened. I checked the nipple and it was all right, but when I gave it to her again the milk dribbled down her chin. She wasn't getting it.

I started to feel helpless panic, afraid I was doing something wrong, but I didn't know what. Patricia screamed louder than ever. Chuck's head popped out from the sleeping bag. He looked over at me, not really awake, then his head disappeared.

I put the bottle back in the saucepan, thinking that maybe it wasn't warm enough. Every few minutes I tested it on my wrist. When it felt warm I gave it to her again. She still wouldn't take it. I tasted it to see if there was anything wrong with it, but there wasn't.

Ten minutes later she was asleep again. I sat looking at her, wondering what could possibly be wrong, if maybe she'd been injured internally in some way. If she had been then there was nothing I could do but sit here and watch her die. I crawled back into the sleeping bag with her and lay there in a half stupor.

The next time she woke I was up before she began to cry. I'd refilled the bottle with fresh milk, and this time I waited for it to heat to the right temperature before I gave it to her. She still wouldn't take it. She twisted and turned, avoiding the nipple, screaming as though she were in pain.

Sick with fear, I sat and stared into space. I couldn't help her. Whatever she needed, I couldn't give it to her.

Chuck's head popped out of the sleeping blanket. He eased himself out of it, shivered, then slipped on his parka. He watched while I tried to get Patricia to take the bottle again.

"Baby no hungry," he said.

"She is hungry, Chuck. That's why she's crying. She hasn't eaten in a couple of days. I don't know what to do."

Chuck wiggled his fingers in front of her. She stopped crying to look at them, then he put a finger in her hand. She grabbed onto it and held it for a few moments before she let it go.

"Tiny liddle baby," he said.

"Did you ever see anything like this happen?" I asked him. "I mean where a baby wouldn't eat?" I was so desperate I was asking an eight year old for help. He shook his head.

I tried the nipple again, but it was the same. She took it, then spat it out and started crying. I handed the bottle to Chuck and put her over my shoulder. The bottle seemed bigger in his hands, awfully big. Maybe that was the trouble. She hadn't eaten in two or three days and she was weak. Maybe she was too weak to hold onto the nipple. "Chuck, get me the first-aid kit. It's over there on the shelf."

He brought it over. There was a medicine dropper in it. Unscrewing the cap on the bottle, I asked Chuck to hold it, pulled some milk up into the dropper and put it in her mouth. She wouldn't take it, but I kept at it. For I don't know how long the milk kept dripping out of her mouth. Then when I was almost ready to give up she began holding on to some of it. First just a few drops, then more.

"She's taking it, Chuck."

He leaned over her, interested. She fussed and fumed, frustrated every time I pulled the dropper out to fill it up again, but she was taking it, all right. When she dropped off to sleep there was about an inch and a half of milk gone from the bottle. She hadn't taken much, hardly more than a couple of mouthfuls, but at least she'd taken something.

I put her back in the fruit crate, then set about getting a meal ready. The dog came over to the stove while I was cooking. I sent him out to do his business and he was at the door again almost right away, scratching and whining to get in.

Ethel woke up just before the meal was ready and the three of us sat down and ate—biscuits and stew. When we were done Chuck and I did the dishes and Ethel sat beside Patricia, talking to her. I couldn't seem to get my mind going. What I needed to clear it was about twelve straight hours of sleep. I felt as if I was going to burst out crying any minute. I wondered where Fred was, how he was making out. If the weather kept up like this it could take him four or five days to reach Forty Mile, with stopovers for sleep. If it eased up he might make it in two.

With the dishes done the three of us sat on the cot while I fed Patricia again with the medicine dropper. Chuck was thumbing through a yellowed magazine. He pushed it over to me and pointed to a page. It was a drawing of a trim, neatly dressed housewife standing alongside of an electric washing machine. She was barely touching the clothes as they went through the wringer and dropped into the laundry basket.

"You like?" Chuck asked me.

"I sure would," I said.

"One day," he said, "I have lotsa money. I buy for you."

"That's nice of you."

"You no more wash and wash and wash." He imitated me scrubbing at the washboard. "How much cost it that?"

I looked at the price. "A hundred and two dollars."

He thought about it, but didn't say anything.

The Terwilligers' dog woke up and sniffed the air. Then it began to whine. A few seconds later a wolf howled somewhere. It wasn't the long lonely cry, but the excited hunting call and it was answered right away by the other wolves. I wondered if they had somehow found their way into the slough bed.

Chuck said something to Ethel in Indian. She answered, "Aha"—yes. I thought it was something about the wolves. I asked him what he'd said.

"I tell Et'el this good place, ask she like stay here. She say yiss."

He was still worried about going back to Chicken. I wondered what *would* happen when we got back, what Mr. Vaughn and Angela Barrett would say. But I didn't really care one way or the other. They didn't seem important anymore, not after all this. The only one I was concerned about was Maggie—what she'd be going through when she found out about Jennie.

Time passed. We couldn't go outside, so we made the best of staying inside. To pass the time we played games—Hot and Cold, Hide the Thimble. Their favorite game was one they made up themselves. They'd run across the room and I'd try to give them a light whack on the bottom as they went by. If I missed they won.

Each time Patricia woke up, every hour or so, she took a little more milk. I kept trying her with the nipple, until finally—it must have been almost a day later —she took it. She finished a whole bottle, then threw half of it back up, but she was getting stronger. In the next few hours she took two more half-filled bottles.

The only thing I'd have wished for was some uninterrupted sleep. Patricia wouldn't sleep for more than a few hours at a time even after she started taking the bottle. Sometimes she'd cry for what seemed hours, and I'd walk up and down with her in a daze until she settled into an uneasy sleep and I'd do the same. I started to get cabin fever, snapping at Chuck and Ethel for no reason at all, then hating myself for it. They were helping out as much as they could, bringing in wood and snow, helping with the dishes and keeping things in order. Chuck even warmed the bottle and helped me feed the baby once.

After two days of it the time came when I just couldn't bring myself to wake up. Patricia began to cry when we were all asleep. I nudged Chuck and asked him to put the bottle in the saucepan, then I gave Patricia to him and told him to wake me when the bottle was ready. I ducked down into the sleeping bag and that was all I remembered until I woke up some time later to hear her crying again. I didn't know how long I'd slept but Ethel and Chuck were awake. She was sitting on their sleeping bag holding Patricia. Chuck was at the stove, warming a bottle.

"Chuck, how long have I been asleep?"

He shrugged. "Long time, I think."

I got up, feeling pretty good. "Don't you have any idea how long?"

He shook his head. "You give me baby. I give milk for him. He go sleep, I go sleep. He wake up, I wake up, Et'el wake up. You not wake up. You have one good sleep."

I took Patricia from Ethel. "You and Ethel fed her?"

"Yiss. I do good?"

I hugged him. "You did marvelous. I needed that sleep bad."

He beamed. "You happy me, I glad."

"Happy? I adore you. And that goes for you too," I added to Ethel.

Only then did I notice how quiet it was. The wind had stopped blowing. I went to the door. Outside the sky was bright with stars, the air still. It was so bitterly cold that my breath snapped into crystals. I came right back in.

From then on I wasn't worried about a thing. I knew we'd make out and that someone would come for us eventually. All we had to do was wait.

The next day the weather was lovely. The sun shone bright in a cloudless sky and it was warm enough to walk around with parka hoods down. Chuck and Ethel went out early and busied themselves building a "road-house," then played hunter for a while. In the afternoon, I brought one of the sleeping bags outside, laid it against a stump and just sat taking in the sun with Patricia on my lap. The sun felt so good that I started to drowse, listening to Chuck make the sounds of a rifle as he tried to "shoot" Ethel the Moose or Ethel the Caribou for the nth time. I heard her squeal with delight as he missed her, then silence as she fell and he started to carry her back to the roadhouse for skinning and eating. Then I heard another sound, a sound I'd become so familiar with the past few months that I knew I wasn't hearing things. It was coming from the direction of the river. I opened my eyes to see Chuck and Ethel standing stock still, listening. They'd heard it too.

It was Mr. Strong's sled. Chuck let out a yell and ran down towards the river and disappeared. A few minutes later I heard him yelling and calling to Mr. Strong, the sound of the bells on the sled getting louder and louder.

I ran into the cabin and put Patricia on the cot, then went out to wait until the two of them appeared, making their way up towards me, Chuck hopping and jumping like a sparrow, Mr. Strong clumping along after him. I was so happy to see him that I threw myself into his arms and almost knocked him over.

"Now, madam," he cajoled, "don't take on so. The situation is well in hand. We'll be out of here in no time."

He hadn't seen Fred, he said, but Fred had left word where I was at Steel Creek.

He stayed long enough to bring Elmer's body into the cabin, and there he left it covered with a blanket, the knife still clutched in Elmer's frozen hand. Then we started out.

We stopped only once on the way, at O'Shaughnessy's, and then only long enough to take a hot meal and a short rest before we went on again.

Later on, a few days after we were back and school was open again, the one thing that stuck in my mind was the moment when the settlement came into view. Ethel and I and Patricia were tucked away on one side of the sled towards the back, where Mr. Strong had made room for us among a whole load of parcel-post packages and dry goods. We were wrapped up pretty warm, the tarpaulin top over our heads like a tent. Chuck was sitting up in front with Mr. Strong. I didn't know we were almost there until the sled stopped and Chuck came crawling back along the side of the sled and pulled up the tarpaulin. He didn't want to be all alone up there with Mr. Strong when we came in.

When he lifted the tarp, there was the settlement in the distance. Chimney smoke had darkened the snow all around it, making it look like a gray little island. Sure enough, everybody was waiting, a bunch of black dots speckled in front of the post office. When we came nearer the whole place looked strange to me, as if I'd been away much longer than five or six days. I felt as if I'd left it a long time ago, almost as a little girl, and now I was coming back all grown up.

The horses started slowing down automatically as we neared the post office, and I lifted the tarp up to let everybody see we were in the back. But we didn't stop there. Mr. Strong let out a shout and I heard his whip crack. The sled jerked forward and I caught a flash of the surprised look on everybody's face as we went by—Mr. Vaughn's all displeased at seeing Chuck and Ethel, Angela Barrett's screwed up in anger. Mr. Strong halted the sled in front of the roadhouse and he'd already jumped down and was pulling the tarp back from us when everybody came running in.

I was too stiff to move, and there everybody was, staring at me and the children, Mrs. Purdy startled, wondering where Fred was, nobody saying a word. I had Patricia beside me, all swaddled in a wolf robe with just an opening for her to breathe, so nobody saw her until I picked her up. Like everyone else, Maggie Carew and her husband had come running. As soon as Maggie saw what I was holding she knew right away it was Patricia and the life seemed to drain right out of her. Everybody else realized it too and they made way for her. I handed the baby down to her and she took her from me, her eyes asking the questions she couldn't bring herself to ask out loud.

Mr. Strong lifted me down from the sled and after

that I hardly knew what was going on. Everybody was pressing forward, Mr. Carew asking me in a croaking voice where Jennie and Elmer were, Mrs. Purdy wanting to know about Fred, all the faces around me stunned, none of them angry anymore. Then Chuck and Ethel were beside me and Mr. Strong was herding the three of us into the roadhouse and trying to keep people back, telling them to give me a chance to get inside and warm up before they made me answer all their questions.

XXIV

For the whole first week I was back Maggie Carew made me and the children come over to the roadhouse for supper. She said that I'd been through an ordeal and that she wanted to make sure I had plenty of good hot food and didn't wear myself out. I didn't want her to go to any trouble for me, but she insisted. Her husband had left with Mr. Strong the next day, headed for Dawson, and she was all alone except for Patricia and the children. Having me there helped her feel better, she said, helped her feel closer to Jennie.

She blamed herself for what had happened. God was punishing her, she said, for something she'd done. He must have been, she insisted, because Jennie was the dearest and sweetest girl in the world, and had never harmed a soul. So she, Maggie, must have done something wrong. She tried not to keep asking me whether I thought Jennie would be all right or not, but she couldn't stop herself. "What do you honestly think, Annie," she'd ask me over and over. "You think she'll pull through?"

No matter how many times I told her I thought she would, she kept torturing herself by asking me more questions: how badly frozen had Jennie's leg been? Her face? If she did pull through, did I think she'd lose her leg or part of her face? All I could tell her was that I didn't know. When I told her how Jennie had tried to smile she broke down and wept.

Even when Fred came back we didn't know much more. He pulled into the settlement in the early afternoon eight days later, completely bushed, and a few minutes later we were all in the roadhouse listening as he told us what had happened. He'd mushed Jennie as far as Forty Mile, just as he'd set out to. There he ran into Percy de Wolfe, which was a stroke of luck. Known as the Iron Man of the North, de Wolfe carried the mail up and down the Yukon between White Horse and Eagle, and he had the fastest team in that part of the country. Almost minutes after Fred arrived, they transferred Jennie to his sled and he'd mushed off with her to Dawson. There was a telegraph station at Forty Mile and they'd wired the authorities at Dawson that Percy was carrying an injured woman who was going to need treatment. "Before I left," Fred said, "Dawson wired back that there'd be a doctor at the hospital ready to work on her right away."

It wasn't until the end of March, three weeks later, that Maggie received a telegram from her husband. By then the days were sunny and long. Gentle chinook winds were melting the snow so fast that traveling by sled was almost impossible except at night when the slush froze up. Mr. Strong brought the telegram in on his last sled trip of the season. It didn't go into any details. It just said that Jennie had been in very serious condition for a while, but that she was going to pull through. Mr. Strong would tell her the details, the telegram ended. Mr. Strong broke it to Maggie as gently as he could. Jennie's face wasn't going to be scarred, he said, but they'd had to amputate her foot to well above the ankle.

Maggie took it pretty hard, as might be expected, and it worked a big change in her. Not that she became soft, just a little more tolerant. I knew that deep down she still felt that I had no business having Chuck and Ethel with me, that I was making a mistake, but

321

she didn't look at them anymore as if they carried the plague or something worse. She even had them come over to the roadhouse every so often to play with Jimmy and Willard. Everybody else who'd been mad at me kind of eased up a little too. Maggie had a lot to do with it, I was sure. She swung weight in the settlement, and when people saw her having me and the children come over to the roadhouse they started acting a little more sociable. Then one night when I went over to the roadhouse to pick up Chuck and Ethel, Maggie asked me a question that surprised me.

Mr. Vaughn and Angela were there playing cribbage, and Uncle Arthur was helping Chuck clean the new .22 rifle I'd bought for him. I'd been so proud of him for how he'd acted during our "ordeal," as Maggie called it, that I'd taken him into Mr. Strong's store and told him to pick out anything he wanted. I'd had some misgivings when he chose the .22, but he knew how to handle it. He'd had one ever since he'd been five.

Ethel and Willard were playing back in the bunkroom, having a pillow fight and Chuck's rifle was all apart, so I had a cup of tea while Uncle Arthur helped him reassemble it. Right out of the blue Maggie popped the question.

"You done anything about buying yourself a cabin in Eagle?" she asked me.

"No," I said.

"How come?" she asked me. "They don't have any teacherage there for ya. You gotta provide your own quarters."

"I know," I said, "but I still don't know whether I'll be teaching at Eagle."

"What makes you think you won't?" she said.

She knew the answer to that as well as I and everybody else in that room did. Angela and Mr. Vaughn didn't look up from their game, but they were listening to every word. They weren't any crazier about me than they'd been before, but at least they said hello now whenever they met me.

"Well, nobody told me I *wouldn't*," I said, "but I didn't think the chances were too good."

Maggie's lip curled into that disgruntled sneer of

hers. "I know everybody on that schoolboard," she said, "and if they got any objections I wanna hear about it . . . How much you want to pay for a cabin if they take ya?"

"I haven't even thought about it," I said.

"How big a one might you want?"

"Well . . . big enough so maybe Chuck and Ethel could have their own room."

She didn't bat an eye. "What do you think, Arnold?" she asked Mr. Vaughn deliberately. "Think it'll be easy to find one?"

He mumbled something and Maggie said, "I didn't hear ya."

"I said probably," he said.

"We'll find you one," Maggie said. "Far as I'm concerned a bird in the hand's worth two in the bush. We know what we got with you. Lord only knows what they're liable to send out from Juneau if we let'm . . . From what I hear about that Rooney, she's a real darb. Pinches the kids till they're black and blue and goes ga-ga over everything that wears pants."

Having Maggie on my side went a long way. Nobody came up to me and told me they thought any better of me than they had before. That wasn't people's way. It was just something I could feel, something in their manner. Like at the next dance we had. We didn't hold one until the Friday after Maggie got the telegram from her husband. Up to then it just hadn't seemed right to have one, to be dancing and laughing and having a good time when almost right next door Maggie would be sitting and wondering if Jennie was going to live or die.

When everybody came in they gave me a big hello or a howdy instead of just a grudging nod as they usually did, and a couple of them even talked about the weather with me. Now that spring was getting close everybody had their own idea about when the river was going to break up or when the creeks would be running so that sluice boxes could be set up. Nobody ever ran out of things to say about it and they didn't generally talk about it with cheechakos or somebody they didn't want to talk with in the first place. One or two even made a point of admiring the map of Chicken on the wall. As big as it was, they'd never seemed to notice it before. Now they said they'd never seen anything like it, and how clever all the kids were to have made it.

Chuck was making out better too. His standing among the kids was upped practically from the first day of school. They stopped snickering at him and making fun of his accent. In fact for the first few days the boys all chummed up to him, wanting to hear all the gory details of how he'd found Jennie and Elmer and how Elmer had looked when he was dead and frozen. Chuck didn't have too much to say about it and didn't do any bragging, which impressed the kids more than if he'd gone on and on about it.

The only thing that didn't change at all was the way things were between Fred and me.

"If you wanna teach in Eagle," Maggie had told me in private, "you better behave. You got away with takin' those kids. Start chasin' after that half-breed again and you won't get away with anything. Now don't go givin' me any Bolshevik speeches. I'm givin' you the straight goods."

I didn't see him again for almost three weeks after he got back, and then only when he came in to pick up some hardware he'd ordered from Mr. Strong. He'd made up his mind he was going to stay away from me for my sake and that was that. No stain on my reputation was going to come from *him,* no sir. He showed up for the dance and when we danced together you'd have thought we were doing a minuet he held me so far away. I had the hope in the back of my mind that maybe Uncle Arthur would put on the *Home Sweet Home* waltz for us, but I wasn't surprised when he didn't. It didn't matter that Fred had saved Jennie's life and even risked his own: he was still a half-breed and I was still pure Northern womanhood.

Sure enough, came mid-April Mr. Strong brought me the news that I'd been accepted to teach at Eagle. I was happy about it. Yet at the same time I wasn't. Chuck and Ethel were worrying me. Ever since I'd brought them back to Chicken we hadn't been getting along.

More than ever, I wished that Nancy was still with me. Between the two of us we'd have been able to figure out what was wrong and do something about it. For the life of me, I couldn't figure it out by myself. I had to keep after them all the time—to dress neatly, to be clean, to help me keep my quarters in order and to mind their manners around people. I wasn't doing it just to be bossy. It was for their own good. Even though the uproar over them had died down, most people still looked at them differently than they looked at other children. If they did something wrong or got into mischief it wasn't because they were kids and didn't know any better. It was because they were Indian kids. Almost everybody felt that way, even people who liked them.

One day when Uncle Arthur gave Chuck some candy, he waved his hand tolerantly when I told Chuck to say thank you. "Don't pay it any mind, missis," he said, "they just don't know any better." He didn't say "he." He said "they"—those Indians. It was the same way with other people. Every time Chuck or Ethel made a mistake it wasn't because things were new to them and they didn't know the ropes. "They" just didn't know any better.

It put me on the defensive. It shouldn't have. I shouldn't have paid it any mind and seen it for what it was, ignorance, but I couldn't. Stupidly, I felt that any criticism of them was criticism of me and I decided I wasn't going to give people a chance to criticize. I made Chuck and Ethel toe the mark. Once we were in Eagle they'd have to take their place alongside of other children and I wanted them to be able to do it as fast as possible. Nobody was going to laugh at them or point out how different they were if *I* had anything to do with it.

I really kept after them. At the same time I nearly worked myself to death ironing dresses for Ethel, scrubbing, washing, and keeping my quarters neat so that people would have a good impression when they came.

I was especially tough with Chuck, always reminding him to hang up his clothes, not to throw things on the floor, to mind his manners, speak correctly, be good.

The two of them kept fighting me on everything, or at least that's the way it seemed. Ethel started soiling her dresses, eating half the time with her hands and getting food all over her. She stopped picking up English too, and pretended she didn't know what shoes or socks were. One time she got up on a chair, pulled down some of her newly-ironed dresses from the wall and stomped all over them. Chuck changed too. I had to force him to wash up all the time and getting him to take a bath was a major battle. He became lazy in his schoolwork and surly around the house. I even had to remind him to bring in wood where before he was always one step ahead of me. I began to feel that he and Ethel were in league against me, whispering together in Indian, laughing between themselves. If I asked Chuck what they were laughing at he said it was nothing. Sometimes I even thought of sending them back to the Indian village I was so disgusted.

Something had to give, and it did.

They both ran away. It wasn't the first time for Chuck. The week before, he'd left the house and not come back until almost nightfall. Fit to be tied, I told him that if he ever did it again I'd give him a spanking.

This time he didn't come back. When dusk settled in at about eight they were still gone. Uncle Arthur and a few others helped me look for them. We tramped through the wet woods, yelling and calling, but there was no sign of them. Around midnight everybody went home, telling me not to worry. "They'll turn up, missis," Uncle Arthur assured me. He and everybody else promised to help me look again in the morning if they didn't. It was the beginning of May, the nights short and kind of dusky—daylight. I stayed out until past two before I gave up and went home to change out of wet footgear and go looking again.

I couldn't think about sleep. Just the thought that something had happened to the two of them kept me on the verge of panic. Over and over I imagined them lying at the bottom of a cliff, or swept away by a swollen creek, or attacked by a bear. And over and over I asked myself why they'd done it. I'd been tough on them, I knew that, but I didn't think I'd been bad enough to make Chuck do something like this. I had a cup of tea and I forced myself to sit down and try to think calmly where they might have gone. The first thought that occurred to me was that they might have headed for the Indian village. A couple of times when I'd bawled Chuck out he'd threatened to. If they were headed there it might take all day to catch up with them.

The sun was nudging in the window, tinging everything with gold. I looked around the room, something I hadn't done before. I didn't see Ethel's little red monkey around anywhere. It wasn't in the schoolroom either when I looked, so she must have taken it with her. I noticed that Chuck's rifle was gone too. And his parka. The last time I'd seen him he'd been wearing his mackinaw, which meant he must have taken the parka out some time before he left. The more I looked around the more I noticed things missing: a few of Ethel's dresses, a dress suit I'd bought for Chuck, a couple of blankets, two pillow cases. There was only a little bread left in the breadbox, and I knew there should have been two loaves. Chuck must have been removing things bit by bit over the last few days and caching them somewhere. My heart started to pound: they'd taken too many things with them to carry them all at once, especially if they were going to the Indian village. If they were anywhere it was someplace in the vicinity. And if I was right there was only one place where they could have gone. I ran out.

The spicy odor of willow buds was in the air when I reached the trail that led down to Mary Angus' shack. The place was in worse shape than ever. Someone had taken out the window frame, and the stovepipe was gone too. As soon as I saw the place, though, I knew they were in there: the wolf robe was draped in the opening where the window used to be.

I pushed the door open and there they were, the two of them lying on a bed of spruce boughs, huddled together under a couple of blankets. Chuck's .22 was on the wall, along with their clothes. The food they'd brought with them was piled in a box.

I bent over them and stared at them a long time before I woke Chuck up. They were beautiful. I'd never realized how beautiful. I remembered them living here with their mother. They'd been cold and hungry more often than not, but that hadn't mattered to them because they'd had *her,* the one person in the world they'd loved and trusted, the one person who knew them and understood them. Here in this shack she'd touched them and held them. Not me. Her. They hadn't asked for me. Even though I was the only one in the world who cared anything about them, they hadn't asked me to take them. I was a stranger to them. I fed them and gave them clothes, but I was still a stranger. So they'd run away from me and come back to where there was nothing but a memory—the memory of someone who'd held them close, spoke to them softly and loved them the way Granny Hobbs had loved me.

"Chuck . . ."

He woke up slowly. I watched his eyes, wanting to see what would be in them when he was aware of me, whether he'd be looking at a stranger or at someone who cared for him. What I saw hurt. He just stared at me the way I used to stare at my father when I wondered if he felt mean, telling myself that I didn't care what he said.

"Morning, Chuck," I said.

"What you want, Tisha?" It was a simple question, no more than that.

"I came to take you home," I said.

He shook his head. "No."

"You can't stay here."

"I stay for a while. Hunt. Get meat. Then I go Indian village."

"The Indian village is pretty far away."

"You think I not find?"

"I guess you could. You're a pretty smart boy. I just wonder why you want to go there."

"I go live with Indian mudda."

He meant Lame Sarah, the old woman he'd lived

with in the Indian village. "I see. I guess that means you don't want to live with me anymore."

"No more."

"Why?"

"I hate you, Tisha," he said simply. "You not nice me. Alla time you *sahnik* me."

Ethel woke up, innocent and beautiful as the morning. She stared at me the way he had.

"Am I angry at you all the time?"

"Alla time. Alla time angry me, angry Et'el too."

"Does Ethel hate me as much as you do?"

"More. Say you white devil-woman. Make scare her. She no more live with you too. We live with Indian mudda. She like us."

"Chuck, will you believe me if I tell you something? I love you. I love you very much. You and Ethel."

"Tisha, you tell one very big lie."

"I'm not lying at all. I mean it."

"Oh, no. You hate me, say I bad boy. All time bad boy." He was getting aggravated.

"Is that what I do?"

"Foreva! All day long you say, 'Chuck, you bad boy, you make floor dirty. Oh, Chuck, you bad boy, you make mud all over clothes. Chuck, you not have good manners, dirty, make table dirty, make big mess, make everything dirty.' Tisha," he spluttered, "soon you tell me I make whole world dirty!"

I didn't want to cry, but what he said next cut the ground from under me.

"Once upon a time, Tisha, you be nice me. You be so nice I love you truly." He shook his head. "No now. Now you shame me. Shame way I talk. Shame everything me. You no love me, Tisha. You hate me."

He said it so simply and honestly that I burst into tears, ashamed of myself. Before I was able to stop, I was sitting on the dirt floor, he and Ethel worriedly patting me. Then we talked. He told me how much I'd picked on him and tried to get him to do things in the past month that were too tough, and the longer we talked the more I realized he was right. I'd been ashamed of him, and of Ethel too. In class I gave everybody extra help but him. At lunchtime I asked

329

nobody else to mind their manners but him. It didn't matter why I'd done it. I'd been wrong. Instead of hugs and pats for the things he'd accomplished I'd given him criticism for the things he hadn't.

In the end he and Ethel came home with me, and I promised him things would be different.

That night when I put him to bed he told me that once when he was in the Indian village he'd chopped twenty cords of wood. I'd lectured him more than once about telling the truth, but this time I kept my mouth shut. I must have shown my doubt, though.

"You no believe," he said.

"Oh, yes I do," I assured him.

He wasn't convinced. "You think I tell helluva lie."

"Let me feel your muscle." He flexed his arm, and gritted his teeth. "That's some muscle, all right. If you say you cut twenty cords I believe you."

He smiled and hunched down, pulling the covers up to his chin. "I fool you," he said. "I not cut twenty cords. Too much for me myself."

"No?"

"No," he said. "Maybe cut ten."

XXV

After that I stopped trying to make Chuck and Ethel into model children. All I had to do was remember how Granny Hobbs used to be with me and I knew exactly what to do. The last thing she'd ever cared about was my etiquette or my cleanliness. The first thing she'd cared about was making sure I was happy. And that's what I did with Chuck and Ethel. If they weren't the cleanest kids and didn't have the best manners, they weren't the dirtiest either and their manners were better than most, so I stopped worrying about it. I stopped worrying about their messing up my quarters, too. Granny would never have given a hoot about something like that, and when it came right down to it I didn't either. As for what other people might think about it, there was nobody I cared that much about impressing anyway, except maybe Fred, so I let them go ahead and mess.

They tested me a few times. They spilled things, splashed water from the barrel and insisted on wearing the same clothes for too long, wanting to see what I'd do. When I didn't pay any attention to it they stopped by themselves. In fact, about a week after they ran away, when I was dumping some of my own clothes in the wash boiler, Ethel came up to me with a little blue dress that was her favorite.

"What do you want me to do with it?" I asked her.

"Do."

"Do what?" I knew full well what she wanted, but I loved to hear her talk.

She pointed to the wash boiler. "Do?"

"Wash? You want me to wash it?"

"Yiss," she said. "Watch."

She followed Chuck's lead and literally worshiped him. If he was happy she was happy. And he seemed to be. It hadn't taken much to please him in the first place, and once he felt I was on his side he settled right down. He had a good sense of humor, too. One time when Jimmy Carew stayed to have lunch with us, Chuck asked for a slice of "brode," as he called it.

"Brode," Jimmy mimicked sarcastically. "It's not brode, it's *bread!*" He chuckled. "Brode . . ."

Isabelle and Joan were having lunch. They started to laugh, and Chuck shot me a quick glance.

"What's wrong with saying brode?" I asked Jimmy.

"It's just wrong."

"Well, where my grandmother used to live in Missouri, the people used to say brayd. Mr. O'Shaughnessy pronounces it brid. What's the difference as long as people know what you're talking about?"

Jimmy shrugged uncomfortably. I hadn't been too

fair to him, but Chuck needed the points more than he did. I put a slice of bread on the plate. "Here's your brode," I said.

"Brode not correct," Chuck said archly, imitating me, "we say bread."

After they'd been back another week, he and Ethel no more wanted to live with anybody else than I'd have wanted to marry Mr. Vaughn. They were with me for good.

It was just around then, in mid-May, that spring came. Up to then the weather had been so change-able you couldn't tell what to expect. March had really been freakish. One day the sun would be out hot and strong—bouncing off the snow, dazzling your eyes and setting eaves to dripping—and you'd be convinced spring was on the way. The next day, and for days after that, gray monster winter would settle back in and you'd be just as convinced that spring would never arrive at all.

April had been a darling. With the class wanting to get in all the last-minute sledding they could, I'd had trouble getting them back in school after lunch. Water had been drip-dripping everywhere, and wet shoes and socks were always drying around the stove. Soon the first crocuses, purple faces splashed with yel-low, had pushed up through the snow, and blossoming crowfoot cascaded down hillsides. After that the creek broke up and everybody became restless. Spring still hadn't been close enough so that we'd been able to shed our winter underwear, and sleds had still creaked by in the half-dusk that was night, but it was closer. It was there in the brown spots that appeared on the hills, and the islands that eddied out around trees. People had scattered ashes in their backyards to melt the snow faster so they could start planting vegetable gardens, and pale green buds sprouted on birches.

Then spring exploded. The sun came and stayed, and soon we were able to open the schoolroom win-dows to the tangy smell of running sap and the spicy odor of willow. Sometimes we'd run out just to see the great flocks of Canadian honkers passing overhead, the loud beating of their wings making the air seem thick as water. The schoolroom felt so musty and confining that I was as glad as the class when Friday came and we could toss our books away. Each long sunny day blended into warm mild dusk, dusk into gentle morning.

And suddenly the snow was gone. Tender shoots of grass sprinkled the hills and wild canaries flashed through trees haloed in green. I started taking the class on field trips again and we'd see rabbits all over the place, their white winter coats already turned ash brown. On one trip we saw a moose, gaunt and needing a haircut badly. It was a bull, his racks still fuzzed with winter white. We even started our own garden. I wouldn't be around when it came up, but it was fun just the same.

At the end of May Nancy came back to take the territorial exam. She took it in my quarters on the last morning school was held, while I rehearsed the class in the schoolroom for the pageant we were going to put on after lunch. For the whole time she sat behind the closed door I was on pins and needles. Even though I knew she'd pass I couldn't help worrying. She'd made all kinds of plans for going to high school in Fairbanks. If she failed I didn't know what it would do to her.

When she was finished she came in and handed the test to me, then went outside while I looked it over. I couldn't grade it for her. That would have to be done in Juneau, which meant waiting six weeks before the official word came back, but I could tell her whether she'd passed or not. She passed, all right, and when I let out a yell for her to come on back in and hear the good news the class let out a cheer.

Before the pageant started we had an exhibit of all the best work the class had done over the school year. Compositions, drawings, book reports, graphs and booklets decorated the walls. Set out on the shelves were fossils and birds' nests, pot holders and samplers, papier mâché masks and everything else the class had made and collected. A couple of Rebekah's papers were on the wall too. She'd already mastered a first-grade

333

reader and her penmanship was so beautiful I'd put up some samples of it.

Seeing it there and watching the kids showing it all off to the parents, I felt proud. Without any fancy equipment, without even all the books they should have had, they'd worked hard and sopped up everything I could teach them. They'd helped each other, taught each other at times, competed and cooperated. And they'd learned. It was a grand day for everyone, including me. The pageant was all about the Gold Rush days and it went off without a hitch. The old-timers enjoyed it more than anybody. After that we served ice cream and cake, and when it was all over everybody helped clean up for the dance we were going to have that night. Maggie Carew was the last to leave.

"Well, that's the end of 'er," she said, looking around the room. " 'No more pencils, no more books,' like the kids say. She's gone now."

She meant the school. There just wasn't enough enrollment to keep it open. There'd never be another school here again.

"What'll happen to it?" I asked Maggie.

"Angela's claimin' it," she said. "Gonna turn it into a roadhouse after I'm gone. You did a good job."

"Thanks." Coming from her it was a high compliment.

"Only thing I don't understand is how come you didn't give the kids marks."

"I didn't see any reason to. They all knew how well they did."

"How'd they know?"

"They just did. I told them where they did well and where they needed improvement, but they already knew."

"Suppose you did give'm marks—what would mine've got?"

"Offhand I couldn't say."

"Suppose you *hadda* mark 'em?" she insisted.

"Well . . . I'd say maybe an A for Jimmy, B for Willard."

"How about the others?"

334

"Maybe an A for Elvira, C for her two sisters, A for Lily, B for—"

"How come you give Lily an A and my Willard a B?"

"Lily's a very bright little girl."

"That don't mean she's smarter'n my Willard. No half-breed's smarter'n a white," she said without thinking. I didn't answer her and she colored. "See y'at the dance," she said as she went out.

It was still light out about 8:30 when everybody started showing up. It would stay light until about eleven when dusk would set in for a couple of hours until the sun came up again in the middle of the night. I still wasn't used to it, going to bed in almost broad daylight and then trying to sleep with the sun nudging at me at two o'clock in the morning. It gave me a kind of a guilty feeling, as if I ought to be awake and doing things. Sometimes I'd only be able to sleep for a few hours and so I'd just get up and start the day at three in the morning, then take a nap later. It was kind of fun in a way because it was the thing you'd always wanted when you were a kid—never to have it get dark. But it was unsettling too, like living in an Alice-in-Wonderland world.

Everybody kept crazy hours. Miners would be out working their claims right through the night, setting up sluice boxes, digging ditches or excavating ground. They only had three good months to get their work done and they didn't want to waste any time. A few of them didn't even bother with dress-up clothes when they came to that last dance. Sprouting beards for protection against mosquitoes, they showed up in clean workclothes, all ready to go back to their diggings when the dance was over. Fred and his mother came too, and that made the evening for me.

Everybody kept asking me if there was anything wrong with me, wanting to know if I was having a good time. I was, but I couldn't help feeling sad. In a few days I'd be leaving, yet when I looked around the room it seemed to me as if it was only yesterday that I'd arrived. In less than a year I'd lived a whole lifetime here. There were still a few papers on the walls and one of the green shades had a message written on it, left over from the class party: "Farewell, Miss Hobbs." Underneath it, Jimmy Carew had scrawled a P.S.: "See you in Eagle."

With Fred playing the banjo during most of the square dances, I only got to dance with him once. If it was up to me we wouldn't have left each other's side. On this night of all nights especially I wanted to be with him as much as possible. Even after Uncle Arthur wound up his gramophone and the round dancing started we didn't get to dance together that much. Since I was going away, Uncle Arthur and Joe and some of the other men insisted I had to dance with them at least once. I didn't mind it early on, but as it started to get late and there was more and more chance that Uncle Arthur would play *Home Sweet Home,* I began to get nervous.

I'd just danced with Jake Harrington when Fred ambled over to me. He looked grand. He had on a starched blue and white striped shirt, and the sun had tanned him really dark. He had a big smile on his face.

"You look like the cat that ate the canary," I told him.

"Funny you should say that. I was just licking my chops."

"Over what?"

"Over the supper you and I are going to have."

Uncle Arthur had already put the next record on and was lowering the needle. The *Home Sweet Home* waltz began to play. Then I saw that there were a whole bunch of people staring at the two of us—Jake Harrington and Rebekah, Ben Norvall and Nancy. They were all smiling. Uncle Arthur gave me a little wink. "We had it all arranged," Fred said.

His arm slipped around my waist, and like the first time we danced that waltz together the walls of the schoolroom moved right back and everybody disappeared. Even the music didn't sound the same. To me it wasn't an old scratchy record playing an old-fashioned waltz, but Paul Whiteman's full orchestra. I was so far away in my mind that not until the record

336

was over and everybody began to clap did I realize that no one else had danced. All of them had stopped to watch Fred and me.

Chuck and Ethel were asleep on the bed along with Joan Simpson, so Robert Merriweather stayed with the three of them while we all went over to the road-house.

It was almost two in the morning and everybody was just about done eating when a couple of chords sounded on the piano. We all turned around in time to see Joe Temple point a finger at the kitchen area, and while he played a march Maggie Carew came out carrying a huge chocolate cake with a candle in the center. She set it down in front of me. "Good Luck" was written on it in icing. I was too surprised to say a word, even more so when Uncle Arthur walked over with a beautifully wrapped box and handed it to me. "We passed the hat around and got this for ya," he said. "A little token of our appreciation."

Inside the box was about the most expensive camera you could buy, all black leather and nickel plate. Everybody clapped and yelled for me to make a speech.

"I wish I could," I said, "but I'm not very good at making speeches. All I can say is, thanks—I appreciate it."

"No more than we appreciate you, Teacher," Ben Norvall said. "There isn't a soul in this room that doesn't think you're a fine honest girl and a true-blue Alaskan to boot."

Jake Harrington said, "Ben, that's the first time in all the years I know you that I heard you tell the un-varnished truth."

Joe started to play *Auld Lang Syne* on the piano, and then Fred and everybody were singing. I never could hear that song without getting a lump in my throat to begin with. By the time they got to the end I was on the point of crying. I wasn't the only one either. Maggie's and Nancy's eyes were wet, and Uncle Arthur burst into tears.

It was almost three in the morning when Fred and I left the roadhouse. We went over to my quarters to see if everything was all right. Robert was asleep on the couch, Chuck and Ethel on the bed, just as I'd left them, so I tiptoed out and Fred and I went for a walk.

As soon as we were out of sight of the settlement Fred took my hand. The woods were as quiet as if the sun in the sky was just pretending to be there and it was really night.

We talked a little about Eagle and what it would be like living there with Chuck and Ethel. I asked him how he thought the kids there would treat them and he said he didn't know. A family with three half-Indian children were already living there, he said, but he didn't know how they got along with the white kids. He said he wanted to come and see me after the freeze-up.

We went on until we came to Fourth of July Pup. Swollen to creek size with runoff, it was too wide to jump across. Before we sat down on the grassy bank we scooped up a drink. The water was cold and sweet, dyed clear amber from roots and dried hillside moss.

"I guess you're relieved," I said, lying back. The ground was warm.

"About what?"

"That I'm going."

"Why should I be?" He lay down on his stomach and leaned on his elbows.

"You won't have me chasing after you anymore."

"You didn't do that," he said.

"Yes, I did. I'm doing it right now. I'll be leaving in a few days, so what does it matter? It's the truth." He didn't like hearing that, but I didn't care. I didn't have a bit of shame left in me and I was glad of it. He could be a gentleman if he wanted. I was sick of being a lady. "I've been chasing after you almost from the time we met."

That made him squirm. "Anne, if I could give you a home, if I had money enough to take care of you, I'd ask you to marry me right now."

I felt like growling, or shaking him, doing anything to wake him up, anything to make him realize I didn't care how much he had or how little, that all I wanted was him. There was no point to it, though. We'd been through all this before, so I just stared at him long enough until he couldn't do anything else but kiss me. From then on I went by instinct. I ran my fingers along the back of his neck and played with his hair. My instincts must have been good because he started kissing me in a way he'd never done before. I felt just the slightest bit scared, but his touch was more pleasantly delicious than anything else. He murmured my name and for the first time in my life it didn't sound plain to me. It sounded lovely, all mixed in with the rush of water running below us and the sweet smell of the earth.

I didn't want to open my eyes. I wanted to keep them closed and feel him touch me. I realized ever so faintly that I wasn't too sure of what I was doing, but I didn't care. Whatever I was doing I was enjoying it. And he was too. When I finally did open my eyes and looked into his I loved what I saw. He wasn't thinking about being noble, or carrying the Holy Grail, or bringing some other kind of prize to me. He was just being *him*. And he wanted *me*. I thought to myself that I sure wished I'd known about this kind of feeling a few months before. At the same time I was glad I hadn't. I'd have been a goner. He said, "Anne," his voice husky and deep, and I could smell that wonderful odor of wood smoke coming from him. My fingers went to his lips. "I want to say something to you," I told him.

He waited while I got it all straight in my mind, and I said, "I don't know what it is you think you have to have before you want to keep company with me, but you just remember this. I love you. I won't be chasing after you anymore because we're going to be far away from each other, but some day, when you get ready, you better come and marry me. Because I'm never going to marry anybody else. I mean that, Fred Purdy. If you don't marry me some day I'm going to be an old maid."

"No you won't," he said.

"Is that a promise?"

"That's a promise."

339

"You better not break it."

"You better not break your promise either," he said.

A little while later we started to walk back arm in arm, stopping every so often to linger and embrace. We went on that way until we came in sight of the settlement, then we let each other go.

September 16, 1975

That's how Fred and I parted those many years ago, with the promise that one day we'd be married. Thinking about that promise now, I almost have to smile. Trying to keep it was like making a trip by dog sled in a snowstorm: you know where you want to go, but you can't be sure how long it's going to take or where you'll wind up along the way.

Fred and I didn't get married until over ten years later, on September 4, 1938. By that time Chuck had graduated from high school, Ethel had entered it, and I'd adopted three more children.

It was worth all the waiting, though. We had a grand life together. Fred mined in the summer, and in the winter sometimes we stayed home, sometimes we packed up the family and went Outside. We did whatever we liked. One winter, maybe the finest we ever spent, we took on the job as teacher and custodian in an Indian village. As for children, Fred loved them as much as I did, so we went ahead and adopted four more.

I'm 67 years old now. Fred passed away ten years ago, and although I've since gotten over the sharp pain of losing him, I still miss him badly at times, mostly when there's a gentle rain falling. I think of it falling

341

so quietly all over the hills, soaking into the ground to bring out new life, and it's hard for me to accept that I'm never going to see him again or hear that wonderful laugh of his. It's as hard as trying to imagine springtime without the sound of birds.

Occasionally I look back on those early years we spent without each other and I feel a little cheated. Then I think about the 28 wonderful years we had together. Everytime I do I realize how fortunate I've been, because as much as I love children and sunlight, I know that the sun would never have shone as brightly for me, nor children's smiles seemed so lovely, had I spent those years without Fred.

—Anne Hobbs Purdy
Chicken, Alaska

ABOUT THE AUTHOR

ROBERT SPECHT was born and brought up in New York
City. A late starter, he graduated from CCNY at the age of
thirty-two after winning top awards in both short story
and essay competitions. Soon afterward he headed for
California, where he became an editor in the Los Angeles
offices of a major book publishing firm. It was then that
he met the heroine of this book and became fascinated by
her story. Not until years later, however, until after he
became a free-lance writer, was he able to sit down and
devote his full energies to writing it. Now a screenwriter,
he lives in Malibu with his wife and two children—and
two horses, three dogs, three cats, assorted chickens, two
tortoises, an ever-changing population of guppies and a
guinea pig named Munch.

He is now working on a sequel to *Tisha*.

SPECIAL OFFER: If you enjoyed this book and would
like to have our catalog of over 1,400 other Bantam titles,
just send your name and address and 50¢ (to help defray
postage and handling costs) to: Catalog Department, Bantam Books, Inc., 414 East Golf Rd., Des Plaines, Ill. 60016.

SPECIAL
MONEY SAVING
OFFER

Now you can have an up-to-date listing of Bantam's hundreds of titles plus take advantage of our unique and exciting bonus book offer. A special offer which gives you the opportunity to purchase a Bantam book for only 50¢. Here's how!

By ordering any five books at the regular price per order, you can also choose any other single book listed (up to a $4.95 value) for just 50¢. Some restrictions do apply, but for further details why not send for Bantam's listing of titles today!

Just send us your name and address plus 50¢ to defray the postage and handling costs.

BANTAM BOOKS, INC.
Dept. FC, 414 East Golf Road, Des Plaines, Ill 60016

Mr./Mrs./Miss/Ms. _____
                        (please print)

Address _____

City_____ State_____ Zip_____
                                        FC—3/84

She looked stunned,

her eyes large and blue, the gold lashes tipped by fiery red. "There is so much to do—"

"It will get done," he said, frowning at her stubbornness. Then he rubbed the oily salve into the skin of one small hand. Her bones were delicate, but the flesh was firm and well seasoned by work.

He finished with the first hand, then had started to work on the second when her chest suddenly rose and a distinctly feminine sound escaped her. Her eyes were closed and she bore an expression he had not seen in years. 'Twas one of ecstasy.

Arousal hit him like a punch.

Her cheeks were flushed and her lips slightly parted. Waves of golden hair framed her face and her pulse beat rapidly in her throat. Still holding her hand, Alex moved closer, feeling quite certain that his very existence depended upon tasting her mouth....

* * *

The Virtuous Knight
Harlequin Historical #681—November 2003

Praise for Margo Maguire's latest titles

His Lady Fair
"You'll love this Cinderella story."
—*Rendezvous*

Dryden's Bride
"Exquisitely detailed…an entrancing tale
that will enchant and envelop you as love conquers all."
—*Rendezvous*

Celtic Bride
"Set against the backdrop of a turbulent era,
Margo Maguire's heart-rending and colorful tale of
star-crossed lovers is sure to win readers' hearts."
—*Romantic Times*

The
VIRTUOUS
KNIGHT

Margo Maguire

HARLEQUIN®

TORONTO • NEW YORK • LONDON
AMSTERDAM • PARIS • SYDNEY • HAMBURG
STOCKHOLM • ATHENS • TOKYO • MILAN • MADRID
PRAGUE • WARSAW • BUDAPEST • AUCKLAND

If you purchased this book without a cover you should be aware
that this book is stolen property. It was reported as "unsold and
destroyed" to the publisher, and neither the author nor the
publisher has received any payment for this "stripped book."

ISBN 0-373-29281-3

THE VIRTUOUS KNIGHT

Copyright © 2003 by Margo Wider

All rights reserved. Except for use in any review, the reproduction or
utilization of this work in whole or in part in any form by any electronic,
mechanical or other means, now known or hereafter invented, including
xerography, photocopying and recording, or in any information storage
or retrieval system, is forbidden without the written permission of the
publisher, Harlequin Enterprises Limited, 225 Duncan Mill Road,
Don Mills, Ontario, Canada M3B 3K9.

All characters in this book have no existence outside the imagination of
the author and have no relation whatsoever to anyone bearing the same
name or names. They are not even distantly inspired by any individual
known or unknown to the author, and all incidents are pure invention.

This edition published by arrangement with Harlequin Books S.A.

® and TM are trademarks of the publisher. Trademarks indicated with
® are registered in the United States Patent and Trademark Office, the
Canadian Trade Marks Office and in other countries.

Visit us at www.eHarlequin.com

Printed in U.S.A.

Please address questions and book requests to:
Harlequin Reader Service
U.S.: 3010 Walden Ave., P.O. Box 1325, Buffalo, NY 14269
Canadian: P.O. Box 609, Fort Erie, Ont. L2A 5X3

This book is dedicated to my middle child, Joseph,
as he embarks on his college career.
Good luck, Joe—and be happy!

Prologue

The Holy Land, April, 1257

Blood pumped from the fresh wound in Alexander Breton's upper arm, staining his sleeve crimson. Ignoring the pain, Sir Alex pulled Roger Kendal—his friend and mentor—from the field of battle. The other knights gave cover as he moved, turning to force the battle away from their fallen comrade.

Using the body of a slaughtered horse to shield them, Alex tore away the edge of his tunic and quickly tied it around the wound in his arm, stanching the flow of blood. Then he leaned over Brother Roger, the monk with whom he had traveled a thousand miles on a sacred mission.

During their journey from France to the Holy Land, Alex had learned of piety and sacrifice beyond what was expected of any knight. He'd witnessed Roger's charity and his humility. And Alexander had decided that when he returned to the monastery at Cluny, he would take the vows that would make him a Benedictine monk.

"Roger," Alex said, his voice low and urgent. "We must get you away from here! To the caves!"

Roger's eyes opened. No longer were they the clear, vibrant blue of the Jerusalem sky, but cloudy and stained, dark with death. Yet they focused intently upon Alex.

"My scabbard…" Roger's voice rasped. His thick, blond hair was muddy with red sand and sweat. Blood gushed from the wound in his side.

"You cannot think to take up arms, Roger," Alex said. The thought of his friend dying was intolerable. He must do something. He must get Roger away from the battle and see to his wound.

Alex glanced 'round. The distance to the caves was great, but he was certain he could carry Roger in spite of the deep wound in his arm.

"Nay, Alex…you must take my…" Roger swallowed dryly. "Take the silver scabbard.…"

Alex pulled the waterskin from the saddle and moistened a bit of cloth. Then he lifted Roger's head and wet his lips. "The scabbard we were to take back to Cluny? We will speak of it lat—"

"Aye," Roger said, struggling for breath. His eyes drifted closed, and Alex took note of the weak, fluttering pulse visible in his neck. There was no time to waste with words, yet Roger continued to speak. "It contains… 'Tis a sacred relic.… Take the scabbard, the sword…to England. To my brother, John of

Eryngton… 'Tis too dangerous to take it to France.…
That is where… Skelton will expect…"

An alarming rattling emanated from Roger's throat.

"Roger, I'm going to move you away from the
fray," Alex said. He kept his voice level and calm,
even though he urgently felt the need to get Roger to
a safe place.

"Keep it hidden.… There are those who suspect…
Lord Skelton will try…to take it from you.…" Roger
continued in a rasping voice, as if he'd not heard
Alex's words. He grimaced with pain and made another ominous sound as he opened his eyes. "Keep
it safe, Alex," he gasped, taking hold of Alex's tunic.
"Do not let it fall…into the wrong hands."

"Roger," Alex said, taking hold of the older
knight's arms, "you must brace yourself, I'll carry
you—"

"Nay," Roger protested weakly. "Do not waste
the effort. I am a dead man. Listen."

Alex stopped momentarily, fully intending to move
his friend as soon as he said what preyed on his mind.

"God go with you, Alex," Roger said. "You are
a good man…but 'tis not clear that you were meant…
for the Benedictines. 'Twas your wife's death…
that drove you to us.…" Roger struggled for breath
as the light faded from his eyes. "Do not…I beseech
you, do not make your vows…until after you've returned from England."

"Roger—"

"When you return to Cluny, if you still…wish to
pledge your life…to the Order…"

"Save your breath, Roger," Alex said.

"Nay," Roger said urgently. "Promise me. 'Tis a dying man's wish."

Alex looked away for an instant, taking in the bright sky, the brilliant sunlight, the sand-washed land. 'Twas a harsh place in which to die. He turned back to Roger with resignation. "Aye, you have it. My promise to take the scabbard to your brother."

"And…your vows… Promise me you will wait until your return to Cluny…."

"Aye," Sir Alexander replied. He took hold of Roger's hands and made his promise, then watched as his most revered friend in all the world commended his soul to heaven.

Chapter One

October 1257

Lucy Kendal rode in the back of the supply wagon and tipped her head, watching the clouds gather overhead. She tried to shut out the sound of Lady Elsbeth's voice, but was unable to eliminate it entirely. Elsbeth always managed to find something to complain of, no matter what her situation, and this lovely morn was no exception.

"You should never have made us ride off without our escort, Sister Gunnora," Elsbeth said from her perch high upon her poor mount. She was the only one of the party riding horseback. "'Tis dangerous to be on the road without prop—"

"We're better off without the drunken oafs," the stern old nun replied. "Such a worthless pair of heathens I should ever hope to…" she muttered, her voice trailing off.

While Lucy reveled in these few days of freedom

from the strict rules of Craghaven Abbey, Elsbeth did not care for the ride, or the weather or the food. The lady disliked the company, the pitted road and the poor horse she'd been forced to ride on their journey to the new abbey in Yorkshire. She deplored the mean inns where they'd been required to pass the nights, and scorned the lackluster service they'd received in those inns.

And Elsbeth took every possible opportunity to berate her spiteful, ungrateful husband, who had banished her from The World, as she called it, to the abbey for her many infidelities.

"Just think, Lady Elsbeth," Lucy said, carefully choosing her words. The abbess had rebuked her all too often for her reckless tongue. "Tonight there will be no impertinent servants, nor bitter mead. We will cook our own provisions and sleep under the stars."

"The clouds, more like," Elsbeth replied with disdain. "And rain. Sleeping out of doors," she scoffed. "'Tis inhumane, forcing us to spend the night without shelter."

Lucy smiled, breathing deeply of the fresh air, full of the promise of a cleansing shower. Rain did not bother her. Being caged behind the cloister walls like some housewife's fowl, and having every day of her life regimented to prayers—Matins in the morn, Lauds and Terce, then Vespers and Complines—did little for Lucy's soul. Aye, she well knew that all these prayers should enrich her soul, but they did not.

Certainly she prayed to Almighty God, and she was as devout as any good Christian, but there were so many other things in The World that manifested God's glory. The beautiful, shimmering, golden elm that stood outside the abbey wall was an exquisite example of God's power and majesty. The ungainly first steps of a newborn lamb, the sound of Sister Maria's voice, raised in song, the color of the sky at sunrise… In Lucy's opinion, 'twas the appreciation of these fine things that gave God his due, so much more than any meager words she uttered while on her knees.

And 'twas this very attitude that made Lucy wholly unsuitable as a nun. She had lived in the abbey in Leicestershire since her twelfth year, but had managed to avoid taking her vows for all these years. And during her time at the abbey, she'd spent many an hour imagining what her life could be, outside the walls.

Lucy was painfully aware that she had no alternative but to remain a part of the nunnery. Still, she had no wish to cloister herself behind the high walls of the new abbey. Holywake, 'twas called, and the new abbey in Yorkshire was said to be even more secluded than Craghaven, which had become overcrowded. The very thought of another thirty or forty hollow years, secluded and barren at Holywake, gave her unease.

"I suppose you care not if you get soaked to the skin tonight," Elsbeth said, "though a person with your infirmities ought to be concerned."

Lucy laughed. She was lame, that's all. She had been sickly as a child, but she'd outgrown it, and become healthy at Craghaven. She had naught to fear from a simple autumn rain.

Lady Elsbeth frowned at her, glancing 'round nervously as if someone might hear Lucy's sparkling laughter. The proud lady had performed many a harsh penance since her banishment to the abbey, but Lucy did not believe the woman had changed in the least. Prayer and suffering had done naught to improve her. Lady Elsbeth had merely become cautious.

"You should be glad the abbess is far away and unable to hear such frivolity from you," Elsbeth said. "'Tis not—"

"Please, Elsbeth," Lucy said. "The abbess *is* far away and…" A strange thought crept into her mind.

What if Lucy went away, and stayed away? What if she made certain that the abbess never had dominion over her again? She might even leave tonight, while the others were sleeping. She had no particular attachment to Lady Elsbeth or any of these nuns—the women of the cloister barely knew each other. They were encouraged to keep apart, and silence was the rule. They would hardly miss her, were she gone from their midst.

What if she made her way to the nearest town or village, or to a manor house or castle? Would she be able to make her way in The World alone? Surely she could she gain employment as a nurse to some noble children, or as a castle seamstress. Mayhap she could earn her way helping a town brewer, or hiring herself out for other domestic jobs.

Lucy bit one corner of her lower lip. Such dreams

were impossible, and she knew it. She was a cripple, and though she was the daughter of an earl, he was long dead, as were her brothers. The cousin who had inherited her father's title had sent her to Craghaven Abbey to absolve himself of responsibility for her. She had no distinguishing skills, and knew naught of The World outside the cloister—other than the intriguing tales of love and lust that Elsbeth had told in secret.

Resigned to her fate, Lucy said, "We have only a few days until we reach Holywake. Let us spend them in peace and in the enjoyment of our free—"

"You two would do well," said Sister Avice, "to engage yourselves in a few moments of prayerful silence."

"'Tis well past time for Terce now anyhow," Sister Gunnora said sternly, as if Lucy did not know their daily routine, as if she had not participated in these prayers every day since she'd recovered from the illness that had caused her cousin to send her to Craghaven.

At that moment, Lucy made her decision. She would go this very night. This would be the last time she ever stopped what she was doing in order to pray Terce.

Sister Gunnora spoke again. "Pull the wagon to the side, Sister Avice, and we—" A startled scream ended the woman's words abruptly, and she collapsed across the bench.

Before Lucy and Elsbeth could comprehend what had happened, the horses bolted and Sister Gunnora was thrown from her seat. Elsbeth screamed. Lucy held on as the wagon careened down the path.

Men on horseback chased them. Lucy could not spare a moment to look behind, for she knew that if the horses continued at this rate, she and Sister Avice would be thrown from the wagon and break their necks. She had to climb to the front and help the old woman regain control of the horses.

An arrow whizzed past Lucy's ear, and she ducked down into the wagon bed. Suddenly, the wagon became airborne. Lucy could no longer feel every bump in the road, and she knew that the worst possible thing had happened. She was not going to look for her freedom tonight. She was going to die.

Sir Alexander Breton heard a commotion somewhere on the road behind him, and turned to see a rough wagon careening toward him, out of control. Then a saddled, riderless horse galloped past him. Two mounted men in decrepit knights' hauberks and helms rode in pursuit of the wagon. 'Twas clear that the men were miscreants, and the women on the wagon their intended victims.

They were obviously not Lord Skelton's well-equipped knights whom he had evaded yestereve at Doncaster.

The wagon hit a deep pit in the road and flew into the air. Horses screamed, and the women were thrown. Alex drew his sword, kicked his heels into his mount and dashed toward the knaves who had caused this disaster. He would secure justice for these women, even though 'twas too little, done too late.

The two scoundrels had a mere fraction of the skill and experience that was possessed by a knight of Alex's stature. Even with a lingering soreness from the wound in his arm, he had no trouble dispatching the two men quickly, and without regret. He took a deep breath, glanced up at the cloud-filled sky, then went to look for survivors.

Alex found the first body near the wagon. The woman had been elderly, and was clearly a nun though she carried a pouch of coins. The second one lay at the base of a giant oak, her neck broken. He looked 'round for the other two—he was certain there had been at least one more body thrown from the wagon, and one from the horse.

He heard a groan.

Quickly following the sound, he came upon a much younger nun, pulling herself out of a murky fen, some twenty paces from the road. 'Twas likely her fall into the bog had saved her life.

She was soaked with the brackish water, her body clearly defined through the worn cloth of her kirtle. Her skin was so pale, 'twas nearly transparent. Her stunned blue eyes stood out starkly—providing the only color in her face, other than a purpling bruise upon her chin. Even her lips were white with shock, but she moved with courage and purpose.

Alex stood with his fists clenched at his sides. Raw emotion knifed through him as he looked at the woman moving clumsily up the soggy bank. 'Twas impossible that he should feel so awkward now, so affected by her feminine vulnerability. This situation was no different from the multitude of times he'd gone to battle in defense of his liege lord, or of the monks at Cluny. And in his recent travels he had defended many a good woman on pilgrimage.

Yet this *was* different. It seemed all too personal this time, and his intense urge to protect and admire her ran contrary to the numbness he'd felt in the three years since the death of his wife, Isabella, and their infant son.

"*Pater Noster,*" he said under his breath, forcing himself to pray rather than gaze upon the woman's comely form, "*qui es in caelis, sanctificetur nomen tuum.*"

The Latin words calmed him, gave him the peace and detachment he craved. He could touch this woman, he could gaze upon her gentle features and feel naught. "*Adveniat regnum tuum. Fiat voluntas tua, sicut in caelo et in terra.*"

Even more composed now, he gave her his hand and pulled her the rest of the way out of the water. She collapsed on dry land and rolled her legs up into her chest, shaking violently. And she said naught. Moisture filled her eyes, yet she did not weep. Light brows, delicately arched, came together in puzzlement as she looked up at him.

Alex knew that a woman would need a strong pair of arms to hold her, to comfort her after such a disaster.

"*Panem nostrum quotidianum da nobis hodie, et*

dimitte nobis debita nostra sicut et nos dimittimus debitoribus nostris,'' he muttered, and turned away suddenly, leaving the woman shuddering and holding on to her limbs, as if they would fall from her body.

He stalked back toward the road and forced his attention to the ground, searching for whoever had been thrown from the horse. He would not allow himself to fall prey to the ways of the world, merely because he was miles away from Cluny. On his own, he must strive for purity of body and spirit, as well as piety and humility. He would defend the innocent wherever he found them, but strictly limit his interactions with the secular world, for he had every intention of taking his holy vows and dedicate his life to the memory of Isabella when he returned to Cluny. His decision to remain celibate had not been made lightly, nor capriciously...even if Roger Kendal had had reservations about it.

Though he was an Englishman, Alexander Breton was the second son of an earl. Alex did not begrudge his elder brother the title or the land. In truth, 'twas never something to which Alexander aspired.

Three years ago, Philip had entreated Alex to return home to Clyfton Castle. Alex had refused. The ability to face Philip's healthy wife and children daily was beyond him.

And now he found himself in York, not far from the home he'd shared with his poor Isabella and little Geoffrey. He intended never again to experience the soul-wrenching grief he'd felt on their deaths.

Alex found the last victim's body on the road, some

distance from the place where the wagon lay broken.
'Twas another young woman, and Alex was uncertain
whether she was also a nun. Like the others, she wore
a wimple that covered her head entirely, as well as
part of her face. But her attire was made of cloth that
was much too costly for one who had taken the holy
vow of poverty, much too fine to have been riddled
by the arrows of those villainous knights. Mayhap she
was a lay sister, or had been relegated to the nunnery
by her family because of past indiscretions.

Whoever she was, Alex picked her up and carried
her back to the wagon, laying her next to the other
dead nuns. Gazing at the grisly scene before him, he
considered what was to be done. The wagon was now
useless, with two broken wheels. Since the horses had
run off, he had no means to carry the women to a
village for a proper burial. It quickly became clear
that he had to bury them here, in the place where they
died.

He had no idea what to do with the waterlogged
woman back at the fen, but with God's mercy, she
would understand that she was on her own now. After
the burial, Alex's obligation would be concluded. He
intended to move on, and would never have to see
her or deal with her again.

From the saddle pack high upon his mare's back,
he took out a small shovel, and began to dig. After a
short while, he removed his hauberk, leaving his
sweat-dampened undertunic rolled up to the elbows.
Keeping one eye upon the road in case Skelton's men
caught up, Alex worked at turning up the soil, and

making the grave deep enough, and wide enough for all three women.

He was nearly finished when a feminine voice cut through the peaceful silence, startling him, shocking him with her brazen words. "Sweet heaven. Are all men as hard as you?"

Lucy had never seen anything as beautiful as the knight whose muscles flexed so tightly as he shoveled the rich, black earth. He was big and broad, though his body narrowed quite elegantly at the hips. His legs were long, with muscles so different from her own, that Lucy had to look down at herself to see if they were even vaguely similar. They were not.

An odd sensation shot through her as she looked at him. 'Twas not exactly pleasant, but somehow... compelling.

Lucy ached. Her shoulder was scraped raw, and bruised. One of her knees—the weak one—was purple and swollen. She felt weak and shaken by the attack, yet there was no time for weakness, for weeping or uselessness. She had forced herself to stand, to wring out her sodden kirtle and compose herself. She could not bear to think of the arrow that pierced Sister Gunnora's neck, or the blood that welled from the wound on Sister Avice's back just before she'd been thrown from the wagon.

For the first time in twelve years, Lucy was all alone, only to find herself beholden to this fierce knight-rescuer. And if everything Elsbeth had said about The World was true, Lucy needed to keep a firm hold upon her wits.

Which was not what she'd done when she'd blurted out the first thought that had come to mind when she'd cast her eyes upon the magnificent knight wearing naught but a damp undertunic and hose. She would be more circumspect in future.

Lucy wrapped her arms around herself and sighed. The knight had given her a fleeting glance when she spoke, but turned back to his task, tightening his muscles even more, if that were possible. She was certain he had heard her question, for she saw his face flush red before he turned back to his work, and Lucy knew then that she'd misspoken.

Feeling heat rise to her own cheeks, she turned away too, and decided 'twould be best to ignore it. The day had been fair strange up until now, and one foolish blush did naught to change matters.

The poor old nuns with whom she traveled were dead. Lucy had not known them well, but she would never have wished such an end upon them. They were good and saintly women, though. Surely the Lord would welcome them into His kingdom.

But Lady Elsbeth... The abbess had called her wicked and wanton. Lucy wondered if Elsbeth would be doomed to spend eternity in Satan's domain. She had not been particularly close to Elsbeth, but the stories of her escapades *had* been intriguing. She had made Lucy yearn even more for the freedom that might be found outside Craghaven Abbey.

Uttering a silent prayer for Elsbeth's eternal soul,

Lucy began to pick up the few items of clothes that had spilled from the boxes on the wagon. All the crockery was ruined, as were the wooden trunks that had been in the wagon. Naught was left intact, not even her spare kirtle, which had caught on something sharp and was torn beyond use.

Life had been disrupted beyond recognition, and for the first time in Lucy's memory, she had to consider what to do.

'Twas a daunting thought. Her course had been so clear a mere hour ago, but now she did not know what to do.

She picked up a dry kirtle from the ground, located a few rags and a chemise from the rubble, and took them to a secluded place near the fen. There, she peeled away her own sodden clothes, wiped herself dry with the rags at hand, and dressed in Elsbeth's clean linen chemise and simple blue kirtle.

Lucy pulled her long braid apart, wincing with the movement of her shoulder. Switching hands, she used her fingers to comb through her mane of curly, light-colored hair, and realized that it was no longer necessary to cover it in the fashion of the Craghaven nuns. Certainly, a head covering would be most appropriate, but if she left the nunnery and went to seek her fortune... Lucy suddenly felt light-headed. She sat down hard on an overturned log and put her head down, taking a few deep breaths.

For years, she had wished to be freed from the confines of the cloister, and this was the opportunity to do so. She was not about to let it pass her by.

Chapter Two

Horses' hoofs pounded the ground in the distance. Alex threw his shovel into his saddle pack, grabbed Rusa's reins and led the sturdy mare into the forest, away from the road. Quickly, he made his way to the mucky fen where he assumed he'd find the young woman. As much as he wanted to, he could not leave her here unprotected, if any more thieves—or Skelton's men—were about.

Alex did not mean to frighten her, but she gave a startled cry when he came upon her, whirling 'round to face him. She was now dressed in something dry, a modest kirtle that contrasted with the golden shimmer of her long, wavy hair.

Alex swallowed. It had been years—mayhap a lifetime—since he'd seen anything quite so lovely and soft as this—

"You—"

He cut her off, grabbing her and covering her mouth with his hand before she could make any other sound. Half carrying her, he started moving, pulling her deep into the forest. She did not struggle against him, and when Alex removed his hand from her mouth, she surprised him by keeping silent, holding still.

"Riders are coming," he said in a low voice, stepping away from her. Keeping his eyes safely averted from her comely form, he tied Rusa in place. "Stay here."

Alex made his way silently back toward the broken wagon and the new grave. He remained hidden and watched as three riders approached the wreckage.

His instincts had been correct. They were the same three who had caught on to him near Doncaster. They had the look of Skelton's knights, wearing black tunics marked with a white lion over their hauberks. 'Twas all the proof Alex needed to confirm that Skelton knew something of the valuable relic that rested within Sir Roger's scabbard.

These men would be well-trained knights, and fiercely loyal to their lord. Alex doubted he'd be the one to emerge victorious from a meeting of these three in battle. Nay, he would have to avoid a confrontation so that he could fulfill his promise to Roger Kendal.

Alex glanced back toward the place where he'd left the woman. If she continued to cooperate, he stood a chance of eluding the men again and keeping her safe. They would keep to the forest paths and avoid the road.

And he would leave her in the first village they came to.

Content with this plan, he turned his gaze on the road and observed as Skelton's men turned over the bodies of the dead thieves, picked through the debris that had fallen from the wagon and spoke quietly together over the fresh grave. One of them pointed ahead, in the direction Alex was taking, and Alex knew for certain that he would have to follow another path to Eryngton. Somehow, they knew his destination.

As Skelton's men remounted, Alex felt something solid touch his shoulder. He whipped his body around, poised to fight, and groaned in dismay when he saw that he'd only managed to knock the small nun to the ground. Her brow creased for an instant, and she looked as if she would call out. Alex dropped to his knees beside her and covered her mouth again with his hand, just as she began to speak.

He shook his head and gestured for her to keep silent. She became still, and he removed his hand. Mindful of Skelton's men standing nearby, Alex put his mouth close to her ear and whispered, "'Twould be best to avoid these men. They…" She turned slightly, putting her face a mere inch from his. Her lashes were dark gold, growing thick around sky-blue eyes. Her breath was warm on his face, her skin flawless.

Alex jerked away from her, and rose quickly to his feet. *"Credo in Deum Patrem omnipotentem, Creatorem caeli et terrae…."* he muttered, turning away to stare absently at the road, toward anything that would force his mind from the unsuitable thoughts that tried to form against his will.

Skelton's men were gone.

In frustration, Alex dug his fingers through his hair, unable to believe he'd missed hearing them mount up and ride away. Something was not right. Why had they left the site so quickly? They'd taken barely a moment to look over the broken wagon, the grave and the debris.

With certainty, he knew they'd be back. The dead thieves in mail hauberks and the fresh grave would make them curious. They would follow the road in hopes of catching up to him, but when it became clear that he had not ridden ahead, they would return.

Alex stole a quick glance at the woman, and saw her rising awkwardly to her feet.

"Come on!" They had to hurry. He pulled her the rest of the way up, then took her hand and dragged her deeper into the woods. When they reached his horse, he wasted no time, but picked her up and tossed her unceremoniously upon Rusa's back. With his heart pounding in his chest, Alex jumped up behind her, reached around her body to grab the reins, then trotted deeper into the woods.

Alex glanced back to assure himself that they were not being followed, and so far, all was well. Then he remembered her wet clothes. She had changed out of her sodden kirtle, and must have left it by the fen. Would Skelton's men discover it? What would they think...that the gown had been thrown when the wagon was smashed?

"We need to put some distance between us and the men on horseback."

"You mean the black knights?" she asked. Alex kicked his heels into the mare's sides, causing the woman to throw one arm around Alex's neck to hold on.

"Aye," he said, clipping the word short. Inuring himself against the sensations that shot through him when her soft body pressed against his, he muttered a quiet prayer. Certainly his reaction to her touch was not the response a monk should have. He drew back from her embrace and tore his gaze from hers.

"Your eyes are the color of the moss by the fen," she said. The clear, rich timbre of her voice vibrated through her chest to his own. Her expression was entirely ingenuous, fascinated. Her stare, unwavering.

Alex's throat went dry, making it impossible to reply. She leaned into him, reaching up to touch his beard.

He grabbed her wrist in his fist and prevented any further stroking, causing a return of the now familiar crease between her brows again. She studied him for a moment, then leaned slightly to the side, her eyes alighting on something over his shoulder.

"They're coming," she said.

The forest was thick enough to provide good cover, but if the nun had seen Skelton's men, the reverse was possible, too. Alex did not stop to think, but urged Rusa into a gallop. Though he was unfamiliar with this part of the Yorkshire terrain, his mare was sure-footed and could be trusted to stay a fair distance ahead of their pursuers. With God's grace, he would find a way to elude the men who would like nothing better than to steal Sir Roger's artifact.

"Hang on," he said.

The nun wrapped both arms around Alex. 'Twas no wonder the Rule dictated that women were to be avoided. If every monk came into such close contact...

"You've lost them," she said against his chest.

He spared a quick glance behind them, and did not see anyone pursuing. Still, he kept Rusa at a full run. He knew the black knights could not be far behind.

"Are they after you or me?" she asked.

"Me, for certain," he said. "Though 'tis possible they seek you as well."

"Why me?"

Alex cleared his throat. The woman was innocent, pure. She'd been sheltered behind her nunnery walls and likely knew little or naught of men's ways. And Alex did not relish the thought of being the one to enlighten her. "These men are ruthless," he said gruffly.

She blinked once, then pulled back to look up into his eyes. She was not as young as he'd first thought, but her naiveté was unmistakable. She had no idea of the perils she would face once he left her.

"If they thought you were a woman alone...er, women don't usually travel without escort. And men— soldiers—have been known to...to..."

"To rape women in my position?" she asked.

* * *

There was that blush again, starting at the knight's neck, rising to his face, and coloring the tips of his ears. Lucy realized that she had misspoken once again. Mayhap rape was one of those subjects that men and women did not discuss together.

But she needed to know. She would not always have this man to protect her, and the abbey had done naught to prepare her for life outside its walls. There would be much to learn, and Lucy believed 'twould serve her well to discover all she could from this noble knight. He was her champion, her guardian, but he would not stay with her forever.

"Have you a name, Sir Knight?" she asked.

"Alexander Breton," he replied as the horse took flight over a fallen log. The jump caused his speech to be cut short and Lucy grabbed his leg to hold on, oblivious to the man's sharp intake of breath. The horse's jarring gait made her shoulder ache, but the joyful freedom and tremendous speed of the ride made her little pains seem insignificant.

"I am Lucy," she said. "Lucy of Craghaven."

She studied his face, watching as his jaw clamped down once more. His cheekbones were sharp, his nose a blade that was neither too long, nor femininely short. Solemn purpose was in his eyes, and in the set of his jaw—what she could see of it past his heavy, dark beard. She wondered if he'd known the black knights were nearby when he'd stopped to help her and the nuns.

"I am sorry you were waylaid by my troubles, Sir

Alexander," she said. "Those men...what do they
want of you?"

He hesitated for a moment. "I...gave them some
trouble last night. They intend to retaliate."

Lucy sensed that he wasn't being entirely honest
with her. Sir Alex may have given the black knights
trouble, but that was not why he thought they were
following him.

"Will they keep after us all the way through the
forest?"

He did not reply directly, but Lucy heard him whispering Latin words to himself in a low voice. He kept
his eyes focused upon the terrain ahead, and very deliberately plucked her hand from his thigh, placing it
upon the edge of the saddle.

Lucy grabbed hold and hung on as they galloped,
frequently looking over his shoulder to watch for any
sign of riders behind them. The ride was exhilarating,
if a bit frightening, and Lucy felt as if she were flying.
She would have laughed aloud, if only the black
knights had not been in pursuit. For the first time in
her life, she was not poor, lame Lucy. She was just
a woman, riding a horse...with her own handsome
knight.

Not that Sir Alexander was hers, but she would
allow herself to dream as long the ride lasted.

His hair was long and sleek, the dark mass held at
the nape of his neck by a leather thong. Lucy wondered how it would feel if she touched it, but she
knew he would not allow it. He held himself distinctly

apart from her—other than allowing the minimum contact necessary to keep her from falling.

Sir Alex finally slowed his horse and turned east. Keeping a steady pace, he took them through a much denser wood, where there was no path and the ground was littered with low brush and new saplings. The mare picked its way across the forest floor until they reached a rocky wall. 'Twas only about twice the height of a man, but impassable.

Lucy glanced up at the escarpment above. "Are we trapped here?"

The knight did not answer. Instead, he shifted his legs and the horse responded immediately by turning and walking alongside the wall. Lucy was astonished by Sir Alexander's movement. She did not know it was so easy to ride and to control such a large beast with a mere touch of the leg. If she had, she surely would have ridden horseback during her journey, just as Elsbeth had done. She needn't have sat with the old women in the wagon.

She'd been "poor Lucy" far too long. In future, no one would ever have cause to call her that, or any of the other pitiful names that had been whispered when she was not supposed to hear.

They moved slowly, but Lucy did not remove her hand from the knight's back or her eyes from the forest behind them. Too much had happened already, in the space of one afternoon for her to feel safe and secure. Lucy forced herself to keep the awful memories at bay, but images of the nuns' screams, their blood flowing...

She shuddered.

"There's a way to climb," Alex said, startling her into the present. She turned to look ahead, and saw that the wall was no longer quite so high. It had gradually declined, but she had not noticed while watching so intently for the black knights.

Alex guided Rusa up the small incline and doubled back toward the place where he'd left the northward path, climbing steadily. The vantage point up there would be excellent, and if Skelton's knights followed, Alex would be able to see them. He would know in advance what direction they took.

It would also afford him the chance to put some real space between himself and the nun. He did not care to put his virtue to the test this way. Celibacy had not been difficult in Cluny, or on the journey to Jerusalem with Brother Roger. Most of Alex's time had been spent in prayer or in training; none of it in the company of women.

He ducked to avoid a low branch, pushing Sister Lucy's head down, too. She remained in that position longer than necessary, with her head pasted against his chest, her free hand going 'round to his back.

Then he realized he still cupped her head. And he did not want to let her go.

"Beati pauperes spiritu," he intoned in a whisper.

"Quoniam ipsorum est Regnum caelorum," Sister Lucy added, finishing the beatitude. She ducked away from his hand and turned away, looking over Rusa's

head. "You did not tell me that you were a priest,"
she finally said.

"Because I am not," he replied.

"But your Latin—"

"I am just a knight, Sister Lucy," he said. "But I
will take my monastic vows when I return to Cluny."

She turned and looked at him then, and the small
crease between her brows reappeared. He did not
dwell upon it, but swung his leg over Rusa's back
and dismounted. Then he set his hands at Sister
Lucy's waist and lifted her from the mare's back. The
ends of her hair brushed his skin as he eased her down
and he suppressed the physical stirring that threatened
to lead his thoughts into sinful paths.

"I might as well tell you then, that I am not a
nun," she said. "Nor will I ever be."

Chapter Three

In the day's fading light, Alexander lay prone at the edge of the escarpment, watching the ground below. It seemed quiet, and he finally allowed himself to begin thinking of settling down to rest for the night. All might have been well, except that Lucy of Craghaven sat waiting, out of sight, in the shelter of a huge pine.

It should have made no difference. Thoughts of no woman other than Isabella had crossed his mind since his marriage six years before. At least, no lustful thoughts had crossed his mind. But now...

The mere memory of Lucy's silken tresses brushing his arm made him quiver with cravings he thought he'd buried three years ago. The feel of her soft flesh against his own seemed more exciting than any physical contact could ever have been.

Alex knew these musings must stop. Prayer and meditation would channel his thoughts in a more suitable direction. He would not give in to the temptations of the flesh because of—

Suddenly, she was beside him.

"Do you see anyone?" the familiar feminine voice asked in a hushed tone as Lucy stretched out next to him, leaving barely an inch between them. But even though they did not touch, Alex could feel her body pulsing with energy and excitement beside him.

Did she not understand how improper it was to lie beside a man? Alex suppressed a groan and forced himself to stay still. He was a strong and disciplined knight. He had the willpower to resist her. 'Twas not necessary to move away.

"Nay," he replied, keeping his eyes on the ground below. Still, he felt her warmth beside him. "They did not follow us."

"It's starting to rain," she said. "Do we dare go back to the wagon for supplies? Or do you carry all that we'll need?"

Mentally, Alex made the sign of the cross. He had not considered what the night would bring. Normally, he would just wrap himself in his woolen blanket and find a bit of cover. Now that he had a woman to protect, he would have to do more to accommodate her needs. "We'll make a shelter under the trees and, uh…spend the night here."

He rose to his feet and gave Lucy a hand up. Deliberately walking away from her, he started back to the place where he'd tethered Rusa, thinking of the night ahead of him.

He had enough food in his pack to last several days. As for blankets, there was only the one, but he was not likely to become chilled, even though 'twas becoming rather cool with the rain. He would give the blanket to Lucy and... He stopped. Where was she?

Looking back, he saw that she was struggling to keep up with him. Her gait was awkward, and she nearly fell in her hurry. Without thinking, he went to her and lifted her off her feet, cradling her in his arms. "Why did you not tell me that you were injured?" he growled. "I'd have—"

"I'm not injured, Sir Knight," she said, pushing at his chest to be let down. The crease between her brows became a cross frown. "I can walk."

Though he did not understand her sudden vexation, he did not put her down. "What happened to your foot then?" He kept his eyes straight ahead and continued carrying her away from the escarpment.

"My leg," she said tightly, "'twas slightly bruised in the fall, but it has not been right since my birth. It means naught. I can still do all that any other woman can."

Alex swallowed. Her words suggested something he had no business pondering, but not a single prayer jumped into his mind to rescue him from his improper thoughts. Her hair trailed across his arm again, sending a shiver of sensation through him.

They reached the stand of trees where Rusa was tied, and Alex let Lucy down. Before he could take her arm to help her, she walked under the boughs of a thick pine, and rubbed her hands over her arms in an attempt to get warm.

Alex glanced 'round. The area was well sheltered from the light rain, and if it did not turn into a downpour, they would be all right here for the night. He pulled his packs off the mare and dropped them near the tree trunk, then unrolled his blanket and shook it out. When he started to place it upon Lucy's shoulders, he thought better of it. The more distance he kept between them, the better.

She took the woolen cloth from his outstretched hand and wrapped it around her like a shawl. He saw her grimace. 'Twas with pain, if he was not mistaken.

"What is amiss?" he asked.

"'Tis merely a bruise," she said. "I must have hit my shoulder on something when I fell into the fen."

Of course she was bruised, Alex thought. And likely on more places than her shoulder and chin. 'Twas surprising she had not broken any bones. He scowled, stepping 'round to look at her back.

A dark stain blotted the area over her shoulder blade.

Alex cleared his throat. "Open your kirtle," he said. "You're bleeding."

Her back stiffened and he could almost hear her protest before she spoke.

"If 'tis bleeding enough to soak through your gown, then it is serious enough to tend," he said. "Open it."

Another moment's hesitation, and she began to unlace the cords that bound the front of the kirtle together. She slipped it off her shoulder, even as she pulled her hair over the other shoulder, out of the way.

Alex forced his eyes to remain upon the deep

gouge that marred her perfect skin. He refused to acknowledge the delicate line of her neck, or the goose bumps that raised the tiny, almost colorless hairs of her nape.

"Stand still." He reached for his pack and took out a stoppered jar, along with his waterskin and a clean cloth. Pouring some of the water on the cloth, he washed the deep wound, then took ointment from the jar and spread it upon her shoulder. The gash was in an awkward place...he did not know how he would bandage it.

She held perfectly still while he tended her, though he knew the ointment had a sting to it, like a hundred bees attacking at once. She was an unusual woman. Mayhap he'd been wrong about her, and she did not require the same kind of comfort that most women would demand. One thing was certain—she was tougher than she appeared.

"'Tis nearly dark," he said. "But I don't want to start a fire...it would show our position too easily."

Lucy nodded almost imperceptibly, keeping her face averted, as if she did not want him to see it. When she raised a hand to her face, he could not doubt that she wiped away tears. And her slight movement drove away all his perceptions about her toughness.

"This should be bandaged," he said, more gruffly than he intended.

She did not reply, but turned her head back and tried to see the injury. Alex took a clean strip of the cloth he'd used on the wound he'd sustained near

Jerusalem and placed one end upon Lucy's injury. He
flipped the other end over her shoulder.

"Can you hold this in place?" he asked.

"What are—?"

"It isn't a good spot to bandage," he said. "But
if you keep this strip over your shoulder, the cloth
should stay in place over your wound. It'll keep the
ointment from rubbing off on to your clothes."

Lucy gave a short nod and did as he instructed.
Then he turned her to face him and he felt her eyes
upon him as he worked to secure the bandage in
place.

"You may...er, lace your kirtle now," he said as
his knuckles brushed the cool, unfettered skin of her
chest. He restrained the urge to run his fingers across
the smooth lines of her collarbone, to touch the intriguing notch at the base of her throat.

She fumbled with her laces. Impatiently, he pushed
her hands away and fastened the kirtle himself, covering her pretty flesh.

Glad to have that chore over, he suddenly remembered the pouch he'd taken from the body of the eldest nun. He had tucked it inside his tunic for safekeeping, until he could give it to this lone survivor.
Now that he knew she was not a nun, he refrained
from handing it to her, wondering at her connection
to the nuns who were killed. Did the valuable contents
of the pouch belong to her now?

"Where were you headed when you were set
upon?" he asked.

"To Holywake Abbey," she replied. "'Tis another two days' journey north of here."

Alex frowned, watching as she tucked in the laces of her kirtle. Two days? He was not about to waste two days escorting this woman to the abbey when he needed to travel due west to Eryngton...and when he needed to put miles between them. "You are not a nun, yet you travel to Holywake with women of the cloth?"

"I have lived at Craghaven Abbey in Leicestershire for many a year, Sir Alex," she said, gazing at him intently. "But I never took the vows. Nor shall I ever."

"I don't understand," he said, clasping his hands behind him and turning away. He paced restlessly, certain his disquiet was due to the proximity of the black knights, and no other reason. They were dangerous men and if they caught up to him when Lucy of Craghaven was under his protection, he would be hard-pressed to keep her safe. By heaven, he would be lucky to keep himself safe.

"Craghaven became overcrowded," Lucy explained, "so the bishop found us a new abbey—Holywake in Yorkshire. A few of us were assigned to go in advance of the others and make Holywake ready—"

"Nay." Alex shook his head. "You mistake my meaning. Why will you not take the vows?" he asked, slipping the pouch from his tunic and handing it to her. Clearly, she would have need of the coin within to make her way to the nunnery.

Absently, she weighed the small leather satchel in her hands. "'Twas never my choice to go to Craghaven. I was sent there as a child to die," she said, responding to his question.

Alex understood even less now and his confusion must have showed upon his face, for she began to explain.

"When my cousin inherited my brother's estate, he and his lady wife wanted... Well, I was a sickly child, and lame, and not expected to last the year." She lowered her eyes and her voice became quieter. "The new earl did not want his first months in...in my home tainted with death."

'Twas an ugly truth, but Alex knew better than most how ugly it could become. His poor Isabella had succumbed to illness, along with their son. But Alex had not sent them away out of fear of contagion. Nay, he'd stayed with them, watched them draw their last breath, one within hours of the other.

Lucy's cousin had had no such regard. The man had sent her to die in the company of strangers.

"This belongs to Sister Avice," Lucy said, turning the pouch in her hands. They were small hands, with slender fingers, but not delicate. Alex saw redness and broken nails—signs of harsh work. She was no longer the sickly child, but a woman fully capable of hard work, and aught else that was demanded of her.

Before his thoughts could once again drift beyond what was seemly, he gestured toward the leather satchel. "'Tis yours now, to return to the abbey."

Reaching inside the pouch, Lucy's eyes grew huge

when she drew out a handful of coins. "'Tis a fortune! What will I..." She drew her lower lip between her teeth and let it slide back out. The movement was slow and sensual, and almost more than Alexander could bear to watch.

"Beati mundo corde, quoniam ipsi Deum videbunt...." he muttered, unable to take his eyes from her mouth.

"Now I suppose I *must* go to Holywake," Lucy said, "just to see this returned to the Order."

Puzzled again, Alex frowned. The woman was a mass of contradictions. "I thought you had planned to go to Holywake."

She shook her head. "No. I... Earlier today, I decided to leave the sisters, and make my way alone. But then—"

"Alone?" he asked, incredulous. "How would you make your way? Were you going to walk until you found a likely village?"

Lucy took a step back and stumbled. Alex reached out and caught her about the waist as the coins spilled out of her hand, on to the loamy soil beneath the boughs of the tree.

Lucy felt his strong hands at her waist, his breath on her face, and she trembled. She licked her lower lip as he held her there, and wished she did not feel so strange every time he touched her.

She was weary and hungry, and now that dusk had fallen, she was more than a little frightened. The day's events were crashing in on her, and it did not help that Sir Alex's gaze made her feel as if someone had lit a torch inside her, and that *both* her legs had gone lame.

She caught her balance and withdrew from him, pulling the blanket more tightly over her shoulders. She glanced at the sky. "Aye," she said in response to his question. "I'll walk."

Sir Alex made no reply, and Lucy was just as glad of it. She did not need him to remind her that she would have difficulty walking any distance. She knew it. She'd lived with it all her life.

'Twas past dusk now, and growing darker by the minute. A few stars were already visible between the clouds, and Lucy realized that what she'd said to Elsbeth all those hours ago had just been bluster. She had never slept out of doors in her life, and now that she was faced with a night without shelter, she felt chilled and afraid.

What if the black knights found them here under the tree, sleeping and unprepared? Could Sir Alexander deal with all three of those men?

Lucy could only wonder. He'd fought the men who attacked the wagon, but Lucy had been thrown a fair distance. She had not seen Sir Alexander in battle. She did not even know how many opponents he'd had—only that one of those men had shot the arrow that had pierced Sister Gunnora's throat. In the moment of the poor old nun's death, her eyes had been wide and horrified. The arrow had made a gruesome sound....

She shivered with the terrible memory, and forced

herself to think of the future, not on the day's events. Crouching down to the ground, Lucy began to pick up the coins. Sir Alexander knelt next to her to help.

"I've never...done this before," she said, looking up and meeting Sir Alexander's eyes. She did not care for the sound of fear that she heard in her own voice. "Sleep o-outside, I mean. I don't know what to do."

He didn't answer right away, and his gaze ignited that strange torch inside her once again.

He turned away abruptly. "Just find a comfortable spot to lie down," he finally said, facing away from her. "Wrap up in the blanket and go to sleep."

"Will you...stay close?"

Lucy heard his sigh and a few muttered words in Latin. "Aye. I'll be here. Beside you."

Chapter Four

Even though Lucy knew she must be in the midst of a horrible dream, she could not shake herself awake. The horses bolted, sending the wagon on an uncontrolled, terrifying flight. The poor old nuns were killed with arrows, and the men on horseback still chased her.

Suddenly, her pursuers became three black knights on massive stallions. When Lucy turned to look at them, the men bared their dreadful, pointed teeth and growled like wolves in pursuit of their prey. They loosed arrows at her, and one found its mark in her shoulder. It stung, and burned with a painful fire that Lucy felt all the way down her back. Her blood welled and dripped, glaring painfully red, draining her life from her.

In despair, she cried out.

She could feel herself trembling, knew she was weeping, but was powerless to stop. A cold chill took hold of her body, making her teeth chatter uncontrollably. Then a sudden warmth enveloped her, soothing her. The shivering and chattering stopped and she began to breathe easily. The awful dream receded.

And she slept.

Alex pulled Lucy into the curve of his body, pressing her back against his chest, bending his knees to lend her as much warmth as possible.

She was having a nightmare. He'd called her name and tried to awaken her, but she was too deeply asleep to respond to him. Not knowing what else to do, he'd moved across the soft pine-needle bed under the tree and pulled her against him.

The ploy had worked. She was quieter now, her body relaxing into his.

A light rain fell all around them. They were sheltered beneath the boughs of a huge old pine, along with the added protection of a wide length of oiled leather that he had hung in the branches to shield them from the dampness.

There was no place for Alex to put his hands. He crooked the elbow of one arm and rested his head upon it, but the other hand seemed naturally drawn toward Lucy's waist. He couldn't keep himself from draping his arm across her, holding her tightly against him, even though he knew he should not. He should never have attempted to soothe away her bad dream. He had no business being this close.

"Credo in Deum Patrem omnipotentem, Creatorem caeli et terrae. Et in Iesum Christum, Filium eius unicum, Dominum nostrum," he whispered as her deli-

cate fragrance drifted through his senses. Her hair tickled his nose.

His body reacted in a way that would have been predictable three years before, but was foreign to him now. He could not push her away, not when he'd found her so cold and trembling, but he *could* control his base urges.

He *would* control them.

Lucy whimpered and stirred against him. "Hush," he whispered. "'Tis all right now. You're safe."

He only wished he could give himself the same assurance.

Lucy burrowed deeply into the warmth, and sighed contentedly. Birds chirped nearby, and the sound of trees rustling in the breeze was soothing. Even the weight across her hip and the soft caress of crisp hair against her cheek felt good. She opened her eyes.

Sir Alexander's chest was less than a hair's breadth from her face, his arm draped across her hip. His chest moved with deep, regular breaths, and Lucy knew he was asleep.

She did not move.

This was the first time Sir Alexander had touched her without drawing back with distaste. Nay, he held her as a lover might, completely relaxed and at peace, the way Elsbeth had described one of her many sinful encounters. She said she always felt "boneless" and serene after a night in her lover's arms.

Lucy would give anything to feel what Elsbeth had felt. Not that she wanted to take lovers...but she wouldn't mind one. A husband. Just one man who would care for her and—

The knight's big hand pressed against Lucy's bottom, pulling her so that her body was flush against his. He began to move his legs, insinuating one of them between hers, then pushing up. Lucy held her breath as he moved against her, unconsciously caressing her.

She did not want him to stop.

Lucy had never felt anything so grand in her life. There was a quickening inside her, a deep sensation low in her body that made her nerves hum. Even more astonishing was the pleasure in the simple physical contact he made. She felt as if she'd been starving, and was suddenly served a feast.

Heat radiated from the knight. His size dwarfed her, and his body felt solid against her. Lucy rubbed her cheek against his chest, savoring the moment. For this one short span of time, she could tell herself that she was not utterly alone in the world. She could pretend that the knight's embrace meant that she was precious to him.

Soon he would awaken and treat her with the same disdain as before.

Alex made a deep sound that seemed to come from the back of his throat, and moved against her. His hand slid down to cup her bottom, urging her closer. Lucy complied willingly. Unfamiliar sensations cascaded through her and her eyes widened as the feeling of comfort expanded into something more.

The knight's eyes opened and he gazed at her from

under heavy lids. His head moved, his lips on a sure path toward hers, and Lucy tingled with anticipation. There was naught in the world that would make her happier than to receive Sir Alex's kiss. His eyes remained trained upon hers, and Lucy allowed herself to believe she heard her name upon his breath.

Her eyes drifted closed. An instant later, a blanket of cold air covered her, and she was suddenly alone. She looked up and saw that Sir Alex had rolled away from her. He sprang to his feet as she watched, picked up his sword and skulked away.

Lucy rubbed her face with one hand and sat up. Pulling the blanket over her shoulders, she winced at the pain that stabbed through her injured shoulder blade.

She bit her lip. She'd been alone before. She'd been essentially alone most of her life. She would not allow Alexander Breton's abrupt departure to hurt. Her imaginings this morn had been foolish, and she'd known it even then. The man had been asleep when he'd made his advances, she told herself, rising awkwardly to her feet. Though it had felt more than wondrous to her, he hadn't even known 'twas *she* whom he had pulled into his arms.

A shaky sigh escaped her. She was the same awkward cripple she'd been the day before, still colorless and unattractive. Naught had changed in Sir Alex overnight, either. He was still destined to become a monk, dedicated to the Rule of his Order. The only thing that had changed since the attack on her party was that Lucy was now free. And she had the abbess's coin to help her make her way.

Unfortunately, she reminded herself, 'twas not her own money. Lucy could not, in good conscience, use the abbess's coin to make her way. She would always feel guilty about stealing from the abbey. She had no choice but to travel to Holywake, to pay the workmen who'd been hired to complete the work needed on the building and to buy the supplies the nuns would need when they arrived.

Momentarily at a loss for what to do next, she glanced 'round, but the woods were so thick, she could not see far. Sir Alex had been gone for quite some time, and since there was no sign of him or his horse, Lucy had to assume that he'd left her. He hadn't disguised his dislike for her, and Lucy knew he'd been anxious to get rid of her.

What better time to do it than now?

He'd almost kissed her.

By the saints, he'd nearly broken the vow he had all but officially made, Alex thought as he scooped water from a tiny stream into his hands to wash his face. Mayhap Roger Kendal's intimations had been correct, and Alex was not well suited to the Order. If he did not exert better control over his urges, even in sleep, then there could be no doubt that Roger had been correct.

Alex wanted to believe he'd been thinking of Isabella when he'd taken Lucy into his arms, but 'twould only be a lie. He'd lain close to *Lucy* all night long, inhaled her scent, dreamed of her flaxen hair. He'd soothed her whenever her bad dreams overtook her, and welcomed the soft pressure of her body lying with his.

But when he'd spoken her name... He prayed she had not heard him. 'Twas lunacy, coming so close to kissing her. There would be only one woman in his life—a raven-haired, brown-eyed beauty—and she was gone. Even though he was only thirty, he would have no other, and would soon take the vows of the Benedictine Order to ensure it. Alex had control over his base urges, and there was no woman alive who could sway him from his blessed purpose.

Rising to his feet, Alex took Rusa's reins and removed the leather hobble from her legs. His packs were on the mare's back, and none of his supplies were missing, except for his blanket and the oiled leather sheet. Both of these were easily replaced after he completed his task at Eryngton.

He would leave from this spot by the stream. There was no reason to go back—in fact, he had every reason not to return to the place where Lucy sat alone, most certainly confused by his behavior.

Leaning his forehead against the mare's flank, Alex felt ashamed. Skelton's men were likely still about, and Lucy would be at their mercy if she fell into their hands. With her lameness, she would never manage to elude them and walk all the way out of the woods to safety.

Alex's first responsibility was to get the scabbard with the artifact to Eryngton. But he could no longer deny that he also felt responsible for Lucy of Crag-haven.

He turned Rusa and led her back toward the place where they'd spent the night, wondering if Lucy had changed her mind about leaving her Order. Now that she'd been on her own for a day and night, mayhap she was reconsidering her decision.

'Twas likely that after the restless night she'd spent, she'd be anxious to return to the security of the nunnery. No woman in her right mind—especially a lame one—would want to strike out on her own, far from everything familiar.

As he approached the stand of trees where they'd spent the night, Alex considered his choices. He could take Lucy to the city of York and find her an escort to take her to Holywake. Or he could take her to the new abbey himself.

Upon further thought, the second idea was not a bad one. 'Twould get him off the road for a time, and out of Skelton's way.

Even if the black knights lost track of him on the road, they would probably lie in wait around Eryng-ton to ambush him there. No doubt Skelton had con-cluded that Alex's task was to take the artifact to Roger's brother at Eryngton.

By all accounts, Eryngton was only a few days' ride north of York. But with Skelton's men so close, Alex knew he would either have to bide a few days time in the forest, or lose himself in the city of York. A few days at Holywake might give him the time he needed. If he didn't arrive at the estate of John Kendal soon, Skelton's knights would be forced to conclude they were wrong about his destination. They would hunt elsewhere.

Alex stopped in his tracks when he saw his blanket neatly folded under the tree.

Lucy of Craghaven was nowhere in sight.

Alex told himself she must have just wandered off for a few moments of privacy before returning to the place where they'd slept. But after several minutes waiting for her, he realized she'd gone off without him.

Her foolishness angered him. What did she know of taking care of herself after her years behind nunnery walls? That kind of life was no preparation for survival outside.

Alex looked down at the damp grass and easily determined which way she'd gone. The little fool! Skelton's men were likely to be somewhere nearby, and Lucy could easily become prey to them. Quickly, he gathered up his belongings, and shoved them in his saddle packs. Picking up his horse's reins again, he followed the bent grass made by the woman's feet as she left the site.

After walking a good distance, Alex wondered if he'd interpreted the tracks correctly. Lucy was nowhere in sight, and he doubted she could have gotten much farther than this, considering her lameness. But where was she? Had Skelton's men already taken her?

Alex quickened his pace as his heart began to race. His eyes bored through the spaces between the trunks and branches of every tree in the forest. Berating himself for leaving her alone for so long, he realized that there were no longer any tracks to follow. By heaven, she was lost.

Alex ran one hand across his mouth and beard and forced out a harsh, irate breath.

He was a fool for allowing her to divert him from his purpose. The danger from Skelton's men was immense. They would kill him and steal Sir Roger's sacred relic without thinking twice, all while he was preoccupied with Lucy's whereabouts, her safety.

If he had any sense at all, he would sneak back toward the road and see if the black knights were still lurking about. Their location would determine the direction he would take with Lucy—when he found her.

The forest was quiet, and Alex could not imagine which way the woman had gone. Annoyed with her for causing this delay... He caught a flash of color out of the corner of his eye, and turned to see Lucy emerging from behind a stand of thick pines.

She began walking toward him and he suddenly realized *she'd been hiding!*

Though her gait was slightly awkward, she did not seem ungainly or ungraceful. She just moved across the forest floor in her own way, while he stood still, utterly confounded by her. He wanted to grab her shoulders and shake her for her foolishness, but he would not. He would keep his distance, as the Rule dictated.

"Do you have any idea how dangerous—"

She silenced him with her hand over his mouth.

"The black knights are just below that ridge," she

whispered, gesturing toward the landscape from which she'd come. "'Twould be best not to let them know we are here, would it not?"

Frowning, he reached up and pulled her hand away. "Come on," he said quietly. Irritated beyond reason, he lifted her up and placed her on Rusa's back, then jumped up behind her. They rode in silence toward the place where they'd spent the night, then continued on in the same direction.

"Where are we going?" Lucy asked, still keeping her voice down.

"To the road," Alex replied tightly, "though I don't intend to reach it until we're quite north of here."

His anger simmered. This woman, who should have no worldly experience at all, had managed to locate the enemy and warn him away before he had a chance to step directly into their camp. She had not relied upon him for her survival, only coming along with him when he'd hauled her away from the black knights.

Didn't she realize he'd saved her skin more than once? Was she too dense to understand the danger posed by the black knights?

"Why did you leave?" he demanded, leaning slightly back in order to have as little physical contact with her as possible.

She turned her head slightly, and he saw that there was a blush of color upon her fair cheeks. Refusing to dwell on her comely charms, Alex watched as she bit her lower lip. "You wanted to be rid of me, and so I left," she said and turned away from him.

Alex felt pressure in his jaws where his back teeth were clenched tightly. He deliberately loosened them. "Where did you think you would go?" he asked harshly. She was too forward, much too blunt. And she had no business anticipating his actions. "You were on foot. You don't know where you are, or where you're going."

She whipped her head around and gave him a scathing look. "I most certainly do, Sir Knight," she said. "I intend to go to Holywake and leave Sister Avice's coin there."

"And how did you expect to find Holywake?"

She hesitated, and he took great satisfaction in knowing that she could not answer him. She *was* lost, and totally dependent upon him.

"The road is that way," she finally said, pointing left, exactly the direction of the road. "I will circle 'round—to avoid the black knights—and follow it north until I reach a lane marked by a shrine to Saint Agatha. Holywake Abbey is down that lane. So if you'll—"

"How far will that be?" he asked, with more ire than necessary. He bent slightly at the waist and leaned toward her and felt some odd satisfaction that she did not back away.

"I do not know," she said.

"But you thought you'd walk all the way?"

"Of course not," she shot back at him. "There will be other travelers—"

"Aye, there *will* be! Wearing black tunics and carrying swords!"

He should not be so upset. If she wanted to be thickheaded about it, 'twas not his concern. He could leave her here and go on to Eryngton himself. The safety of Lucy of Craghaven would be in God's hands.

She frowned slightly. "I—I'm sure I can avoid them," she said.

Alex laughed sharply. "You were lucky this morn. You are no match for Skelton's ruthless men."

"I never planned to engage them in battle," she said, caustically. "Only to see where they were, and then find my way around them."

Alex shook his head at her naiveté. Only an inexperienced, overly sheltered woman would use that kind of harebrained strategy. Not even the hapless women he and Roger had encountered on pilgrimage were so witless. Lucy of Craghaven should consider herself lucky that she had him to look after her for the time being. Without his expertise at survival, she would be lost.

"*You* never saw me," she said, breaking into his reverie, "until I wished to be seen, is that not true?"

Chapter Five

Lucy gathered her hair in her hands and pulled it over one shoulder, then settled herself more comfortably in the saddle. Sir Alex gave her plenty of room, leaning away as if he could not bear to touch her. She did not understand what made him so determined to keep his distance, but he never relaxed his posture, and they rarely came into physical contact with one another.

They stayed off the road, keeping to the trees just east of it, to stay out of sight of anyone traveling north. Lucy was glad of the ride, for it was proving to be a long way to the path that would take her to Holywake.

"What kind of preparations were you to make when you reached the abbey?" he asked.

Lucy was surprised that he bothered to speak to her after an hour of silence. "I'm not quite sure," she replied. "Sister Avice was in charge. I was only told that the new abbey had not been used in years…that there was cleaning to do, some repairs that would have to be made.''

"Surely you were not expected to make repairs."

"I suppose that's why Sister Avice carried so much money—to pay carpenters or laborers to do whatever was necessary."

"When will the other nuns arrive at Holywake?"

"Let me think," Lucy said. So much had happened since the attack, it seemed impossible that it had occurred only yesterday. "Mother Superior and the rest of the nuns won't leave Craghaven for at least a fortnight. We were to have plenty of time to make the abbey ready."

"And no one is there now?" he asked.

Lucy turned to look at him. "No. Why?"

He did not answer right away, and she had a moment to admire his green eyes while he kept his gaze upon the terrain before them. His lashes were thick and dark, and there were faint lines of pale skin emanating from the corners of his eyes.

"I thought mayhap 'twould provide us shelter for a day or two while the black knights—"

"Sir Alexander?" she said, looking past him now.

His eyes met hers then and Lucy knew he looked at her only because he heard an urgency in her voice.

"They're on the road."

She did not need to say any more. The knight quickly turned the horse and rode into the deep shadows of the woods, finding a spot where 'twas not likely they'd be seen from the road. They sat quietly and waited, watching as the black knights rode slowly in front of them. Lucy was certain that she and Sir Alex had retreated before the men had a chance to see them. Still, she sat quietly, without moving a muscle.

Even if her knight-rescuer had not pulled her back to his chest and held her close, she would have known she needed to remain still. With Alex's strong arms around her and his warm breath disturbing the hair across the top of her head, Lucy did not feel as frightened as she should.

She shivered once and his arms tightened around her.

The black riders were in no hurry. Lucy and Alex watched as the men meandered closer, talking quietly among themselves. She had trouble hearing exactly what was being said, but their words were issued without humor or amusement. The men were dead serious and their intensity did not bode well for her and Sir Alexander.

Eventually, the black knights rode past, and Alex dismounted, helping Lucy down after him.

"I'm hungry," he said, as if he had no care in the world. He pulled a leather satchel off his horse.

"Sir Alexander, shouldn't we go deeper into the woods?" Lucy asked, glancing warily in the direction the knights had gone. "What if those men come back?"

"They're going to York," the knight replied.

"How do you know that?"

"I heard them," he replied as he pulled bread and cheese from the pack. He tore a piece of bread from the loaf and handed it to her. "They figure we got ahead of them somehow and rode into York. They'll follow and see if they can locate us."

"They are quite determined to catch up to you," she said, marveling that he'd been able to discern their words. "Are you certain they only want to avenge some minor trouble you gave them?"

Alex shrugged and handed her a piece of cheese, and Lucy knew she would not get more information out of him this way. She took the food he offered and ate her fill, then drank from the waterskin while she considered what to do.

She supposed it was safe—at least for her—to go into York, because the black knights had never really seen her. Nor were they after her. Clearly 'twas Sir Alex that interested them, though she did not understand why.

His plan to go to Holywake was a sound one. With luck, they could travel to the new abbey and arrive without notice. Lucy had no intention of staying there, but would make an assessment of the work that needed to be done and hire men to do it.

Then she would go to York and make her way in The World. She was five and twenty and as capable as any woman her age. Surely it would not be too difficult to find employment.

"You say we follow this road to Holywake?" Sir Alex asked.

Lucy nodded. "I'm not sure of the distance, but when we set out yesterday morn, Sister Avice told us we would spend another two nights before reaching the abbey.''

Sir Alexander narrowed his eyes. ''Two nights if you'd covered a significant number of miles.'' He was clearly dissatisfied with the notion of spending the next two days with her. And his reaction angered her.

She had asked him for naught. She'd been cooperative, and had even warned him of danger—on more than one occasion. She did not believe she'd been any trouble at all, yet the knight clearly disliked her. Swallowing the hurt caused by his unwarranted enmity, Lucy turned away to gaze at the road visible through the trees.

She decided to follow her earlier plan, when she believed he'd left her. Since the black knights had ridden ahead, travel by road would be safe enough, and 'twas possible that she would meet and join other friendly travelers on their way to York. She had no need of this taciturn, bad-tempered knight-monk.

''Now that the knights are gone,'' she said, facing Sir Alex once again, ''I'll bid you adieu. Thank you for your assistance, and the loan of your blanket.'' She gave a slight bow and turned, walking away from him, keeping her temper under tight control. 'Twould serve no purpose to call him an ill-mannered blockhead to his face, even if that was what she wanted to do.

The abbess would be proud of her disciplined tongue.

Lucy found it somewhat awkward to walk over the uneven ground of the forest, but she felt Sir Alexander's eyes boring into her back, so she forced herself to minimize her limp. She did not want him coming after her for any reason—but especially not for pity's sake.

The distance to the road was farther than she had judged it, but she made it there without incident, and without Sir Alexander. She turned to walk upon the road, which was a good deal smoother than the forest floor had been, and began working her way north.

'Twas ridiculous to feel guilty.

The little nun would manage. There were plenty of others in this world who were much less fortunate than she. By the grace of God, her life had been spared, when all in her party had perished. Surely the Lord would protect her now.

Alex turned away when she stumbled, afraid that he might jump to her assistance in spite of himself. Taking more care than was necessary, he tied his food satchel to his saddle and led Rusa farther away from the road, toward the stream.

There was no hurry now. Alex could take his time watering his horse before he set out for Eryngton. With Skelton's knights safely on their way to seek him out in York, there was no reason to delay his mission.

He looked back through the trees toward Lucy, and saw that she had just reached the road. And her shoulder was bleeding again.

Her small wound did not concern him. 'Twould

stop bleeding soon and heal well enough without his assistance.

Alex knelt to refill his waterskin. He was anxious to complete his task and return to Cluny, though he might make a visit to his brother's estate before he returned to France. After all, it had been nearly three years since he'd seen Clyfton Castle. He wondered if it had changed, and how Philip and his family fared. Last Alex knew, Philip's wife, Lady Beatrice, had borne him four daughters.

He forced his thoughts from his own manor house on the Clyfton estate, the home where he and Isabella had lived with their son. Nay, if he visited Clyfton at all, he would be sure to avoid that sad house that overlooked the sea.

Sensing movement across the stream, Alex looked up into the eyes of a young doe, who had come down for a drink. She showed no fear, but stared at Alex with a mixture of curiosity and wariness...

Just like Lucy.

The doe finished her drink, and when she lifted her head, she perked her ears and stood perfectly still, listening to the silence of the forest. In another instant, she turned and sprinted away, limping noticeably. One of its hind legs was malformed. Alex stood abruptly and mounted his horse. Disconcerted, he rode Rusa deeper into the woods, far from the direction of the road.

'Twas more prudent for him to stay out of sight, and away from Lucy. She seemed to know where she was going, and would make it there in due time...if Skelton's men did not circle back and find her alone.

Alex refused to entertain the thought of anything else happening to her, but considered his own plans. Once he left Roger's scabbard with the earl of Eryngton, he would travel to Clyfton and visit with Philip and his family before returning to France, for 'twas unlikely he would ever return to England once he took his vows.

That thought gave him pause. For the first time, he reflected on what it would mean to go away from home forever. To look, for one last time, upon the ground he'd trodden as a lad. To bid farewell to Philip, once and for all.

He shoved his fingers through his hair and looked up. Somehow, he'd returned to the road, but Lucy was nowhere in sight. *"Agnus Dei, miserére nobis,"* he prayed, searching for signs of her. Surely trouble hadn't found her so quickly.

Alex dismounted. Taking the mare's reins in one hand, he drew his sword and proceeded slowly, cautiously. He'd not heard any disturbance, but he'd been distracted by his own thoughts and hadn't even realized he'd come back to the place where he'd left her. 'Twas possible he would not have heard anything.

He turned his head and peered into the dark forest on both sides of the road, and traveled some distance before he saw her, sitting in the shadows on a fallen log. She'd pulled her skirts up, and was examining a scrape on her knee when she saw him.

Though she quickly shoved her kirtle back into

place, 'twas not before he'd seen much more than he should have.

"Sir Alexander!" she cried, awkwardly rising to her feet. She lost her balance and would have fallen backward, but Alex caught her hand and righted her.

Her fair skin flushed with color, and she was more flustered than he'd ever seen her.

"You've hurt yourself," he said.

"'Tis naught," she replied, removing her hand from his grasp. "A slight scrape is all."

"Nay…your shoulder," he said.

She lifted her hair away and turned to look at the stained area below her shoulder. Her lashes were long, golden crescents upon her cheeks. As was her habit, her straight, white teeth bit into her lower lip while she strained to see behind her.

"I'm certain it's all right, Sir Alex. I'll just be on my—"

"You'll come with me," he said. "But I'll tend to your wound first."

A fleeting frown crossed her brow and she gave a slight shake of her head. "I have no wish to be a…a burden to you, Sir Knight. I will manage on my own."

"And fall again?"

Her lower lip trembled slightly, and she bit it again to gain control over it. Her reaction to his cruel words made him feel like a churlish beast. She had done naught to raise his ire, and he knew he ought to treat her more civilly.

He took her arm, only to have her shake it off.

"Go on your way, Sir Alex," she said, swallowing thickly. "You have been m-more than kind and I re-lease you from any—"

"Sit down, Sister Lucy," he ordered, his voice sounding harsh, even to his own ears. "Please."

The woman sat back down on the log and crossed her arms over her chest. Alex pulled his saddle packs to the ground in front of her and located his jar of Persian ointment. Still crouched, he lifted her skirt to her knee.

She gasped and tried to pull away, but Alex circled her ankle with his fingers and held her fast. "This one first."

"Sir Ale—"

She hissed when he spread a thick coating of oint-ment on the scrape on her knee, but did not try to pull away again.

To Alex's eye, naught was wrong with either of her legs. They were both smooth and soft as a woman's legs should be. *"Uni trinoque Domino,"* he prayed. *"Sit sempiterna gloria. Qui vitam sine ter-mino. Nobis donet in patria."*

A moment later, he had the knee bandaged and his wayward thoughts under control once again.

"Will you open your laces or shall I?"

She turned away to protect her modesty as she loosened her bodice and let it slide off her shoulders. The bandage he'd fashioned the night before was sat-urated with blood, and it slipped off when she low-ered her kirtle to expose the wound to his eyes.

"Your fall opened your shoulder wound," he said,

then realized she must have scraped her hands as well as her knee. He turned her in order to examine them, and forced his attention to remain upon her injured hands, and not upon the feminine flesh that rose enticingly above her lowered bodice.

But time seemed to stop. His gaze was drawn to her throat when she swallowed. When his eyes dipped lower, he saw a tiny mole lying nearly hidden within the deep cleft between her breasts. Her hands, still resting in his, trembled slightly.

Alex's mouth went dry. The desire to taste the small brown spot was nearly overpowering, but he tore his eyes away and released her hands. He barely refrained from making the sign of the cross before he turned her, though he did utter a silent prayer for strength. He had disciplined such carnal needs from his body, his soul. He was capable of rising above these base desires.

Still, his body reacted in a way that had become entirely foreign to him. He could not remember the last time he'd experienced such raw lust.

He wiped the fresh blood from her shoulder and applied ointment to the wound. Lucy tipped her head to one side, pulling her silken hair away from the gouge in her shoulder. In spite of himself, his eyes wandered, and so did his mind.

He caught himself imagining how her soft skin would feel against his roughened hands, and whether she would tremble if he touched his lips to the enticing bend between her neck and shoulder. Remembering the crease that often formed between her brows,

he considered how 'twould feel to soothe it away with
a kiss.

Alex clenched his jaw tightly and closed his eyes.
"Ostende nobis, Domine, misericordiam tuam," he
said in an inaudible whisper. Surely God would show
his mercy and remove these tempting thoughts from
his mind.

He tore a length of cloth and placed it over the
wound, then pulled the stained kirtle over it.
Abruptly, he stood and strode away. And he did not
look back.

With shaky fingers, Lucy fastened her clothes.

Though he'd made it clear that he could barely tolerate her presence, *something* had come to pass between them just now. She frowned with the effort to
understand what had happened.

Lady Elsbeth had told her and some of the other
novices about kissing. But the idea of touching
mouths with a man was embarrassing and distasteful,
even though Elsbeth had highly extolled the practice.

Yet Lucy had felt absurdly drawn to Sir Alex just
now, hungry for more than the casual touch of his
ministrations. Had she desired his kiss?

She felt her face heat when the answer became
clear. To her shame, Lucy had desired more than a
kiss. She had enjoyed the admiring gaze of his eyes,
and would have welcomed a caress. She could not
help but remember how it had felt to have Sir Alex's
arms 'round her, to have the heat of his powerful body
wrapped around hers.

Straightening her kirtle, Lucy walked to the place where the knight had tethered his horse. Unmindful of her approach, Sir Alex ran his hands over the mare's flanks and spoke quietly to her while Lucy watched with fascination. His hands were so much larger than her own. They were hard and strong, yet easy with the mare, and gentle when he'd tended Lucy's wound.

She had planned to travel to Holywake alone, on foot, because 'twas clear he did not want to accompany her. But something had changed.

And Lucy intended to find out what the change meant.

Chapter Six

Alex knew he was out of his mind when he lifted Lucy into his saddle and mounted behind her. Hours in close proximity with her was the last thing he needed. He should have let her continue alone on the road to Holywake.

"This is the wrong way, Sir Alexander," she said.

He did not reply, but kept going in the opposite direction of their respective destinations.

"We're headed south, as you can see," she continued, turning to look at him with puzzlement upon her face.

"With the black knights gone," he said, "it might be possible to retrieve some of your belongings from the place where you were attacked."

"Oh, I had not thought of that. Haven't we gone too far to go back?"

"No."

She remained silent until they reached the site, then slid off Rusa with his assistance, and went to the grave where the nuns were buried. Alex left her to search for anything of value in the broken boxes. The food the nuns had carried had been spoiled by small animals, but he found several articles of clothes and a few blankets scattered among the ruins. He gathered whatever might be useful, and stuffed it into his packs.

When he was ready to go, he glanced at the grave site and saw Lucy struggling to stand. She wiped a tear from her face and turned away from him, as if she did not want him to know how she grieved for her sisters.

He came up behind her.

"Sister Avice was just about to stop the wagon," she said, sniffling once, "so that we could say our morning prayers. Then the arrows c-came."

Her voice started to wobble at the last few words, and Alex fought a reckless urge to pull her into his embrace. He had seen grown men break down after such an attack, but Lucy held on to her composure, as if she could not bear to have him see her tears.

"One pierced Sister G-Gunnora...through the throat...." Her voice was unsteady. "There was so much b-blood. The horses w-went wild then...."

Alex walked around to face her. She did not look up, but closed her arms around herself, as if to contain the horror she'd experienced. A tear fell when she blinked, following the tracks of the others she'd shed.

"Lady Elsbeth...she rode b-beside us... S-she... she was not to have come w-with us...but the abbess...she..."

Her voice broke and she closed one hand over her mouth. Alex pulled her into his arms and she wept.

"Do you smell food cooking?" Lucy asked.

He did.

They had covered a good many miles and the smell of a campfire and cooking meat was clear. So were the sounds of music and voices.

It occurred to Alex that he might leave Lucy with this group of travelers that camped nearby, and he was near desperate to do so. He did not know how many more hours he could continue to ride with her sitting practically across his lap. Turning off the road, Alex followed the aroma of the cooking food until he reached a small clearing.

All music and talk ceased.

Two burly young men stood and challenged their approach. Behind them were wagons, where women and children stood waiting with three other men. There was a familial resemblance among them.

Alex dismounted and assisted Lucy down, then placed his hand on the hilt of his sword. Eyeing the men, he stepped in front of Lucy to keep her safe in case of a confrontation. There were few weapons about, though Alex did not doubt that these men would be proficient combatants.

He took a step forward, but was interrupted by Lucy's hand on his arm. She walked around him to stand in front.

"Good evening to you," she said to the people in the clearing.

The men relaxed visibly, though they still maintained a protective stance.

"We are peaceful travelers," she continued as she made her way toward the men. Alex would have grabbed her and pulled her back until they understood the situation here, but she slid past him to stand directly in front of the men. "I am Lucy of Craghaven," she said. "And behind me is Sir Alexander."

The men remained wary, though the tallest of them stepped forward and spoke. "We, too, are peaceful travelers," he said, then looked past Lucy to Alex. "Lay down your arms and be welcome."

In the moment that Alex hesitated, Lucy turned and looked at him with trusting eyes. Making what he hoped was not too hasty a decision, he unfastened his sword belt and placed it behind his saddle, next to the scabbard that held Brother Roger's relic. Taking Rusa's reins in one hand, he went to Lucy and placed her hand upon his, then entered the campsite.

"I am Gilbert Bavent," the leader said.

The two men near the campfire picked up the lute and pipe they'd been playing before Alex and Lucy arrived, and resumed playing. The women returned to their task of preparing and serving the meal from a large kettle suspended above the fire.

"Three knights harried us in our camp this morn," Bavent said.

"The black knights?" Lucy asked. She cast a quick glance toward Alex, and he saw her dismay.

"Aye," the man replied. "You know of them?"

Alex began to reply, but Lucy spoke first. "Did they do you harm, sir?"

Bavent shook his head. "There was naught here of interest to them," he said. "But their visit reminded us to be wary. Who do you serve, Sir Alexander, and where are you headed?"

"Our business is our own, Master Bavent," Alex said. "But we intend no harm to you. We saw the black knights ourselves and stayed clear of them."

One of the women, young and pretty, handed Lucy a bowl containing a thick, savory stew. "Come and sit by me, Mistress Lucy," she said.

Lucy took the bowl and followed, going to a place next to one of the wagons. All of the women seemed to be gathered there, along with several children. Alex counted six of them, although he could hear other childish voices in the woods nearby.

Satisfied that Lucy was safe for the moment, Alex joined Bavent with the other men by the fire. He accepted a bowl and a crust of bread, and began to eat.

He learned that this was a family of mummers, on their way south to a noble estate where they would entertain during the wedding festivities of the lord. Unfortunately, they traveled opposite the direction Lucy needed to go.

Alex paid little attention to his meal, keeping one eye on Lucy and the other on the road in the distance. He wanted no surprises. If the black knights returned here...if aught were to happen to Lucy...

The sudden wail of a newborn cut through the air.

Alex looked toward a large canvas tent set up beyond the wagons.

"My newest son." Henry Bavent tipped his head in the direction of the sound. "My wife was close to her time, so we had to stop here yestermorn. She birthed the lad a few hours later."

Alex congratulated the man and muttered a quiet *Gloria Patri* in honor of the bairn.

"Without meaning to pry, Sir Alexander," Rolf Bavent said, "are you headed to York?"

Alex gave a curt nod. He was going in the direction of York, if not the town itself, though these men did not need to know that. He wanted no one to know that he was going to Holywake with Lucy, and he would certainly not divulge his errand at Eryngton.

"We did not stop in town," said Rolf.

"Our travels brought us from a castle on the seacoast," said Henry. "A fine place—Clyfton. Have you heard of it?"

Alex gave a nod and struggled to contain his intense interest in any news of Clyfton.

"We spent nearly a month there…festivities every day for the christening of the earl's sixth child."

Alex was dumbstruck. Philip and his wife had had *two* more children during the time he'd been gone. There could be no doubt that God smiled upon Philip and his family.

"Beautiful place," Gilbert remarked.

"The sea air was beneficial to my wife," Henry added. "It eased her discomfort during her last month."

"Your lady is bruised, Sir Alex," said the more serious brother, Gilbert. "And there is blood on her gown."

"An attack yestereday," Alex replied. He did not correct the man's misapprehension that Lucy was *his* lady. Since the Bavent troupe was not going north, he would not send Lucy with them.

"The black knights?"

He shook his head. "A couple of rogues looking for coin, or some such. They are no longer upon the road."

"'Tis good to know, for we still have a fair journey ahead of us," Gilbert said.

"The black knights were headed north," Henry said. "They are far along now.... I doubt they will harry you when you continue your travels."

Alex doubted it, too, but he would not relax his vigilance. Skelton's knights were not the only dangers on this road. He glanced to the place where Lucy sat with the women and children and vowed to keep her safe.

Until they reached Holywake, Lucy of Craghaven was his charge.

Lucy had never seen a newborn bairn before.

Carefully, she took the tiny lad from his mother, who showed her how to support his wobbly head and still hold on to his body. Gazing into his perfect little face, Lucy knew she witnessed one of God's true miracles.

"You're a fine one, Little Bert," she said quietly

to the bairn, taking in the wonder of his rosy lips and miniature nose. His hair was thick and dark like his mother's, but it stuck out in wild tufts all over his head. His eyes were closed, and Lucy could detect no lashes, but his face suddenly contorted. A tiny furrow appeared between his pale brows while his chin quivered.

"Oh, he's about to tell you something," Mathilde said.

The infant made three short cries, then opened his lungs and wailed as loudly as his little voice could manage.

"Oh!" Lucy said as she started to hand the infant back to his mother. "You'd better take him."

Mathilde guided Lucy's hands so that she changed the bairn's position, cradling him on her shoulder.

"What do I do?" Lucy asked.

"He's just been fed," the mother replied, "so that's not the problem. Just bounce him a bit."

Lucy tried it, but the lad continued his cries.

"Now pat him…here, on his back."

She did so as she started to walk with the bairn in her arms. Tucking his head under her chin, she spoke softly to him as he cried, and suddenly he gave out a loud belch that startled her.

"There's a lad," said one of the men, and they all laughed.

The infant quieted, and Lucy looked up to find Sir Alex watching her. She hugged the bairn closer to her breast and quietly sang a nonsense song to him as he drifted off to sleep, even as the knight's intense gaze bored into her.

This was not the first time she'd felt disquieted by Sir Alexander, but she had never had this odd flush of yearning before—for a husband, for a child of her own. Being with this large family made Lucy realize all that she'd missed over the years, living in her harsh and barren surroundings.

If she'd felt torn about leaving the abbey before, Lucy was certain now that it was the right thing to do. Cuddling Little Bert in her arms, she thought of her journey beyond Holywake, and what kind of life she would make for herself.

How did a woman alone find a husband? Lucy knew that families usually arranged marriages, but how would she go about it herself? She supposed the question was premature, since she had not even reached York yet. Once she arrived in town, she would find some sort of employment, and perhaps meet a likely suitor.

"Ah, you've a knack for it," Emma Bavent said. "You and your husband should have fine, sturdy bairns, what with the way he's made." She gave a nod in Alex's direction, and Lucy realized the woman believed that she and Alex were man and wife.

She opened her mouth to correct Emma's misconception, then changed her mind. Pressing her lips to the infant's head, she inhaled the scent of him, unlike anything she'd ever encountered before, and thought of the children Sir Alex would sire.

Like the infant in her arms, they would have dark

hair. Their eyes would be as sharp and green as blades of grass, and would turn fierce when challenged or perplexed. His sons would be physically powerful, though kind. 'Twas difficult to imagine how his daughters—

Lucy gave herself a mental shake. Sir Alexander was a monk...or would be, as soon as he returned to France. All that was missing were the vows that would bind him to the monastery forever. He would never sire children.

Certainly not Lucy Kendal's children.

Alex walked away from the camp. He should have told the Bavents that he and Lucy were not wed, then he would not be expected to sleep with her in the small tent the family had provided for their use.

Too edgy to take his rest, Alex prowled the perimeter of the camp, as if the light rain could rid him of his unwelcome thoughts. He should not be thinking of the way Lucy had felt in his arms the night before. If there was any woman to occupy his thoughts, 'twas his beloved Isabella, the mother of his son.

Alex began his *Pater Noster* more times than he could count, but never managed to get past the first few words of the prayer.

He could not remember Isabella's face.

Her scent, the memory of which he'd carried with him for three years, was gone, too. As was the sound of her voice, and the bitter ache in his heart whenever he thought of her.

A cold sweat broke out over Alex's skin and his

head throbbed from forcing his thoughts to the direction they should take. 'Twas not possible that he was forgetting Isabella, or their years together at Clyfton House.

His reaction to seeing Lucy with the bairn had only demonstrated how callous and unfaithful he was to the memory of his wife and son. He had allowed a multitude of earthly concerns to interfere with his memories as well as his chosen vocation.

He scrubbed one hand across his heavy beard. He'd had no idea that this task set by Brother Roger would be so difficult. It had seemed simple enough.

Yet now, when he was merely days from completing his mission, his life was fraught with complications. The dead nuns on the road, Lucy, and now the Bavent mummers... He swallowed. Never had he striven more to be an honest and virtuous man. Yet he had been possessed by lust since the moment he'd set eyes upon Lucy of Craghaven. And he'd committed the sin of omission, by neglecting to correct the family's impression that Lucy was his wife.

'Twas true that it had seemed safer at the time, to let them believe they were wed. But that lie would lead to the commission of yet another sin. Alex was going to have to lie with the woman again. And conquer his lust as he did so.

He looked up at the moon, shadowed by the clouds gathering in the sky. *"Beati mundo corde, quoniam ipsi Deum videbunt,"* he whispered, praying for purity in his own heart.

The unfamiliar stirrings of desire were entirely unacceptable. He was beyond such feelings, such needs. He'd been certain they had died with Isabella.

He stayed away from the tent long enough for Lucy to have fallen asleep, but finally resigned himself to joining her inside. They had many miles to cover on the morrow, and he needed to try for a few hours' sleep.

When he found Henry Bavent sitting near the smoldering fire, he pulled his leather tarpaulin from his pack and unfolded it.

"This will keep the rain out of the fire." Alex tossed one end to Henry and the two men strung it up in the trees.

"I don't mind the rain as long as it stays warm as it is." Henry sat down beside the fire when the tarp was in place.

"I'll keep watch if you care to sleep, Master Henry."

The mummer shook his head. "Nay. 'Tis my duty tonight. Go find your woman and seek your rest," he said, then added with a grin, "or your pleasure."

Alex rubbed the back of his neck, and as he approached the tent, he tried to think of an excuse to stay away.

The tent flap was closed, and all was quiet within. Seeing no choice in the matter, Alex pulled his wet tunic over his head and lay it under the tarpaulin to dry near the fire. After giving a nod to Henry, he crawled into the tent.

The fire cast a dim light upon the walls of the tent, so Alex could see Lucy lying on one side. As quietly as possible, he picked up his blanket and wrapped it around his shoulders, then stretched out on the ground beside her.

"Take your rest...or your pleasure," Henry Bavent had said.

He grunted and turned away from the woman, presenting her with his back. Not that she would notice, for she appeared to be sleeping soundly, which was more than Alex was likely to do this night. He doubted he would rest easily until he had left her at her destination.

"...or your pleasure..."

She made a small sound and Alex felt movement beside him. She must have turned over, for he sensed her body lying much closer now. 'Twas no wonder that thoughts of her were so often in his mind. All day, her hair had brushed his arms and grazed his nose. Her scent had inflamed him. And whenever she spoke, her husky voice fascinated him beyond reason.

And that little brown mole...

"...or your pleasure..."

Alex sighed and moved away to the farthest edge of the tent.

"You smell like the rain," Lucy said when he stopped moving. Her voice felt thick with sleep, for she had almost drifted off when he'd come into the tent.

She'd been thinking of Mathilde's newborn, and all the strange, new things she'd learned about him tonight.

"Did you know that when a bairn is newly born, there's a cord that attaches him to his mama?" she asked.

"Of course."

"Oh!" He sounded as if 'twas something so commonplace that any fool would have known it. "I was so surprised by it."

"Go to sleep. You'll need your rest before we ride tomorrow."

Silence blanketed them once again, though the rain came down harder than before. Lucy was grateful for the canvas tent that Emma had given them, though its small size made it necessary to sleep close to Sir Alexander once again.

She had loved holding Mathilde's bairn and had watched with wonder when the infant had suckled at his mother's breast. Lucy would give anything to have a child of her own one day, to hold and suckle. And love.

It suddenly occurred to her that she might bear a child before she'd had a chance to find a husband.

"Might I get with child from lying with you, Sir Alex?" she said abruptly, concerned about what she'd been told over the years. "We've lain together twice—"

He sat up abruptly, coughing. He was choking! Lucy moved close and struck his back several times.

"Are you all righ—"

"You cannot conceive by merely lying with a man," he growled. She shifted her position to face him and then they were sitting knee to knee.

"But Father Boucher said th—"

"'Tis impossible," Alex countered. "Whoever told you such a tale is..."

She heard him take a deep breath, then he grabbed his blanket and lay down again.

"Is what?" She remained sitting and watched him cross his hands over his chest. A few muttered words in Latin came to her ears.

He did not answer her.

She supposed this might not be a fitting subject to discuss with a man, but she was confused. Lady Elsbeth had spoken of some very strange practices that contradicted everything Father Boucher and the nuns ever said about procreation.

"I did not believe Lady Elsbeth...." She whispered absently. But it must be true. Now that she'd seen Mathilde's babe out of his swaddling, Elsbeth's words made sense. She looked at Sir Alex and felt her face flush with heat when she thought of the babe's male part and wondered if Sir Alex was similarly made. Certainly the thing would be much larger on a grown man, particularly a man of Alex's size.

Would it fit?

Lucy wondered if, when they'd awakened in each other's arms this morn, Alex would have done what Elsbeth had described. Though the act had seemed altogether distasteful and embarrassing when she'd first heard of it, Lucy had not felt degraded or uncomfortable when he'd pulled her close. She had not been embarrassed when he'd almost kissed her.

'Twas after he left that she'd felt embarrassed.

''This morn,'' she said, ''when you…when we…''
She hesitated, never more aware of the abbess's admonitions to guard her tongue. Yet how was she to know and understand unless she asked questions? Sir Alex was clearly not inclined to offer her any enlightenment without her prodding, therefore, she *must* ask.

She lay down and faced him, her body close enough to feel his warmth. Slightly breathless now, she felt overwarm remembering the details of their near tryst.

''What I mean to ask is…if you had not awakened, would you have started a bairn in me?''

He made a strange noise and Lucy wondered if he was choking again. She was just about to get up to assist him when his hand shot out and held her in place.

''By all that is holy, woman,'' he snarled, ''go to sleep!''

Chapter Seven

"I bid ye, Archangel," Rolf Bavent pleaded dramatically to his masked brother, Gilbert, "heal our champion, our hero, the revered and most holy, George."

Gilbert, the archangel, looked up to the cloudy heavens and then back at the mere mortal who asked for a miracle. And he tripped over a log and fell on his rump.

The children sitting 'round Lucy laughed and pointed at their uncle.

In spite of himself, Alex smiled at the sight of her, holding the newborn in her arms, her eyes lit with joy as she watched over the children. While the two uncles rehearsed their play, the rest of the adults packed up the camp. The infant was now three days old and its mother had deemed herself ready for travel.

Alex himself was ready to go, with his belongings—along with Lucy's few measly items—already tied on Rusa's back, and he was impatient to leave.

They had another day and night to pass before reaching Holywake, and who knew how much time upon the morrow. He'd considered having Lucy ride the mare while he walked, but 'twould take that much longer to reach Holywake. Mayhap *two* nights.

He had no choice but to ride with her, unless he wanted to draw out the journey. Remembering their conversation the previous night, and now watching her jest with the Bavent children, it was abundantly clear to him that the less time he spent with Lucy of Craghaven, the better. He needed to put some space between them in order to bolster his resolve.

Gilbert got to his feet again and resumed his lines, while Lucy skimmed her lips over the infant's dark head. She turned to one of the other children and gave a wink. The gesture itself was innocent enough, but to Alex, it seemed a slow and seductive move. 'Twas a promise of fiery pleasures and passionate devotion.

"Credo in Deum Patrem omnipotentem...." he whispered.

The actors broke into song when the hero was healed. The children joined in, urging Lucy to do the same. 'Twas apparent that she did not know the words or the tune, but she managed to follow, her voice ringing pure and true.

The sound washed over Alexander and he closed his eyes to listen to her voice as it rose above the others. He did not think he'd ever heard any music so moving as that of the monks at Cluny, but he knew now that he was mistaken. Her feminine tones reached something hidden deep within, and he believed he could remain there forever, listening.

Except that he knew such feelings were wrong. He would not betray his commitment to his wife, his Order. Getting hold of himself once again, he turned away abruptly and walked toward the family members who were packing the wagons. He bade farewell to the Bavent brothers in turn, thanking them for sharing their meal and their fire.

Then he went to Lucy. He extended his hand to assist her, but she handed him the infant instead. It surprised him, and sent a stab of pain, as well as one of unexpected pleasure through him. He'd not held a bairn in his arms since his own son was an infant.

"Why, you're quite good at that," Lucy said once she was standing.

Alex could not say what caused the tightening in his chest—whether it was Lucy's smile or the child in his arms. He only knew that it was time to leave. He gave the bairn to its mother.

"Take care of your lady, Sir Alexander," Mathilde said. "God be with you, and may he bless you with many children."

Lucy beamed at the woman's benison and turned to say farewell to the others. When she was finished, Alex placed one hand at Lucy's back, near her waist. With the smallest pressure, he guided her toward his mare and lifted her into the saddle while the Bavent family called out their good wishes.

Alex said naught, and refrained from looking back, although Lucy leaned to one side and waved until the road curved and the Bavents were out of her view. Then she sighed happily and let her hands fall into her lap.

Late into the afternoon, Lucy was still thinking about ways that she might join up with the Bavent family again, even though she knew it would be impossible. There were too many reasons why it would never work.

Still, she knew she could have been very happy with them. Though she would never be a performer, she might help mind the children for their mothers. She could most certainly cook and clean, and help make the actors' costumes. Emma Bavent had shown her the brilliant masks that would be worn when they performed *Saint George and the Dragon,* and Lucy could only imagine how wonderful it would feel to be a part of that kind and generous family.

Not that she would truly belong, but life with the Bavents would be exciting and interesting...visiting new places, meeting new people. If only she did not have to go to Holywake, she'd have asked Master Gilbert if she could join the troupe.

She became drowsy with the rocking movement of the horse, and fell asleep for a time. When she awoke, she became aware of Sir Alex's arms around her. Up until now, he'd kept his distance—at least, as well as he was able while they rode. Yet as Lucy awakened, she sensed his beard brushing the top of her head, his heart beating in his chest at her back.

'Twas amazingly pleasant to be so embraced, however inadvertently it occurred. Nestling into his body to glean more of his heat, Lucy heard his breathing change. It seemed harsher, deeper. She kept her eyes closed, her body relaxed, and tried to imagine how his embrace would feel if it were affectionately given.

Sir Alex was a hard man, both in muscle and in spirit. He was fierce, but Lucy felt perfectly safe with him, even when his hands shifted. His thumbs brushed the undersides of her breasts and she felt the tips harden. 'Twas suddenly difficult to breathe. An odd sensation flared at the base of her spine, and heat pooled low in her belly. She felt boneless, just as Elsbeth had described, and she wanted to curl ever more deeply into Alex's heat.

He somehow realized she was awake and shifted his body. "We'll make camp soon, beside the river," he said.

Lucy had heard the flow of water nearby, but she'd been too distracted to pay attention to it. She wanted Sir Alex to move his big hands back to where they were, wanted to know if it was his touch that made her feel so strange.

But he did not. He leaned away from her now that she was awake, and Lucy forced her tired muscles to support her as she sat up straighter. She felt travel-worn and dirty, and her scalp itched. Her stomach growled with hunger. She wanted to ask him to pull her close again, but knew that she must guard her speech or else risk his anger again.

"I would like to walk for a while," she said instead.

Sir Alex did not answer, but pulled up on the reins

and stopped the horse's progress. He dismounted and helped her down, holding her when her unsteady leg threatened to buckle under her.

"I'm just a little stiff," she said, embarrassed that he had seen her weakness in its worst form. She was not usually so clumsy, and to a man as perfectly made as Sir Alex, Lucy felt she must seem horribly flawed.

She started to move away from the knight, but he stayed with her, keeping his hand at her elbow while she walked.

"Let's go this way," he said, leading her away from the road.

There was no forest path, but the going was fairly easy with Sir Alex to keep her from tripping and falling as she'd done before. They followed the sound of the river in the distance and eventually reached a rocky bank in a bend of the river, where it ran deep and fast.

Alex looked 'round. "This will do," he said. "We're far enough from the road that we won't attract any unwanted attention." He took his packs down, then pulled the saddle off his mare while Lucy went to the water's edge.

She knelt and scooped some of the fresh, cool water into her hands and washed her face. It felt wonderful after the long, unseasonably warm day riding on the back of Sir Alex's horse.

"Here are your things," the knight said, coming up behind her. He handed her a package wrapped in one of the Craghaven blankets, then walked away again. Lucy opened the bundle and found several items gathered there. A tin cup, a comb, a sliver of soap wrapped in a thin leather pouch, and a delicate silver chain with a small locket. All these things had been folded inside Lady Elsbeth's favorite dark-red kirtle.

Lucy felt a pang of sorrow for Elsbeth and the nuns. They hadn't deserved their violent end, not even Elsbeth.

The journey to Holywake was not at all what she'd anticipated. Looking at Sir Alexander as he pulled items out of his pack, Lucy felt fortunate to have such a powerful escort. There could be no doubt that he would keep her safe from the dangers on the road.

Quietly, Sir Alex walked around the small clearing, gathering firewood. Keeping his back to Lucy, he afforded her a degree of privacy, but Lucy needed more. She had decided to change into the fresh kirtle since hers was filthy, as well as stained with her blood. She picked up her belongings and stood, then followed the riverbank around its curve, finally stopping at a place where she would be able to step into the water.

She was a good distance from Sir Alex and completely out of his sight, so she slipped off her shoes, then unlaced her kirtle and removed it. Still wearing her linen underkirtle, she stepped into the water.

'Twas cold, but since Lucy had felt uncomfortable and sticky for two days, the water felt wonderful. She wondered if she should consider dousing her hair—mayhap her entire body—but the deeper water was rushing too fast and Lucy decided not to risk it since she could not swim.

Instead, she crouched in the shallows and scooped water into her hands, then washed as well as she could, using Lady Elsbeth's soap. Moving quickly, she removed her underkirtle and tossed it over a tree branch so that she could wash more thoroughly. Somehow managing to cleanse herself quickly with her tiny piece of soap, she rinsed off and reached for the thin linen garment.

It fell into the river and was caught up by the current.

Lucy reached for it and lost her footing, sliding on the slippery rock bottom. Pulled into the rushing water, she struggled desperately to right herself or grab on to something. She flailed her arms and legs ineffectively and could not manage to keep her head above the water.

She tumbled wildly in the current, sputtering and gasping for air whenever her head reached the surface, certain that she was about to die.

Alex wondered what was taking Lucy so long.

They'd both needed a few minutes of privacy, but he'd already removed Rusa's saddle and brushed her down. He'd found a secure place for Brother Roger's scabbard, and gone to set a few snares with the hope of catching a hare or two for their supper. And still Lucy did not return.

The last thing he wanted to do was intrude upon her, but as he stood with his hands on his hips, he began to think he had no alternative. He called out her name, but got no response. He turned to head in her direction, but something in the river caught his attention.

Driven by dread, Alex did not think twice. He unbuckled his sword belt and jumped over the boulders at the riverbank. Running awkwardly through the water, he dived across the surface and swam in the same direction as the mass of golden hair that had just passed by. His arms cut through the water while he allowed the current to help carry him to his goal, though 'twas difficult to navigate the fiercely rushing water.

By the way Lucy's body was tumbled by the waves, Alex could see that she was helpless, perhaps even unconscious. There was naught she could do to help herself.

He made a grab for her, but the current carried her out of reach. Something heavy knocked into Alex and stunned him momentarily, causing him to lose precious time as well as space, putting distance between himself and Lucy. He sputtered back to the surface and doubled his efforts to reach her, using his powerful arms and legs to propel him through the water.

Finally, his hand brushed her hair and he grabbed it. Holding on, he pulled her toward him. Her body was deathly cold when he drew her close, but he refused to believe she'd drowned. He would get her to dry land and she would recover.

And he would never let her out of his sight again.

He hauled her into his arms and staggered up the

rocky embankment, then lay her on the level ground. When he turned her over and pressed the heels of his hands into her back, she coughed up the water she'd swallowed. He repeated the pressure once, then again.

Alex did not let up until she braced herself on her forearms and started to breathe more easily. Then he turned her over. Carefully, he brushed her hair out of her face.

She was pale, but the bluish discoloration around her nose and lips was gone. There was a new scrape on her cheek to go with the bruise on her chin, and her eyes were open and vacant.

"Lucy!"

He shook her when she did not respond. He glanced down at her chest and saw that she was breathing…and at the same time he realized that she was naked.

"Lucy!" he said again, taking her chin in his hand.

Her eyelids fluttered, then closed for a moment. When they opened again, they were focused on him, and the crease between her brows was back.

"C-cold," she whispered hoarsely.

He remembered that her body had been as cold as the snow in winter, but the fear that had driven him had kept him from noticing her lack of clothes.

"In nomine Patris, et Filii, et Spiritus Sancti." Making the sign of the cross, Alex lifted her into his arms.

When he reached the place where he'd left Rusa and their belongings, he knelt and picked up his blanket, then wrapped it around her. Alex knew the air would cool significantly once the sun had set. He would have to make haste and get a fire going or Lucy's chill would deepen.

Gently, he set her down on the grass and went to the place where he'd piled wood for a fire. Ignoring his own saturated clothes and the setting sun, Alex made a small fire. Once it caught, he added a few of the thicker branches and fanned the flames until the fire blazed. Then he went back to Lucy, picked her up and carried her to the heat.

She was shivering, and her eyes were open.

"What happened?"

"You nearly drowned," he said, hardly able to absorb all that had happened since they'd stopped for the night. The woman was a walking disaster, from all her mishaps to her intemperate speech.

"I slipped," she said. "And the current caught me."

Alex looked up at the sky. No sign of rain tonight. The sky was so clear that the temperature would drop after sunset. He had no tent to sleep in, and no extra blankets. She had to get dry and warm, soon.

Certain that a hot meal would help her, Alex quickly changed into dry clothes, then left Lucy to check his snares. He found them empty. 'Twas likely they hadn't been in place long enough to catch anything. Still, he had bread and cheese, and some stew that the Bavents had given him.

Lucy was asleep when he returned to the campsite. He dug out a small cookpot and poured the stew into it, and once it was cooking, checked on Lucy.

She was still cold, so he added another blanket to the one already covering her. He could not stop himself from lingering near her, touching her hair, watching her breathe. Kneeling beside her, he wanted to gather her up in his arms and protect her from harm.

Alex knew that such a thing was impossible. He'd done all in his power to safeguard his wife and son, yet he'd lost them.

"Lucy," he said, "you need to eat something warm."

She looked up at him drowsily. "I'm not hungry, Sir Alex."

"'Tis not for hunger, but for heat."

She nodded once and struggled to keep her eyes open. "I'll try."

Alex managed to get only a few bites into her before she succumbed to sleep. The ordeal in the river had sapped all her strength. Worried that she would not manage to stay warm though the night, he rearranged the blankets to make a bed for them both, then lay beside her and pulled her close.

He had enough heat to warm her.

It grew cooler as night progressed, but within their cocoon, Lucy's shivering subsided and her skin began to warm. They both slept fitfully.

Alex dreamed of soft curves and sweet-smelling skin, of golden hair that swirled around his wrists and bound him. He dreamed that he buried his nose in that hair and fondled the lush curves of feminine breasts. He felt the smooth skin of buttocks while his fingers dipped into their crease.

Small sounds of pleasure, bodies moving together—

Alex awakened to daylight and sprang to his feet.

He was fully aroused and desperate for completion.
In three years he'd not experienced such intense need,
and it appalled him to know that he had so little control over his base urges.

His heart pounded and his breath came in short
pants as he looked down into Lucy's puzzled eyes.
'Twas no more than his male nature that had reacted
to her. Yet when he felt her gaze traverse the length
of his body, he felt powerful and potent.

The blanket slipped down to Lucy's waist. Alex
stood rooted to the ground for an instant, reacting to
the sight of her breasts, their pink tips pebbling in the
cool morning air. His eyes were drawn to the small
mole at the top of her breast, and again, he felt an
undeniable urge to taste the spot. He swallowed and
suddenly came to his senses.

This was not what he was about.

He turned away and quickly left the campsite. Determined to remain celibate, he would master this attraction, no matter how comely Lucy was, no matter
how intensely he wanted her.

After an hour spent in prayer, Alex was certain he
would have control once again.

Lucy lay back and wondered what had just happened. The strange sensations that had welled up in
her chest took her breath away. Feeling as if she'd

been in the sun too long, she sat up again and saw
that she was without any clothes.

She stood and wrapped herself in the blanket, then
glanced around the area where they'd slept. Frowning, she saw no sign of her things and realized that
her clothes must still be where she'd left them when
she'd tried to bathe in the river.

Keeping the blanket around her, Lucy went to the
place, walking with some difficulty over the rocky
ground. She tried to remember everything that had
happened after she'd fallen into the river, but could
not. All that was left in her mind was the memory of
a terrible cold that seemed to go through to her bones.

Lucy found her belongings—all but the tiny piece
of soap that must have washed away when she'd
fallen. Her underkirtle was lost forever, so she had no
choice but to wear one of Lady Elsbeth's gowns without the benefit of underclothes. When she slipped the
red kirtle over her head and pulled the bodice laces
tight, she was chagrined to see how immodest a garment it was. Eyeing the blue one, Lucy saw that it
was even worse, with the neckline cut much too low,
and the sleeves partially unattached.

Pulling at the bodice, she raised it as high as it
would go, but it still left her far too exposed for comfort. She remembered some of the things Elsbeth had
said about the ladies at court, and knew that this gown
was no worse than some. Still, Lucy decided she'd
use the blanket as sort of a shawl for the day…that
is, if Sir Alex was willing to travel with her.

Well aware that she had been nothing but trouble

for him since the moment they'd met, Lucy did not blame him for wanting to be rid of her. Sitting down upon a nearby rock, she vowed to be no more trouble to the man if he stayed. She would guard her tongue, and avoid any further incidents—like falling into the river.

How embarrassing to have to be rescued in such an ignominious manner. 'Twas clumsy to have lost her footing in the first place, then to be unable to swim to safety…that was almost worse than being carried out of the water entirely naked.

But not quite.

She had always kept herself modestly covered, though she had to admit that vanity made her hide her lame leg. 'Twas the last thing she wanted anyone to see, especially a man so well made as Sir Alexander Breton.

The rushing water caught Lucy's attention and she shivered when she looked at it. The cold depths, the treacherous rapids… She told herself 'twas better not to dwell on what might have happened, and to be thankful that Sir Alex had been there to pull her out, no matter what the circumstances.

If he still planned to escort her to Holywake, Lucy was sure they would arrive at the abbey sometime today. And Sir Alex, who had never wanted to be saddled with her in the first place, would leave her then. Lucy had no doubt it would be difficult to watch him ride out of her life, and she felt bereft already, just knowing he would go.

Lucy could not remember ever feeling this way

about anyone else. Years ago, when Roger had gone away on Crusade, she had missed him, but there was naught to do but go on without him. The deaths of her parents had been devastating, but she and John had still had each other. They'd made a proper life for themselves at Eryngton, and, though Lucy had been sickly, she'd never felt she was a burden to her brother, or an impediment to his life. John had even been in the midst of negotiating his marriage when he'd been thrown from his horse and broken his neck.

Life had changed drastically for her then. Everyone she'd known and loved had been taken from her, and she'd been left at the mercy of her cousin, Hugh Kyghley. She had missed John desperately. Her first few years at Craghaven had been dismal and bleak.

Somehow, she had survived. And she would survive again. When Sir Alex rode away from Holywake, Lucy would hold her chin high and smile as she bid him farewell.

Chapter Eight

"'Tis a warm day for autumn," Alex said, wondering why Lucy was still wrapped in her blanket.

She nodded absently.

"You are not still chilled?"

"Nay," she replied. "I, er...lost my..."

Not her clothes. He could see a skirt of crimson underneath the blanket.

She blushed and turned away. Alex would not allow himself to care. If she wanted to swelter beneath the woolen blanket, 'twas her own concern, and none of his.

She cleared her throat. "My underkirtle was lost, sir," she said, "if you must know. While I was washing in the river, it fell in, and when I reached for it, I lost my balance and—"

"Fell in, yourself."

"Aye," she replied in a small voice. "And you pulled me out."

"I did more than pull you out," he said, though he regretted his words as soon as he uttered them. He did not want to engage her in any more conversation than was absolutely necessary.

"You kept me warm," she said.

"I had to swim downstream to get you," he countered, anxious to change the topic. "You were caught in the current, and would have been lost if I hadn't noticed you tumbling by."

"That's twice you've saved me, Sir Alex. I wish there was something, some way to repay you for every—"

"'Tis not necessary," he said abruptly. "I would have done the same for anyone in need."

She bit her lip. "Aye, but—"

"Speak no more of it. 'Tis done. And your lack of…er, underskirt…means naught to me. You are clothed, are you not?"

He felt her eyes searching his face, but he kept his own gaze trained upon the road ahead and wondered how much longer 'twould be before they reached Saint Agatha's shrine and the lane that led to Holy-wake Abbey.

Lucy settled into the ride again, and only then did Alex allow himself to glance at her. He'd done everything possible to avoid thinking of his fear when he'd carried her out of the river. When all he'd been able to feel was the deathly chill of her skin.

It had only been the result of that fear that made him lie down with her and hold her through the night. He'd needed to keep her near to ease his worry. Alex readily admitted it had been a kind of madness, but it had passed.

He was fully composed now, and had been, ever since he'd left their bed that morn. His senses had returned and she could do nothing else to cause him to stray from his purpose.

Lucy let the blanket drop, baring a large portion of her shoulders and chest. Alex swallowed thickly and understood her concern over the missing under-clothes, but he refused to say another word about it. 'Twas too warm to stay covered by the heavy wool, and he'd already told her that her garb meant naught to him.

"Gloria Patri, et Filio, et Spiritui Sancto," he be-gan silently, averting his eyes.

Holywake Abbey was a long, low building with dingy walls and only a few narrow windows. Its roof was not thatch, but made of some other material that had suffered the damage of neglect. The grounds were overgrown with brush, and a rickety barn stood among the weeds and sapling trees. The main door of the abbey was scarred by the blows of someone who'd tried to break the lock to gain entry.

'Twas an altogether dismal place.

Alex remembered seeing a heavy brass key inside the nun's money purse. He took it from Lucy and unlocked the door, pushing it open on creaky hinges.

He noticed a hesitation in Lucy's step as she went inside. Though he had planned on saying adieu and going on his way, he found himself tying Rusa and following Lucy into the building, pulling down cob-webs and adjusting to the gloom as he went.

She did not speak, but as he followed her through the entrance and the various rooms, he could see that Lucy's task was overwhelming. She could not possibly make this place ready for habitation in a fortnight.

"Now I understand why there's so much coin in that purse," he said, tipping his head back to look at the ceiling, then down to the floor. "You will need all of it to hire help for this."

Lucy gave a quick nod and turned away from him, her shoulders visibly slumping. Alex set his jaw, unwilling to involve himself any more deeply in Lucy's affairs. What she did here was her concern. They'd seen a tidy village in the distance, and that was where she would find laborers to help her with her task. 'Twas not up to him to offer further assistance.

A rodent scurried by, startling Lucy. She jumped away from it and lost her balance, falling into a rotting table that collapsed in a dusty heap on to the floor. Alex caught her arm and kept her from falling, and when he felt her trembling, he could not let her go.

"There will be workmen in the village," he said. He felt his pulse in his throat, and it was beating much too fast. His hands were moist and his tongue grew thick.

Lucy nodded and walked away. Alex clenched his fists and watched as she rubbed the grime from the corner of a nearby window and looked outside.

He could not leave her like this.

Her shoulders were far too bare without the undertunic that he'd never noticed before this morn, too delicate to shoulder the burden of Holywake alone.

"I'll ride into the village at first light and hire laborers for you," he said.

"I'll go with y—"

"No!" he said more vehemently than he intended. But she could not go into the village dressed as she was. Every man within miles would find his way to her, just for a glimpse of her lovely form, of which too much was left uncovered. And when they discovered that she was staying alone at Holywake...

"But you..." she frowned and shook her head slightly. "I did not think you would stay beyond—"

"And I won't," he said gruffly. "I'll be gone tomorrow, after I find men who can clear out this mess for you." And after he found someone willing to sell him some more suitable clothing for her.

He couldn't leave until he was certain that all was secure here at Holywake. That Lucy would be able to accomplish what she'd been sent to do before she went on her way.

Sir Alex stalked away from Lucy again, muttering his Latin prayers, and she smiled tremulously. She considered following him, but she knew that he was disconcerted. His Latin prayers were a sure sign of it, and he would appreciate her company even less than usual just now.

She knew she was the cause of his dismay, or rather, 'twas his own reaction to her that upset him. Yet Lucy had never experienced anything so stirring as the way his appreciative gaze had made her feel. She had wanted him to touch her, to lower his head and touch his lips to hers. She had wanted to feel his strong arms around her...and more.

They were foolish desires. Sir Alex had made his intentions plain. He had wished to be rid of her almost from the moment they'd met. He was going to leave her here at Holywake. And sometime later, he would travel to France and take his monastic vows.

Lucy took a deep breath and walked farther into the abbey, in the direction opposite Alex. She was a mere stranger who happened to cross his path. She meant naught to him, and the fact that he'd rescued her twice had no particular significance. As he'd said himself, he would have helped anyone in her situation.

In the handful of days they'd been together, she had foolishly allowed tender feelings for Alex to develop and grow, and she knew those feelings were not returned. But knowing it didn't make it any easier. In another day—mayhap two—he would be gone, and somehow, Lucy would have to adjust to her life without him.

Misgivings arose in her chest. Was she hopelessly naive to think she could survive alone in The World? In the last few days, she'd lived through one disaster after another, surviving only because of Sir Alexander's intervention.

And now, this mess at Holywake—Alex would help her find men to put it right before the Craghaven nuns arrived.

Squaring her shoulders, Lucy turned her attention to the walls and floors. She was no stranger to hard work, and as soon as she had buckets and rags, she would get to it. With help, 'twould take no more than a few days to make Holywake habitable, and then she could move on.

Without Sir Alex.

"Must be our week for his majesty's knights to be riding through," said Father Robson, the priest of Saint John's Church.

Alex raised a questioning brow.

"Aye." The man had a comely face and a trustworthy mein. "They were here not two days ago. Fierce-looking men, though. Black livery, black horses, all three."

"Where are they now?" Alex asked.

The man shrugged. "Stayed one night at Ada Lampet's inn. Then they were gone. Never stopped in church."

"Do you know what direction they took?"

"North," he said. "Toward York."

And toward Eryngton. What bothered Alex most was that they'd stayed so close to Holywake. There was a possibility that they would backtrack some time in the future and discover Lucy alone at the abbey.

Nay, that would not happen. Alex was going to find men to help put the old building to rights, and Lucy would be safe enough for the time being.

"I'm looking for men to hire," he said to the

priest. "Do you know of any who would care to earn a day's wage up at the old abbey?"

The man shook his head. "Not with the harvest," he said. "No. And old Artie Carpenter didn't even finish the work he'd been hired to do before he managed to kill himself falling off Wickers's roof."

Alex scratched his beard. He'd noticed the golden fields when they'd ridden to Holywake, but it had not occurred to him that all the villagers would be occupied with cutting the wheat.

"Who was Artie Carpenter?"

"I had word from the bishop some time ago," the priest elaborated, "that the old nunnery was to be opened again. Some work was needed out there, so I bade Artie to build beds and tables, fix the windows...whatever else was needed."

"But he died."

"Aye. Helping old Wickers patch his roof."

Alex made the sign of the cross and said a silent prayer for the carpenter.

The man had gotten quite a bit done before his death, Alex thought. There were new bed frames in the dormitory, and the main door had obviously been repaired recently.

"What about women?" Alex asked. "Are there any who would wish to earn a few coins for their labor?"

"Sir Knight, you must know better," Father Robson chided in a friendly tone. "The women work the fields alongside the men. 'Tis our way."

'Twas the way in most places Alex had known.

Everyone had to help bring in the grain in autumn, else the crop would not be cut in time, and be ruined when winter came.

"So 'tis you who have come to open up the abbey?" the priest asked.

Alex gave a noncommittal grunt, unwilling to tell the priest any more.

"Is there a place where I might buy some provisions?"

"Might be that Ada Lampet has extra over at the inn," he replied. "It's not far…just follow the lane and after you cross the bridge, you'll see it. The inn stands just beyond the square."

Alex received the priest's blessing and took his leave. Picking up Rusa's reins, he led the mare down the lane, following a low stone wall that bordered the narrow road. He did not notice the pretty shrubs or the late blooming flowers in tiny gardens near front doors. His eyes were trained straight ahead, toward his destination, as he mulled over what the priest had told him.

Arriving at the inn, he tied Rusa and opened the main door. The common room was dark and the fire threw smoke as well as unnecessary heat into the room. An assortment of travelers sat eating at long, scarred tables, and two young women served them. The two turned to look Alex over when he stepped inside.

Both were comely wenches. The younger of the two had russet hair braided and twisted on top of her head. The other wore her dark hair tied at the back of her neck. Their kirtles fit low, showing more chest than Lucy did in her scarlet gown, but they weren't half as alluring as the woman he'd left behind at Holywake Abbey.

"Lookin' fer a good meal?" the red-haired one asked, smiling seductively.

"I'm looking for the proprietress," Alex replied.

"Ada?" the other serving girl asked. Smiling, she took his arm and looked at him coyly while rubbing her bosom against him. "Come on wi' me and I'll take ye to her."

Alex extricated himself from her grasp and said, "I can see you're busy. Just tell me where to find her and—"

"Ceily! Lizzie!" a sharp voice rang out. "Get to yer chores!"

A tiny woman came into the room wielding a long, wooden spoon. She waved it at both girls, who hurried away to the far corners of the common room while the lodgers at the tables laughed. Alex concentrated his attention on the newcomer.

"Ada Lampet?" he asked.

"Who's askin'?" she replied, looking up at him, and squinting one eye.

"I am a knight of the realm, which is all you need know," he answered, to which she gave a short bark of laughter.

"Well then, Sir Knight," she said, looking him over. She licked her lips, then turned and walked toward the back room. It was dingy and poorly lit, and Alex detected a coating of soot on all four walls.

Leaning over a pot that hung over the cookfire, the woman stirred its contents. "What is it ye want of me?"

"I'm told you might have provisions to sell."

"And what kind of provisions would ye be wantin'?"

"Bread. Cheese and meat if you have any," Alex said. "And I would buy a bucket from you if you have one to spare."

He told her all the other things Lucy would need and found the woman willing to part with some of her goods for far too many of the coins in his purse. Seeing no choice but to give in to Ada Lampet's avarice, Alex paid her. He gathered up the food and placed it in the bucket, along with several rags, then went outside to the place where his horse stood waiting. He tied it all to his saddle.

"All that clutter makes yer fine mare look like a peddler's mount," Ada said, laughing at her clever insult.

Alex was not amused by her jest, or by her greed. Nor was he pleased when the dark-haired serving wench came out and whispered an improper suggestion in his ear. Not tempted in the least, Alex did not dignify her proposition with an answer, but mounted his horse and rode away from them.

He had planned to ask if there was anyone who would be willing to sell him a bit of linen, or a woman's underdress, but knew that these coarse hens would have nothing appropriate for Lucy. And even if they'd had something for her, his Lucy was too pure to wear their sullied garb.

He would think of some other solution to her clothes.

'Twas nearly dark when Alex left the village, and he rode carefully up the narrow path that led to Holywake. He was certain that the most prudent course would be to remain at Holywake for the time being. He had no connection to the abbey, so Skelton's men would have no reason to look for him there.

The fact that Lucy would be left alone if he went on to York or to Eryngton played no part in Alex's decision to stay. She was a capable woman. She would do what needed to be done whether he stayed or not.

However, if he was going to remain with her at Holywake, they were going to have to do something about the state of her clothes. 'Twas possible that a ride into York was needed. He might have better luck there in finding men or women to come and work at Holywake, and he was sure to find someone who would sell him something more modest for Lucy to wear.

With a solid plan in mind, he spurred Rusa on her way.

Lucy awoke alone the following morn in the room that would be the nuns' refectory. She'd fallen asleep there the night before, waiting for Sir Alex to return. She knew she would have to accustom herself to being alone, but she'd felt his absence acutely last night. She relied upon him far too much.

Biting her lip in consternation, Lucy decided that would have to change. Starting today, she would keep to herself as much as possible and figure out a way to get the work done at Holywake so that she could leave. Sir Alex had likely found men in the village who would come and work for a day's pay, which would hasten her own departure from the abbey.

Then she could get on with her life.

She got up from the bed she'd made upon the floor and pulled the braid out of her hair. There was no sign of Alex, and Lucy wondered whether he'd come back from the village. If he'd hired laborers for her, there would have been no reason for him to return.

With that thought, a lump of dread formed in her throat. Her heart ached and tears filled her eyes. She would never see him again.

The man who had twice saved her from certain death, who had held her and cared for her when she'd needed him... She had come to mean naught to him. And it hurt to realize that.

Brushing the tears from her eyes, Lucy swallowed the lump. She gathered herself up and looked around, taking stock of what needed to be done, where she should begin. 'Twas no use grieving over what had never been...what could never be, even though Sir Alex's absence left a gaping hole in her heart.

She had plenty to do to keep her occupied, and when she was finished here, she would be free to go.

Though she knew not what her destination would be, or how she would make her way, she was certain—

A furtive noise in the entryway startled her. Someone, or some*thing* was there. In silence, Lucy crept toward the door to see if an animal had found its way inside, or if it was a more dangerous intruder. Flattening herself against the wall next to the door, she peeked around the corner and saw a strange man setting a bucket of water on the floor.

She whipped her head away, concealing herself again, and held her breath, wishing that he would just go away. If he came any farther inside, he would notice her in the refectory since she could not creep quietly or quickly enough to get away.

Her heart beat painfully in her chest and her palms became moist as she waited for the man to leave. She could not imagine why he would have shown up at the abbey today, of all days, carrying his water and—

She frowned. The man's movements were vaguely familiar. And since she only knew one man...

Lucy peeked around the corner again and released the breath she'd been holding. She frowned as she observed the familiar colors of his clothes, his dark hair, his shoes that had been nearly ruined by river water.

Sir Alexander's appearance had changed drastically and her heart jumped at the sight of him. Expecting never to see him again, she would have run to him and cried out her joy as well as her relief, but somehow managed to keep her feet upon the ground.

"What's wrong?" Alex asked gruffly when he saw her.

His jaw was clean-shaven and he'd tied his hair neatly at his nape. He wore a clean tunic of dark green rather than the rough brown wool he'd been wearing when she last saw him.

"I...I thought..." A tear spilled from her eye just then and she turned away.

"What is it?" he asked, coming to stand behind her.

"Naught," she said. "I m-must have raised some dust and it got in my eye. And then I thought you were..."

"Who did you think I was?" he asked.

"I— I don't know," she said, composed now. She turned to face him again. "You came so quietly...I thought 'twas someone from the village. Or an animal come to nest. I didn't know you."

"I, er...shaved my beard."

If she'd thought him magnificent before, she could think of no better word to describe him now. The skin of his strong, angular jaw was soft and smooth, his chin slightly cleft.

Lifting her hand, Lucy touched his naked cheek with the back of her hand, his lips with her fingers. And wanted more than ever for his lips to touch hers. For his arms to pull her close.

But he stepped away.

"I'll be riding to York today," he said, turning his back to her, "and if I meet up with the black knights, I don't want them to recognize me."

Chapter Nine

She was so beautiful that Alex could hardly catch his breath when he looked at her. 'Twas a good thing he'd planned to go away for the day. He did not think any number of prayers could keep him from touching her.

But his touch would not be the light, guileless caress she had given him.

Once he returned from York with laborers, the situation would solve itself. His impious attraction was only due to their solitude. When they were surrounded by workers and occupied every hour of the day, 'twould disappear.

"I— I did not recognize you," Lucy said. "Those knights will never know you."

Her swollen eyes and red nose were those of a weeping woman, and Alex wondered what had upset her. But he was not going to ask. Her troubles were her own, and he had no part of them, no matter how strongly her tears tugged at him.

"I found some supplies in the village, but no one

to come and work for you," he said. "The village is in the midst of the harvest, so there is no one to spare."

"Oh," she said simply, her gaze making him uncomfortable. He felt naked without his beard, shaken by her gentle touch on his face.

"When I go into York, I'll find workers for you," he said. "And I'll get whatever supplies they did not have in the village."

He went to an old wooden stand where he'd placed the items he'd already purchased for her in the village. "Is there anything more that you want?" he asked.

She looked through the rags and the hard soap he'd gotten from Ada, then noticed the food at the bottom.

"A broom," she said, though he could see that she was distracted.

And so was Alex. By her eyes, deeply blue and still moist. By her silken hair flowing loose about her shoulders, so soft, so bare. And most of all, he was distracted by her vulnerability.

She needed him.

Alex suddenly pulled his knife from its sheath and began cutting pieces of cheese from the brick he'd bought in the village. Then he tore a couple of pieces of bread and handed them to Lucy.

'Twas time to go. He did not want to be needed by her or by anyone. He had a clearly defined task and in God's good time, he would complete it. In the meantime, he would give assistance to this woman who'd been stranded, through no fault of her own.

He went outside and started to mount Rusa, but

Lucy stopped him with one hand upon his forearm. "Please do not g-go until I have thanked you for all you have done, Sir Alex," she said, blinking back tears, "and b-before I can wish you Godspeed on your journey."

When she raised herself up and kissed his cheek, Alex realized she believed he was leaving her. Permanently. "I wish you well—"

Drawing away, he took her hands in his own and said, "I'm coming back."

The familiar crease appeared between her shapely brows and she appeared not to understand his words. When she swallowed back her tears, an odd sensation crept from Alex's belly to his chest.

"I'll be back before nightfall with the supplies you'll need, and laborers to help you."

"But I...I thought you did not plan to stay."

He took another step away. "I do not. But it suits me to remain here at Holywake for now."

Lucy worked all day, scrubbing floors and washing what tables and other furniture had been left by the order that had abandoned Holywake only a few years before. The Craghaven abbess expected the new abbey to be adequately furnished when she arrived, and it mostly was. New bed frames lined the dormitory walls and some of the windows had been repaired. There were water marks on the floor of the chapel and the refectory that Lucy assumed had been caused by a roof leak. She could not see whether it had been repaired, too.

The tables in the refectory seemed to be newly

made, but there were no benches. There was still much that needed to be done, and Lucy could not fathom why some of the work had been completed, but not all.

Nor could she understand why Sir Alexander had decided to stay. Somehow, she needed to be better prepared for his eventual departure from her life. She'd nearly wept on him this morn when she thought he was leaving her forever.

It would not happen again.

Lucy spent most of the day with her hands in soapy water, scrubbing windows and floors. She thought about the possibilities life would bring once her task was completed here, and where she would go. York seemed the most likely place, where there would be many wealthy merchants' families who needed nurses or servants of any other sort.

She did not allow herself to think of the yearning she'd always had—that of having a family of her own. She was well beyond marriageable age and 'twas unlikely that any suitor would take an interest in her. At least she might enjoy another woman's infant—like tiny Bert Bavent. Lucy had no doubt that she could learn what needed to be done for a bairn, and she would love doing it, so much more than her dreary life at the abbey.

Many were the times the abbess had admonished her to be grateful for her place at the abbey, for no man would want a crippled wife. Naturally, she'd had a dowry when she'd been sent away from Eryngton. Craghaven Abbey had been the beneficiary, so Lucy did not have even the slightest wealth to tempt a husband.

She would not allow herself to brood over it. Lucy was determined to live as full a life as her lame leg allowed. Even if she was not to have a husband and family, she planned to live without walls and restrictions.

The weather changed in the late afternoon, becoming more seasonably cool, and threatening rain. Wondering when Alex would return, and whether she should prepare a meal for them, Lucy collected wood for a fire and carried it into the kitchen. She picked up her blanket from where she'd left it in the refectory, and made herself comfortable in the kitchen.

'Twas not until it had grown dark that Lucy heard the sound of hooves on the road and the creaking of wagon wheels. Alex was back, and he'd brought help.

Alex's mood was foul when he returned to Holywake in the pouring rain. He drove his new-bought wagon into the leaky barn and found a relatively dry spot to stow it, then unhitched Rusa. As he was pouring grain for the mare, Lucy rushed in, shielding her head from the rain with one of the blankets.

"Sir Alex, you're—" She stopped and looked around. "Where are the… You found no one to help me?"

He shook his head. "They're building a new church in York," he said. "There's not a spare carpenter in the town, or any other kind of worker, either…at least, none willing to travel all the way to Holywake for work."

All was not lost, though. Alex had found lumber at the site of the new church building, and the priest had been willing to part with some of it for a pretty price, along with an old horse cart. Alex had stopped at various shops as well, and purchased more of the items Lucy would need. 'Twas fortunate he'd had the wagon, else he'd have had difficulty carting everything back to Holywake.

When he looked across the wagon, he saw that she was crestfallen. He caught a glimpse of the crease between her brows before she turned away, gathering the blanket around her.

Alex reached her before she got to the door, and took her arm. She turned and looked up at him.

"'Tis not so bad," he said. "I'm no stranger to a carpenter's tools."

The expression that came into her eyes took his breath away. 'Twas full of hope and gratitude and… He took a deep breath and moved to the back of the wagon.

"Since I'll be staying here for a few days," he said, picking up parcels from the wagon, "I can make some repairs, build a few benches."

He'd been proud of the comfortable chair he'd fashioned for Isabella when she'd been with child, and he'd built his son's cradle with his own two hands. Once the lad had grown, he'd enjoyed the little pull-cart Alex had made him, and the toys he'd carved from wood.

Alex had forgotten all that. Since he'd left Clyfton, the only times he'd looked back were when he prayed for the souls of his beloved wife and son. It had always been too painful to do more than that.

"What is all this?" Lucy asked, standing beside him. He'd been so immersed in his thoughts, he hadn't heard her move. And he was suddenly very angry that 'twas Lucy next to him, and not Isabella.

"Grain, some vegetables, candles, a cookpot," he said, gathering the goods he could carry in his arms and starting for the door without her. 'Twas up to Lucy whether or not to follow. He did not want her to rely upon him for anything more than he'd promised—a few benches, repairs to some of the windows and to the roof.

Intentionally ignoring her, Alex went out into the rain and walked through the grass and high weeds. He would not worry about Lucy. She had managed to come out to the barn alone and she could get herself back the same way.

The main door was ajar so he pushed inside, stopping abruptly before he tracked water into the clean entrance hall. Even in the meager light, Alex could see that the hall was spotless. He craned his neck to look into the refectory, and saw that it was the same. Lucy must have worked all day to rid the place of the dirt and clutter.

She came in just behind him, slightly breathless, and carrying a wrapped bundle in each hand.

"Oh!" she said when she saw him standing just inside the door. "Are you going in?"

"The floors..."

"They look much better, do they not?" she asked, seeming pleased that he'd noticed.

"Lucy, I would rather not track water all across the clean floor," Alex said impatiently. "I'll just leave these things here and go check my snares."

"You set snares?"

He gave a curt nod. "Before I left this morn."

She set down her parcels, and before he could leave, she placed her hand upon his arm and used him for balance while she removed her shoes. A moment later, she'd disappeared into the refectory or somewhere beyond, lifting her skirts to avoid dripping on the floor, and carrying her packages with her.

Alex went back into the rain while he squelched the ridiculous sensation of coming home. It made no sense whatsoever, since they'd arrived only yesterday, and he'd spent precious little time here. Clyfton House had been his home, and it was no more.

He collected the two hares that had been ensnared near the burn that trickled through Holywake's grounds. Before carrying them to the abbey, he stopped in the barn and picked up the last package he'd bought in York.

When he returned to the main building, Alex stopped under the low overhang outside the nunnery's kitchen. He stood there protected from the rain while he dressed his kill. Eventually, he rinsed his hands in the pouring rain and pushed the door open.

This room had been cleaned, as well. And there was a warm, welcoming fire in the hearth.

"Are your dry clothes in your saddle packs?" Lucy asked. She stood up from a place she had made near the fire and started for the door. "I'll get them and you can change here, by the fire."

He started to tell her not to trouble herself, but she hurried out of the kitchen with that uneven gait of hers before he had a chance to tell her he'd go 'round and get it himself. And standing in the warmth of the stark and unfurnished kitchen, he realized how cold he was. He would just warm himself until Lucy returned—

"Here you are, Sir Alex," she said, handing him his pack. "I'll leave you to it."

A moment later and she was gone again, giving him the privacy he required. He stripped to the skin and put on a dry tunic, along with new hose and braes. His shoes were sodden again, so he left them near the fire to dry, along with the rest of his clothes.

When Lucy returned, he was dressed.

"Shall I cook some of this meat for supper?" she asked, carrying the pot and one of the bags he'd left at the front door.

A hot meal for his belly would suit him well, after being out in the cold rain for hours. But Lucy must be weary after all her obvious toil today.

"I'm a fair cook," she said cheerfully.

"I have no doubt of it," he replied, "and a hot meal sounds good. But I will help you."

"There is no need," Lucy said. "You've labored all day for my cause, and 'tis only right that you rest now."

He would not have her waiting upon him. While she poured water into the cookpot, he took his knife from its sheath and cut the meat. He tossed the pieces into the water, and Lucy began to cut onions and garlic. When she added them to the pan, Alex noticed the condition of her hands. They were beyond chapped. Red and swollen, the knuckles were cracked and seeping blood.

Alex hung the pot over the fire and took hold of her wrist. "Your hands," he said.

"Oh, 'tis naught," she replied as she tried to pull away.

He knew by her blush that she was embarrassed, but he did not release her. "You've ruined them," he said. "You cannot possibly think you can do all the work here yourself."

"Well…"

"You'll be no good to anyone if your hands get any worse," he said. "Come here."

While the pottage cooked, she sat down on the blanket she'd laid near the fire and Alex took his jar of ointment from his pack. "This will help ease the pain and soften the skin."

"Who would ever believe an earl's daughter would need such a remedy?" she said with a laugh.

He looked up at her then and frowned. She'd said something of her background, but he hadn't given it much thought before.

"You mentioned a cousin who inherited the title?"

She nodded as he wrapped a clean, thin cloth around her hand. "Yes. Hugh. He became earl when my brother, John, died," she said. "My brothers were very devout knights. I often think they should both have gone on Crusade."

"And left you alone?"

She shrugged as if it did not matter, but Alex saw

the shadow of an old sadness in her eyes. "They left me alone anyway."

It angered him to think how it must have been for her as a child, weak with her infirmity and illness. Could not the younger brother have remained at home to care for his sister who clearly needed him?

He finished wrapping her hands and she sat still, looking at them as she held them out in front of her. "You have defeated me, Sir Knight."

He gave her a puzzled look.

"I won't be able to get any work done at all, with my hands bound so."

"Mayhap 'twas not meant to be done entirely by you."

She laughed. "Then by whom? You said there were no laborers to be found."

"Neither in the village nor in York."

"Then who... Surely not you? A great knight on his knees—scrubbing floors?" She chuckled.

Alex felt the tug of a smile coming to his lips. "Mayhap the Craghaven nuns will have to take to *their* knees when they arrive."

Still smiling, she tilted her head and gave him a puzzled look. "Do you jest, Sir Alex?"

He hesitated, abashed by his mirth. He could not remember the last time his heart had felt so light. "I believe I do."

Chapter Ten

The meal was better than any Lucy had had in days. Their thick soup, eaten with bread, was filling and satisfying. And they were able to wash it down with mugs of ale from the cask that Alex had purchased in the village.

Sir Alex would not allow Lucy to clean up after the meal, but rinsed their bowls and mugs himself. Then he brought in more firewood and they sat quietly in the warm, dry kitchen while the rain continued. She cringed a little when the lightning and thunder began, but was so astounded by Sir Alex's tender care of her hands that she did not experience the usual terror that accompanied a violent storm.

She was even more bewildered by the knight's small attempt at levity. Lucy would suffer any injury if it would bring a lightening of his spirit. She did not think she'd ever known anyone whose soul was so sadly burdened.

She wondered what evil thing had befallen him to make him so somber. For some reason, he planned to give up arms and become a monk. Lucy could think of no reason a powerful man would do such a thing, especially one so comely as Sir Alex. She had no doubt that there would be many a young maid willing to become his wife.

Studying him covertly, she admired the strong lines of his face. His jaw bore the shadow of his beard and Lucy wondered if 'twould be necessary for him to shave it daily. She was unsure of such things, having had no contact with men since her childhood.

"Years ago, when I was a child and it stormed," she said quietly, breaking the silence, "my brothers used to take me into my father's study and hide me under his big oaken table. One would close the curtain and the other would cover the table with a blanket so that I wouldn't be afraid of the lightning."

Bright light flashed in the small window behind Sir Alex, and Lucy braced herself for the thunder that would follow. Her fear of storms had abated over the years, but they still made her uneasy, even now, when she knew she was safe in Holywake's kitchen.

"They were good enough not to tease me," she said, drawing her legs up under her and wrapping her arms around them, "even though they were much older and absolutely fearless."

"Were they not gone to foster?" Sir Alex asked.

She shook her head. "Only for a short time," she replied. "My father brought them home when our eldest brother died while fostering at a nearby estate. My father said he would not risk his heirs to the care of any other man."

Though Alex did not turn to look at her, Lucy saw that he was perplexed. As any knight would be, Lucy supposed. Lads did not stay at home once they reached the age of reason. They were sent away to becomes squires in the households of great lords.

She was certain that Alan's death, along with her own infirmity, had given her father reason to keep his other two sons close, instead of following the usual custom. Lucy was glad of it, too. She'd gotten to know and love her brothers, and had mourned them well when they died.

"Have you any brothers or sisters, Alex?" she asked.

The muscles of his throat worked before he answered. "One brother," he finally said. "Philip."

"And he is well?"

"Aye," Alex replied. "Last I heard."

"When was that?"

"Three years ago," he said. "When I left England."

"'Tis a long time," she mused. Her hip had begun to ache, as it often did during wet weather, and she shifted her position. "Have you been in France all this time? At Cluny?"

He shrugged. "Only for the first two years. Then I escorted one of the monks to Jerusalem."

"His own pilgrimage?"

"I suppose you could call it that."

"When I was ten years old, we received word that one of my brothers had died en route to Jerusalem," Lucy said, remembering that sad day. She'd been in her bed, lying ill from one of her many maladies when the messenger had come. And she had been too sick to attend the requiem said in his honor, though she'd said many a prayer for both her brothers in the days since then.

"John was thrown by his horse not a year later," she said, as Sir Alex turned his intense green gaze on her. 'Twas not without sympathy, but he said naught. "It killed him."

"And you were sent to the nunnery."

She shrugged. "'Tis a woman's lot," she said without bitterness. "To do as her master bids."

"Your cousin."

"Aye," she replied. "I had no choice but to go to Craghaven when he ordered it."

"But you will not stay with the nuns."

Lucy shook her head. "Though I will never be able to do what really suits me, I will find work somewhere and make my own way."

Alex stood up and added a log to the fire. Though 'twas comfortably warm in the kitchen, if the fire went out, the cold and damp would quickly find them. Alex pushed the logs around and made the flame flare. Then he turned to look at her.

"What suits you?" he asked, though it seemed to Lucy a reluctant question.

Had anyone else asked, Lucy might have worried about ridicule. But Sir Alex was not a man to sneer at another's weakness.

"I would have a husband," she said. "And children. But, as my cousin—and the abbess herself—

often told me, there isn't a man in England who would knowingly take a lame and sickly wife of my advanced age and no dowry to speak of.''

Alex's tongue felt thick and as dry as leather. Only a fool would look at Lucy and see naught but an awkward gait. She had a kind of beauty that was more than just the silken tresses that fell in waves to her waist, more than comely features and a fetching form that ought to tempt any man.

He turned away and looked into the fire again, afraid that if he gazed at her any longer, he'd fall into the depths of her eyes and never be able to come out again.

She was as robust as anyone he'd ever known—man or woman. Alex had no doubt that she would be able to make the voyage to Jerusalem and back—as arduous and dangerous as anything he'd ever done—without complaint.

But Alex had met many a fool in his life, so he knew that Lucy's cousin and the abbess had not been mistaken. Once Lucy left the abbey, she would have to make her way alone.

He stood abruptly.

"I'm going to take a look around and see where the roof leaks," he said. He picked up one of the new candles and strode from the room before he could think of her on the streets of York, looking for work.

Or for a husband who would deign to have her.

A loud crack of thunder shook the abbey before

Alex reached the main hall. A moment later, Lucy was right behind him.

She made a valiant attempt to hide her nervousness in the storm, but Alex saw the way the flame of her candle quivered. She was just as frightened as when she was a child and her brothers had made a safe place for her to hide.

But there were no brothers to care for her now.

A sharp edge of protectiveness surged over Alex. And if his good sense had not prevailed, he might have fashioned some small shelter for her as her brothers had done in the past. Chivalry had been deeply bred into him, and that was the only reason he felt such a strong urge to take care of this woman.

But it did not explain why his arms ached to pull her close, or why the air suddenly seemed too thin to breathe.

"I think the roof leak is t-the worst in the dormitory," Lucy said, holding her blanket close.

She took the lead and kept going until they reached the large room where the beds were lined up against the walls.

"At least the water isn't pouring in," Lucy said. "It's just a steady drip."

"Enough to damage the floor."

"Can it be fixed?" she asked.

He nodded just as lightning flashed and a fierce clap of thunder startled her. Lucy jumped, dropping her candle in the puddle on the floor.

"I'm sorry!" she cried, covering her mouth with one hand. "I didn't mean to—"

"'Tis all right." He retrieved the candle, then took her arm. "Let's go back to the fire."

She went without hesitation, and they used the light of his candle to return to the kitchen, stopping in the front entry to pick up the bundles Alex had left there earlier. One of the packages contained the items Lucy would need to make her wardrobe more suitable for the day she ventured out of the abbey. Alex did not want to have to think of her going out in the streets of York or any other town, dressed as she was.

She was much too alluring for any man to resist.

As Lucy sat down by the fire, Alex knelt and slit the string that held the package closed. When the cloth wrapping fell away, he pulled out a deep-blue woolen shawl. Refusing to admit that he'd purchased it because it made him think of Lucy's eyes, he handed it to her without looking at her.

"For me?" she asked. She let the blanket fall and wrapped the shawl around her shoulders.

He nodded. "You can't wear that blanket forever."

"But I... What's this?" she asked.

"Cloth," he replied, watching her unfold the linen. Fortunately, the merchant had reminded him of the need for thread, as well as needle and shears. "You can sew something to wear while your hands mend."

"Sir Alex," she said softly. If he was not mistaken, she sounded a bit breathless. "You..."

"'Tis naught," he said, opening the other packages and ignoring her gratitude. "Winter will soon be upon us. You have only the gown you wear, and it—"

"Is indecent," she said, sounding embarrassed. "I know."

She crouched down beside him and pressed a kiss to his cheek, then stood and walked away.

He felt a lightning bolt shoot through him and his face burned where her lips touched. Though she'd kissed him in the same manner once before, the heat of this kiss stunned him. He placed one hand against the spot she'd touched with her lips while he watched her leave the warmth of the kitchen.

Mortified by her rash gesture of gratitude and affection, Lucy stayed away for as long as she thought it would take Sir Alexander to fall asleep. She could not face him, not after such boldness.

Pulling her new shawl tightly around her, she sat huddled in a dark corner, well aware that she had committed a grave error. Sir Alex wanted as little to do with her as possible, yet she'd not only made him feel responsible for her, she'd made him uncomfortable with a kiss that was entirely unnecessary.

A simple thanks would have sufficed.

Some time later, when the storm had abated, Lucy returned as quietly as possible to the kitchen. Relieved to find her knight asleep, lying on his side facing the wall, she settled herself into her own blanket.

The night passed fitfully, her dreams mingling reality with the outlandish stories told by Lady Elsbeth. She dreamed of lips touching sensitive places, of hands giving pleasure, of tender words spoken. She felt agitated and overheated, and it did not help that

when she awoke the following morning, Sir Alex was
pulling off his tunic and the light shirt he wore underneath.

She lay staring at him, and as she became aware
once again of the striking differences between them,
her breath caught in her throat. His chest was big and
broad, and it narrowed to a hard belly, ridged with
muscle. The muscles of his arms were thick and well
defined, hard as if hewn from stone. And much of
that masculine flesh was covered by a layer of coarse,
dark hair.

Lucy felt her face heat. She knew she should allow
him his privacy, yet she could not turn away.

In all her years at Craghaven, she had seen no more
of any man than their priest's face and hands. Elsbeth
had said men were made very differently. But besides
their lack of bosom, Lucy had not understood what
the woman had meant.

She had begun her education with little Bert Bavent. Now she wanted to know more.

Lying perfectly still, Lucy felt oddly disappointed
when Sir Alexander took the clothes he'd dried overnight by the fire and slipped outside, being careful not
to disturb her. She wondered if he'd have blushed
pink had he noticed her eyes on him. And it occurred
to her to wonder if he felt the same fascination when
he saw her bosom half bare as it was in this kirtle.

She stayed where she was for a few moments,
mulling over her strange thoughts, then rose from her
bed, feeling overly warm and uncomfortable.

Lucy's hands were still bandaged and she knew she

could accomplish naught if they remained bound this way. She unwrapped them and saw that they were not as red as they'd been, and the skin was smoother than before. She should have known Alex's ointment would help—her shoulder wound was almost healed because of it.

She looked for the bucket and realized that Alex had taken it with him. The rain had stopped and 'twas a beautiful morn, though much cooler than it had been during their travels. Gathering her shawl about her, she opened the kitchen door and went outside.

A little while later, she found Alexander filling the bucket in a narrow river. To her disappointment, he was fully dressed.

"Good morn to you, Sir Knight," she said.

He gave a brief nod but did not look at her.

Lucy crouched and dipped her hands in the cool water, then washed her face. The little river was a good deal wider now than it was the day before, and the water rushed wildly past her. She could only imagine how much more treacherous the river where she'd fallen in would be today.

Alex picked up his sword and started to walk away.

"Where is your other sword?" He always had two swords with him, though why he would need them was beyond Lucy.

He stopped in his tracks, then turned slowly toward her, buckling his sword belt 'round his waist. To Lucy, it seemed that he was unsure how to answer her, though she thought her question had been simple enough.

"The other sword... 'Tis a relic brought from the Holy Land," he said. "Not a sword to be used in battle."

Lucy stood abruptly, excited by the prospect of seeing a precious piece of antiquity. "Where is it?"

"Hidden safely away."

"Why?"

Alex did not respond to her question, but turned and started to walk back to the abbey. Lucy hurried to catch up to him. "Are you afraid someone will try to steal it?"

"There have been several attempts since I left Jerusalem."

"You mean someone— The black knights?"

"Aye." The word was clipped short, as though he did not want to speak more of it, but Lucy was determined to see the sword that was held within the beautiful silver scabbard.

"And you've found a safe place in the abbey where it cannot be found?"

He nodded.

"In the cellar?" she asked. "Hidden in the rafters?"

Alex stopped abruptly. Turning to face her, he took her by the shoulders. "How did you know?"

She shrugged. If she'd had anything of value to hide, she supposed the foundation of the building would have been the choice place to hide it. "I just guessed."

Her answer clearly disturbed him and he stood looking down at her for a short moment before turning away and heading back to the abbey. Lucy followed as closely as she could.

He went through the kitchen and beyond, into a storage room where a trap door in the floor led to the cellar below. A thick rope hung from one edge of the opening, and Lucy watched as Alex descended into the darkness. She heard his feet touch ground.

Lucy knelt at the opening and saw the top of Alex's head in the gloom. He looked up. "Hand me a candle, would you?"

She reached for one of the lamps he'd brought from York and lit the candle. After she gave the light to him, he disappeared, though she could hear his footsteps in the dirt floor of the cellar. A few moments later, he reached up through the floor and handed her the lamp, then climbed up after it.

The silver scabbard now rested in his sword belt. "There must be a place around here where no one would think to look for it."

Lucy frowned. She could think of no secret niches in any of the rooms. "You will have to make a secure place."

"What do you mean?"

"You brought tools from York, did you not?" she asked.

The glimmer of a smile crossed his face and he narrowed his eyes when he looked at her. "You are a very keen woman, Lucy of Craghaven."

She felt her heart flutter in her chest and stopped herself from thanking him for the compliment. Her kiss of gratitude had not been welcome, and Lucy did not think he'd appreciate her words, either.

"Who owned the sword, Sir Alex?" she asked, standing aside when he closed the trap door.

"I do not know."

"Then you know naught of the sword's history?"

He shook his head and walked from the kitchen to the nuns' dormitory. "Only that I am to deliver it into the hands of a Yorkish earl for safekeeping."

"Why?" Lucy asked, beyond curious now that she'd gotten him to talk.

"I can only imagine that it is a relic of untold value," he said. "Its heft is not that of a battle sword, so it is probably an honorary weapon, given to a king of old."

"Do you mean Herod? Or *David?*"

"I don't know," Alex replied and it seemed to Lucy that his curiosity was piqued as well. Standing beside a window, he pulled the scabbard from his belt and then tugged on the handle. It did not budge. Upon further examination, Alex noticed that 'twas not a sword handle at all, but a cap, a decorative cover, fastened into place over the scabbard. As he opened it, his brow furrowed and Lucy read the puzzlement on his face.

"What is it?"

"Not a sword," he said, pulling something from the sheath. "'Tis soft. Cloth."

A long roll of stained and discolored linen slid easily out of the scabbard. Alex crouched and set the scabbard on the floor. Lucy knelt beside him and watched him unroll the linen.

"Gloria Patri, et Filio, et Spiritui Sancto," he whispered in awe, then made the sign of the cross.

The image on the cloth appeared similar to a wood-cut. 'Twas brown and the lines of the image were blurred, but the cloth clearly bore the distinct imprint of a man's face. Lucy's mind raced with the knowledge that she was looking at something that was profoundly sacred. Was it the face of—

"The Mandylion," Alex whispered.

Neither of them moved, but just looked upon the fabled cloth. "'Twas lost more than fifty years ago," Alex said, "when the city of Constantinople was invaded."

"Where did it come from?"

Bewildered, Alex spoke as if he had not heard her question. "I had no idea this was the reason we were sent to Jerusalem," he said with awe in his voice. "I was never told what we sought. Nor do I know exactly which of the sultans gave us the scabbard."

"I don't understand," she said. She had never heard of any Mandylion, but she did not need to be told what lay before her. 'Twas obvious. But she knew naught of sultans or Constantinople.

"This is the Edessa Cloth," he explained, sitting back on his heels. "With the face of Christ upon it."

Awe and wonder pulsed through her at the sight of the sacred relic. That she should be here in the same room with it—

"Skelton's men will kill for it," Alex said, "and take it to the Turkish emir, Mehmet."

"Skelton?"

"Lord of the black knights," he explained.

One more thing that Lucy did not understand. If Lord Skelton was an Englishman, why would he be dealing with a Turk? The Turks were the enemy were they not? "Why would Lord Skelton want to give such an important Christian relic to this...emir?"

"For rewards," Alex said. "Land and power. Riches."

"Oh." She supposed these were not such unusual motives for betrayal. But this was not a common breach of faith. 'Twas sacrilege.

Alex rolled the cloth tightly and slipped it back into the scabbard for safekeeping.

"You must build a hiding place when you repair the wall or the floor. Mayhap you can slip it inside."

"The cloth was kept hidden in a wall at Edessa," Alex said. "I might be able to do something similar here."

Emotion welled in Lucy's heart. If he built a special place to hide the scabbard, he must be planning to stay.

Alex resigned himself to passing a few days at Holywake, but no more. "I'm going to start work on the roof before it rains again," he said. And until he had a new place to hide the scabbard, he would put it back where it had been in the cellar.

By the time he had stowed it below the abbey and

returned to the kitchen, Lucy had sliced bread and poured mugs of ale for them. She had tied the shawl so that she was modestly covered, but her hands were bare. They looked better than they had before he'd wrapped them, but not altogether healed.

"You will keep your hands out of water today," he said, sounding unintentionally harsh.

She looked stunned by his words, her eyes large and blue, the gold lashes tipped by fiery red. "But there is so much to—"

"It will get done," he said, frowning at her stubbornness. He picked up the jar of ointment from the hearth and, as they stood before the fire, he rubbed the oily concoction into the skin of one small hand. The bones were delicate but the flesh was firm and well-seasoned by work.

He finished with the first hand, then started to work on the second when her chest suddenly rose and a distinctly feminine sound escaped her. Her eyes were closed and she bore an expression he had not seen in years. 'Twas one of ecstasy.

Arousal hit him like a punch.

Her cheeks were flushed and her lips slightly parted. Her pulse beat rapidly in her throat. Still holding her hand, Alex moved closer, feeling quite certain that his very existence depended upon tasting her mouth.

Lucy took a deep breath and when her breasts touched his chest, Alex slid one hand around her back and pulled her against him. The heat of her body

washed over him. Lightning bolts of sensation flowed
through him, shocking him back to reality.

He was Alexander Breton, a man immune to the
needs of the flesh. A man whose life had ended with
the death of his wife and child.

In haste, and without a word, Alex released her and
took his leave. Determined to put some space between
himself and Lucy, he did not bother to break his fast,
but went directly to the barn. His horse nickered and
snorted but he hardly heard the sounds. Placing his
trembling hands on Rusa's flank, he took a deep
breath.

No prayer came to mind.

Work was what he needed. Hours of hard labor
would wipe the memory of her scent, of her touch,
from his mind. They had just spent too much time in
close quarters and needed to go their own separate
ways, at least for awhile.

He patted the mare, then opened the barn door and
led her out. Once he'd hobbled the horse, he let her
roam free in the overgrown pasture and returned to
the barn for the tools and supplies he'd purchased in
York.

An old ladder, missing a couple of rungs, hung on
the wall of the barn, along with a rusty scythe which
he would use to clear the yard of its weeds. Carrying
the ladder to the abbey wall, he set it against the eaves
and climbed.

Chapter Eleven

Lucy sat quietly in the refectory, stitching her new chemise while Alex worked on the benches he made. Her hands had improved significantly in the two days she'd kept them out of soapy water and used Alex's ointment on them.

His sword lay on one of the tables nearby, but Lucy did not know where he'd hidden the scabbard with the Mandylion. Possibly on the roof where he'd spent an entire day making repairs.

He had naught to say as he worked, but Lucy enjoyed his company nonetheless. He was very clever with his hands, and the muscles of his shoulders and arms bulged quite pleasingly. He'd kept his beard shaved, and Lucy could not imagine a more comely face on a man. Her heart pounded just thinking about the way he'd held her, had almost kissed her.

Months ago, Elsbeth had told Lucy a tale that made her blush even now. Whether 'twas entirely true or not, Lucy would never know. But Elsbeth had admitted to seducing a duke while she was at court.

Her method had been simple, though Lucy had thought it crude. Elsbeth had managed to lure the duke to her chamber one night. When he'd arrived, she'd met him alone, wearing naught but a thin shift. She'd plied him with kisses and tantalized him with her nearly naked body.

Lucy wondered what Alex would do if she kissed him. She glanced down at her chest, modestly covered by her shawl, and wondered if she could bring herself to flaunt it the way Elsbeth had done with her duke. Was that what she would have to do to gain his attention, his affection?

Blushing at the thought, Lucy knew she could not.

What she needed to do was to get through the next day or two, then bid farewell to Sir Alex and watch him ride away.

"You are surprisingly good at that," she said. Their remaining time together was so limited that Lucy did not want to spend it in silence.

"Why surprising?" he asked, planing the wooden bench to a smooth surface.

"Well, I just never thought of a knight with carpentry skills." She took another stitch in the linen underkirtle. "I thought that knights wielded swords, not hammers."

He planed in silence for another few minutes and Lucy continued sewing.

"I once made a cradle for my son."

Lucy's breath caught. Unsure that she had heard him correctly, she put down her sewing, stood up and went to him. "Your...son?" she asked quietly.

He nodded and continued working.

Drawing the logical conclusion, she realized his son would have a mother. But Sir Alex intended to become a monk.

"I don't understand," she said. "If you take the vows of your Order, then what will happen to—"

"He is dead," Alex said without inflection. "Along with my wife."

A heartfelt sadness welled up in Lucy at his stark words. "I am so sorry. When…?"

"Three years ago," he replied. "There was a fever. Geoffrey became ill, then Isabella. I lost them both inside a week."

"How terrible for you," she whispered, watching the muscles of his back flex as he worked. Lucy had been ogling the man and wishing for his kisses whilst he mourned his wife and child. She felt ashamed.

"I have not been back to England since then."

She nodded, certain that she would also have difficulty returning to the site of a loved one's death. She had no wish ever to see Eryngton again, not after losing everyone who was dear to her there.

"My brother and his wife wanted me to stay…."

"I can see how you would not."

He lifted the bench and turned it so that it fit under the table. Then he moved to the other side of the table and started on another of the long seats. "They've had two more children since I've been gone."

"Will you see them before you return to France?" she asked.

"Mayhap, though I know all is well at Clyfton."

"Clyfton?" Lucy frowned. Was this not the estate mentioned by Henry Bavent?

"Aye," he said, answering her unasked question. "The estate lies east of York, on the coast. My brother, Philip, is earl."

"Then 'tis not very far from here."

He shook his head and applied himself once again to his work.

"'Twould be wrong to leave England without seeing him," she said quietly.

He did not answer, though Lucy knew he'd heard her words.

"Your family would wish to know how you fare," she said. "I wondered about my brother after he went on crusade. For more than a year, we heard naught. Then there was word that he had perished when his ship sank in the Aegean Sea."

Alex paused to look up at her. "I knew a man whose ship sank in the Aegean...but he survived."

"I wonder if 'twas the same ship."

He shrugged. "That would have been many years ago."

Lucy nodded. She'd been a child when they'd learned of Roger's death at sea. "Still, I think you should go to Clyfton before you leave England."

"Philip will pressure me to stay."

"Would that be so bad?" She spoke quietly, her heart wishing there was some way to convince him to remain in England.

Alex lifted the bench onto the table. He took a nail from a pouch and began to pound it into one of the legs. Then he tested its sturdiness by trying to wobble it.

"My brother would see me remarried," he said casually, but Lucy detected a stubborn set to Alex's jaw and knew that he felt anything but casual about it.

She swallowed. Any dreams she might have had— no matter how foolish and impractical—were over.

There was less than a day's work to be done, and then Alex felt he could leave without deserting Lucy. He'd kept his distance from her for the last few days, and pretended naught had occurred when he'd touched her, when he'd rubbed her hands.

He had come unbelievably close to kissing her. And he had not been drowsy with sleep when it had happened. He'd been fully aware of her. Painfully aware.

He wanted her.

His gaze followed her when she left the refectory, and he forced his attention back to his work. 'Twas a challenge, overcoming his lust, especially when Lucy was so appealing in her innocence, her artlessness.

She could not have been more different from Isabella. Alex sat down on one of his new benches and thought of his wife, of her dark hair and teasing eyes, and remembered the way she used to manipulate him, used to entice him to her will with her feminine wiles.

'Twas something Lucy would never do. She was of a more honest and straightforward nature.

He heard a door close in the distance and realized that she must have gone out. A quick glance at the window told him that dusk had fallen. Lucy had probably gone out to get fresh water to use for their supper.

He folded his hands and bowed his head, and prayed yet again for the strength he needed to resist her charms. She was as worthy as any woman he'd known, and Alex had no doubt that she would freely give him what he craved most.

The grief that had driven him for years had strangely abated in the days since he'd been at Holywake, and he'd not found himself seeking solace so often in prayer. But his plans hadn't changed.

After Lucy had been gone for quite some time, Alex began to wonder what was keeping her. He lay down his tools and went to the kitchen, thinking that perhaps he had not heard her return, but she was not there. Concerned that something was amiss, he strapped on his sword belt and went out to find her.

The path to the river was not long. 'Twas overgrown with branches and weeds and Alex intended to trim them before he left. Sunlight was fading fast, and he hurried toward the riverbank before it became fully dark. There was no worry about her falling in and being carried away, because the river was much too shallow here. But—

A low-pitched sound stopped him in his tracks.

Whether 'twas a man's voice or something else, Alex could not say. But he felt a new urgency to get

Play the Lucky Hearts Game

and get...
2 FREE BOOKS
and a FREE MYSTERY GIFT...

yes! YOURS to KEEP!

I have scratched off the silver card. Please send me my *2 FREE BOOKS* and *FREE mystery GIFT*. I understand that I am under no obligation to purchase any books as explained on the back of this card.

Scratch Here!
then look below to see what your cards get you... 2 Free Books & a Free Mystery Gift!

349 HDL DU63   **246 HDL DU7K**

FIRST NAME   LAST NAME

ADDRESS

APT.#   CITY

STATE/PROV.   ZIP/POSTAL CODE   (H-H-08/03)

Twenty-one gets you
2 FREE BOOKS
and a **FREE MYSTERY GIFT!**

Twenty gets you
2 FREE BOOKS!

Nineteen gets you
1 FREE BOOK!

TRY AGAIN!

Offer limited to one per household and not valid to current Harlequin Historicals® subscribers. All orders subject to approval.

® and ™ are trademarks owned by Harlequin Enterprises Ltd.

DETACH AND MAIL CARD TODAY!

The Harlequin Reader Service® — Here's how it works:

Accepting your 2 free books and mystery gift places you under no obligation to buy anything. You may keep the books and gift and return the shipping statement marked "cancel." If you do not cancel, about a month later we'll send you 6 additional books and bill you just $4.47 each in the U.S., or $4.99 each in Canada, plus 25¢ shipping & handling per book and applicable taxes if any.* That's the complete price and — compared to cover prices of $5.25 each in the U.S. and $6.25 each in Canada — it's quite a bargain! You may cancel at any time, but if you choose to continue, every month we'll send you 6 more books, which you may either purchase at the discount price or return to us and cancel your subscription.

*Terms and prices subject to change without notice. Sales tax applicable in N.Y. Canadian residents will be charged applicable provincial taxes and GST. Credit or debit balances in a customer's account(s) may be offset by any other outstanding balance owed by or to the customer.

BUSINESS REPLY MAIL
FIRST-CLASS MAIL   PERMIT NO. 717-003   BUFFALO, NY

POSTAGE WILL BE PAID BY ADDRESSEE

HARLEQUIN READER SERVICE
3010 WALDEN AVE
PO BOX 1867
BUFFALO NY 14240-9952

NO POSTAGE
NECESSARY
IF MAILED
IN THE
UNITED STATES

to Lucy. In absolute silence, he crouched and drew his sword, then inched toward her.

Lucy stood in the river, some distance from the bank. The water swirled around her skirts, but she managed to keep her balance on the rocky bottom. She held the wooden bucket in front of her chest like a shield against the threat of a ragged and wounded gray wolf that stood snarling on the bank.

In the near darkness, Alex could see that the wolf had been injured, probably in a fight. His coat was ragged. One ear was torn and he had a gash in one shoulder. He was so thin that he was probably starving, though Alex would not like to have to test the animal's strength. The wolf had been large in his prime, and his wound had likely made him vicious.

Alex said a silent prayer thanking God that Lucy had had the presence of mind to remain where she was, and to use the bucket as a weapon or a shield, as the case might be. In the meantime, he crept closer. By God's grace, he would be able to kill the wolf before it lunged.

The animal moved slightly, his muscles tensed in a stalking position. Alex prayed that Lucy would not move before he could get to her, or the wolf would give chase.

He moved closer, taking care to remain perfectly quiet, though the wolf's low growl chilled his blood. The animal was poised to leap at Lucy and though Alex could see fear on her face, 'twas clear that she was ready to fight for her life.

The beast snarled and leapt. Alex moved at the same time, reaching Lucy just as the animal attacked.

The wolf knocked Lucy down into the icy water. She screamed and protected herself from its jaws with the bucket, and Alex speared it with his sword. It yelped in agony and he speared it again to be certain of its death.

Quickly sheathing his sword, Alex pushed the carcass off Lucy and lifted her into his arms. 'Twas only a few steps to the riverbank, but he carried her all the way up the path and did not stop until they'd reached the back wing of the abbey. He kicked open the door and stepped inside, then shoved the door closed again.

Only then did he loosen his hold upon her and let her slide to the floor.

Soaked and shaking, she held on to him, needing his warmth…and his comfort. Her head fit neatly under his chin, and he ran his hands across her back, pressing her ever closer.

"You must now…be accustomed…" she said, her voice small and tremulous, "to dealing with all m-my mishaps, Sir Alex." She started to move away, but he kept her in his arms in spite of her attempt at levity.

He was *not* accustomed to her all too frequent brushes with death, nor was he ready to part with her just yet. No doubt she should change into her dry gown, but he had to hold her now, had to feel her body alive with breath and the chill of the river upon her skin.

"I was so frightened," she murmured in a quavering voice.

He touched the crown of her head with his lips and closed his eyes, feeling her heart beat against him.

She sighed and he pressed his mouth against her forehead, then her temple. "Lucy," he breathed, just before tasting her lips.

They were cool and soft, and he barely restrained himself from devouring them.

Alex heard her whimper, then felt her arms tighten around him. Needing no further urging, he pressed his lips against hers, tipping his head to increase the contact.

His blood boiled with need. He opened his mouth slightly and deepened the kiss, sipping, tasting her sweetness.

Needing no prompting, Lucy pressed against his length, slid her hands up his chest, then farther, cupping the sides of his face. She opened to his kiss, and he sucked her tongue into his mouth.

No longer did she feel cold to him. He breathed in her heat while he seduced her mouth, first suckling, then thrusting, imitating what he would do when they were both naked, both writhing with pleasure in the warm cocoon of the kitchen.

He broke the kiss long enough to lower her to the blanket that lay on the floor before the fire. His own passion was reflected in her eyes when she reached for him, pulling him over her, positioning her body to accommodate his.

"You are so beautiful." He dipped his head and

caught her lips again, and drowned in the sensations caused by her touch.

She slid her fingers through his hair, then down to his jaw, his neck, his chest. Her hands encircled the muscles of his arms and he felt her breasts rise against his chest in a sigh. Alex unfastened her wet laces and opened her bodice.

Her breasts spilled free, and he trailed kisses down her throat and licked the little brown mole that had tantalized him so. Then he moved down to one cool, rosy nipple. When he sucked it into his mouth, her breath caught in her throat. She cupped his head in her hands.

Alex could not imagine a more responsive woman. She nearly came out of her skin when he touched her, and her reactions only inflamed him more.

"Lucy." She was a fever in his blood, a tempest in his mind. He closed his eyes and shuddered with his burning arousal. Pure instinct drove him now. He was male, she was female, and he wanted her with greater urgency than he wanted his next breath.

Until a chilling howl penetrated his hazy consciousness. A wolf—a pack of wolves howled— somewhere outside their door.

Alex came to his senses abruptly. He could not remember if he'd secured the door when he'd carried Lucy inside. Though he was still intensely aroused, he pushed himself up on his hands and reached for his sword. Lucy sat up and tried to pull the blanket around her.

"Is it wolves?"

He barred the door and nodded. "They probably found their brother in the river," he said. "I'm going to go check the barn to be sure Rusa is safe."

Lucy grabbed his arm. "But—"

"'Tis unlikely they'll come close to the abbey," he said. "Stay inside."

A faint light shone through the cracks in the barn door. Lucy could see it through the window of the refectory, so she knew Alex was still safe inside. With his horse.

She'd waited more than an hour for him to return, pacing the length of the kitchen, then doing the same in the refectory. Waiting expectantly, yearning for him, for his kiss, his touch.

But she'd finally faced the fact that he had no intention of returning. If anything, he wanted to avoid her.

Naught had changed since he'd first stumbled upon her over a week before. He'd accompanied her reluctantly, and even been stuck here at Holywake with her—due more to chivalry than affection, she was sure. No knight in Christendom would have left a lame woman to complete these tasks alone.

She wiped away her tears and slipped out of her wet clothes. After putting on her dry gown she spread her wet things out to dry. A while later, she curled up in her blanket by the fire and felt more alone than ever before.

Alex was a free man. He had not yet made his monastic vows, so he was free to choose. But he had not chosen her. He'd had a family already…a wife, a child. Lucy could not imagine the pain of his loss, but 'twas clear no one would ever be able to take his family's place in his heart.

He would spend the night in the barn to keep himself from doing anything that would tie Lucy to him. Though she wished she could believe 'twas sheer piety that kept him from her, she knew better. When the intensity of the moment had passed, he'd regretted his actions. And in the morning, Lucy had no doubt that Alex would throw his saddle packs upon his horse's back, and take his leave. He might even bid her an awkward farewell.

Lucy could not fault him for having done what was right. Her virginity was not something to be taken lightly, yet she had not given it a moment's thought once he'd kissed her. The feelings were exactly as Elsbeth had described. Lucy had been lost in a fevered haze, wanting and needing naught but his hands and lips upon her.

But Alex had been the one to halt the lovemaking. According to Elsbeth, a man in the throes of passion could not stop. If he was truly enamored of the woman, 'twould be impossible for him to cease until he reached completion. Lucy swallowed hard, dejected by the realization that he must not have wanted her at all.

Presently Lucy dozed, but 'twas not a peaceful sleep. Her new bruises were painful and terrifying dreams assailed her. She ached for Alex and yearned for him to care for her.

When Lucy finally awoke, 'twas near dawn and she was still alone. She did not bother to build up the fire, but sat in the dark, chilly room gazing at the glowing embers and thinking about what to do.

She could not face Alex after what had happened. To have behaved like a harlot—holding him, urging him on, moaning in rapture... A heated blush rose from her chest to her face and she pressed her cool hands against her cheeks to relieve it.

Standing abruptly, she gathered her few belongings in the blanket and tied it into a bundle. There was no reason for her to stay at Holywake. The place was now habitable.

She found the money pouch. There was more than enough for a carpenter's services, if the abbess was able to find one when she arrived. Lucy kept a few pennies for herself, then set the pouch upon the hearth where Sir Alex would find it. He could either stay at Holywake and give it to the abbess himself, or keep it. He had earned it.

Lucy wiped her eyes and stepped out of the abbey. She could not go into the barn, could not bear to look upon Alex's countenance once before leaving. Nay. She would make it easy for him and take the decision out of his hands. Taking a steadying breath, she found the path that led to York, and started out upon it.

Chapter Twelve

Alex felt as if he'd drunk too much ale. His head ached and his body felt as tense as an archer's bow string. Sleep had eluded him for most of the night, and he'd battled fiercely against the urge to return to Lucy and finish what he'd started.

Beyond killing the wolf for Lucy, his actions the night before were shameful. He had succumbed to temptation of the worst sort—he'd given Lucy reason to believe he had tender feelings for her, even when he knew that would never be possible.

She was hardly more than a girl, naive and untutored in the ways of the world. 'Twas highly doubtful she would understand that he'd reacted in the heat of the moment. They'd faced a dangerous enemy together and survived without injury. He'd been exhilarated by the fear, then the kill, and finally by her courage and fortitude.

'Twas no wonder he'd nearly taken possession of her.

He put his hands together and bowed his head in

prayer, begging forgiveness for his transgression. By the time he said amen, he had a clear idea of what he had to do.

He packed what belongings he had in the barn and tied them to Rusa's saddle. Leading the mare into the dawn, he picked up the ladder and quietly placed it against the roof where he'd done repairs. The scabbard containing the Mandylion was hidden in a protected part of the eaves, where the black knights would never think to search.

Alex retrieved the precious relic, slid it into his belt and mounted the mare. He sat still for a few moments, debating whether he was doing the right thing. Leaving Lucy without a word... He did not think he could stand to look upon her face and know that he would never see it again.

He'd done that once before, with another woman....

Rusa snorted and tossed her mane, anxious to move. Alex gave one last look 'round, making certain that the wolves had gone, though he'd heard their howls fade in the distance sometime during the night. He saw no tracks, so he knew they had not come close to the buildings.

Once he knew the area was safe for Lucy, he kicked in his heels and started off at a trot. With his life unfettered, he would go directly to Eryngton and deliver the Mandylion to Roger's brother. Once his task was complete, he would ride south. There was no reason to delay his return to France. 'Twas important that he get back to Cluny and take his vows as soon as possible. The events of the previous night were proof of that. He needed the monastery, he needed the fasting and prayers, and the company of the monks to keep him from sin.

A fine mist covered the ground, but Rusa was sure-footed, and traveled the road without mishap. As the morning progressed, a light rain began to fall, and Alex was glad he'd repaired the abbey roof right away.

With his mind well occupied by thoughts of Lucy, he was surprised by the sight of a lone figure in the mist some distance ahead. He slowed Rusa to a walk and placed one hand upon the hilt of his sword while he glanced all 'round.

The mist was thick here, and 'twas difficult to see if there was more than just one rider, if indeed the man was on horseback. Alex approached cautiously, taking note of the woods that lay east of the road. As he weighed the risk of taking his horse into that unknown terrain, he saw something that gave him pause.

The person ahead of him was on foot, and had an unusual gait. The form was not that of a man, but a woman, and she'd covered her head with a dark-blue shawl against the mist.

Lucy!

She'd left him.

Alex stopped in his tracks and jabbed his fingers through his hair, praying silently for the strength to face her. Either she would realize he'd intended to abandon her...or she would think he'd come looking for her.

He groaned.

Turning back to avoid facing her was never an option, so Alex rode closer and dismounted, then caught up to her on foot. Though she kept her face forward and did not stop walking, he saw the muscles of her throat working as if something were caught there. Her face was moist, but so was the air. He did not like to think it was her tears, and he felt ashamed to know he'd driven her from the safety of the abbey.

Had it been the earlier intimacy or his later abandonment that had caused her to run away without speaking to him? Alex was fairly certain of the answer, and something twisted in his chest when she licked her lips and shifted her bundle.

"Might I carry that for you?" His voice sounded odd in the mist.

She shook her head and kept walking.

Lucy would feel much better if he would just mount his horse and ride away. He had to get the Mandylion delivered safely to his Yorkish earl, and it had naught to do with her. She'd resigned herself to losing him, and she could only hold back for a few minutes more before she succumbed to her tears and begged him to take her with him.

She swallowed thickly and resolved to do no such thing. She would manage on her own. Life in The World was much more complicated and difficult than Lucy had ever imagined, but she would somehow find her place in it. Sadness and disappointment were all

part of it. She could not dwell upon her foolishness
of the night before.

Alex walked slightly behind, leading his horse.
'Twas late for him to worry about her. She might have
been eaten by wolves last night for all he knew. Or
cared.

Lucy would not allow him to see how much it hurt
to know she meant so little to him. Yet he had never
lied to her. She'd known his intentions from the first.

But things had changed between them in recent
days.

"'Tis a long distance to York," he said. "Another
hour at least, on foot."

Unsure of the steadiness of her voice, she did not
reply. She moved the bundled blanket with all her
possessions to her other shoulder and readjusted her
shawl, surreptitiously wiping away one foolish tear
that had escaped her resolve.

"Lucy, I—"

"Please, Alex," she said as steadily as possible. "I
understand that your commitments lay elsewhere, and
I thank you for all your assistance—"

He took her pack from her in spite of her protests,
and threw it upon his horse's back. Suddenly, he had
her in his arms and was lifting her up, too. She landed
on Rusa's back and felt him mount behind her.

The warmth of his body flowed into her chilled
bones, but Lucy resisted becoming too comfortable in
his arms. Since she was weary and knew she would
soon need to rest, she did not object to the ride. But
when they reached the city gate, Lucy was determined

to walk through it on her own, without Sir Alexander Breton's escort.

Fortunately, he did not speak as they rode, nor did Lucy. They just braved the rain, which worsened as they approached the city. She did not want to lean into him, but found that the only way to avoid shivering was to let him warm her.

Alex slipped one arm around her middle and pulled her closer. Lucy's eyes slid closed with the sheer pleasure of it, but she quickly jerked herself out of her absurd contentment.

"You risked walking out among the wolves when you left this morn," Alex finally said.

"I heard their howls fade in the night," she replied. She'd known exactly when they'd run off, having been awake most of the night. "Is that the wall of the city?" she asked.

"Mmm." Lucy felt his affirmation as much as she heard it.

"You can let me down now." She leaned away from him and braced herself against the cold.

"But there is still some distance to go."

"Sir Alex," she said without turning to look at him, "please let me down. You have your own journey to follow, as I have mine."

"Lucy—"

"Nay, do not argue." She forced herself to speak lightly. As if it did not matter that she had no choice but to leave him. "We must part now. I am firm on this."

"What reason—"

Turning now to face him, she said, "There is naught between us. 'Tis time to go our separate ways!"

And if she did not leave him now, she did not know if she ever could. She grabbed the edge of his saddle and started to lower herself from the horse, but Alex reached the ground first and helped her down.

"At least let me help you find a room," he said gruffly. Lucy could see that he was perplexed by her demand to be left alone, perhaps nearly as much as she was.

She pulled her rolled-up blanket off Rusa's back and held it between them. "Nay," she whispered.

With her dignity miraculously intact, she turned and walked away, as gracefully as her limp would allow. And prayed that he would not follow.

She was adamant, so Alex complied with her wishes, although he was not pleased to do so. He stayed back and waited until she'd entered through Mickelgate Bar before following her into the city.

Clouds remained overhead, hanging low and threatening, but the rain finally subsided. From a distance at the far end of the lane, Alex watched a bedraggled Lucy walk from shop to shop, looking more and more dejected each time she exited one. 'Twas clear she was having little success finding gainful employment.

He had no doubt that she would find something eventually, and Alex intended to remain in York only long enough to see that she was settled. Within two days, he could be on his way to Cluny.

'Twas odd that the prospect of returning to the monastery did not hold the same appeal that it had only a month before…only a fortnight before. He refused to believe his change in attitude had anything to do with Lucy. 'Twas more likely due to his proximity to Clyfton and the manor where he'd lived with Isabella. Thoughts of returning home, of seeing Philip and Beatrice…

Alex frowned. When had his mind been freed of constant thoughts of Isabella and life as it once had been? And how had he become so neglectful of his prayers?

'Twas wrong and he would remedy it as soon as he left York and Lucy's welfare no longer preyed upon his mind. That was all it was…with Lucy, there was always some disaster looming, something from which Alex would have to rescue her. Soon none of that would be his problem, and his life could return to what it was…hours following minutes of quiet meditation. Years of prayer and penance for the benefit of his beloved family.

Alex realized that Lucy had been in the weaver's shop for some time. He supposed 'twas possible the man had hired her to spin wool or to card it, and there was no reason for him to remain there, watching to see that she was all right. The shop had an upper floor and she might even be given a room.

So all was well. He could leave.

He took Rusa's reins and started to lead the mare away, but could not keep from stopping before he got to the end of the lane. Turning to look back at the shop, he could see no one inside. Naught was amiss, though. Lucy was doing what she'd intended from the first. She was making a life for herself outside the nunnery, and he said a silent prayer of thanks that she'd found what she was looking for.

Mayhap in time, some young man would offer to wed her. Lucy was far too passionate a woman to remain confined behind convent walls. She should become a wife and bear children—a good number of them—and raise them with all the delight and joy he'd seen in her eyes when she'd held the mummer's infant.

Alex swallowed and turned to go toward the northern end of the city. If he left York now, he'd be able to travel several hours before night fell.

He had gone quite a distance when a brightly painted sign showing two crossed swords below the image of a man caught Alex's attention. The savory aroma of cooked meat emanated from the building and he realized he was hungry. He stepped inside.

Saint George's Inn was a hostelry with several rooms abovestairs, as well as a courtyard and stable. Alex sat down in the crowded main room and ordered a meal, and decided to take a room for a day or two, until he'd decided what to do about Skelton's men.

'Twas possible, too, that he would run across Lucy one last time before he left for Eryngton.

Chapter Thirteen

"Come away from that spindle, girl," Giles Falk croaked ominously. He sniffed and wiped the back of his arm across his nose.

Lucy would never have taken this position if there'd been any other choice. But she'd had no luck in finding employment anywhere else in York. Master Falk had not only promised to pay her in coin, but to provide her board, and a small chamber with a cot, besides.

But the weaver was a one-eyed man with a temper. A bad temper. And he kept his one good eye upon her in a manner that made her distinctly uncomfortable. She found herself dreading the moment she would be left alone with him when it became fully dark.

Suppressing yet another shudder, she looked up at him.

"Yes, Master Falk?" she asked respectfully. He was hovering over her now and if she stood up to move away, he would be unpleasantly close. Already, he'd managed to touch her shoulder, her bottom and the side of her breast *inadvertently*. She was going to have to move adroitly to avoid anything more, and that was a difficult task with her lame leg causing her to move awkwardly.

The man's hair was long and hung untidily over his shoulders, and smelled of mutton grease. As a weaver, his clothes were stylish, she supposed, and of good quality wool. But the skin of his hands and neck was marred by ugly, dark red cankers—she had never seen anything like it before.

"You can make me my supper," he said, barely moving away so that she could stand.

Lucy swallowed hard and scooted away from him. His good eye, so black she could see the reflection of the candles in it, followed her as she moved toward the fire at the back of the shop. Her skin crawled when she thought about spending another hour here in this man's company.

But what else could she do?

Why had she been so stubborn about allowing Alex to help her? It had been foolish to send him away when he'd so clearly wanted to stay and see her suitably situated. Or mayhap he hadn't exactly *wanted* to stay, but felt responsible for her.

By now, he was well away from York.

Glad to have a moment away from Giles Falk's leering scrutiny, Lucy stoked the cookfire and found the man's food stores. 'Twas a meager collection of moldy cheese, some beans and a heel of bread. The combination turned Lucy's stomach, and she knew she would not be joining the weaver in his meal.

She poured water into a pot and added the beans, then began to sweep the floor with a broom she'd found standing in a corner. The place was a mess—mayhap worse than Holywake.

After one afternoon spinning wool, Lucy's hands were raw. She wished she had some of Alex's ointment to soothe them, but knew she would have to make due without it. Somehow, she would manage.

The beans started to boil, and she moved the pot out of the fire so they wouldn't burn. As she did so, the weaver stepped up behind her, startling her so that she nearly dropped the pot.

"I'll want butter for my bread," he said, throwing Lucy into turmoil. She had not seen any butter when she'd looked through his stores. "Go down to the baker's shop," he said, tipping his head toward the door at the back. As was his way, he stood too close to her. "Find his wife. Berta. She's most often in the back of the shop, and give her this," he said, placing a red silk ribbon in her hand.

Lucy shuddered at the gleam in the weaver's eye. He reminded her of a cat that had just caught a mouse and was playing with it before killing it. But she didn't know if she were the mouse, or if 'twas the baker's wife.

"Comely, was she not?"

Lucy set a plate of beans and cheese on the table before the weaver. "Who?"

"The baker's wife!" By his tone 'twas apparent he thought her a dim-witted dolt. But Lucy had not taken note of the woman's appearance. She'd been dumbfounded by the wife's cloying, secretive manner when she spoke of the weaver. 'Twas as if...Elsbeth had told her about trysts between men and the wives of other men. Elsbeth herself had admitted to such illicit behavior, which was the reason she'd been banished to Craghaven in the first place.

"Aye, she is a beauty." The master's red spots seemed to pulse in the candlelight, and Lucy averted her gaze from the appalling sight.

Falk narrowed his good eye into a gaze that made her skin crawl. Lucy stepped away from the table. "Sit here and eat with me."

"Nay, I am not hungry," she said. She picked up the broom again for something to do, some way to mask her unease. "I'll just clean up when you're finished and retire to my chamber."

"Your chamber?" He laughed. "You'll have a pallet under my workbench and be thankful for it!"

"Aye," Lucy replied in a whisper. "I will." He'd promised her food and a room of her own.

Lucy rued her naiveté. Here she was with food—which was entirely unpalatable, and a room—space on the dusty, cold floor of the workroom. No doubt his promise of coin for work was exactly the same.

At first light, she would leave the shop and look for some other employment. She'd been too tired, too wet and uncomfortable to do an adequate job of it today.

Her best plan had come to her when she was walking back from the baker's shop. When she left the weaver, she would find a nearby church and ask the priest for help. Surely he would know what households and shops were respectable, for clearly, Master Falk's was not. He seemed to be engaged in some sort of flirtation with the baker's wife, though Lucy did not understand exactly what part she was to play in their game.

All of it made her feel sick inside, from the moment she'd walked away from Alex, until now, watching Master Falk wipe his nose once again, upon his sleeve.

She shuddered and continued to sweep.

"Take that broom up front and make use of it there, girl," he commanded, and Lucy did as she was told. Every surface was dusty and there were small snips of thread on the floor beneath the two looms. Lucy did not think anyone had ever swept beneath the workbench—the place where she was expected to sleep.

She dislodged several spiders from their webs and cleaned out the space, wondering what she was to use as a pallet, for she had not seen anything vaguely resembling a mattress or bed. It did not matter. Lucy had long since realized she would not be able to sleep easily in Falk's shop, no matter what the accommodations. 'Twas likely she would sit up all night, wrapped in her blanket, awaiting daybreak.

A soft sigh escaped Lucy's lips. There had been a deep hole in her heart ever since she'd taken her leave of Alex. When a well of tears threatened to spill from her eyes, she brushed them away. She missed him desperately. But no matter how intensely she loved Alexander Breton, he was gone. She would never see him ag—

A shove from behind knocked the air out of her and she fell to her knees.

"Ha!"

A heavy weight fell upon her, and she hit her chin on the floor. She gasped for air and cried out.

"Master Falk!" He managed to pin her arms behind her so that the only way to struggle away from him was with her legs. 'Twas ridiculously ineffective against the man's weight and strength.

Still, she tried with all her might to get away.

He grabbed her hair close, at the roots, then pressed his knee into her back. Tears came to her eyes with the added pain.

"Let me go," Lucy demanded.

He laughed aloud and grabbed her skirt. Lucy heard the fabric tear and she became even more alarmed. "Not until I've gotten—"

With a massive effort, Lucy shifted position, knocking Falk to the side. One of her hands came free and she took hold of the table leg and began to kick more effectively now.

"For a cripple," he snarled, "you put up a good fight. Wait until Berta sees how you— Ahh…" Using one hand to hold her two, he got his free hand under her dress and slid it up her bare legs.

Lucy yelped and twisted away from his groping,

though her only hope was to get her hands free so that she could push herself to her feet. Once she was standing, she would have a fighting chance against him, but she was having little effect against him while he was lying on top of her.

With both her hands, she pulled his bare arm close to her face. While he was distracted with pulling at her gown, Lucy sank her teeth into his arm and bit down as hard as she could, taking as much flesh as would fit in her mouth.

The weaver roared in pain and released her long enough for her to scoot away and get on to her knees. As he yelled with pain, Lucy felt some primitive satisfaction at the blood running down his arm. She'd taken a goodly chunk from him.

He started to come after her again. The broom was beside her, and Lucy picked it up to use it as a crutch to help her up. The weaver reached her before she'd gained her feet, and started to grab for her again.

On her knees, she swung the broom, using all her strength to hit him in the knees.

"Ye bloodthirsty wench!" he yelled, lifting his arms to protect himself from her blows. "I won't be making it easy fer ye now!"

Lucy felt an irrational bubble of laughter rise in her chest. *Easy?* She had not been able to get off her knees, and he was limping toward her. She swung again and he almost caught the broom in his hand. Quickly, she jabbed with the broom handle, and speared him in the belly.

This slowed him, and while he was doubled over,

she managed to get up on her feet. She did not waste a second, but hobbled over to the corner where her belongings remained in their blanket bundle, and picked it up.

Falk grabbed her hair while she was turned, but Lucy spun around and thumped him hard against his head with the broom handle. He released her to grab his wound, and Lucy hastened for the door before he could do anything else to her.

'Twas dark outside and she did not know where to go, but there could be no doubt that anywhere else was better than remaining at the weaver's. She hurried down the lane, glancing behind her frequently, to see if he followed.

She caught sight of a sudden movement and knew she would have to get off the street. But there was nowhere to go, no signs of life anywhere. Every shop was dark.

With no choice but to keep going, Lucy slipped into a narrow break between two buildings. She made her way down the passage as quickly as possible, aware that Falk would discover it and close in on her.

When she got to the end, she found a place to conceal herself. Crouching, she made herself as small as possible and covered her head with her dark bundle. She hoped that by dropping out of sight, he would be thwarted.

Finally, her breathing settled to a normal rate, but her shivering seemed uncontrollable. Why had she insisted on leaving Alex? The weaver could beat her, or even kill her, and no one would ever know. She sat in the silence of the night and prayed that Giles Falk would go on past her. If he did, then she would leave this spot and walk as far as possible from his miserable little shop.

Chapter Fourteen

Alex broke his fast in the same room where he'd had his supper, though the men present that morn were unconscious—incapacitated by their revels of the night before. He ate and went out, leaving Rusa in the stable while he walked in the direction of the weaver's shop.

When he reached the shop where he'd last seen Lucy, he stood on the opposite side of the lane, hoping to see her through the front window pane. When he saw no one and no sign of life, he began to pace back and forth.

Finally, he crossed the road and tried the door.

'Twas locked.

He pounded on the door and waited impatiently for someone to answer. When no one did, he pounded again, then stood with his feet braced apart, his hands upon his hips.

If she was not here, then where…

Too anxious to wait any longer, he put his shoulder to the wood and shoved hard. The lock easily gave way, and Alex was suddenly standing inside the weaver's shop, looking at the startled face of the one-eyed man.

"What do ye want?" he croaked.

He appeared ill. The red welts on the man's neck were more angry-looking than when Alex had first come to the shop, and the man had a dark, purple bruise upon his forehead.

"The woman who came here yesterday, looking for employment," Alex said, perusing every corner of the weaver's workroom. "Where is she?"

The man moaned. "Gone."

"Explain yourself." Alex's worry turned to anger, and he put one hand on the hilt of his sword. "She stayed here with you, did she not?"

"Attacked me in my bed, she did," the weaver moaned, putting one hand to the side of his head. "Vicious—"

"You lie!" Alex took the man by the throat and shoved him up against a workbench. "The woman is a nun and incapable of hurting—"

"Bashed me...on the head..." he rasped. "Ran off...in the night."

With ease, Alex tossed the man to the floor. It took all his restraint to keep from drawing his sword and running the man through when he considered what must have transpired to make Lucy run away.

If this malt-worm had violated her...

'Twas only by the grace of God that he managed to keep his sword in its sheath and turn away. Alex stepped outside, wondering how far Lucy would have

gone last night, and where she might be now. With
absolutely no clues to go on, he started walking.

Lucy had been put right to work, doing laundry.
The inn where she was now employed had fourteen
beds, and seven of them needed their linens washed.
When she was through with that task, she'd been
given other menial chores, but Lucy did not mind
them. This was all work she knew, though she was
not particularly fond of it.

The man who owned Saint George's Inn was gruff
and unfriendly, and his wife was even worse. They'd
had no help at the inn since both their daughters had
drowned during the summer, and they were bitter and
short-tempered with her. It seemed to Lucy that they
were angry with her for being alive when their own
girls were gone.

And Lucy knew she could easily have met the same
fate as the two girls, if not for Alex. Since meeting
him, he'd saved her from one disaster after another,
and she knew she needed to take care now. He was
nowhere near York and she could not rely upon him
to rescue her again.

Still, no matter how unkind she found the innkeeper and his wife, they did not attempt to rip her
clothes off her, or abuse her in any other way. At
Saint George's, she had food and a place to stay, and
all they expected was a good day's work from her.
Lucy was weary from lack of sleep the past two days,
and she missed Alex unbearably. But she would manage to get through the evening. Her last task was to

help Maude serve the patrons in the tavern until Alf closed up for the night.

She hoped it would be early.

Saint George's Inn was very different from the small country inns where Lucy had stayed with Elsbeth and the nuns on their journey from Craghaven. Elsbeth had complained of them, but Lucy had found most to be comfortable. None of those inns had had taverns—there had been only a common room where travelers could get a simple meal. At Saint George's, the visitors came and went, and so many stayed until finally there were no seats to be had.

They drank copious amounts of ale and sang bawdy songs while musicians played. It all seemed very jovial until the room became overwarm and crowded with men. Lucy could hardly move past them with her tray of drinks without stumbling into one or another.

And they encouraged it, laughing uproariously when she lost her balance and stumbled, sometimes falling into one of them.

She quickly discovered that the jostling was intentional. But she gritted her teeth and learned to dodge past their groping hands, grateful that at least these were impersonal hands, and generally harmless.

Maude came out from the kitchen with a large platter laden with food. She caught Lucy's attention and shouted above the din in the room. "Take this to the burly light-haired fellow by the window. And give a care, cripple—do not spill it." The woman passed the heavy platter to Lucy over the heads of the men at the nearest table. ''Be quick about it!''

Lucy took it in one hand and balanced her pitcher of ale in the other. She looked at the tables before her, the unruly men jesting and singing…'twas so different from the neat aisles of the refectory at Craghaven and the clean faces of the nuns she'd known most of her life. Lucy began to doubt she was made for this kind of work.

The noise and confusion in the tavern made her dizzy and she wondered again how she could have erred so badly in the first two days she'd spent on her own. Mayhap she should have remained at Holywake and awaited the abbess. Surely that would have been a safer course, for she knew what was expected of her there, and none of the nuns had ever willingly harmed her.

A hand shot out as she made her way through the crowd and pinched her breast. Lucy yelped and dropped the clay pitcher, which shattered. Ale splashed everywhere as men jumped out of their seats. The platter flew out of Lucy's hand and the burly man who had ordered the meal grabbed her wrist and yanked her off her feet.

''Ye damned froward giglet!'' he thundered. '''Twas *my* mutton ye spilled!''

Worried and discouraged, Alex shoved open the door of Saint George's tavern and nearly turned around to leave again. The place was as boisterous and as full of fools as it had been the night before. Nay, 'twas even more so.

A fierce brawl had broken out and fists were swinging in every direction. The fight seemed to be centered on the far side of the room, near one of the dingy windows. And in Alex's present mood, he was just ripe for a fight.

He'd had no luck finding Lucy, though he'd gone up and down most every street of the city, and questioned every shop owner and tradesman he could find. One or two had seen her, but had not paid any attention when she'd left. They could not tell Alex where she'd gone.

As he pushed his way through the crowd, Alex hoped that one of these blockheads would throw a punch his way. He'd never been more ready to crack some heads.

The innkeeper tried to break things up, but was having little success on the fringes of the fight. The brawlers merely tossed him aside.

Alex searched the periphery, and then the crowd, for the innkeeper's wife, but he did not see her. And he began to suspect the woman had gotten caught in the thick of it.

Using his size and strength to push through the crowd, Alex took great satisfaction in wrestling and battling the men who crossed his path.

Finally he reached a brawny, light-haired fellow, bent over the struggling woman in a crimson gown. Alex grabbed the man by his collar and yanked him away.

"*Alex!*" the woman cried.

His heart twisted painfully. God in heaven, 'twas Lucy!

And as he stood gaping at her, the big fellow threw his fist and caught Alex on the jaw. Lucy screamed and scooted away, straightening her torn clothes as she moved. Alex turned into the fight, pummeling the man who thought he could violate Lucy with impunity. But before he could murder her assailant, several of the men pulled him off. The music stopped as Lucy threw herself at him, weeping.

He closed his arms around her and led her from the fray. As soon as they were away from the crowd, Alex guided her to the staircase. Keeping hold of her, he climbed the steps and did not stop until he reached his room.

'Twas cold and dark inside, but Alex did not leave Lucy to start a fire, but sat on a chair by the bed and pulled her onto his lap. It seemed that she would never stop trembling, and Alex felt somewhat unsteady himself. They did not speak, but as he tucked Lucy into his embrace, his heart pounded heavily in his chest.

He'd searched for her all day, and now that he found her, he did not know what he would do with her.

With Lucy's penchant for finding trouble, Alex could not leave her alone. At least, not until he'd helped her find an appropriate method to support herself. It might delay him for another day or so, but after his months of travel, such a short span of time did not seem to matter. He'd hidden the Mandylion well, and if the black knights came to York, they would not find it.

Nor would they find him. 'Twas doubtful they would even recognize him with his shaved beard and the new tunic he wore.

He rested his chin on the top of her head and held her while her sobs subsided. It had been a long couple of days and Alex doubted Lucy had slept much—if at all—the night before. She'd been on the run from the one-eyed maggot who'd tried to molest her.

"Tell me, Lucy...what did you do to the weaver?"

"What did I do to *him?*" she asked, wondering how he knew about the weaver.

She felt his throat move as he swallowed thickly and pulled her closer.

"Nay," he whispered. "Do not tell me, for I may have to kill him."

Lucy saw the tradesman's face in her mind, felt the grasp of his strong hands holding her down, and she shuddered. His ill treatment was much worse than the incident that had just occurred in the tavern, though she was more than grateful for Alex's timely arrival just now.

"I did not know where to go last night when I ran from the weaver," she said quietly. "I walked for a long time... Did you know there are watchmen who walk the streets at night?"

"Aye." His voice was low and warm. Reassuring. She felt him stroke her hip where he held her.

"I stayed out of sight as much as I could, but there

was nowhere to go...." She could not make her voice any louder than a whisper. "I was afraid...."

A sound from somewhere deep in his chest rumbled through her.

"The weaver did not f-follow me very far." She curled into him even more if that were possible. "I think I m-must have hurt him when I hit him with the b-broom. And I think he was w-waiting for someone else to come...."

She stopped speaking when tears threatened again, and her voice failed her. She did not want to think what might have happened if the baker's wife had come to help him with whatever debased act he had planned.

The hours since leaving Holywake swirled together in Lucy's mind like a terrible dream. And the nightmare ended only when Alexander intruded upon it. She did not know how he happened to arrive at the inn when he did, but she was grateful, and would allow herself a few moments of comfort in his arms.

The heat from Alex's body seeped through Lucy's skin and finally deep into her bones. She felt weightless and free in his arms, on his lap, and wished he would never let her go.

Never in her life had she been so glad to see anyone as when Alex rescued her in the tavern.

'Twas not only because he'd saved her from being assaulted by the drunken townsman, but because she'd missed him more than she ever could have imagined.

* * *

It seemed far too natural to hold Lucy in his arms, to comfort her. But Alex could not stay with her indefinitely and keep her from harm. There had to be some wholesome and reputable place in York where she could remain and earn her keep while she stayed out of trouble.

Unfortunately, Alex did not want to leave her.

He could not put off the inevitable any longer. He had to leave for Eryngton soon.

Without thinking, he rubbed Lucy's arms. She was much too cold, and still shivering. Her breathing was uneven, and Alex heard the occasional sniffle. Her weeping had not yet subsided.

The bastard in the tavern had torn her gown and bruised her throat. Or mayhap the weaver had done that. Either way, she'd experienced too much of the world's evils since her arrival in York, and Alex would prefer that she see no more of them.

He supposed he could take Lucy with him when he went to Eryngton. If he purchased another wagon and they rode together, any onlooker would assume they were man and wife. Skelton's men would not recognize him without his beard, nor would they associate him with a wife—or a woman of any kind. 'Twas likely they could ride right in front of the black knights, and the men would not know him.

Satisfied with his plan, he leaned back and relaxed in the chair, pulling Lucy close. Absently, he caressed her, he closed his eyes and nuzzled the hair at her crown, content now that he had her near. He would not leave her again until he was satisfied that she'd found a situation perfectly suited to her, something that placed her with a family, with children. She would make a fine nurse.

Or wife.

Her breathing settled down and when she finally slept, Alex allowed himself to doze. Sometime during the night, he carried Lucy to the bed and lay down, keeping her in his arms until morning.

Chapter Fifteen

Lucy awoke to a feeling of warmth and comfort that was entirely unfamiliar, especially of late. Pulling the warm quilt around her, she sat up in the bed and looked at her unfamiliar surroundings. Her heart sank when she realized that Alex was not there.

The windows were shuttered, so she could not tell how long she'd slept. A healthy fire blazed in the grate, and there was a tray on a table nearby, covered by a cloth. The rips that Giles Falk had torn in her blue kirtle had been mended, and it lay draped over a chair. The red one was nowhere to be seen.

'Twas with relief that Lucy's eyes alighted upon Alex's leather saddle packs, lying on the floor near the chamber door. He had not left her.

Giddy with relief, she threw off the bedcovers and got out of bed, only to discover several new bruises in addition to the ones she'd acquired at the weaver's. But the worst was a small lump at the back of her head, where she must have hit it the night before.

She stepped over to the window and opened the

shutters. Bright sunlight shone in and Lucy guessed
it must be near noon, if not already past. She was
hungry, but the fatigue that had plagued her the day
before was gone. The day was new, and Alex was
nearby.

It took but a moment to strip off her clothes, and
Lucy quickly washed with the water in the pitcher.
She dressed in the clean blue kirtle and was assessing
the damage to her head and hands when a quiet tap
at the door claimed her attention.

'Twas Alex.

"You're awake," he said when she opened the
door.

She nodded, feeling absurdly shy. He seemed ret-
icent, too, which made things much easier for her.
While she was asleep, he'd shaved and put on clothes
Lucy had never seen before. He wore a tunic of deep
green and trimmed in gold. A short cape in comple-
mentary colors was slung over his arm and he looked
like a prosperous nobleman.

"Have you broken your fast?" he asked, coming
into the room.

"Not yet," she replied. "I have not been awake
for long."

He nodded and his eyes lingered on hers a moment,
then skipped down to her shoulders and the rest of
her body before glancing toward the tray of food.
"You needed to sleep. How is your head?"

"Better, I think," she replied, catching her breath
when he ran his hand gently across the back of her

head. She would not mind if he pulled her to his chest and held her there until she felt steady once again.

"You need not worry about finding employment now." He stepped away and stood next to the chair where they'd sat together the night before.

Or had that just been a dream?

"I have a plan," he said. "Eat."

Alex had always struck her as a determined man, but there was something different about him now. 'Twas as if he'd settled himself somehow and was more certain of his task. Or mayhap the new clothes had made him seem different to her. Lucy took a bite of the bread on the tray and waited for him to explain what he intended.

"'Tis my task to get the Mandylion to safety," he said. "But the black knights will interfere, and steal it if they can."

She sat down on the bed and listened.

"They may not recognize me without my beard," he explained, "but they will surely not know me if I travel openly with a woman. With you posing as my wife, and—"

"As your…?" Lucy felt the blood drain from her head. She had never dared think of herself as Alex's wife, though being wed to him was her heart's deepest desire. To pretend such a thing… She swallowed and tried to ignore the fluttering in her chest. "Your w-wife?"

"Once the Mandylion is safely delivered—" he stood and faced the window, clasping his hands behind him ''—I will see that you find proper employment for a woman of your station.''

Tears clogged her throat. He could not have asked anything more difficult, but Lucy could not refuse him, no matter how much it would hurt when he finished his ploy and sent her on her way. And if 'twould give her another day or two with him, she would do it.

Her stomach churned and her appetite disappeared. And since there was no reason to linger, Lucy rolled up her blanket along with her few other belongings and tied the bundle neatly. He slipped her shawl about her shoulders and they walked together to the main floor of the inn. They did not go through the tavern, for which Lucy was grateful.

''Oh, Sir Alex!'' The innkeeper's wife encountered them near a door that led to the courtyard. She seemed breathless, as usual, and no friendlier to Lucy than she'd been before. She was more than civil to Alex, though. ''Alf fetched the wagon ye bought. He's just hitching it now to yer horse.''

Alex gave a curt thanks and led Lucy from the inn. They walked across the courtyard to the stable where the landlord was leading Alex's horse outside. The mare pulled a large wagon behind her.

Alf said naught, and by the sullen set of his face, Lucy surmised that his exchange with Alex had not been a pleasant one. In spite of that, Alex dropped a coin into the man's hand, then lifted Lucy onto the wagon. He dropped her bundle into the wagon bed, then climbed up after her. Sitting side by side, they set off.

With Alex next to her, she felt safe and protected. Naught could happen to her while he was there, other than having to suffer a bit of ridicule for being dressed like a beggar next to her fine knight. Though her sleeves had been reattached to the gown, and the tears had been patched, she and Alex could not have appeared more mismatched.

Lucy ignored the stares of the people they passed on the street, and without thinking, moved closer to Alex on the seat. She did not recognize the area of town in which they rode, but she had not seen much of York in daylight. She felt she'd covered all of it during the night when she'd run from Master Falk.

Alex stopped the wagon and jumped down. He tied Rusa, then came around and helped Lucy out of the wagon. He treated her as though her shabby attire meant naught to him, holding her by the waist as he lowered her to the ground. Lucy gazed up at him and when their eyes met, a heavy ache of yearning formed in her chest.

She did not know 'twas possible to care so deeply for another. His heart was clearly engaged elsewhere, but that did not seem to matter to Lucy's own heart. She loved him.

He found a boy to watch over his horse and the wagon, then took Lucy's arm and led her down the narrow lane full of shops.

''What is this place?'' she asked to take her mind off the flood of emotions coursing through her.

"The tailor's shop is down this way," he replied. "I stopped here earlier, while you slept, and made some arrangements."

The shop was very different from the one where Lucy had worked. 'Twas clean and orderly and smelled of cider and cinnamon. "Good day, good day, Sir Alex!" said a round little woman with bright red hair. "Is this your young lady?"

Lucy heard Alex clear his throat and mutter affirmatively.

"Well, come in, come in!" she said. "My brother is not yet returned, but we have all that you'll need. Hmm…she's a good bit smaller than my niece. Ah, 'tis no matter. We've got the means to alter the lot."

The woman's words puzzled Lucy, but when she felt Alex's hand at the small of her back, urging her forward, she went along without question. They walked into the workroom where two large tables were situated. Folded piles of colored cloth were stacked on shelves against one wall and three women sat at the tables sewing and chattering among themselves. At the other table, a man stood cutting fabric with a pair of shears. Lucy wondered if her gown had been mended here this morn.

"'Tis fortunate that my niece will not be wed until next month," the red-haired woman said to Alex as she poured a cup of cider for Lucy. "So we can replace these two gowns and all the rest of it well before she'll be needing them." She turned to Lucy. "Just go through there and take off your clothes."

Lucy did not move. Too much had happened of

late for her to follow instructions blindly and she could not fathom what was going on here. *"Wait."*

Everyone in the room became silent at her forceful command and she felt her face heat with the blush of embarrassment. She turned toward Alex. "May I have a moment?"

He did not hesitate, but went with her into the small chamber where she was supposed to have disrobed. When he turned to face Lucy, he was frowning. "What is amiss?"

"I don't understand what I'm to do here. Why must I…must I…"

"Remove your clothes?"

Embarrassed all over again, Lucy nodded. She well knew 'twas unseemly to speak of such things to Alex. Intimate matters were to be left between husband and wife, and Alex's wife was dead. The only wife Alex wanted now was a temporary one. A fake. A sham.

"'Tis a tailor's shop. They have some women's clothes that were made for another purpose," he explained, "that the tailor is willing to sell to us."

"But Alex—"

"I arranged it all earlier. You may break your fast, then let the woman fit you and we can be off."

There was no reason to argue. The only clothes in Lucy's possession were fit for a beggar's wife. She would never find suitable employment in such garb, so she accepted the new kirtles.

By late afternoon, the women in the workroom had altered two gowns and a warm, woolen cloak so that they fit Lucy. Alex paced impatiently as they worked, and even left the tailor's shop for a short time. Lucy did not know where he'd gone, but she was ready to leave when he returned.

Instead of the travel-worn, abused kirtles she'd worn since meeting him, Lucy was now fashionably dressed. Her gown was a very fine velvet of brilliant blue, with decorative trimmings in gold and a darker blue. Underneath it, Lucy wore a delicate silk chemise.

She had never worn anything so fine.

Once the final fittings had been done, the ladies in the shop amused themselves with Lucy's hair, putting it into braids and weaving it intricately about her head.

She was certain the mirror in the tailor's shop reflected some other woman within its glass. Though Lucy had rarely had occasion to look into a mirror, she could not recall a time when she'd looked—or felt—so feminine.

Never in her life had Lucy dressed for a man, and she was not quite sure that was what she'd done this time. But she was suddenly very glad that she would no longer appear to Alex as a ragged waif.

If only she could have cured her damnable limp as easily as her wardrobe had been corrected.

When Alex returned to the tailor's shop, Lucy found herself suddenly shy and hesitant to make her appearance in the anteroom. The tailor's sister was oblivious to Lucy's consternation, ushering her toward the entrance of the shop where Alex awaited her.

"Well then, Sir Alex," the proprietress said, "our task is complete and well done, wouldn't you say?"

Alex said naught, and Lucy began to feel as if something was out of place. Or mayhap she still looked like a stray waif dressed in finery that was far above her.

"Aye," he finally said. "Your task was well done."

His voice sounded strange, and Lucy did not know if he spoke the truth, or if he'd just given an expedient reply so they could leave right away. Expedience was the more likely explanation, since he'd barely given her a glance.

Alex paid the woman and took possession of her new cloak and a parcel that contained the other clothes that had been altered for her. He said naught to Lucy, but opened the door for her and took her arm to escort her to their wagon.

"One more stop and we'll be on our way," he said after mounting the wagon behind her. Lucy assumed he meant they'd be on their way to take the Mandylion to its destination, for that was the only reason Sir Alex was in England.

In silence, they rode through the streets until they reached a church with a walled cemetery beside it. Alex drove the wagon to the front and stopped. Jumping down, he quickly tied his horse, then helped Lucy down. He did not say what he was about, but walked up the stairs beside her, and went inside.

Alex kept his eyes straight ahead since he could barely breathe when he looked at Lucy.

She'd been lovely even in her disheveled and ill-fitting clothes, but now that she wore garments better suited to her form and her fair complexion, she was breathtaking. He'd devised the perfect plan for her future, but doubt entered his mind whenever he looked at her.

Alex walked up through the nave of the church he'd visited several times as a child, with Lucy right behind him. There were windows of colored glass in the tower over the altar, but 'twas getting late so the light did not shine through as it did when the sun was high. Still, Alex knew he would have no trouble finding the place where he'd hidden Roger's scabbard.

Fortunately, the church was empty. Alex did not want to encounter anyone who might remember him and speak of the knight who'd drawn a scabbard from a concealed place at this altar. He lit a candle and climbed the one step to the chancel.

"What are you about, Alex?" Lucy whispered. She did not follow him up, but remained behind, appearing ill at ease in the empty church.

Yet she looked as innocent and vulnerable as a bride, standing in the aisle before the altar. Alex could not imagine a more beautiful bride....

"My scabbard is hidden here," he said, certain she would understand what he meant. "Once I have it, we can leave York."

Many years before, during a visit to York, Alex and his brother had gotten into mischief while their father had met with the priest. 'Twas because of that foolishness that Alex knew the statues of Mary and

Joseph were hollow. He also knew that they were not terribly heavy. He approached Joseph and tipped the statue to one side, reaching underneath with his free hand. A moment later, he drew out Brother Roger's silver scabbard, containing the Mandylion.

Alex replaced the statue of Joseph and slid the scabbard into his belt.

"Halt, you thieving—"

Lucy gasped and Alex spun his body 'round to confront the intruder. He found himself facing the priest, dressed in a traveling cloak and carrying a satchel. The man held up a lamp, illuminating Alex's face.

"Alexander Breton, is it not?" the priest said at length.

Alex gave a quick nod. He recognized the priest, too. The man had been Clyfton's cleric for several years. At one time, they had known each other well.

"Father Massey."

"'Tis been a long time, lad," the priest said more gently.

Alex nodded. Father Massey had prayed over the graves of Isabella and Geoffrey. Alex had not seen him since then and wondered why he was here in York, and why he was dressed for travel.

Regardless of the answers to those questions, Alex could not regret this chance encounter with the priest. Father Massey had hardly aged in the past three years. His hair was the same sandy-brown color, although strands of white had appeared at his temples. The man's expression was one of kindness and tolerance and he looked much as he had when he'd presided over Alex's wedding.

And a strange thought came into Alex's mind when he remembered that day so many years ago.

"I would stay and speak of old times," Father Massey said. "But the master of Mannington Manor lies dying and I must go to him."

"I understand," Alex said. He'd noticed Lucy's sudden pallor, and he took her hand in his own to reassure her.

"We must be on our way soon, too," he said.

"In what direction do you travel? We might go together."

"North," Alex replied noncommittally. And he was suddenly in no hurry to arrive at Eryngton with the Mandylion. 'Twould mean his parting with Lucy for the last time.

"Last I heard, you'd gone to Cluny," Father Massey said quietly. "What brings you—and your lady—to York?"

Alex took Lucy's hand and placed it in the crook of his arm. "We wish to be wed."

Chapter Sixteen

What was he about? The blood drained from Lucy's head and she felt as if she would faint. 'Twas only Sir Alex's grip on her that kept her upright. Was this some new ploy?

"Ah," the priest said. "What of the banns?"

"You know I am widowed," Alex replied.

"But three years is a long time," Father Massey countered. "How am I to know that there is naught impeding you—or your lady—in matrimony? I had not even heard that you'd returned to Clyfton."

"There is no time to argue." Alex pulled Lucy forward, keeping his hand at her waist. "You are leaving for Mannington and we must leave York. This woman will be my bride. Today."

Neither man moved, though Lucy felt the cool, assessing gaze of the priest's dark eyes as they roved over her. He rubbed one hand over his face, clearly torn. It seemed obvious to Lucy, too, that though he was in a hurry, he did not wish to part with Alex so soon.

"I will petition the bishop for a dispensation. In one week's time, I can have his permission—"

"Father, Lucy and I must leave York *today*. I would be lawfully wed before we take our leave." He turned and caught Lucy's gaze. "Do you agree?"

"I...yes." She wanted to cry out with joy, but somehow remained outwardly calm in the face of his puzzling behavior.

"Then you will have to wait until my return from Mannington Manor," Massey said. "The lord lays dying, and I must attend him."

"Nay. Before you go," Alex said adamantly.

Lucy did not understand why he was insisting upon this. They had already traveled miles together, and stayed at Holywake without benefit of holy matrimony. She wondered what had suddenly changed, why he wanted to make their ploy a reality.

Father Massey sighed audibly. "You were always the stubbornest lad... I'll have your solemn oath that there is no lawful reason why you should not be wed," he finally said. "Both of you."

Lucy swallowed. She thought Alex had intended for them to *pose* as man and wife on their journey. She'd had no reason to believe he'd changed his mind about taking his monastic vows. Yet here she stood before a priest, her heart pounding, wearing fine new clothes, on the verge of becoming Alexander Breton's wife.

"Nay, I am no man's wife, nor promised to anyone," she heard herself say.

"And Sir Alexander," the priest said. "What of your vows to the Benedictine Order at Cluny?"

"I have taken no vows, Father," Alex said quietly, "other than one that I made to a dying friend in Jerusalem."

"And this vow does not hamper your marriage to this woman?"

Alex shook his head. "No, Father. It does not."

Massey shrugged off his cloak and draped it over a chair beside the pulpit. He placed his satchel beside it. "Come, stand before me," he said. "Unfortunately, we must be quick."

A few minutes later, Lucy was Alexander Breton's wife.

Lucy had never witnessed the marriage ceremony before, and she was struck by its stark simplicity, its basic honesty. She had freely given her vow to remain a faithful wife to Alex for as long as she should live. He had given his vow to be her husband.

But she did not know what that meant to him. He'd already dedicated his life to his wife's memory, and had planned to become a monk. What would happen now that he'd taken another wife? Did he mean to keep her with him?

She dared not hope.

Elsbeth had often spoken of husbands who left their wives at home and went about their own business. Yet a wife was never allowed to do the same. She was bound to remain at home keeping the master's house and bearing his children.

Would Alex go to Cluny and leave her here in England? Her heart sank at the prospect of being abandoned by him.

They followed the priest into the vestry where he found quill and ink and etched documentation of the marriage into the church record. Lucy felt strangely numb as she watched, and her eyes refused to come into focus.

The day had been all too confusing and she wondered if the bump on her head had caused some damage to her mind. She glanced down at her clothes and saw that they were real, as was the pressure of Alex's hand at her back.

They went back into the church.

"You cannot plan to ride to Clyfton tonight?" the priest asked as he pulled on his cloak once again. He picked up his satchel and started toward the door. "'Tis a distance from York."

Lucy nearly collided with the priest when he stopped and turned toward them again. "I'll likely be at Mannington two or more days...you might consider staying in my cottage, waiting 'til daybreak before leaving town."

"My plan was to go this afternoon."

Lucy was surprised that Alex did not correct the priest's misapprehension. Their destination was not Clyfton.

"'Tis beyond afternoon," Father Massey said with a quick glance toward the windows. "It will be dark before long and there is no suitable inn on the eastern road where a man might take his wife. Especially a *new* wife."

While the priest let that thought drift between them, Lucy noticed a reddening of Alex's ears. She tipped her head down and felt her own face heat.

Alex drew in a deep breath. To Lucy's ears, it sounded like resignation. "Aye," he said. "We'll stay the night."

Father Massey pointed out his small house beyond the church.

"There's a bit of food and ale, and you're welcome to it," the priest said. "Stable your horse in the shed." He seemed to regret being unable to spend more time with them, but made his farewell, leaving Lucy alone with her husband on the church step. She shivered and pulled her cloak tight against the sharp wind. And when Alex started down the steps, she followed.

'Twas a short walk to the cottage. When they arrived there, Alex left her at the door. He barely looked at her. "I'll, er...put Rusa in the shed."

Unsure what to do, Lucy went into the cottage. With daylight waning, she lit a lamp and looked 'round. There was no fire in the hearth, so she started one to take the chill out of the house before exploring any further.

It seemed strange to perform the mundane tasks of lighting fires and looking for food stores. She was Alex Breton's wife—a rank to which she had never hoped to aspire except in the deepest recesses of her heart.

'Twas long past time to go into the priest's house. Rusa had been unhitched from the wagon some time ago, but Alex stood with his forehead resting against her flank, wondering at what he had done. What of the monastic vows he'd planned to make?

What of Isabella's memory?

Lucy awaited him in the cottage and was likely even more unsure of their situation than he was.

Now that the deed was done, Alex could not say why he'd told Father Massey they'd come to the church to be wed. He could have come up with some other tale to cover his retrieval of the Mandylion.

But he had not. He had made Lucy his wife. And he did not regret it.

He gathered up his packs and headed for the house. It had started to rain and Alex was glad the priest had offered his cottage. 'Twas far better to retire here for the night, rather than trying to sleep in some make-shift shelter on the road to Eryngton.

That thought gave him pause. He and Lucy would share a bed tonight. The unrelenting desire he'd felt since their days at Holywake would be—

The sound of riders caught Alex's attention before he reached the house. In the distance were three knights in black, riding south into the city from the direction of Bootham Bar. Light from the setting sun glinted off their helms and swords and Alex could make out a pattern of white upon their chests. He did not doubt that they were Skelton's men.

While they were still a fair distance away, Alex returned to the shed and crouched near one wall so that he could see them without being seen. Within a few minutes, the knights rode past in silence.

Alex set his packs on the ground. Lucy awaited him in the cottage, and every instinct urged him to go to her. But he did not want to lose sight of the knights. He had no choice but to follow, even though he carried the Mandylion. But there was no time to replace it in the statue or find a hiding place in the cottage.

Keeping to the shadows of the trees and buildings on the way, he followed the black knights. He wanted to know exactly where the men were going and if they were staying in York or heading in some other direction.

'Twas only by the grace of God that he and Lucy had not encountered the knights on their way out of the city, for they, too, would have left by way of Bootham Bar. It would not have been possible to avoid the men as they returned to the city via the northern road.

Their pace was unhurried so 'twas not difficult for Alex to stay with them. He kept a fair distance between himself and the knights, and followed as they kept to the main streets. Eventually, they came to a tavern near the center of the city where all three dismounted. They tied their horses and went inside.

Alex paused and considered what to do next.

The most logical course would be to return to Father Massey's cottage, saddle Rusa and leave York immediately. As long as Skelton's men were here in York, he could be certain that the road to Eryngton was safe.

But logic had not dictated his actions in several

days. Especially not since last night when he'd pulled Lucy from the fray at Saint George's Inn. He'd felt no overwhelming desire to pray. He'd barely given a thought to Cluny and the vows he intended to take.

Alex's mind had been fully occupied by thoughts of Lucy.

She'd spent half the night upon his lap, the other half in the bed, lying in his arms while he resolved never to leave her unprotected again. He'd inhaled the scent of her hair, felt the curves of her body, guarded her while she slept.

He would not leave her tonight.

Certain that Skelton's knights intended to stay in York at least until morning, Alex headed back toward Massey's cottage. He remained as concealed as possible, reluctant for anyone to note his passage, in case the black knights heard of a man wearing two scabbards. They might not recognize him with his beard shaved off, but there was no doubt in Alex's mind that they would suspect a man who carried two swords.

He was anxious to get back to the priest's house. Eager to see Lucy dressed in the gown he'd bought for her at the tailor's shop, and even more eager to help her out of it.

Lucy could not imagine what was keeping Alex. He was probably regretting their impulsive marriage and trying to figure a way out of it.

That would not be too difficult. If Elsbeth were to

be believed, then a husband could take his leave whenever it suited him and never explain his absence to his wife.

Her hands shook as she sliced bread for their supper and she wished she knew what to do. Was there a way for Alex to dissolve the marriage before it had even begun? Was he preparing to leave her already? No matter what Alex intended to do, Lucy would show him how suitable a wife she could be. She would prepare his meals and…and find out exactly what else wives were expected to do. What little she'd learned about wifely duties from Elsbeth was probably not accurate. She did know, however, that she would share a bed with Alex, and they would continue what they'd started on their last night at Holywake.

Breathless anticipation flooded Lucy's senses and emotion swelled in her heart. She longed for his kiss, for his intimate touch. She'd never experienced anything to compare with the sensations she'd felt when Alex had begun to make love to her. And he'd been tender and protective of her last night at Saint George's Inn.

As darkness fell, Lucy doubted that Alex would ever return. He'd broken his promise to the monastery at Cluny and likely regretted it. If he was not in the church doing penance for his offense, then she guessed he must be on the road to the estate where he was supposed to take the Mandylion. Then he could be off to Cluny. Certainly the abbot of such a large Order would find a way to nullify Alex's marriage vows.

Still carrying the knife and heel of bread, she went to the single window that faced in the direction of the church, hoping to catch sight of Alex. It was nearly dark now, and had begun to rain and Lucy was nearly positive that he would not return. Why should he, when—

"Oh!" she cried when the door opened with a blast of cold, moist air. "You…"

"Skelton's men are here." Tossing his packs inside, he removed his wet cloak and hung it by the fire, then pushed his wet hair back from his face.

Lucy dropped the knife. Her panic must have shown in her eyes, for Alex came to her and placed his hands upon her shoulders. She wished he would take her into his arms, but he did not.

"Rest easy. They do not know we're here."

Her breath returned and she gazed questioningly into her husband's eyes.

"I saw them as I was coming to the house earlier." Alex released her and closed the shutter over the window. "I followed them to a tavern down near the Shambles," he added, reaching down to pick up the knife. "They'll never know we're here."

"But shouldn't we leave York while they're in town?" Their course seemed clear to Lucy. "As long as they're not lying in wait for us upon the road—"

Alex laughed aloud. 'Twas the first time Lucy had seen his face aglow with mirth, and it warmed her even though she did not understand its cause. She thought there was some urgency to getting the Mandylion to its destination.

"I had the same thought."

"Then why are we not leaving? We can be—"

His hands closed around her upper arms and his mouth came down on hers, silencing her, melting her with his heat.

He pulled away slightly. "The journey can wait." His voice was deep and quiet. "This cannot."

His hands slid behind her back and he pulled her close, even as he deepened the pressure of his mouth on hers. If Lucy was melting before, she ignited when his hands moved ever lower, pressing her hips to his. A soft groan slipped from her throat. He teased her lips apart with his tongue and she opened to him.

Sensation coursed through Lucy and she felt as if she were floating. Alex's tongue danced wickedly, enticingly with hers, and she felt his hand move to the back of her head. He cupped her cheek, then moved to her throat and down the bodice of her gown.

When his hand closed over her breast, Lucy gasped, breaking their kiss. Immersed in the intensity of his touch, she hardly heard him when he spoke.

"Is there a bed somewhere?" His voice was a low rasp that resonated through her body.

"In back, I think," she said, "past the curtain."

Alex took the lamp in one hand and kept his other arm around Lucy as they sought the priest's bedchamber. She took no notice of her surroundings, but after finding the small room with its narrow bed and rough wooden trunk, turned her attention to Alex. She slipped her hands to the back of his neck and tangled her fingers in his hair. This was what she wanted—warmth and intimacy, a chance to show him what he meant to her.

He made a sound of approval that was cut short when Lucy raised herself on to her toes to kiss him again. She felt the muscles in his shoulders and arms tighten as he put his arms 'round her again, and she felt his strength envelop her.

A pleasant heaviness swirled in the lower part of Lucy's body and she pressed against Alex to increase the lovely tension growing there. His chest was broad and hard, his abdomen unyielding. When she felt his hands moving at her shoulders, she realized he was loosening her sleeves, removing her bodice.

She shivered with anticipation when her gown dropped to the floor.

And then he touched her naked breasts.

A heated flush spread from her nipples to her neck, then to her cheeks. She broke the kiss to catch her breath.

''Ah, Lucy,'' he breathed in her ear. She felt his mouth move down to her jaw, her neck. Her skin, already warm, turned fiery when his mouth reached the tip of one breast and he pulled it into his mouth.

She took his head in her hands and held him in place while he stroked her nipple with his tongue. A soft groan sounded in the room and Lucy did not know if 'twas she or Alex who'd made it.

When he moved to treat her other breast to the same tender attention as the first, Lucy felt as if her bones had turned to dust. Before her knees gave out from under her, Alex lifted her into his arms and carried her the few steps to the bed. He lay her gently upon the simple quilt and jerked his tunic and linen shirt over his head before coming down to her.

Reaching for him, she breathed his name. Her breasts brushed against the mat of hair on his chest when he hovered over her. She encircled his neck with her arms, then slid her hands across the taut skin of his broad shoulders and down his back. Alex shuddered and tipped his head down to meet her lips in a fierce encounter of tongues and teeth.

He filled Lucy's senses completely. Alex's hand touched her knee, then moved upward. She felt no shyness, no shame when his fingers reached the part of her that ached for his touch.

She opened to him. Body, heart, and soul.

"You are so soft...." His whisper penetrated the sensual haze that surrounded her and she responded with quiet, inarticulate sounds that seemed to inflame him even more.

He continued to kiss her as he shifted his position, placing his body in intimate contact with hers. When he moved again, Lucy felt him press against her, his flesh as naked as her own.

"Alex?" Her voice, soft as a whisper, was full of emotion, her body full of yearning. She needed him....

"Don't be afraid."

"I could never— Oh!"

He moved quickly. A burning pain lasted only a second and Alex held perfectly still within her.

As the pain subsided, Lucy was certain there must be more. Sensing that he awaited her acceptance, she moved her hips, taking him deeper. Alex made a low sound in his throat and braced himself over her. Slowly, he began to move with tight, deliberate strokes.

Lucy matched his rhythm, digging her fingers into the thick muscles of his upper arms, her body aching for something she could not name. She began to move faster, and Alex coaxed her legs around his waist. When he slid a hand down between them and touched her intimately, Lucy was plunged into a maelstrom of sensation, like naught she'd ever known before. She cried out with the pleasure, cupping Alex's face in her hands.

And as he drove into her one last time, shuddering with his own completion, Lucy brought his face down to hers and melded her lips with his.

Chapter Seventeen

The lamp cast a flickering light into the room while rain pelted the windows.

Alex gathered Lucy into his arms and held her as they lay together weakly, and vainly tried to force himself to think about the task that had brought him to England, and not the raw, mind-numbing pleasure he had just experienced with Lucy.

His wife.

He watched her eyes flutter closed, her thick lashes resting like golden half moons on her cheeks. Her lips, lush and giving, were parted in sleep, and Alex saw that the pulse in her throat had slowed to normal. He wondered if his own had.

His body still hummed with the intensity of their lovemaking. That should not have been unexpected, he supposed. He'd been without a woman for several years. That alone had made the experience with Lucy beyond memorable. So there was no point in making more of it than it was. Marital relations would certainly become calmer after this.

Lucy's lower body nestled into him. She slipped one arm across his middle and her breasts pressed against his side. He pulled the blanket over them and lowered his face to her hair while his body became immediately aroused again.

'Twas too soon to take her again. Besides, she had just fallen asleep. Alex could not imagine any woman who would care to be awakened so that her husband could make love to her. Again.

He'd been careful of her new bruises, though she had not seemed to mind their vigorous lovemaking. Nay, she'd been as enthusiastic and giving as he could have wished. She had responded to every kiss, every caress, as if starving for him. She made him feel alive.

His demand to be wed by Father Massey...Alex could not say what had come over him. But the thought of leaving Lucy at Eryngton had become every bit as abhorrent as leaving her in York. He could not do it.

He could hardly accept what he'd done, either.

What of his commitment to Cluny? What of his intentions to become a monk? And Isabella... His grief over the loss of his wife and child had changed. Since meeting Lucy, his memories of Isabella and Geoffrey were more tender than sad. He could think of them without pain, and remember the life and love they'd shared.

Though he doubted he'd ever feel the same about another woman, some bright part of Alex that had been deeply buried had begun to emerge. And Lucy was the cause.

Yet he did not think he could be a husband to her. His course had been set too long ago to change now. He could not return to Clyfton House with a wife in Isabella's stead. 'Twould be a betrayal of all he'd shared with her.

Nay, he would set aside funds for Lucy's keeping. He'd find her a house in York if she wanted to stay here, or mayhap there would be a comfortable cottage closer to Clyfton, where Philip could see to her well-being. Alex would see that she had servants so that she would never have to work her hands raw, or strain her weak hip.

A cold finality seeped into his soul as he mentally arranged things, and Alex wondered if 'twould actually be possible for him to leave her. When her hand shifted and came to rest over his heart, he placed his own atop it.

She made a small sound and turned her head to look at him. Her eyelids were heavy with sleep, but she smiled softly. Alex found himself bringing her hand to his lips for a kiss.

'Twas not at all what he intended, but while he did it, Lucy pressed her lips to his chest. She kissed him again, her mouth touching one of his nipples. He groaned, but she did not stop.

If she had, he would have begged her to continue.

Turning to lie upon him, she straddled his leg and pressed her breasts to his belly while she teased his nipples in turn, just as he had done hers. She'd learned well, for Alex was fully aroused instantly.

"You have so much hair, Sir Knight," she whispered. "'Tis thick on your arms...your chest...."

She rubbed her nose against it and trailed her tongue down his breastbone to the center of his abdomen. He shuddered with anticipation but she stopped.

"I would touch you..." she said breathlessly, "as you touched me...."

"Aye." He took her hand and guided it to his most sensitive place and squeezed his eyes closed at her gentle touch.

Her shuddering breath was warm on his abdomen when her hand encircled him. "Teach me to please you," she whispered, "to give you the same pleasure you gave me."

"Ah..." He could hardly speak. "Just...continue... what you are doing...."

Lucy slid farther down in the bed and when her breasts grazed his thighs, Alex nearly came out of his skin. She stroked him tentatively at first, but her touch quickly became bolder. Her fingers learned how and where to apply pressure but when he groaned, she stopped abruptly. "Did I hurt you?"

Alex could not reply. Instead, he guided her hand back to where it had been and encouraged her to resume what she'd been doing. 'Twas as if she knew exactly what he needed, what he craved. "You are so smooth...yet so hard."

He groaned. His blood pounded in his ears and his entire body clenched.

With one swift move he shifted their positions until

she was beneath him and he was poised to enter her. He'd been quick and forceful the first time to minimize her discomfort. This time, he planned to go slowly and torturously, to maximize her pleasure.

"Oh!" She put her hands on his buttocks to try to pull him in, but he kept his control. Somehow.

Lamplight flickered across her features. Their eyes met as Alex braced his arms on either side of her head and finally plunged.

"Kiss me," she whispered.

He looked down and saw her full lips slightly parted. A deep rose hue painted her cheeks, and her brows were raised in anticipation. She was so beautiful his heart tightened in his chest and he could do naught but what she requested.

He kissed her.

Their mouths met, their tongues coming together in a mating dance that echoed the movement of their bodies. She gave so generously, Alex did not know if he could ever get enough of her. Certainly one night would not be enough.

He savored every sensation: her softness, her shy sensuality, her eager response to his touch. She was more passionate than any woman he'd ever known, more fiery than he could ever have imagined.

When the movements of her lower body became frenzied, Alex knew she was close to reaching her peak. She held his hips in her hands and bucked against him, her muscles suddenly tightening around him. She tore her mouth from his and cried out.

Alex could hold out no longer. He lunged and

surged within her, his pleasure cresting in mind-numbing pulsations that went on endlessly. 'Twas almost as if their first encounter had never occurred.

But it had. The sweet innocence of their first time was etched upon his mind, his heart, forever.

He felt her heart beat against his chest and realized that he was crushing her with his weight. He pushed up onto his arms again, but was not ready to leave her. He kept them joined.

Lucy took a quivering breath and her muscles clenched around him again, sending waves of pleasure through him.

"Are you all right?" he asked when he could breathe again. He'd been more forceful than he'd intended, and he frowned with concern that he may have hurt her.

Lucy nodded bashfully, her eyes skittering away from his. Gently, he took her chin in his hand. "What is it, Lucy? What's amiss?"

She bit her lower lip. "I should not have... I forgot myself, Alex and I—"

"Could not have pleased me more, if that is your worry."

A deep breath escaped her. "I..." She swallowed. "When we're joined this way...'tis the most wondrous thing I've ever known. Does it...is it always this way?"

Her question was innocent enough, and Alex could do naught but answer her honestly. "Nay," he whispered. "'Tis rarely so uncommon."

Alex had never had reason to believe Isabella

hadn't enjoyed their trysts in their bedchamber. Yet his experiences with his late wife did not compare to what he'd just felt with Lucy.

He moved aside and she turned to curl into him. He did not want to feel anything toward Lucy. He did not want to relive the overpowering sensations of joy and satisfaction that he had just experienced with her, the sensations that had been banished from his existence during these long, solitary years.

Lucy awoke alone.

The curtain was drawn so she could not see into the rest of the cottage, but she could hear no movement on the other side and sensed that she was alone.

She did not know where Alex was.

Quickly, she washed and dressed, then pushed back the curtain to find that the fire had been built up recently. Alex's packs were next to the door, but his sword and the scabbard were gone.

Still, she did not think he'd gone far.

The pottage she'd cooked the night before was still in the pot, lying near the fire. Lucy stirred it and put it back in to cook, then went to each of the windows to look outside.

'Twas still raining, and there was no sign of him.

Lucy pulled her shawl around her shoulders and sat down on a stool by the fire. She was glad for a few moments to herself, to reflect on all that had happened since leaving Saint George's Inn.

Though she did not understand why Alex had made her his wife, she was certainly glad he did—*and* that he'd returned to her yesterday. Though they had made love twice last night, and again before dawn, Lucy still did not know what was in his heart, or what he planned for them.

She got up to stir the pottage and decided that this would be her choice. She'd seen Lady Elsbeth banished to the nunnery when she had not pleased her husband, and the misery she'd suffered for months afterward. Lucy was not going to succumb to the same fate. She was going to do whatever was necessary to stay with him.

Mayhap if Elsbeth had used some of her experience in the bedchamber with her husband, she would still have been with him rather than with the Craghaven nuns. Lucy remembered every word of Elsbeth's tales...and 'twould be her pleasure to experience everything the lady had spoken of...with Alex.

"'Tis still raining," Alex said, pushing open the cottage door. "And there is no sign of the black knights anywhere in town."

He pulled off his long, dark cloak and spread it out by the fire while Lucy wondered if he would offer her a husbandly kiss. When he did not, she decided to go to him.

"Good morn, husband," she said, placing her hands upon his shoulders. She rose up on her toes and pulled him down, enabling her to reach his lips with hers. Lucy gave him the kind of kiss she'd learned during the night, one that she hoped blistered his soul as much as it seared hers.

A moment later, Alex pulled her into his arms and

returned her kiss with the kind of ardor he'd shown her last night.

His eyes were unfocused when he finally drew back. "I missed you in our bed," she whispered as his thumbs grazed the lower part of her breasts. She slipped away from him. "'Tis time to break our fast."

Lucy took the cookpot from the fire, then ladled the soup into two bowls. She handed one to Alex, who still remained silent after their kiss.

"Shall we leave after the meal?" she asked.

Alex sat down across from her. He shook his head. "I think we're safe to stay here another day. Massey won't travel in this rain, so he won't be back. And Skelton's men will spend another day at the tavern wondering where to look for me."

He warmed his hands by cupping the bowl. They were large and the skin rough, but they'd been naught but gentle with her. A shiver ran through her when she remembered some of the things those hands had done, and when she thought of the way they might spend the day.

There was only one way in which Alex wanted to spend the day. But there were good reasons why he should not. Instead, he turned away from Lucy and opened the shutters that faced the street. "If Skelton's men ride toward the northern gate, we'll see them," he said.

"Will you watch the road all day?" she asked. She wore the second gown that had been altered for her. 'Twas a bright russet with gold trim that suited her fair coloring perfectly. The neckline left her delicate neck and shoulders bare, and hinted at the fullness of her breasts. Her hair was loose, flowing in soft, golden waves to her waist. Without thinking, Alex could almost feel it brush across his belly as it had in the night.

"I think we'll be able to hear anyone riding past," he said when he was able to find his voice.

"Will we leave here when it stops raining?"

Alex did not want to commit himself to taking her with him. The journey to Eryngton would be dangerous with Skelton's men pursuing him. 'Twas even possible the knights would recognize him.

The more he thought of it, the greater his worry for Lucy's safety. Mayhap 'twould be better for her to remain—

Alex's breath caught when he turned to look at her. She wore naught but a thin silk chemise and her mantle of beautiful, wavy hair. Her gown had fallen and was pooled at her feet.

Seduction was in her eyes, and Alex was powerless to resist. All morn, he'd thought of naught but the woman who'd moaned with pleasure and warmed his bed all night long. His fingers itched to touch her, his arms ached to hold her. He could almost taste her.

"Did I tell you how much you please me, husband?" Her voice was soft, her words flowing through him as though she'd touched him with her lips, her hands.

Somehow he found himself standing before her with one thumb touching the elegant notch at the base of her throat. From there, his hand slid down and found the distinctive mole nearly hidden between her breasts. Her eyes slid closed and when her head fell back, Alex pressed his lips to her neck.

''Aye,'' she whispered. ''Touch me.''

He untied the fastening that held her chemise closed. When it slipped away from her breasts, he cupped them and teased their tips with his fingers. She trembled, and he felt her lips on his forehead, then near his ear as she sought his mouth.

Alex was already so swollen, he was near to bursting. He moved his head and caught her lips in a searing kiss, even as her fingers slid through his hair, loosening it from the thong that tied it neatly at his nape.

She broke the kiss and touched her tongue to his chin, then his neck. Her lips moved to his chest and every muscle, from his feet to his neck, tensed. A shudder of anticipation ran through him.

Lucy's chemise dropped to the floor. She pulled at Alex's tunic until he lifted it over his head and threw it aside. When his chest was bare, she devoted her attention to his nipples, now pebbled with arousal.

Her hands worked at his braes, and Alex groaned when her fingers found him. They slid across his engorged length, then encircled him, even as her mouth moved downward.

Chapter Eighteen

"I wish we knew where the black knights were," Lucy said, running one finger absently across Alex's chest. He turned over in the bed and propped his head on his hand to look down at her. She was not the only one who wanted to know where they were, but Alex did not see how it would be possible to find out.

"They could be anywhere in York," he said. "Or they might have left town by one of the other gates."

"We could go to the tavern where you saw them. Ask if they've been seen lately."

"They'd recognize me right off."

"Then *I* could ask."

Alex frowned. "Absolutely not. Women do not go into taverns and they—"

She covered his lips with her fingers. "What if I just looked about...tried to see if they were inside?"

"Too dangerous," he said, taking her hand in his and lowering it to the bed. "Besides, you cannot walk so far."

"Of course I can," she protested. She sat up and

threw her legs over the bed. She picked up her chemise and slipped it over her head then tied the lacing
at the neck. "I am perfectly capable of—"

"Nay, Lucy, 'tis too dangerous."

Alex slid out of the bed, too.

"You forget...I spent one entire night in the streets
of York, looking for a safe place to stay."

"Nay. I have not forgotten. Nor will I ever."

"Come with me, Alex," she said. She drew out
her old, mended kirtle from her small bundle of possessions. "If they happen to see me, they will never
recognize me. I can go where you cannot."

She pulled on the gown and began to fasten it. Alex
moved her hands aside and tied her laces himself. Her
idea was not entirely without merit, though he'd have
preferred a seasoned fighter to venture into town with
him. The idea of Lucy in danger again was abhorrent
to him.

"Come. If we are to leave tomorrow, 'twould be
good to know where they are, and if they keep watch
over the northern road. Besides, it has stopped raining, and the timing could not be more perfect."

Reluctantly, he agreed with her plan. They would
not risk taking his horse into the city streets, for Rusa
was a war horse and would never be mistaken for
peasant stock. They would walk, and he would allow
Lucy to set the pace, certain that his own gait would
be much too fast for her.

Alex dressed quickly in his darkest tunic and
watched as Lucy made herself ready to go. She

slipped on her old shawl, pulling it up to cover her head. ''Ready?'' she asked.

They left the priest's house and took the same path Alex had used when he'd followed the knights to the tavern the day before. The night watchmen were out, so they took care to avoid them. Alex preferred not to be stopped and questioned, drawing attention to them.

''I'll walk by the window and see if they're there,'' Lucy said when they reached the tavern. It seemed to be a smaller and quieter room than the one at Saint George's Inn, and though Alex did not like sending Lucy unescorted, he had no alternative. They stood on the opposite side of the lane and looked over at the building.

''Do not tarry,'' he said, holding one of her arms. ''Take a look and go on by.''

She agreed and crossed to the other side of the lane.

Lucy could not deny that she was nervous. Knowing the location of the black knights was extremely important. She and Alex did not want to be surprised on the road when they left York.

This had been her idea, and she was going to see it through. She walked as evenly as possible across the lane, arriving on the other side, at one edge of the tavern. She made her way to the steamy window, where she slowed and looked in.

'Twas impossible to see.

Determined to get something out of this trip, she turned back to look at the windows, and saw that water had dripped down in one area, clearing the glass. Bending slightly to put her eye to it, she looked over the crowd of men gathered in the room.

'Twas not as crowded a place as Saint George's had been, and Lucy was able to see every man inside. None wore the black tunic emblazoned with a white lion. Lucy guessed the knights might not always wear their livery, especially if they—like she and Alex— did not wish to be recognized. But there was no man inside who had the look of a knight.

She straightened and went back to Alex.

He took her arm and pulled her into a concealed space under the eaves of the building. ''You are supposed to walk past once,'' he said. ''Not flaunt yourself to the crowd.''

''They did not see me, Alex,'' she said. Even without touching him, she felt the tension coiled in his body. ''And there were no knights inside.''

''Are you sure?''

''Aye,'' she replied and he relaxed slightly. ''Shall we keep walking? They might have gone to Saint George's if they were looking for rooms.''

He did not respond right away and Lucy knew his hesitation was because he did not want her to have to go back there. ''Nay. We do not need—''

''Alex, you know 'twould be best to see if they are still here in York.''

''Men come and go from Saint George's too frequently to risk having you seen by that buffoon who assaulted you.''

''No one will see me.'' She grabbed his arm and

made him to go along with her, enjoying the feel of
his arm entwined with hers, and the protectiveness he
showed her.

'Twas a very foreign feeling, indeed, and Lucy
could not feel afraid when Alex hovered so close.

When they arrived at Saint George's Inn, Alex led
Lucy 'round to the back of the building, where the
courtyard and stable were located. "Wait here for me.
I'm going inside to speak to the proprietor."

"What if the knights are there?"

"I'm going in the back way, and I'll wait for Alf
to come into the kitchen. No one else will see me."

"Be careful," she whispered, watching him disappear into the dark.

Lucy hovered close to the back wall, unwilling to
be discovered by a patron coming out to relieve himself. She could hear the music and the raucous laughter that had gone on the night she'd worked in the
common room, and a shudder ran up her spine at the
thought of it. If Alex had not arrived when he did,
and taken her away from those men...

"They haven't been here," Alex said, coming to
her so silently that she had not heard his footsteps.
"They might have left York already."

"But not by way of the church. We'd have seen
them."

"True," he replied. "Come on. Let's get back.
We're taking too great a chance of being seen."

They turned back toward Father Massey's cottage,
moving as quickly as Lucy's weak leg allowed. 'Twas
not a direct route, since they'd walked to the center

of town, but fewer people were out and about now. 'Twas not as frightening to be out while Alex was with her.

"What's that smell?"

"'Tis the butchers' district," he answered.

"Let's hurry past. It stinks."

Lucy grabbed Alex's hand and tried to run ahead of him, but he suddenly grabbed her and pulled her into a niche, flattening her into the narrow crack between two buildings. The scent of butchered meat was nearly overpowering and she fought the urge to gag, aware that Alex had gotten her off the street for a reason. As he pressed his body against hers, neither of them breathed as footsteps came closer and they heard men's voices in the air.

"...is not here in town, if he ever was," one of them said, his voice low and gruff.

"Where do we look now?"

"You said he'd be here in York."

"Well, 'tis clear I was wrong," a third man said, his words clipped, his expression irritated.

"We've looked in every tavern and inn, and visited every church. If the Cluny knight had come to York, we'd have known about it."

Lucy nearly gasped when she realized who these men were, but she remained perfectly still, and they continued past.

"Then what shall we do?" the first voice asked. "Wait for him to turn up at the King's Inn...?"

The words became muffled as the men continued,

but though she could not hear the men's plans, she was able to breathe with relief. Inadvertently, they had accomplished what they'd set out to do!

When the dark knights stepped out of the lane and out of sight, Alex pulled Lucy from their hiding place and moved her in the opposite direction. Feeling safe and elated now that she knew where the black knights were, Lucy fairly skipped back to the cottage. When they arrived in Father Massey's yard, she threw open the door and waited for Alex to bar it behind him.

Then she tossed off her shawl and flew into his arms, laughing. "We did it!"

Her laughter made their dangerous excursion worthwhile, even more than learning the black knights' location. Alex's heart felt strangely light and the corners of his mouth turned up in an uncharacteristic smile.

"Ha!" she grabbed his hand and kissed the palm, then giggled and pressed her face to his chest. "They never saw us!"

"They very nearly did."

"But you saw them first and got us out of harm's way," she said, undaunted. "My mighty protector!"

She danced away from him, and no matter how awkward her gait, Alex found her graceful. Delightful. Beautiful.

"Your *lucky* protector." He could think of naught but spending the rest of the night indulging in the pleasures they'd discovered together in their marriage bed.

Her hair swirled around her as she swayed, pulling off her kirtle as she moved.

"They have no idea where you are!" She laughed aloud again, clearly exhilarated by their near encounter with Skelton's men. "And so we are safe tonight in our bed!"

"So you think, my winsome one."

Alex threw wood on the dying fire, and watched as her kirtle dropped to the floor. She was giddy with relief, and her playfulness was contagious. He lunged for her, but she skittered away, laughing.

Lucy taunted him with bared shoulders as he unbuckled his sword belt and set it upon the table. Smiling wickedly, she held her silken chemise so that it just covered her breasts, then bent down to remove her shoes.

When he grabbed for her again, she squealed and skirted around to the far side of the table. He played along with her chasing game until he could stand it no longer, then, taking exquisite care not to hurt her, he made one quick move and scooped her up in his arms. He tossed her over one shoulder and patted her soft rump.

"You think to defy me, wench?" he jested.

"Alex!" she cried, laughing and screeching. Squirming provocatively.

"One more wiggle, and I shall lay you on the floor and have my way with you!"

She did it again and he slid her slowly, torturously, down his body while he fought to maintain control. He was hard and wanting, but he reveled in her scent, her softness, her feisty demeanor. He would have her frolicsome mood continue…for a time.

When her bare feet had nearly reached the ground, Lucy tipped her head for his kiss. Their lips were a breath apart when she whispered, "I'd prefer the bed, Sir Knight!"

Alex slept fitfully. He had been sated within Lucy's body so many times that his nerves hummed with an odd restlessness. The fire had burned low, so he climbed out of bed and walked across the chilly room to add more wood.

Lucy slept soundly. Her playfulness had been more arousing than anything he'd ever experienced. He'd laughed with her, allowed her to tease and taunt him, and had seduced her in turn.

He had never known such pleasure or contentment with Isabella.

Alex shoved his fingers through his hair. He had resisted temptation for three years.

Until Lucy.

"*Deus meus,*" he whispered, suddenly aware of how remiss he'd been with his prayers, with his true purpose. "*Ex toto corde poenitet me omnium meorum peccatorum.…*

Lucy lay peacefully with her beautiful hair spread under her, and one pale arm flung wide. Her hand was smooth and soft now, the hand of a lady unfamiliar with the kind of work she had done at Craghaven. She was his wife now, in the eyes of God and man.

And Isabella was dead and buried.

Chapter Nineteen

They left the priest's cottage at daybreak the following morn. Alex had concealed the Mandylion somewhere… Lucy thought it might be in the same place where he'd hidden away his affections, too.

He'd been quiet and distant since leaving York, hardly speaking, never touching. Lucy did not understand what could possibly be amiss, not after the experiences they'd shared over the past two nights. She was certain that Alex had begun to feel something for her—something more than an inconvenient responsibility for her.

But after spending a day in the wagon with him as taciturn as ever, she was not so sure. She'd even heard him muttering in Latin, which was something he had not done since their earliest days at Holywake.

The rain held off most of the day, though the clouds hung low and threatening while they rode north. Lucy felt fortunate to have her new, thick woolen cloak to wrap around her, its hood keeping her head warm.

Alex did not remark upon their good luck in finding the black knights, nor had he shown her any of the sensual tenderness she had expected after all that had passed between them in the priest's cottage. He was cool and remote, and his mien did not invite discourse.

Lucy chewed her lip and wondered if aught had happened to upset him.

She had assumed there would be time for talking later, as they traveled. But if Alex had thoughts on anything that had transpired between them, or what he intended for their future, he kept them to himself, and hardly spoke to her all day.

It was near dusk when he drove the wagon into an inn yard. A light rain began to fall just as Alex stopped in front of the inn and jumped down. In silence, he helped Lucy out of the wagon and went inside with her.

The main room was warm and comfortable, with a blazing fire in its massive fireplace.

"Ah! Come in, come in!"

They'd walked in upon a family sitting together for their evening meal, but no one seemed particularly annoyed by the interruption. While three children remained seated, a man and his wife arose and came to the door to greet Lucy and Alex. The wife carried a small, yellow-haired child in her arms. "Ye must warm yerselves by our fire," said the man.

"Have you a room to let for the night?"

"Oh, aye," he replied. "No one here but we Mortons."

Carrying the child in her arms, Anna Morton left the other children to show Lucy to a chamber on the second floor where she and Alex would spend the night. In the meantime, the woman's husband went out with Alex to stable the horse and wagon.

"While you settle in, I'll get yer supper for ye," Anna said. "Ye must be famished, travelin' all the way from York."

"Aye, they were here...." Edmund Morton said, holding the lantern high so that Alex could see where he was leading Rusa and the wagon. "Three nights ago...er, maybe four. Quiet men, the lot of them."

"And dressed in black."

The landlord nodded. "Fancy livery 'twas—with a white lion on each chest. Anna didn't want to take 'em, but what are we in the business for, if not to take in strangers? Fierce men, though. We kept our counsel when they were near."

There could be no doubt that they were Skelton's men. Alex wondered if the three would remain in York, or return to the northern road to await him. 'Twas likely they would stay in York for a time, but he had been unable to hear enough of their conversation to know what they would do.

He and Lucy could not dally here. It had probably been a mistake to bring her along, but he'd been unable to face leaving her.

'Twas clear that Lucy cared for him. This was not at all what he had intended when he'd wed her, though he was still unsure exactly what he *had* intended. Security against the world was his primary reason, he supposed. Being the wife of Alex Breton would afford her some protection. Philip would accept her at Clyfton and she could live at the castle with his family while Alex…

Alex did not know what he would do after the Mandylion was safely delivered to Eryngton. Brother Roger had been right. But Alex was not yet ready to abandon his plan to devote his life to prayer and penance.

What he'd begun to feel for Lucy was…was not yet definable. She was beautiful and giving, as generous as anyone he'd ever known. Their hours in the cottage the previous night had been playful and carefree—unlike any he'd ever known. Lucy was a fitting wife for any noble household. Yet a wife was the last thing Alex needed. Or wanted.

He did not know what he would do with her.

"'Tis certain my Anna has a meal ready for ye," Edmund Morton said once Alex had unhitched Rusa and seen to the mare's water and feed. "Shall we go inside and see?"

"You go on ahead," Alex said. "I'll just gather our things."

Alex took the Mandylion from the place where he'd concealed it in the wagon, then picked up his saddle packs and walked through the rain toward the inn. He heard laughter and song as he approached, and wondered if the innkeeper's children were entertaining Lucy.

He stepped inside and found her sitting near the

fire. She'd shed her cloak and was wearing the blue gown he'd purchased for her in York. Her hair glowed like burnished gold in the firelight and her smile tugged at the restraint he'd maintained all through the day.

She was lovely.

"Ah, here y'are!" The innkeeper's wife carried two bowls and a loaf of coarse, brown bread from a back room. "'Twill take but a minute to fetch the rest of yer supper. I hope ye don't mind that yer wife is keeping the children for now."

"No, I—"

"'Tis so much easier to fetch and carry when I haven't got one or t'other of 'em attached to m'apron."

She was suddenly gone from the room again, and Alex was left watching Lucy as she clapped and played with the children. The Mortons' eldest girl was showing Lucy some game with her hands—each one held her hands up and clapped the other's in rhythm while they sang rhyming words.

It struck Alex then that Lucy's girlhood had been cut short with the deaths of her brothers. She'd likely had a nurse who'd attended her, but afterward, there would have been little opportunity for play in the nunnery.

Not that Lucy would have been well enough to play. He remembered her saying she'd been a sickly child. That the cousin had sent her to Craghaven to die.

A cold fist tightened around his heart at the thought

of Lucy dying among the Craghaven nuns. He uttered a quiet prayer of thanks that she had not, and that God had sent him on this path to Eryngton.

Else he would never have met her. Would never have saved her from the brigands who'd attacked her party on the road. Would not have been there to pull her from the river when she nearly drowned. Alex would never have learned the taste of her sweet lips, or the exquisite pleasure he'd found in her body.

Alex swallowed. He had kept his sensual thoughts at bay throughout the day and he would not think of her now, lying naked beneath him, her eyes sparkling playfully as they had last night, or sensuously as they'd been during the countless hours they'd spent entwined in their marriage bed.

"Anna's bringin' out the pot," Edmund said as he set two mugs of ale on the table. "Hope ye don't mind 'tis naught fancy. Since we weren't prepared for yer comin'."

"I'm sure it will be satisfactory," Alex replied absently. He could not take his eyes from Lucy and the glow in her eyes. They'd finished the clapping game and now she held the youngest child upon her lap.

Was it possible that she already carried their child within her? The thought gave him pause.

He'd never considered the possibility of having another family...a wife, more children...

The ale in Alex's cup disappeared in one long gulp. He'd never had any intention of replacing Isabella and Geoffrey. They'd been his family, and he needed no other. *Why had Brother Roger insisted that he wait to take his vows?* Because of that promise, Alex's life, his plans were now in chaos.

"All right, here 'tis!" Anna Morton set the heavy pot in the center of the table. She served Alex, then filled a bowl for Lucy, who came to the table with the children following.

Scowling at his meal, Alex hardly heard the questions the little ones asked. They were excessively interested in Lucy, but she seemed happy enough to indulge them. Anyone could see that she'd enjoyed their songs, their games.

As Lucy took her seat next to Alex, the children gathered 'round her and asked if she'd been to the fair and whether she'd seen York Minster.

"N-nay," she replied. "I was there for only a very short time."

Being abused for a goodly part of it, Alex mused, his dark thoughts worsening. And then he had made her his wife and taken her to the priest's cottage from which they had hardly emerged for two full days.

'Twas likely she did not fully grasp all that had happened to her in the short weeks since the Craghaven nuns were killed on the road. Alex certainly did not. Since that day, naught had gone according to any of his plans.

"We weren't allowed to sit with our last visitors," the younger girl said. "Papa made us stay in the kitchen. But 'tis warm there, too, so we didn't mind too much."

"That's enough now, children," said Anna. "Ye

must leave our guests in peace, or I'll shoo ye back into the kitchen.''

"Oh, I don't mind them," Lucy said. "Let them stay."

"Have ye far to go, then?" asked the innkeeper. He'd poured a mug of ale for himself and sat at the end of the table near Alex.

"I'm not sure," Alex said. "We travel to Eryng-ton. Do you know how lo—"

Beside him, Lucy choked.

Alex moved quickly and gave her a firm pat on the back.

"I'm all right," she said, catching her breath. "Eryngton? *Eryngton* is nearby?"

"Aye, 'tis," answered the innkeeper. "On horse-back—half a day's journey north."

"What do you know of Eryngton?" Alex asked, frowning. By her reaction to the name, Alex was cer-tain she was somehow familiar with the place.

He watched as she swallowed visibly. "'Twas my home...." she said quietly. "A lifetime ago."

Her words struck him like a blow to his chest. It could not be. Somehow, the estate he'd named was... Nay, there could only be one Eryngton. The Kendal family seat. "Roger Kendal was...was your brother?" he asked.

Her head dipped slightly and Edmund Morton slapped his thigh. "Ah, ye're the lass was sent down to a nunnery when Lord John died and Hugh Kyghley became earl. Lady Lucy!"

"Aye," she replied soberly. She pushed away her

bowl, apparently no longer interested in her food. "Lord Hugh is my cousin. Still Earl of Eryngton, I suppose."

"I remember ye well," the man said. Caught up in his own memories, he did not notice the change in Lucy's mood. "Ye stayed here—'twas m'father's inn before me, for I was just a lad at the time—ye stayed here with the old abbess and a couple o' younger nuns."

"I don't remember it well."

"Nay, ye wouldn't," Morton remarked. "Ye were too ill, even to know where ye were."

Alex's hackles went up at the thought of cousin Hugh sending Lucy off when she'd been so clearly ill. She'd just lost her only brother, and was close to death herself. Couldn't the man have shown some compassion for his ailing little cousin? When Alex got to Eryngton, he would see that—

The thought hit him like a blow—*Roger's brother was dead.* And Roger himself had been believed dead for a number of years.

Alex was going to have to tell Lucy that her brother had only recently died. That he'd gone away on Crusade and left her at the mercy of her coldhearted cousin.

Alex did not understand why Roger had not contacted his family after he'd survived the shipwreck. He could not figure why Roger had let them believe he was dead.

It made no sense. Roger knew he was his brother's heir. He had to have known the estate—*and his young sister*—would become his responsibility if John died. Had Roger been at Eryngton at the time of John's death, Lucy would never have been sent to Craghaven.

"Ye stayed here an extra week with the lung fever. They called in the priest one night, for fear ye wouldn't last 'til the morn."

Lucy stood abruptly and stepped away from the table, gathering the children 'round her. "Come," she said. "Shall we sing some more? I'm sure you have songs you have not yet taught me."

"But you have not finished—"

Lucy interrupted the eldest daughter. "Aye, I have." She picked up the bairn and went back to the hearth. "Let's sing the one about the merry summer. You said there was a dance, too."

Anna Morton smacked her husband's head. "Ye've made her weep," she said in a hushed tone, clearly angry with him.

"My apologies, Sir Alex," he said. "I spoke without realizing...."

"'Tis not your fault. My wife has not thought of her brothers in some years," he said, arising from his place at the table. He had not seen Lucy's tears, but the set of her shoulders told him that she was upset. She had gone along with the children, but her heart was elsewhere. "Had I known this place would bring back memories..." He shook his head. "'Tis only natural that coming here would sadden her."

He followed Lucy and the children, reaching over

the Mortons' smallest girl to take Lucy's hand. "Time we retired for the night."

When she looked up at him, the only evidence of her distress was her slightly reddened nose and the unshed tears in her overly bright eyes.

Lucy did not argue or resist, but went with him easily, bidding the children good-night. Alex picked up a lamp, then took her hand and placed it in the crook of his elbow. "Which way to our chamber?"

A fire burned brightly in the hearth of their room. The large bed was piled with soft quilts and rested against the far wall. Alex followed Lucy inside and barred the door behind them.

Lucy felt ill. Feeling a deep chill, she stood in front of the fire, unable to move, to speak. She faced the fire with her hands clasped tightly at her waist. She thought of Roger, and the farewells he'd made before going on Crusade. He had promised to return once he'd made his pilgrimage.

He'd lied.

"Some time ago, you spoke of a man who survived a shipwreck in the Aegean Sea...." she finally said. Her voice was not as steady as she would have liked, but she needed to ask. "'Twas Roger, was it not?"

Alex nodded. "Aye."

She had suspected as much when she learned that Alex's destination was Eryngton. Alex had spoken of a Brother Roger when they'd discovered the Mandylion inside the silver scabbard. Who else but Roger would have sent Alex to Eryngton?

Emotion welled in her heart and threatened to spill over. "Why did he never...."

She turned away from Alex to face the darkness beyond their window. Her eyes were trained upon the glass, but she stood unseeing, her pain mixed with confusion.

"During my first year at Craghaven," she said, "I prayed every day that Roger would intercede for me— I knew he was in heaven, of course. I asked him to help me find a way out of the nunnery."

She remembered all those prayers. On her knees every morn, noon, night, in spite of the excruciating ache in her hip; regardless how much her lungs had to strain for every breath. All those words...prayed in vain.

"I was certain he looked down upon me from Saint Peter's knee, else he'd have returned to me...." She swallowed. "To us, at Eryngton."

"Lucy..."

"Did you know?" she asked, turning to look at him. "All along, did you know that Roger was my brother?"

She barely saw him shake his head. "Nay. Roger never spoke of his home. I did not know he had a sister."

His words felt like a knife in her heart. Roger had said naught of her to his closest friend.

He had abandoned her and his responsibility to Eryngton. He had become a man of the Church, with no earthly cares beyond those given him by his Order.

And his small, unprotected sister was not one of them.

Chapter Twenty

Alex undressed her slowly, using great care, leaving her in her chemise. He turned down the bed and guided her into it. A moment later he'd shed his own clothes.

He slid into the bed, pulled her into his arms and held her until she fell asleep.

Yet sleep did not come to him. Lucy did not weep, but her distress cut him deeply. He could not keep from thinking Roger should have stayed in England. Undoubtedly, his presence would have eased his sister's life.

But Roger had gone away, and in the years Alex had known him, the man had barely given her a thought.

Had Roger's religious calling been more important than Lucy's well-being? 'Twas a shocking thought for Alex, who had been about to follow Roger's example.

Now he wondered how 'twould go for his own brother's family if Philip should die. When Alex had left Clyfton three years ago, Philip had had four daughters—and no male heir. For all Alex knew, *he* was still Philip's heir. Had he turned his back upon his own responsibilities, just as Roger had done?

He tucked Lucy's head under his chin and thought about what he needed to do. His charge to deliver the Mandylion to Eryngton was null, now that he knew John Kendal was not earl. Alex would not leave it with a man so callous as Lucy's cousin.

But what would he do with it? Take it to France and leave it at Cluny?

Skelton's men knew only two things about Alex. That he'd been Roger Kendal's escort from Cluny to the Holy Land, and that Roger would have sent Alex with the Mandylion to a secure place—his former home in England.

If Alex never arrived at Eryngton, mayhap the knights would assume they'd been mistaken, and abandon their search in England to pursue him in France. If that occurred, Alex might still be able to find a suitable place for the ancient cloth in England.

He believed there was a monastery somewhere north of York. 'Twould be easy enough to determine its location, and possibly travel there to leave the Mandylion with the abbot.

But Alex was loathe to leave it with someone he did not know, or someone who had not been recommended to him. Monasteries were subject to politics as well as plundering. What if the abbot were an unscrupulous man? That was known to happen on occasion, and could be the case at the Yorkshire abbey.

Roger had not wanted the cloth to go to the monastery at Cluny. Had his only reason been because he knew Skelton would assume Alex would take the Mandylion there? Or were there some conflicting politics within the monks' ranks of which Alex was unaware?

Mayhap the current earl of Eryngton was not as evil a man as Alex had been led to believe. If John Kendal had left some provision for his sister to be removed to Craghaven in the event of his death, then the cousin would have had no choice but to send Lucy there. If that happened to be the case, then mayhap the Mandylion could be safely left in the care of the earl.

Alex supposed he should find out.

Lucy stirred in her sleep and absently, Alex pulled her deeper into the warmth of his body. The black knights were nowhere near, they were warm in their snug room, and she was safe in his arms. He drifted into sleep, feeling peaceful and secure, though he still had not determined what to do with the Mandylion.

Or with Lucy.

Roger had been dead—at least for Lucy—more than ten years. There was no reason for grief to take hold of her so painfully now.

Except that he never sent word that he'd survived the shipwreck. For all those years, Lucy had believed Roger's bones lay at the bottom of the Aegean Sea, while his soul was in heaven with God and all His archangels. She could not imagine why Roger had not contacted her.

In truth, she did not wish to face what she knew was true...that to Roger, his religious calling was of greater importance than anything that could possibly occur at Eryngton.

'Twas still night when she awoke with Alex sleeping soundly beside her. One of his arms lay draped over her middle, his leg resting between hers. His breathing was rough in her ear.

Lucy knew that Alex's religious calling was important to him, too. Once he delivered the Mandylion to Hugh, would he forsake her and return to Cluny according to his plan when he set out from Jerusalem? She had had her doubts right after the marriage, and now they came back to her, worse than before.

She did not know how she would face living without him.

With his features relaxed in sleep, Lucy admired each one in turn...his long, dark lashes; his nose, straight and masculine; lips that were deceptively warm and soft; his jaw, dark with the whiskers that grew every night...

She touched his hair and longed to press her lips to his, to make love with him before he—like Roger—decided that his duty to God was of greater consequence than anything he might feel for Lucy.

She loved the way they'd laughed together after their excursion into York the previous night. The weight of responsibility had been lifted from Alex's shoulders for that short interlude, and his playfulness had delighted her. His smiles had touched her heart, his laughter had melted it.

But it would not last. Lucy sensed that they had few days left together. Her heart, which had felt so light only the day before, was weighted by sorrow now.

"I'll be back as soon as I decide whether I can leave the Mandylion with Eryngton," Alex said.

Lucy nodded and watched him mount Rusa in the inn yard. The ornate scabbard containing the Mandylion was hidden beneath his saddle packs. She felt afraid, though she had no solid reason for it. *He was coming back.*

She watched him ride away, then returned to the inn, to the main room where the older children worked at their chores while they minded the younger ones. Somehow, Lucy got through the day, going to the window to look for Alex mayhap once in every hour.

"It may be a greater distance than Edmund told him," Anna said. She stirred the pot over the fire and handed her eldest daughter some bowls to take to the table. 'Twas past dark and nearing supper time. "He's never been to Eryngton himself—only heard the tales of the road from travelers who've stayed with us."

That did not ease Lucy's mind at all, for as it grew darker, she worried that Alex would not return to the inn until the morn.

"Ah! Is that him I hear?"

If 'twas, then he was on the wrong side of the road. This rider was approaching from the south.

"Nay, 'tis more than one rider," Edmund said, en-

tering the kitchen. "'Tis those knights who stayed a
few days ago. They're back."

Lucy jumped up from her stool by the fire. "The
black knights?"

"Aye, I suppose you could call 'em that."

"They cannot discover us here!" Lucy cried.
"They'll track down my husband and..." She did not
know what they would do. She could only assume
they would fight to the death for possession of the
Mandylion.

Edmund and his wife exchanged a glance while
Lucy stood in one corner of the kitchen wringing her
hands. Clearly, she had to do something.

"Get ye to yer chamber then, lass," he said. "And
don't come out 'til one of us comes to tell ye it's
safe."

"Children, come!" Anna said, gathering them together in the kitchen. Lucy headed toward the main
staircase while Anna admonished the children to stay
in the back and eat their supper.

Lucy's room was not the only one on the second
floor. There were other guest chambers, and if the
knights were planning to let rooms—which, of course
they were at this time of night—then the men would
be situated right next to her. Worse, they would hear
Alex's approach and attack before Alex even knew
they were there.

Lucy had to do something to prevent that.

The sound of the knights' voices spurred her to
action. She unlaced her kirtle and pulled it off, then
changed into an old gown. A moment later and she

had her belongings, as well as those that Alex had left behind, tied together in her blanket.

The men were still outside, so Lucy hurried out of her chamber and down the stairs while she had the chance. She crossed the main room and went into the kitchen where the children had gathered for their supper. "What are ye…?"

Lucy took Anna's arm and stepped away from the children. "I must go," she said, "and find my husband."

"Aye, I understand," Anna said. "D'ye have all yer things?"

Lucy nodded and drew out several coins from the pouch Alex had left her. She placed the coins in Anna's hand and started when she heard the front door of the inn open and the men enter.

"I can hear their voices."

"Aye," Anna replied. "The sound carries in here."

"Mayhap 'twould be best if I stayed here for a bit to listen and see if I can learn their plans."

"I doubt yer husband would approve, Mistress Lucy," Anna cautioned. "And what if he arrives just as these knights sit down to their meal?"

"I'll listen with both ears," Lucy said. "One on the road, and one on the knights."

Anna shook her head, but protested no more. She went out to join her husband in welcoming the three men, and seeing them settled in rooms. Lucy talked quietly with the children while she waited for the knights to return to the main floor. All she wanted was to hear a few minutes of their conversation, to know what they'd learned about Alex, if anything.

'Twas strange that they'd returned here. Lucy guessed they must have surmised that Alex would arrive eventually—or they'd heard something of him in York. She glanced at the door and listened for him. Surely Alex would be cautious in his approach.

It was ages before Lucy heard footsteps on the stairs again. While the men shifted chairs, Edmund came into the kitchen for ale and mugs. He shook his head at Lucy, but said naught before returning to the knights.

Lucy knew that staying was risky. But going on without knowing these men's plans might be worse.

"...and Eryngton will hold him as long as it takes..." The man's voice rose and faded, depending upon which way he faced when he spoke, Lucy supposed.

Garbled speech followed, words that Lucy could not understand, no matter how hard she strained to hear.

"...a wife..."

"...cloth back to London..."

"...wait another day for him to..."

Anna bustled into the kitchen and took Lucy's hands. "I'm a wreck from worry," she said in a low voice. "Ye've got to go now. What if yer man returns and the knights..."

Lucy nodded. "I'll go," she whispered. "It sounds like they plan to stay here for one day, anyway."

"Aye. That's what they said."

Lucy picked up her bundle.

"Go on past the stable and keep walking 'til ye find the path," Anna said. "Be careful when ye first get on to the path. There's a steep drop on the left side that ye don't want to fall into."

She disappeared from the kitchen, only to return half a second later. "And find yerself a big stick. There'll be wolves hunting out there sometimes, but they're more likely to be wary of ye than y'are of them."

Lucy did not take time to be frightened. She said a quick goodbye to the children, then slipped out the back door.

Taking Anna's advice, she found a stout stick and picked it up, her memory of the wolf at Holywake too fresh in her mind to neglect her own protection. She pulled her cloak 'round her against the chill of the night, and hoped it would not rain—and that Alex had not decided to stay the night at Eryngton.

In truth, she hoped that any number of mishaps would not occur, but that she would meet up with her husband sooner, rather than later.

The clouds cleared away occasionally, and the half moon was bright, so Lucy managed to walk quite a long way without incident. No wolves, no encounters with people upon the road.

Until she heard the approach of a horse and rider. There was no certainty that 'twould be Alex, so she left the path and concealed herself to await him.

Nothing could induce Alex to leave the Mandylion with Hugh Kyghley. The earl was a man without principles, without conscience. Roger would never have wanted Alex to entrust the Mandylion to Hugh's care.

The trip to Eryngton had not been a waste of Alex's time, however, for now he had a better understanding of the situation from which Lucy had escaped as a child. She had no idea how fortunate she was, to have been sent away from Eryngton.

Though he knew her life had been harsh and lonely at Craghaven, Alex was certain she had fared better than the earl's daughters. He did not believe he'd ever met two more slovenly, cruel or irreverent wenches in his life. He did not like to think of Lucy at Eryngton, at the mercy of those two.

At Craghaven, Lucy had become a kind and compassionate woman. She was full of joy in spite of the hardships she'd suffered over the years, in spite of the misshapen leg that marred her perfect beauty.

Except that if Alex noticed it at all, he thought it added to her perfection. She required no pity.

He spurred his mare to a faster trot, anxious to return to her. She'd had a difficult night, learning that Roger had only recently died. He'd been the rightful earl of Eryngton for years, and never known it.

He'd left his sister unprotected, and had not realized that, either.

Alex rode on, glad of the moonlight, and decided they would remain at the Mortons' little inn for another day or two—long enough for Lucy to recover from the news of Roger. It would give him time to decide what to do about the Mandylion, too. 'Twas obvious he could not ride the countryside indefinitely, carrying it from place to place.

Eryngton had spoken of Rievaulx Abbey, mentioning that he was on close, personal terms with the abbot. Which made the abbey a very unlikely place for Alex to leave the Mandylion. Still, he did not know that the abbot was a dishonest man. It might behoove him to see if he could find out if...

"Alex!"

He pulled up and listened.

A moment later, Lucy came toward him from the shadows beside the narrow road. Alex dismounted quickly and went to her.

"What's amiss?" he asked, taking her arms in his hands. She dropped the bundle she carried. "Is aught—"

"'Tis the black knights," she replied. "They arrived at the inn a couple of hours ago, and I was worried you'd ride into the yard and they'd see you."

"*Gloria Patri...* Where are they now?"

"At the inn," she said.

"*Deus meus.*"

"Waiting for you, or..."

"Lucy, it is dangerous for you to be—"

She kissed him. Rising onto her toes, she'd reached up to pull him close and give him a searing welcome.

But Alex was angry. She'd risked too much, coming out into the dark...walking this road alone.... He shuddered to think what might have happened.

He set her away from him and picked up her bundle. "You should have waited at the inn."

''But Alex—''

''Do you think I've lived more than thirty years without learning to be cautious?'' he growled, even as he lifted her off her feet and set her upon Rusa's back. ''You risked too much, coming for me.''

''But I—''

''And your leg…'' He mounted behind her. ''You've already walked so far, you would never have been able to outrun a predator.''

The thought of another wolf threatening her was almost more than he could bear. And his reaction alarmed him. He had begun to care too much.

He had to put some distance between himself and Lucy, for he would not suffer the same pain when—

''I do not understand why you are so angry,'' Lucy said, turning to face him in the dim light. ''When the knights came, I knew I had to warn you somehow. I am not some helpless—''

''Aye. You are!''

He heard her sharp intake of breath and knew that his words were too harsh.

'''Tis true, you've had to save me from more than one disaster,'' she said in a firm voice. ''But this time, 'twas *I* who saved *you!*''

''Ha!'' The day had not yet come when one small, lame woman needed to rescue *him* from a catastrophe. He would certainly have noticed something different about the inn when he rode into the yard.

''Alex?''

Skelton's men would never have been aware of his presence—

"Alex!" She grabbed his tunic. "Someone's coming!"

Lucy did not have time to think about Alex's cold reception. He moved so quickly, she could barely catch her breath, much less put together any coherent thoughts.

He spurred Rusa into a gallop. They rode for only a few minutes, until they reached a bend in the road and Alex used one arm to ease Lucy down. He tossed her pack to her. "Hide!"

Staying on horseback, he drew his sword, then turned to face whoever 'twas that had followed him from Eryngton.

Lucy did naught to conceal herself, but remained at the roadside, standing amid some low brush. Two men rode toward Alex, wearing dark clothes. Their swords gleamed in the moonlight, but Lucy could not see their faces. She flinched when she heard the first clang of weapons, and dropped her bundle.

Sword met sword as the two men tried to unseat— *to kill*—Alex, but he did not waver. With Rusa moving as though she were part of his body, and Alex using his sword so powerfully, the two attackers were at a disadvantage. Alex moved aggressively, forcefully challenging every thrust, every parry.

When one attacker's horse reared, nearly unseating its rider, Alex took advantage of the mishap. He thrust his sword, and with a sickening sound, the rider slumped and fell to the ground.

Lucy kept her eyes on Alex and bit down on her

fist to keep from crying out. The blows came faster
and harder, his attacker fighting even more desperately now. Rusa moved forward as Alex fought the
other man, and in the moonlight, it seemed that Alex
was in control. Yet Lucy could not trust her impression of the battle in the dark. As long as the swords
clashed, she remained terrified.

She heard words exchanged between the two men,
but could not make out what was being said.

Alex's remaining assailant suddenly fell from his
horse. Without delay, he took up his sword and went
after Alex, who also dismounted.

The fierce battle continued with both men on foot.
Alex was the more powerful of the two, and it seemed
to Lucy that he dominated the battle, although she
was still frightened that Alex's assailant might somehow deliver a lethal—mayhap fatal—blow. Unable to
tear her eyes from the sight of her husband fighting
for his life, she wondered if there was something she
could do to help him.

He'd told her to hide, and she supposed that was
what she should be doing—staying out of sight in the
event that he was—

Alex fell to the ground and the attacker lunged.

But instead of impaling Alex with his sword, he
missed his target when her husband rolled away and
swung his own sword upward. Alex managed to jump
quickly to his feet but the two men turned so that the
attacker's back was toward Lucy and she could not
see. Her breath caught in her throat as the fighting

resumed, and it seemed that she held her breath for an age.

She was tempted to move closer to the fray, but Alex had clearly wanted her to remain out of sight.

Muted sounds mixed with clanging swords and suddenly all was silent. One man fell to the ground and Lucy cried out.

"Alex!" Her voice was unsteady. She stood at the roadside, her mind numb, her body immobilized by the shock of the sudden attack. She felt light-headed and faint, but did not waver when Alex gathered up Rusa's reins and walked toward her, sheathing his sword.

She could not keep from launching herself into his arms. "I was so afraid!" she whispered, her mouth against his hard hauberk.

She felt his hand cup her head, then he staggered against her. "You're injured!"

"'Tis just…a small…"

"Let me help you," she said, moving to support him. She could not tell where he'd been hurt, but the injury was severe enough to keep him from moving easily.

"Nay," he replied and she saw his grimace. "I must deal with these bodies and then get us away from here."

"But the black knights will not be coming—"

"Wolves, Lucy… We need pull these blackguards off the road, and then get ourselves far from this place."

Taking the horse's reins in hand, Lucy retrieved her

pack from the ground while Alex performed his grim task. She looped her blanket-pack over the saddle and led the horse back to Alex.

"Where are you hurt?" she asked. He had already moved the first man off the road and was grabbing the other one's arms to complete his task.

"My wound is of little consequence." Grunted mutterings of Latin prayers accompanied his efforts, which were quickly completed.

"Help me round up the two horses," he said. "They're too valuable to let run free and they'll be likely to have food in their saddle."

They had not wandered far, and before long, she and Alex had the three horses together and were ready to leave.

"No!" Lucy cried as Alex lifted her into the saddle of one of the spare horses. "I cannot ride alone."

"You'll manage, Lucy," he said, not unkindly. But in his voice, she heard his eagerness to be away.

The panic she felt was nearly as bad as when she'd watched Alex confront his two attackers. She had spent many an hour upon Rusa's back, but Alex had been there to guide the horse. How would she do it on her own?

"Tell me what to do," she said, settling herself in the saddle.

With a grunt of pain, he mounted Rusa and gave instructions to Lucy. "Just hold on to your saddle, and I'll do the rest."

"Alex, I would see to your wound."

"Not now," he said, keeping Lucy abreast of him

while he led the spare horse behind them. They rode slowly, but did not stop for many miles as the moon arched and set.

''There's a path somewhere near here,'' he finally said, ''where someone pulls carts into the field,'' he said.

The light hue of a grassy field was easily visible. And Lucy could see Alex studying the roadside as they went past.

He eventually found the tracks he sought, and turned Rusa and the other horses into the field. ''The wolves will be occupied far from here,'' he said.

Lucy shuddered at the gruesome thought, but was grateful the fearsome animals would be unlikely to bother them now. She rode silently beside Alex, until they reached some bracken growing near a hedgerow. Finally, he stopped and dismounted.

''This will have to do,'' he said. In the dark, Lucy could see that he was moving slowly, painstakingly. He came 'round and helped her to dismount, then unhooked her pack from the saddle. ''You brought everything in this one pack?''

''Aye,'' she replied. ''''Tis not so much, and at least we'll have blankets.''

He did not respond, but lay the woolen spread out on the bracken and dropped on to it. Lucy hobbled the horses as she'd seen him do many times, and took his packs from Rusa's back.

''Where were you hurt?'' she asked, kneeling next to him on the blanket.

''Leg.''

"Let me see it."

"'Tis too dark," he said curtly.

She ignored him and put one hand upon his leg, skimming upward from his shin to his thigh until she found the area wet with blood. "Alex, this needs to be washed out."

"Leave it."

Undeterred, she searched through his saddle packs until she found his water bag. She gently pushed up his hauberk and untied his hose, which she assumed had been sliced open as well. "How did he slash through your hauberk?"

"He caught it on his upswing and sliced my leg," Alex said, then muttered, "Nearly unmanned me."

Lucy did not state the obvious, that once he returned to Cluny, the state of his manhood would be of no consequence.

Working nearly blind, she washed out the wound, then dug through the pack again to find the ointment that had helped to heal the injury on her shoulder. His muscles were tense under her ministrations, and she knew from experience how badly it stung, though she could not determine how deep a wound it was. "I may have to sew it closed in the morn when there's enough light."

"Nay. Leave it." His voice was tight with strain.

"I cannot believe a bit of stitching would worry you, husband."

"Hmmph."

"If there's anything clean in here to use for wrapping it, I cannot find it," she said, digging through the pack once again. "Your torn hose will have to do for tonight."

He did not reply, but pulled her down next to him.

"I am not going to apologize for coming after you," she said, careful not to bump into his wound.

"Nay?"

"I did what I thought necessary."

"Mmm..."

She knew she should help him pull off his hauberk and try to make him comfortable for the night, but he seemed exhausted, and Lucy had no energy, either. She'd walked for miles, then stood watching in terror while he fought for his life. All she could do was curl up against Alex and share his warmth, and hope that it would not start to rain.

She yawned and placed one arm across his chest. Each beat of his heart pulsed through her soul, and Lucy closed her eyes, cherishing the life that flowed through his veins. She snuggled closer. "I could not let you ride into the inn yard to be so outnumbered and trapped...."

He said naught, and Lucy thought he might well be asleep.

"Stay angry with me forever, if you will, husband," she said on a sigh. "But that is how long I will love you...."

Chapter Twenty-One

By dawn, Alex's wound throbbed unmercifully. As light broke, he peeled his hose away from the sliced muscle and determined that it would not need stitching. The bleeding had stopped and the salve was doing its healing work.

Lucy was still asleep, and he did not want to wake her. Leaving the inn, and walking miles to find him in the dark had been foolhardy...and heroic.

And she'd done it out of love for him.

He looked at her, sleeping soundly on the blanket among the bracken. Her features were not relaxed—her little frown line was deeply etched between her brows, and her mouth, always so lush and giving, was now a somber crescent. Loving him had brought danger to her. He thought he'd been protecting her when they wed, but naught had gone according to plan. He closed his eyes and prayed.

"Deus, qui corda fidelium Sancti Spiritus illustratione docuisti. Da nobis in eodem Spiritu recta sapere, et de eius semper consolatione gaudere."

The familiar words did not bring the same peace he'd experienced only a fortnight ago. And his thoughts of Cluny were hardly comforting when he considered leaving Lucy here in England while he traveled to the monastery.

"How does it look this morn?" Lucy asked, stretching. She sat up and looked at the wound.

"Not as bad as it feels," he replied lightly.

Lucy rubbed the sleep from her eyes and knelt beside him, pulling his tunic away to look at the wound. Alex nearly smiled at the expression she made while she struggled to avoid an actual grimace.

"Have we anything to use to bind it?" she asked, leaning across him to reach for her pack.

"Lucy."

"I can tear my chemise—"

"I would rather have your kiss," he said, pulling her onto him.

Clearly surprised by his ardor, she fell into his arms readily. "Alex, I don't—"

"Kiss me, wife."

When she gave him an insignificant peck on the side of his mouth, Alex took charge. He slid one hand around her and turned her so that she was on her back looking up at him, startled. He lowered his head and gave her the kind of kiss he'd craved ever since hearing that she loved him.

She cupped his head with her hands, then slid her fingers through the hair at his nape, sending a tremor of exquisite pleasure through him. He slid his tongue into the welcoming warmth of her mouth, and was rewarded with Lucy's sough of arousal.

With his eyes closed, he tasted her mouth, then moved to her jaw, her neck. He pulled her kirtle away from the notch at her collar and kissed her there.

"Alex, should we...?"

He answered with the touch of his tongue upon her nipple. Lucy squirmed under him, her hands seeking his belt, careful to avoid his injury, but never wavering in their purpose.

He was more than ready when she took him in her hand and skimmed his hard length from base to tip. He groaned and rolled to his side, taking Lucy with him.

She continued her sensual foray, taking his breath away with her touch. He nuzzled her breasts, and pulled the blanket over them so she would not become too chilled by the cool dawn air.

"I love to touch you," she breathed.

He shuddered and nearly lost his control.

"Lucy," he said, swallowing hard. "Straddle me."

She shifted, carefully swinging one leg over his waist. The weight of her body grounded him while her touch sent shocks of joyful pleasure through him. She moved against him and he shuddered as she slipped over him, on to him, becoming one with him.

Lucy tried to slow the pace with her movements, adjusting her rhythm to accommodate his wound. But Alex was desperate for her, beyond caution. She lay across his chest as he bent one knee and drove into her again and again, whispering her name.

He was beyond holding back when she suddenly cried out and he felt her muscles contract around him. They crested together, their hearts racing as one with their chests pressed against each another.

Still joined, Alex ran his hand down Lucy's back, soft and feminine, her silken hair warm under his palm. And he wanted to hear those words again, the ones she'd whispered when she believed he was asleep.

"What did you learn at Eryngton?" Lucy asked, kneeling on the blanket beside him.

"Only that your cousin is an avaricious worm."

Lucy had assumed as much, but she also understood that Alex had needed to go to Hugh Kyghley and see for himself, because of his promise to take the Mandylion to Eryngton.

"I could not leave the cloth with him."

She nodded, understanding completely. "Who were the men who attacked you last night?" She could hardly believe he'd survived the attack with only the superficial wound in his thigh. One end of the slash was fairly deep, but she'd removed her old kirtle and torn it into strips to wrap tightly around the wound.

"They were Eryngton's men, I'm sure."

Lucy began to wind the cloth around Alex's leg.

"I have no doubt that the black knights promised to reward the earl if I showed up and he managed to keep me at the castle until their arrival."

"But when you would not stay..."

"He sent those two rogues after me."

"Alex," Lucy said, tying the bandage together, "those men meant to kill you, not just bring you back."

"Aye." He rose to his feet and tested his weight upon the leg. "'Tis likely Skelton's men told Eryngton that I carried something of great value, but did not say what."

He was so casual about it that Lucy was taken aback. "You might have been killed." *While she watched, unable to do one thing to help him.*

"Nay. There was never any danger of that."

Lucy had seen various scars upon his body—some serious—and knew that last night's attack was not the first time her husband had faced peril. And now that she was not watching in terror, she realized that Alex was a master swordsman. Not many men would be able to best him in battle. 'Twas likely the reason he'd been chosen to travel to Jerusalem with her brother and escort him back to England with the Mandylion.

In an impulse she could not explain, Lucy threw her arms around Alex and hugged him tightly, shuddering at the thought of what might have happened to him through all his travels. She nearly spoke the words she'd said the night before when he was asleep and did not hear. But Lucy kept her silence instead and released him after a moment. She knew he would not care to hear of her love. 'Twould only make everything more complicated for him.

Alex did not let go of her. He looked down into her eyes, then kissed her lightly.

"We've got a long ride ahead of us," he said.
Can you manage this horse alone for a distance?"

"We cannot return to the inn," Lucy said. She was
mounted upon one of the spare horses and would
manage to ride alone, as long as they kept a slow
pace. "The black knights will be there."

"Or they'll be on the road to Eryngton today, so
we don't want to encounter them."

"Where will we go?"

"East."

Lucy could not imagine where Alex thought they
would find refuge, unless there was another inn—or
perhaps an abbey or convent nearby.

He led the way through the field, staying as close
as possible to the tall hedgerow. If anyone came up
the road, she hoped their eastward path would not be
obvious, and that they would not be easily seen.

"I should have moved the two dead knights farther
afield," he said.

"Alex, you could not. Your leg—"

"If they are found too soon..."

She sighed. His concern was not ill-founded, but
there was naught to be done about it now. They'd
ridden too far to go back and bury the two men.

Their path took them across beautiful green and
gold farm fields, each one squared off by a row of
rocks, or another hedgerow. The land rolled gently,
and they continued to ride eastward. Lucy did not
know where Alex was leading them, nor did she think
he was even certain where they were going. But they

continued on, stopping only twice to rest, sharing th
meager rations they found in one of the packs.

By the time the sun was at their backs, Lucy fe
sore and out of sorts, and did not understand how
Alex had managed to ride so long with the wound i
his leg. She was hungry and wanted something to ea
other than a piece of the hard brick of cheese they'
found in one of the Eryngton knights' packs.

And she felt small and petty for thinking her con
plaints while Alex had to be suffering a great dea
more than she was.

"Lucy." He stopped at the crest of a hill an
pointed into the distance. "Not much farther, now."

She saw a massive castle in the distance, encircle
by a high wall with towers placed at intervals.

"Darington Castle," Alex said. "I fostered there.

"Did you know we were coming here?" Luc
asked.

Alex shook his head. "I only hoped our path woul
bring us close." He kicked his heels and rode ahea

Alex's memories of Darington Castle were most
fond ones. His father and Viscount Darington had fo
tered together many years before, and were as clo
as brothers. Darington had one son who was an as
but the other two were fine men and Alex had n
doubt that he and Lucy would be given a warm we
come.

They entered through the western gate.

"Alexander Breton!"

Alex turned to the voice and saw an old, familiar face.

"Theo Croke!" He slid off his horse and greeted the man who had trained him as a youth, embracing him fondly.

"How many years has it been, lad?" Theo asked. "Ten? Twelve? Ye've not changed in the least."

"You're looking fit, old man," Alex said, more pleased than he'd have thought to revisit the friends of his youth. He slapped Theo's broad back affectionately.

"Ye wouldn't be callin' me old, would ye?"

Alex laughed aloud and denied saying such a thing, then turned to help Lucy down from her horse. "My lady wife," he said. "Lucy of Eryngton."

The expression she wore was one of astonishment—at his lighthearted demeanor, he supposed—but she greeted Theo graciously, took the arm Alex offered, and began their walk through the bailey to the keep. Theo summoned grooms to deal with the horses, but pulled the saddle packs down himself.

"Viscount Darington is away," the old knight said, catching up to them. "Gone to see his grandchild christened at Pickering."

"Whose child?"

"Lady Alice wed Lord Pickering a year ago at Eastertime," Theo said. "Bore one child that died the day it was born, and now this one."

Alex did not need to be reminded of the fragility of life. He gave up a silent prayer for the health and well-being of Alice's child, and started up the stairs to the keep. When they reached the top, Theo put a hand upon Alex's forearm. "Only Roland is at home," he said.

"Does Meg still run the household?"

"Aye," Theo replied. "And everyone in it. She'll welcome ye like a son, lad." He pushed open the door to the great hall, and allowed Alex and Lucy to pass in front of him.

Servants were lighting candles and adding wood to the fire that already blazed in the massive fireplace. Theo walked past the massive oaken table and shouted Meg's name. "She's likely overseein' the supper preparations, though they be small with Lord Darington away."

"Meg!"

She soon appeared, looking much as she had a decade before, only smaller. Her shoulders were stooped and she had a few extra lines on her friendly face, but Alex would have recognized her if he'd seen her on the streets of York.

"Why, Alexander Breton!" she cried. "What brings ye here to Darington?"

"A...slight mishap upon the road, Mistress Meg," he replied. He had long decided not to mention the circumstances of his travels, and even hoped that word of his arrival at Darington would not reach Skelton's men. He doubted they would associate Alexander Breton and his wife with the Sir Alex they sought, but Alex would be cautious.

He wished there was a way to avoid Roland, but

Alex was a guest in the man's home. He could not very well shun his host.

"This is my wife, Lady Lucy," Alex said. "She has traveled many a mile with me, and is weary. Have you a—"

"The Tusk and Ale is another mile down the road, Breton. In case you did not remember."

Alex turned to see Roland—the heir of Darington—descending the staircase. The man was a good deal shorter than Alex remembered, but then Alex had been a younger, more impressionable man when he was squire to Roland's father.

"I remember it well, Roland," he said, ignoring the sneer that curled the other man's lip. The Tusk and Ale was an inn in the village, the kind of place where a man could find a harlot or two to quench his appetites. 'Twas not the sort of place where a man would take his wife. "But I thought better of it. Roland, meet my wife, Lucy."

Theo remained standing behind Alex while Meg set off somewhere, calling for servants to help her above stairs. Lucy greeted Roland with polite reservation. Alex cleared his throat to cover a smile and her reticence. She was very perceptive, though 'twas likely she'd never met anyone like Roland before this.

Except mayhap her cousin, Hugh Kyghley, a petulant and peevish man if ever Alex had met one.

"Alice's child is being christened yet you do not attend your sister and her family?"

"Bah!" Roland said. "Alice is…I cannot abide her husband, so I did not go." He threw a pair of gauntlets upon the table. "Where is supper? 'Tis late, is it not?"

Alex and Lucy joined him at the table in the great hall while servants brought the meal, course by course. Lucy remained quiet, only speaking when Roland asked her a direct question. And then she kept her responses short and on point. She did not invite conversation.

But she ate as though she had not seen food in a week.

It had been a long and tiring day, especially for Lucy. She was unused to riding a horse, and along with the miles she'd walked the night before, Alex was certain she must be in pain.

"Your chamber has been made ready, Lady Lucy," Meg said as she came into the hall carrying a blazing candelabra. "I shall take you if you are ready."

Alex pushed his chair away from the table and arose, even as Roland groused about being left alone in his hall. Spending an evening in Roland's dour company was the last thing Alex wanted to do, and he walked alongside Lucy as she climbed the stairs behind Meg.

He stopped suddenly and realized that the company in the hall did not make the difference. Alex would have chosen to go with his wife, even had there been a grand fete going on here.

Lucy's love had changed him.

He hardly heard Meg's friendly chatter as he gazed up at the landing where Lucy lagged behind, surreptitiously rubbing her hip. Without considering the aching wound in his own leg, he bounded up the stairs and lifted her off her feet.

"Lead on, Meg," he said, ignoring Lucy's squeal of protest.

'Twas another flight of stairs before they reached the tower. Their belongings were already inside, and the chamber was warm with a glowing fire. Meg took one candle to light her way down the stairs, and left them. In the meantime, Alex carried Lucy to a large, curtained bed that dominated the room and set her down gently.

"Your hip is bothering you."

"'Tis naught, Alex," she said.

Of course she did not complain. Alex had never once heard Lucy utter a word of discontent, yet he knew she must be sore. She'd done much more than she should have, and he was going to do what he could to ease her discomfort.

"Lie down."

"Nay. I would look at your wound and—"

"Lucy." He slid his warm hands under her skirts, startling her. But when he began to rub the muscles of her weak leg, she lay back on the bed and sighed with pleasure.

"You walked a long distance last night. For my benefit. And I gave you grief for it."

"I know you were worried."

"Aye, I was. Scared of what might have happened to you."

She sighed. ''I know 'twas foolhardy, Alex, but I could not let you ride into the inn and—''

He kissed her. Leaning on one arm braced next to her head, he continued to stroke the tense and aching muscles of her hip as his lips gently plied hers. She made the small sound that he loved and wrapped her arms around him, but Alex did not want to tax her now. She needed to rest.

He eased her out of her kirtle and chemise, then pulled the quilts over her. In another moment, he had undressed too, and had pulled her against him in the bed.

Chapter Twenty-Two

Clyfton was only a day's ride from Darington. If they left at dawn, they could reach the castle by sunset. And Alex would be able to see Philip and Beatrice, and all their children.

He knew the Mandylion would be safe in Philip's care. Alex's brother was a just and honorable man, as well as a fierce warrior, who could take the Mandylion into Clyfton Castle and protect it from any who would steal it for nefarious purposes.

Alex had resisted this solution to the Mandylion because of the danger it could pose to Philip and his family. And because of the sorrowful memories he associated with his home.

He did not think he'd be able to return to Clyfton House. Facing those empty rooms, knowing that Geoffrey had been born in one of them, that his little son had played in the nursery, and on the stairs... Remembering how Isabella had commanded every aspect of the household—including himself and their son.

Lucy shifted restlessly in her sleep and Alex pulled her back against his chest and groin, slipping his arm around her waist and sliding one leg between hers. She sighed and breathed his name without awakening, while he inhaled her familiar scent.

An odd sensation arose when he thought of going back to Cluny. The feeling turned to confusion when he considered his life as a lay brother at the monastery, and his weeks in Lucy's company...his short tenure as her husband.

Alex swallowed. He had to make a decision soon. And once done, 'twould be final, for he could spend months, even years, debating the question. The easiest course would be to leave the Mandylion with Philip....

And he had to come to some decision about Lucy.

She moved again, turning in his arms to face him. They were warm and comfortable in their bed, but Lucy was restive. When he felt her take a shuddering breath, he wondered what was amiss. She often dreamed in her sleep, difficult, troubling dreams, judging by the movements and sounds she made.

He ran his hand down her back to soothe her, but it seemed only to make her unease worse.

"Lucy," he whispered, hoping to awaken her gently.

A sob escaped her, and she turned away from him abruptly.

"What is it?" he asked, certain that she was now awake.

"'Tis naught," she replied. "A...a b-bad dream."

* * *

Lucy gave a quick shake of her head and drew another shuddering breath. She knew 'twas foolish to weep over a dream, but the overriding helplessness and feelings of isolation were not easily put aside.

She felt exhausted and boneless as Alex pulled her back to face him. "Tell me." He used his thumbs to brush her tears away. His voice was low and seductive, and should have soothed her.

But it did not.

The images were too fresh in her mind, the emotions too raw. "Something was chasing us…"

Alex smoothed her hair back from her face while the firelight flickered over his comely features. She sniffed once and tried to distance herself from the terrible images.

"Fierce gray wolves tore at us from a thick mist. They seemed to…to grin their wicked grins at me." She took another shaky breath. "They grabbed my leg, but…suddenly they were not wolves anymore. They were the b-black knights with white lions emblazoned upon their chests. The men's teeth were yellow and sharp like the wolves'. I ran…tried to run," and she added in a whisper, "but I couldn't catch up to you. You were t-too far ahead."

"Lucy." His hands were upon her back, and he tried to soothe away her distress.

"I could not keep up. My…my leg…it gave out and I fell…."

She held back a sob of despair, even as Alex

touched his lips to her brow. He was here now, and Lucy knew she should take pleasure in the moment.

Yet she could not help but feel that the dream was a presage of what was to come. Still trembling, she tried to hold back her tears, to shake off the dream. She told herself 'twas not real. The black knights were far away, and unlikely to find them. And there were no wolves at Darington. She was safe in their bed in the tower, with Alex's strong, warm arms wrapped around her.

"Hush, I'm here," he said.

"Nay, Alex..." she whispered, unable to deny the truth of her dream, "you left me behind."

"I need a day to give my wound a chance to heal."

Lucy had cleansed it and covered it with the Persian ointment. Now she was wrapping it carefully with the bandages Meg had provided. "We'll leave upon the morrow."

They would have one day of rest at Darington. The strain of the past two days had made Lucy's limp more noticeable, which indicated that she was in pain, though she said naught about it. Alex knew she'd have mounted her horse and spent the day in the saddle without complaint if it had been necessary.

Fortunately, 'twas not. Alex thought it very unlikely that the black knights had found their trail across the fields and through the bracken. He assumed the knights had spent half the day traveling to Eryngton believing naught was amiss. Once they learned that Hugh had sent two scoundrels out to waylay Alex on the road, there would be hell to pay.

And Alex hoped they would be confounded enough to be further delayed.

He would not tarry more than a day at Darington, though. If Skelton's men managed to track him here, he wanted to be well away, leaving no indication of his direction. The worst possible thing would be to lead them to Clyfton, where they would learn that Sir Alexander was brother to the earl. He had no doubt they would draw the natural conclusion.

"Is your sister's child a girl or boy?" Lucy asked Roland. She sat opposite him, near the fire in the great hall, and was mending the hose Alex had worn when he'd been slashed.

She'd spent the morning being pampered by Meg, sitting in a tub of hot water to ease the ache in her hip, then dressed and coifed by the lady's maid who had not gone to Pickering with Lady Darington. Alex had never seen her so beautiful. He wanted to lift her out of her chair and carry her away from Roland, who looked at her as if she were the choicest, sweetest berry on the vine.

And she was.

He settled for taking her walking in the garden, where men were clearing out the summer's dead stalks and raking out the flower beds. They walked to the far edge of the garden, where the shrubs and trees grew thick, and ivy climbed the walls of a small, stone chapel.

"You managed to charm Roland," Alex said, feeling as possessive as he had in York, when she'd fallen prey to the drunkard at Saint George's.

"He's not as black-hearted as you let on," Lucy replied. She bent down and picked a small, solitary white flower that had somehow escaped the colder weather. "In fact, he's been naught but kind to me."

Alex did not want to hear of his, or any other man's kindness to her. He stepped closer and took her chin between his fingers. "You are mine," he said, surprising himself by how much he meant it. His heart, so painfully empty until now, was replenished. His soul, so lonely, was no longer so isolated.

Lucy filled him in a way that he could not have imagined even a month before.

"Aye, husband," she whispered. Her eyes welled with moisture, but Alex thought no more of it when she pulled his head down to hers and took his lips with her kiss.

The weather held for their departure, though the mist was thick around Rusa's hooves, and the sky threatened to open up at any time. Alex had decided against taking all three horses, arranging instead, for Theo Croke to have riders take them to Clyfton.

Lucy was happy to ride with Alex, though she did not know what to make of their destination. Why had he chosen to go to Clyfton? She wanted to ask if he planned to leave her and travel on to the monastery with the Mandylion, but was afraid of the answer. To her mind, 'twas better to put off the bad news until the last moment.

"It smells different here," she said.

"Aye, 'tis the sea."

"We're that close?"

She felt him nod behind her. "Clyfton Castle stands upon a hill that overlooks the North Sea. When I lived there, I used to go up to the battlements and watch the sun rise and feel the salty wind off the water."

Lucy thought it would be lovely to live so close to the water, but not without Alex. If he left...

"I don't remember much about Eryngton," she said to change the direction of her dismal thoughts. "I spent my days indoors, mostly in my own chamber, unless my brothers came to rescue me."

"Like I've had to do so many times these past weeks?"

"Aye," she said with a sad smile. "Though I don't recall that I was such a pest to them."

"Ah, Lucy," Alex said. "'Tis part of your charm."

"Oh!" She jabbed an elbow into his hauberk and laughed. She knew she'd disrupted his life, and could not blame him for lamenting the changes she'd wrought.

Outside of any plans he'd made, he was saddled with a wife he'd taken for some reason she did not come near to understanding, and the Mandylion was still vulnerable. At least she did not have to take responsibility for the latter. If only Roger had been in contact with Eryngton, he'd have known that Hugh Kyghley was earl now, and the Mandylion would never be safe in his hands. Alex would have been somewhere other than the York road when she and the Craghaven nuns had been attacked.

And Lucy would never have met him.

Once they were on the beach, they still had several miles to go. Alex intended to bypass the manor house and go straight to the castle, unwilling to face the memories that were sure to linger in the home he'd shared with Isabella.

There was no reason he and Lucy could not live at the castle with Philip and his family. The living quarters were plenty large enough, even for a family of six children and another…

Children.

Imagining the child that might already be growing within her, he pulled Lucy back against his chest and fit her head under his chin. He did not know how he could ever have considered leaving her for the monastery. He'd wed her to protect her from the harshness of the world outside the nunnery. He'd taken her to his bed because he'd been unable to resist her.

And he would stay with her out of love.

He did not know why the decision had been so difficult. 'Twould clearly be wrong to abandon her— even to the care of his brother—as many of the lay monks did with wives they did not want. Even her brother, Roger, had deserted her when she needed him.

Alex would not do the same. *Jesu, he wanted her.*

They would make their plans this eve, after he made love to her in the seclusion of his chamber at Clyfton.

Lucy turned and slipped her arms around his waist. "Make her gallop, Alex! I want to fly!"

Happy to oblige her, he dug in his heels and Rusa responded instantly, speeding across the sand and scrubby grasses as if she were a winged creature. Lucy laughed and clutched Alex tighter, her delight a contrast to her quiet mood since their arrival at Darington.

"Is the sea always so...*wild?*"

"'Tis the storm," Alex shouted above the wind and the waves. "See those low clouds over the water? If we hurry, we might outrun it."

The wind became fiercer and Alex began to doubt that they'd reach the shelter of the castle before the rain came. They were likely to be soaked when they arrived at Clyfton.

'Twas no matter—there'd be warm fires and mulled wine to welcome them, as well as Philip and the rest of his family. Now that they were so near, Alex was anxious to get there. He kept Rusa at a gallop, while Lucy laughed and held on, her hair loose and whipping him mercilessly.

"It's starting to rain!" Lucy cried.

They were pelted at first, by large, icy drops of rain that penetrated their clothes and slid down their collars. It soon became a deluge and Alex knew he would have to lead them to shelter.

"So cold!"

Rusa tore up the sand with her hooves, galloping

southward, her gait fast and sure. When Clyfton House came into sight, Lucy made a small squeal and pointed to it, and Alex knew then that he had no choice but to make a run for it. If he'd been alone, he'd have gone on to the castle.

But he did not want Lucy to take a chill. Continuing their swift pace, he turned Rusa toward the house near the beach and kept going until they reached the yard. Quickly dismounting, he helped Lucy down. Keeping his hand around her waist, he led her to the back of the house, where he found the door locked.

"Don't worry," he said in response to her cry of dismay. "This lock never held very well."

He stepped back a pace, then kicked the door and it crashed in on its hinges.

Lucy rushed inside.

"Wait here and I'll get Rusa settled," he said. He took only a few minutes to stable the horse and grab the packs, returning across the yard in the driving rain to get back to Lucy. And the house.

With her wet cloak still wrapped tightly around her, Lucy was shivering in the buttery, right where he'd left her. "Come on, let's get you warm."

He took her hand and led her through the main floor of the house, out of the buttery, past the pantry, down a long hall, and into the first drawing room. Since it was smaller than the great hall, it would be easier to heat.

Wood was stacked nearby, and Alex arranged it in the fireplace. Soon, a fire blazed in the grate, and he was rubbing Lucy's hands to warm them.

"You'll feel better in a minute," he said.

"This is your house," she said quietly. "Isn't it?"

He nodded.

He had not wanted to look 'round, to see all the familiar objects that had been part of his old life. Yet now, the most important thing was to get Lucy warm, to make her stop shivering.

"Warmer now?"

"Aye," she replied. "But 'tis strange to be standing here…in the house where your life once was.…"

He allowed himself a quick glance across the walls, the floors, he took note of the hangings, the chandelier, the furniture. 'Twas all the same—yet somehow different.

The pain he thought he'd feel… It did not occur.

As the room warmed, he stepped away from Lucy and walked to the window that overlooked the back acreage. The barn stood with its door gaping open, falling off its broken hinges. He would have to repair that. The roof of the sheephold needed thatching, and the dovecotes were also in need of repair.

Lucy stood with her back to the fire, eyeing him gently. "Needs a good cleaning in here," he said, taking note of the stale rushes upon the floor and the dust on every surface. He lit a taper in the fire, then took her hand and led her into the great hall.

"My sword used to hang there," he said, indicating a place on the wall beyond a cluttered trestle table. "Geoffrey was anxious to be allowed to touch it."

"And was he ever? Allowed to touch it?"

Alex shook his head. "Nay," he whispered, his

memory of his son warming him from within. "He was too small, the sword too sharp."

He could almost see the lad, his dark eyes gleaming, his hair thick and dark as he ran off with his own wooden sword to fight some imaginary enemy upon Clyfton lands. Alex smiled with remembrance and far less pain than he'd expected.

He took Lucy's hand again and led her to the far end of the hall to the thick stone staircase that led to the upper floor. They climbed the stairs slowly, allowing for Lucy's difficult gait. The air was thick with dust here, too, and on every surface.

Alex pushed open the door to the nursery and walked across the room where his son had slept and played. Everything was in order, every toy upon a shelf, his other belongings presumably folded neatly and placed in the trunk at the foot of the small bed.

He opened the window and looked out at the rain, and felt his heart cleansed of the pain of loss. The memories that stayed were sweet, unencumbered by the harshness that had driven him so hard for the last three years.

Lucy's expression was one of puzzlement, as well as worry. She did not understand, and Alex did not think he could explain it to her.

In the bedchamber he'd shared with Isabella, Alex took one long glance at the bed and chair, at the trunks that held their clothing...

He set the candle on a table, then turned to Lucy and took her hands in his. They were still icy cold.

Her eyes were moist, her nose red with the strain of holding back tears.

And in that moment, he knew he had never loved anyone more.

"Can you be content here in this house?"

She swallowed and her mouth dropped open. "Alex," she whispered his name in an unsteady voice while her chin wobbled with emotion. A thick tear spilled from one of her beautiful eyes.

"Lucy." He lifted her hands to his lips and kissed them. "Will you bear my children and be wife to me here?"

Without hesitation, she slid her arms around him and pressed her cheek against his chest. They stood together silently for a moment, then Alex set her away from him.

"Lucy, I..." He caressed her jaw with his fingers. "Will you go downstairs and await me there? I just need... I'll meet you there in a moment."

Her understanding was one of the things he loved best about Lucy. She withdrew, giving him a moment of privacy in the chamber he'd once shared with Isabella.

Naught had been changed since the day she was buried. The clay pitcher he'd thrown at the wall still lay shattered on the floor. The rich, gray velvet tunic he'd worn was still lying across the bed, no doubt covered in dust.

And Isabella was gone.

He dropped to his knees and prayed for her soul, then folded his hands and touched his forehead, add-

ing a prayer of thanks for Lucy. He realized he
wanted to make something of the life God had given
him, starting now, with Lucy.

With his full attention upon his prayer, and the rain
falling in sheets against the house, Alex did not hear
the disturbance outside. He made his peace with the
past and was rising to his feet when he heard a crash
and Lucy's terrified scream.

Lucy struck the first man in the forehead with the
poker and he went down hard. The second one
dodged the blow, and when he started to grab the
weapon from her, she threw it at him. She managed
to run to the far side of the trestle table, certain that
as long as she stayed there, he would not be able to
get to her.

Just as she wondered where the third black knight
was, he came in through the back hall, the way she
and Alex had done when they'd first arrived at the
house. When he came toward her, she knew she was
cornered.

But a second later, Alex dashed down the stairs,
his sword drawn. Instantly, he engaged the newcomer
in battle, while Lucy tried to slip away from the
knight who held her hostage behind the table. She had
to ensure that the man she'd downed with the poker
remained down. Alex was capable of dealing with
two attackers, but 'twould not do to have the third
man join the fray.

With a quick glance to the hallway, Lucy saw that
the knight was still unconscious. But the one who'd

tried to grab her had drawn his sword and was going for Alex. Lucy grabbed a heavy, iron candlestick from the table and went after him. She struck him, but the blow glanced off his shoulder ineffectually.

He turned on her then. She screamed and started to run from him, but her foot caught in her skirt and she started to fall. He caught her by the arm.

Lucy whimpered with pain when he yanked her arm behind her, holding her tight against him with his sword at her throat.

"Enough, monk!" he shouted at Alex.

In the instant Alex glanced over, his attacker lunged, spearing Alex's side. The color drained from his face and Lucy's heart leaped into her throat when the blood gushed from his side.

Alex staggered, but stayed on his feet, clutching the bleeding wound. "Let her go! Your fight is with me!" he called out, his voice harsh and rasping.

"Your fight is over," one of them said.

"Hand over the cloth."

"Release my wife."

"When the cloth is in our hands, the woman will go free," Lucy's captor said.

The man on the floor groaned and pushed himself up. With murder in his eyes, he started for Lucy, but the leader of the three halted him with a look.

Lucy quivered with fear. The black knight would slice her throat if she moved, yet if she did not help Alex…

With great difficulty, her husband pulled the silver

scabbard from his belt and started to hand it to the knight who'd stabbed him.

"Nay! It could be a trick!" called the man with the sword at Lucy's throat. "Open it and take out the cloth."

Alex struggled to do as he was bid. His fingers were awkward at their task, and Lucy's heart cried out to go to him, to do something about the wound that bled so profusely. She started to speak, but the sword bit into her neck and she knew the knight would kill her without hesitation if she struggled.

But Alex's wound needed immediate attention, or he would die.

With shaky breaths, Lucy watched him pull the Mandylion free of the scabbard and let it drop open. To Skelton's men, 'twas no precious relic, but only a treasure to be plundered and sold.

Still holding the cloth, Alex fell to his knees. Lucy cried out.

The front door burst open. Several knights in blue livery swarmed into the great hall with swords unsheathed. Her captor shoved Lucy aside and she dropped to the floor. In the midst of the melee, she crawled to Alex, who lay at the foot of the stairs in a pool of blood. The Mandylion lay beside him while the battle raged 'round them.

Picking up the precious cloth in one hand, Lucy lay it upon his chest while she reached across him to press her skirt against the wound.

An odd heat, taut and vibrating, shimmered up her arm and into her shoulder. "Alex!" she cried, terrified that the strange sensation she felt was his soul passing out of his body.

The heat filled her, shot through her arms and legs, neck and head, until she was no longer aware of the men fighting around her. There was only the heat.

And Alex, lying beneath her, bleeding, groaning.

"What...Lucy?" He was frowning, dazed.

"Lie still and let me—"

He sat up suddenly, bringing her with him.

"Alex, you—"

He moved quickly, agilely, helping her to her feet. Lucy did not understand how he had the strength to half carry her up the stairs, away from the fray, yet there was no weakness in him. He did not act as though he'd been mortally wounded. "You were near death," she cried. "Skelton's man...he k-kept me from you."

"I'm all right," he said, hugging her close. "And the Clyfton men have settled matters."

She looked down the stairs, and through her tears, saw that the men in blue had defeated Skelton's knights. They stood silent over the bodies with their swords at their sides.

"Alex Breton?" one of them called in surprise.

"Aye." Alex went halfway down the steps to meet the other knight.

"We were on patrol and saw these men riding toward Clyfton House... I had no idea you were back."

"'Tis good to see you, too, Stephan."

Lucy watched Alex descend the rest of the stairs and embrace the man at the bottom.

"Your brother will be pleased to see you."

"And I, him."

Stephan glanced up at Lucy. Alex turned to her and she started down the stairs. Her gait was oddly steady and she walked without pain as she approached her husband, whose hand was outstretched to take hers. There was no blood at the foot of the stairs, none on Alex's tunic.

And her lame leg seemed...

She looked up at Alex, and with tears filling her eyes, took his hand. They were home, and here they would stay.

"My wife, Lady Lucy," Alex said. "Meet Sir Stephan of Clyfton, an old friend."

Epilogue

"One would think that after four children, a husband would have learned to deal with having his wife in childbed," Beatrice muttered, carrying clean cloths into Lucy's bedchamber. "'Twill not be long now, Alex."

Alex could not keep himself from pacing the hall while his eight-year-old sons, John and Roger, kept apace beside him. His two younger sons played outdoors with their nurse, happily oblivious to what was taking place behind this closed door.

"When will she be finished, Papa?" Roger demanded.

"This has been going on far too long," John asserted, crossing his arms over his skinny chest.

Alex had to agree with John. Lucy had been in labor for too many hours with this one, and he could not help but worry that all was well, even though she'd not had a moment of illness in all the years of their marriage.

They'd been blessed from the very beginning of

their life together at Clyfton House, saving the Mandylion from mercenaries who would have sold it to the highest bidder. And they continued to be blessed every day.

"Go outside with your brothers, lads," he finally said, jabbing his fingers through his hair. He had to go to Lucy and see for himself, and the bedchamber was no suitable place for the twins now.

"But—"

"No arguments. I'll come down after I've seen to your mother."

Alex patted each blond head and the boys obeyed him reluctantly. As their footsteps faded on the stairs, he turned the door handle and stepped into the chamber he'd shared with Lucy for nearly nine years. He offered up one more prayer before stepping to the bedside where she labored to deliver their fifth child.

"One more push, m'lady!" said the midwife as Alex knelt beside the bed and smoothed the damp hair away from his wife's forehead. She was completely immersed in her task, but he knew she was aware of him by the way she took his hand and held on.

Alex prayed for a girl this time, but he had said naught to Lucy. As long as she and the bairn were all right, he would be satisfied.

She made a sound that was half cry, half grunt and pushed again, her shoulders tensing, her body contracting with exertion.

"Aye, Lucy...she's coming now," Beatrice said crouching to help ease the bairn from Lucy's body.

A tiny cry filled the room, and Lucy let out a small cry of relief.

"'Tis the lass you've been wantin'," said the midwife.

Lucy said naught, but turned to gaze into Alex's eyes, showing him all the love and joy they'd shared over the years.

"Your daughter, my love," she finally whispered. Her voice was weak from exhaustion, and Alex touched his lips to hers and cupped her face in his hand. Her eyes drifted closed.

"Lucy," he whispered. Emotion welled up in his chest, his heart taut with love. He felt satisfied, complete. Lucy was so much a part of him, he could not imagine how desolate these past years would have been without her.

And he'd come so close. He kissed her temple. "I love you."

She smiled, depleted.

And then her eyes flew open. *"Ave Maria,"* she cried. "Beatrice!"

As Lucy gripped Alex's hand again, Beatrice quickly placed the new bairn into his free arm and went to help the midwife. His worry was cut short, for the infant was squalling madly for her mother's breast. He rocked his new daughter gently while Lucy gave out another cry and pushed.

"Beatrice?" he croaked.

"'Twould seem you've been doubly blessed, once again, Alexander," Beatrice said as Lucy pushed out a second bairn. "What would you say to two daughters?"

Savor the
breathtaking romances
and thrilling adventures
of Harlequin Historicals®

On sale November 2003

MY LADY'S PRISONER by Ann Elizabeth Cree

To uncover the truth behind her husband's death,
a daring noblewoman kidnaps a handsome viscount!

THE VIRTUOUS KNIGHT by Margo Maguire

While fleeing a nunnery, a feisty noblewoman
becomes embroiled with a handsome knight in a
wild, romantic chase to protect an ancient relic!

On sale December 2003

THE IMPOSTOR'S KISS by Tanya Anne Crosby

On a quest to discover his past, a prince masquerades
as his twin brother and finds the life and the love
he'd always dreamed of....

THE EARL'S PRIZE by Nicola Cornick

An impoverished woman believes an earl is
an unredeemable rake—but when she wins
the lottery will she become the rake's prize?

Visit us at www.eHarlequin.com

HARLEQUIN HISTORICALS®

HHMEN

eHARLEQUIN.com

Your favorite authors are just a click away
at www.eHarlequin.com!

- Take our **Sister Author Quiz** and
  we'll match you up with the author
  most like you!

- Choose from over 500
  author **profiles!**

- Chat with your favorite authors
  on our **message boards.**

- Are you an author in the making?
  Get advice from published authors
  in **The Inside Scoop!**

- Get the latest on **author appearances**
  and tours!

*Want to know more about your
favorite romance authors?*

Choose from over 500 author profiles!

**Learn about your favorite authors
in a fun, interactive setting—
visit www.eHarlequin.com today!**

INTAUTH

If you enjoyed what you just read,
then we've got an offer you can't resist!

Take 2 bestselling
love stories FREE!

Plus get a FREE surprise gift!

Clip this page and mail it to Harlequin Reader Service

IN U.S.A.
3010 Walden Ave.
P.O. Box 1867
Buffalo, N.Y. 14240-1867

IN CANADA
P.O. Box 609
Fort Erie, Ontario
L2A 5X3

YES! Please send me 2 free Harlequin Historicals® novels and my fre
surprise gift. After receiving them, if I don't wish to receive anymore, I ca
return the shipping statement marked cancel. If I don't cancel, I will receive
brand-new novels every month, before they're available in stores! In the U.S.A
bill me at the bargain price of $4.47 plus 25¢ shipping and handling per bo
and applicable sales tax, if any*. In Canada, bill me at the bargain price of $4.9
plus 25¢ shipping and handling per book and applicable taxes**. That's th
complete price and a savings of over 10% off the cover prices—what a gre
deal! I understand that accepting the 2 free books and gift places me under
obligation ever to buy any books. I can always return a shipment and cancel
any time. Even if I never buy another book from Harlequin, the 2 free books a
gift are mine to keep forever.

246 HDN DN
349 HDN DN

Name	(PLEASE PRINT)	
Address	Apt.#	
City	State/Prov.	Zip/Postal Code

 * Terms and prices subject to change without notice. Sales tax applicable in N.Y.
** Canadian residents will be charged applicable provincial taxes and GST.
 All orders subject to approval. Offer limited to one per household and not valid to
 current Harlequin Historicals® subscribers.
 ® are registered trademarks of Harlequin Enterprises Limited.

HIST02   ©1998 Harlequin Enterprises Limited

PICK UP THESE HARLEQUIN HISTORICALS®
AND IMMERSE YOURSELF IN RUGGED
LANDSCAPE AND INTOXICATING ROMANCE
ON THE AMERICAN FRONTIER

On sale November 2003

THE TENDERFOOT BRIDE by Cheryl St.John
(Colorado, 1875)

Expecting a middle-aged widow, a hard-edged
rancher doesn't know what to do when his new cook
is not only young and beautiful, but pregnant!

THE SCOUT by Lynna Banning
(Nebraska and Wyoming, 1860)

On a wagon train headed to Oregon, an independent
spinster becomes smitten with her escort,
a troubled army major.

On sale December 2003

THE SURGEON by Kate Bridges
(Canada, 1889)

When his troop plays a prank on him, a mounted
police surgeon finds himself stuck with an unwanted
mail-order bride. Can she help him find his heart?

OKLAHOMA BRIDE by Carol Finch
(Oklahoma Territory, 1889)

A by-the-book army officer clashes with a beautiful
woman breaking the law he has sworn to uphold!

Visit us at www.eHarlequin.com

HARLEQUIN HISTORICALS®

HHWEST28

COMING NEXT MONTH FROM

HARLEQUIN HISTORICALS®

- **THE IMPOSTOR'S KISS**
  by **Tanya Anne Crosby**, Harlequin Historical debut
  On a quest to discover his past, the Prince of Merrick masquerad
  as his highway-robber twin brother and found the life and the lo
  he'd always dreamed of in Chloe Simon. But would Chloe forgi
  him when she learned his true identity?
  HH #683 ISBN# 29283-X $5.25 U.S./$6.25 CAN.

- **THE EARL'S PRIZE**
  by **Nicola Cornick,** author of THE NOTORIOUS MARRIAGE
  Ever since her father ruined them at the gaming tables,
  Amy Bainbridge has lived in genteel poverty and has vowed nev
  love a gambler. But when she meets Joss, the Earl of Tallant and
  unredeemable rogue, she risks losing her heart and becoming th
  rake's prize!
  HH #684 ISBN# 29284-8 $5.25 U.S./$6.25 CAN.

- **THE SURGEON**
  by **Kate Bridges,** author of THE MIDWIFE'S SECRET
  When his troop played a prank on him, John Calloway, a mount
  police surgeon, found himself stuck with an unwanted mail-orde
  bride. Though he wanted nothing more than to send the stubborr
  beauty back home, he needed to know if she could help him fin
  his long-buried heart....
  HH #685 ISBN# 29285-6 $5.25 U.S./$6.25 CAN.

- **OKLAHOMA BRIDE**
  by **Carol Finch,** author of BOUNTY HUNTER'S BRIDE
  Feisty Karissa Baxter wanted to secure land for her injured brot
  by illegally sneaking into Oklahoma Territory, but Commander
  Rafe Hunter stood directly between her and her crusade. Thoug
  she was breaking the law he had sworn to uphold, Rafe couldn'
  deny his smoldering passion!
  HH #686 ISBN# 29286-4 $5.25 U.S./$6.25 CAN.

KEEP AN EYE OUT FOR ALL FOUR
OF THESE TERRIFIC NEW TITLES